*TRANSRACIAL AND
INTERCOUNTRY ADOPTIONS*

# Transracial and Intercountry Adoptions

*CULTURAL GUIDANCE FOR PROFESSIONALS*

*Rowena Fong and Ruth McRoy*
EDITORS

 COLUMBIA UNIVERSITY PRESS   NEW YORK

COLUMBIA UNIVERSITY PRESS
Publishers Since 1893
New York   Chichester, West Sussex

cup.columbia.edu
Copyright © 2016 Columbia University Press
All rights reserved

Library of Congress Cataloging-in-Publication Data
Transracial and intercountry adoptions : cultural guidance for professionals / edited by Rowena Fong and Ruth McRoy.
   pages cm
 Includes index.
   ISBN 978-0-231-17254-7 (cloth) — ISBN 978-0-231-17255-4 (pbk.) — ISBN 978-0-231-54082-7 (electronic)
  1. Intercountry adoption—United States.  2. Interracial adoption—United States. 3. Intercountry adoption—United States—Case studies.  4. Interracial adoption—United States—Case studies.  I. Fong, Rowena.  II. McRoy, Ruth G.
   HV 875.5.T73 2016
   362.734089—dc23

                                                    2015017338

Cover design: Rebecca Lown

TO ALL TRANSRACIAL AND INTERCOUNTRY
ADOPTIVE FAMILIES AND CHILDREN.

## CONTENTS

FOREWORD   IX

ACKNOWLEDGMENTS   XI

**INTRODUCTION**   1
*Rowena Fong, Ruth G. McRoy, and Ann E. Schwartz*   1

**ONE**
▸ Overview of Intercountry Adoptions   19
*Rowena Fong, Ruth G. McRoy, and Hollee McGinnis*

**TWO**
▸ Legal and Policy Issues Affecting Intercountry Adoption Practices   38
*Karen Smith Rotabi and Carmen Mónico*

**THREE**
▸ Legal and Policy Issues Affecting Transracial Adoption Practice   69
*Ruth G. McRoy, Amy Griffin, and Hollee McGinnis*

**FOUR**
▸ Interculturally Competent Practice with Gay and Lesbian Families   90
*Devon Brooks, Doni Whitsett, and Jeremy T. Goldbach*

**FIVE**
▸ A Neurodevelopmental Perspective and Clinical Challenges   126
*Bruce D. Perry, Erin Hambrick, and Robert D. Perry*

**SIX**
▸ Ethnic Identity Formation   154
*Ellen E. Pinderhughes, Jessica A. K. Matthews, and Xian Zhang*

**SEVEN**
▸ Mental Health Issues   193
  *Amanda L. Baden, Jonathan R. Mazza, Andrew Kitchen, Elliotte Harrington, and Ebony White*

**EIGHT**
▸ Medical Issues   237
  *Dana E. Johnson and Judith K. Eckerle*

**NINE**
▸ School Issues   274
  *JaeRan Kim and Beth Hall*

**TEN**
▸ The Need for Adoption-Competent Mental Health Professionals   315
  *Debbie B. Riley and Ellen C. Singer*

**CONCLUSIONS**   359
  *Rowena Fong and Ruth G. McRoy*

**LIST OF CONTRIBUTORS**   371

**INDEX**   383

# FOREWORD

TWO OF THE WORLD'S LEADING authorities on adoption, Drs. Rowena Fong and Ruth McRoy, have coedited this impressive volume, which focuses on two significant and controversial contemporary issues: transracial adoption (the domestic adoption of children whose racial or ethnic background does not match that of his or her adoptive parents) and intercountry adoption (the adoption of children across national lines, regardless of race or ethnicity). This work draws on the extensive research experience and broad social work practice experience of coeditors Fong and McRoy, in combination with the expertise contributed to specific chapters by a veritable "who's who" of other researchers and practitioners who are leading figures in the world of transracial and intercountry adoptions.

Readers will find that the volume is both evidence based and accessible. Authors come from disciplines that include social work, sociology, psychiatry, pediatrics, and psychology (clinical, counseling, developmental) and work in diverse applied settings serving children and their families. The research cited in their chapters reflects the authors' multidisciplinary backgrounds and the growing interdisciplinary nature of the field of adoption research and practice. The authors present and critique existing research, while noting the significant gaps in our current knowledge base. Students and researchers looking for underresearched topics will find that many opportunities await them.

Chapters focus on the needs of children (e.g., mental health, medical, ethnic identity, developmental, from neurobiological to social) as well as the contexts in which children grow up, especially their families, schools, and communities. Children's needs and vulnerabilities are explored in the context of current controversies, including child trafficking, rehoming, and child laundering. The needs of adopted persons, adoptive parents, and birth parents are explored through the lens of the well-known seven core issues of adoption, updated by giving attention to the special issues raised by transracial and intercountry adoption.

The volume also attends to issues of policy, because it is policies (whether at the agency, local, state, federal, or international levels) that embody society's values and provide direction to service providers. Authors help readers navigate the alphabet soup of the many policies that govern adoption practice, including, for example, MEPA (the Multiethnic Placement Act), IEP (Interethnic Adoption Provisions), ASFA (Adoption and Safe Families Act), IAA (Intercountry Adoption Act), ICWA (Indian Child Welfare Act), and HCIA (Hague Intercountry Adoption Act). Readers are provided with context for how these policies arose as well as information about their current implementation and, as seems all too frequently to be the case, unintended consequences.

Fong, McRoy, and their authors portray the contemporary world of adoption in its great complexity. Nevertheless, they also take a pragmatic approach, acknowledging that children have been and will be adopted across racial and national lines and that professionals in the field must develop best practices for care providers and parents so that the needs of these children—who themselves did not choose adoption—can be met. Permeating the volume is their call for an attitude of "cultural humility," committing to self-reflection and continuing critique of existing social arrangements on behalf of the best interests of children worldwide.

Harold D. Grotevant, Ph.D.
Rudd Family Foundation Chair in Psychology
University of Massachusetts Amherst

## ACKNOWLEDGMENTS

SPECIAL THANKS TO MALLORY ANDREWS and Allison Marshall, MSSW students at the University of Texas at Austin, who assisted in the research for chapter 1, "Overview of Intercountry Adoptions."

The authors wish to thank Heidi Bruegel Cox, executive vice president and general counsel for the Gladney Center for Adoption, and Addie D. Williams, LMSW, JD, president and chief executive officer of Spaulding for Children, for their legal consultation on the development of the policy sections in chapter 3, "Legal and Policy Issues Affecting Transracial Adoption Practice."

Special thanks to the incredibly talented clinical staff at C.A.S.E. who contributed to this work: Sean Delehant, Lisa Dominguez, Valerie Kunsman, Susan LaVigna, and Laura Arroyo for her administrative support.

*TRANSRACIAL AND
INTERCOUNTRY ADOPTIONS*

# Introduction

▸ ROWENA FONG, RUTH G. McROY,
AND ANN E. SCHWARTZ

THE AMERICAN FAMILY IS BECOMING more diverse as parents are choosing more frequently to adopt children not of their same race through intercountry adoption and domestic transracial adoption. The term "transracial adoption" (TRA) refers to the legal placement of a child of one racial or ethnic group with adoptive parents of another ethnic group. Often in the United States, these adoptions typically refer to the "placement of children of color either from the U.S. or from another country with Caucasian families" (Child Welfare Information Gateway, 2013). According to the findings from the 2007 National Survey of Adoptive Parents, "four out of ten adopted children were in TRAs—that is, their parents reported that both adoptive parents are (or the single adoptive parent is) of a different race, culture, or ethnicity than their child. The majority of adopted children have non-Hispanic white parents, but are not themselves non-Hispanic white" (Vandivere, Malm, & Radel, 2009, pp. 5–6).

Although TRAs can apply to both domestic and international adoptions, in this book, TRA refers to domestic adoptions that occur in the United States. Adoptions that occur in international countries are referred to as "intercountry adoptions" (ICAs).

Since the Adoption and Safe Families Act was passed in 1997, the number of domestic adoptions reportedly has increased nationally because of the mandated expedited permanency for foster children (Coakley, 2005). An increased pool of adoptable children, including children who are older and with special needs, are available for parents willing to adopt from child protective services in public child welfare systems.

Since 2006, however, the availability of children to be adopted internationally has decreased steadily (Selman, 2012). Reasons for this decrease range from economic stability and an increase in domestic adoptions within the international country (Groza & Bunkers, 2014) to unethical fraudulent practices of child laundering and the illegal abduction of children (Gibbons & Rotabi, 2012; Roby & Maskew, 2012).

Concerns about rehoming, the illegal practice of finding and placing a child in a new adoptive home, raise the question of the inadequacy of postadoption services that might prevent these tense disruptions from happening (Pinderhughes, Matthews, Deoudes, & Pertman, 2013). Also, fraud and coercive practices have been associated with rehoming, child trafficking, and global surrogacy in some international countries (Gibbons & Rotabi, 2012; Punaks & Feit, 2014). Although these complex problems may not apply to all families who have children through ICAs or TRAs and successful adoption experiences are occurring, more information still is needed about TRAs and ICAs as the complexities and challenges increase, and recommendations for strengthening postadoption services and for solutions for addressing these problems are often sought.

### OVERVIEW OF THIS BOOK

This book is designed as a useful day-to-day reference for professionals who work with families who have adopted transracially or internationally, such as child welfare workers, therapists, physicians, teachers, and others who provide services to these adoptive families. Limited information is currently available to professionals to help prepare and assist families postadoption so that they can address issues specific to TRA and ICA, such as identity formation, understanding adoption, and dealing with the experience of loss and trauma. Many adoptive families seek services from educators, therapists, and medical staff, and often find that these professionals have only limited knowledge about adoption in general, and even less about the unique issues associated with TRAs and ICAs. Information about the history of policies related to TRAs and ICAs, trauma, fraud and coercion, ethnic identity formation, gay and lesbian adoptions, adoption issues in school settings, working with doctors and medical practitioners, and adoption-competent mental health professionals is provided.

In this book, TRAs typically refer to situations in which African American children are adopted by white families, which account for the majority of TRAs in the United States. It is acknowledged, however, that TRAs also occur in and with Asian American, Native American, and Latino and Mexican American children and families.

ICAs refer to the placement of children from one country (sending country) with a family from another country (receiving country). Six international countries were chosen (South Korea, China, India, Russia, Guatemala, and Ethiopia) to exemplify the range of complexities faced by triad members in ICAs. These situations range from growing domestic adoptions occurring within international countries to dramatic decreases in the numbers of placements from sending countries, which historically were responsible for the largest numbers of ICAs in the United States. Strained relations between international countries because of child abuse and neglect of adopted children by U.S. parents, rehoming of children, child laundering, and trafficking—as well as fraud and coercion practices, including ethical dilemmas in global surrogacy—are all challenges that are discussed in the chapters specifically about ICAs.

In chapter 1, the authors present the rationale and need for a book on TRAs and ICAs using a systems and intersectionality framework to explore challenges triad members face in mental health, health, and school systems. Issues such as disproportionality and kinship care, which affect the need as well as options for permanency for African American children in foster care are discussed. A brief introduction is also provided about fraudulent and coercive practices in ICAs. Chapter 1 includes an overview of ICAs, with a focus on history and demographics, as well as adoption challenges within the following countries: China, South Korea, India, Russia, Guatemala, and Ethiopia. The legal and policy issues related to ICAs are the main focus of chapter 2, with a critical analysis of the Hague Convention Intercountry Adoption (HCIA) and its impact on fraudulent and coercive practices, such as abduction and child laundering. Chapter 3 provides an overview of TRAs and explains the legal and policy issues related to the Multiethnic Placement Act (MEPA) and the Indian Child Welfare Act (ICWA). Issues associated with TRAs and ICAs by lesbians and gays are discussed in chapter 4, and chapter 5 provides a neurodevelopmental perspective on the role and impact of trauma and early life adversities on child development. Ethnic identity formation in TRAs and ICAs is addressed in chapter 6. Chapters 7, 8, and 9 discuss from a single systems perspective, the challenges ICA and TRA triad members can face when seeking services from mental health, medical, and school professionals. Chapter 10 makes a strong plea that adoption-competent professionals be trained especially in specific mental health services that triad members seek. Case examples are provided. The concluding chapter suggests updates and expansions needed in the seven core issues of adoption teaching curriculum, as well as additional frameworks that need to be added to attachment theory, to make these theoretical approaches more relevant to TRAs and ICAs. The authors conclude with a call for cultural humility and culturally competent practice approaches to work with the complexities faced by individuals and families in TRAs and ICAs.

## DISPROPORTIONALITY AND KINSHIP CARE

One factor that has led to TRAs is the disproportionate representation of African American children in the U.S. public child welfare system (Fong, Dettlaff, James, & Rodriguez, 2015). To address this challenge to promote permanency, safety, and well-being of the child, kinship care has become a growing option in which kin keep children and youth close to their biological family members through kinship foster care and in adoptive placements.

### Disproportionality

Disproportionality is the over- or underrepresentation of a group of people within the public systems (child welfare, schools, courts, hospitals) compared with the size of the same group of people in the general population (Wells, 2011). The public child welfare system has a disproportionate number of African American children in foster care and in need of adoption. For example, although in 2013, African American children represented only 13.7 percent of children under 18 years old in the United States, they represented 24.9 percent of children in care, and 25.7 percent of children waiting to be adopted (Wells & Girling 2014). This disproportionately high number of African American children needing permanency leads agencies to consider varying types of adopters of various racial backgrounds, as well as considering adoptions by relatives or kin.

### Kinship Care

Kinship adopters represent a growing population of adoptive families. Kinship care may be understood broadly as "any living arrangement in which a relative or someone else emotionally close to a child (e.g., friends, neighbors, godparents) takes primary responsibility for rearing that child" (Leos-Urbel, Bess, & Geen 1999, p. 1). The increasing use of kinship foster care in the United States over the past three decades has led to a long-term growth in kinship placements (Geen 2003). The last available federal statistics from 2013 reported that 28 percent of children in care reside in a relative placement, up from 23 percent in 2007 (U.S. Department of Health and Human Services [HHS], 2014). Adoptions from foster care by relatives have also increased. In 1998, only 15 percent of these adoptions were by relatives, but in 2013, this number reached 31 percent (Maza, 2006; HHS 2014). Kinship foster care also has become a more prevalent child welfare practice in other countries like England, Scotland, Ireland, Norway, and Ghana (Hong, Algood, Chiu, & Lee, 2011).

In the United States, the majority of children in kinship care are racial–ethnic minorities (Children in Kinship Care, 2002). Although kinship foster care as a social service practice is a recent phenomenon, among many minority groups, there is a long history of informal or private kinship care—that is, care with no involvement by child welfare authorities. This developed as a result of both cultural heritage and structural conditions. For example, in West African societies, different members of kinship networks commonly have cared for children whose parents were unable to provide care (Hegar, 1999). In the United States, slave children, separated from their parents, learned to depend on both blood relatives and symbolic or fictive kin, individuals not related but with close, emotional ties (Gutman, 1976). Continued economic difficulties faced by many African Americans since have placed continued importance on kin networks and shared parenting (Stack, 1985). In the past, informal kinship care was also necessitated by the exclusion of African American children from the child welfare system (Billingsley & Giovannoni, 1972). Likewise, traditional child-rearing practices among Native American children have emphasized the roles and responsibilities of extended family, clan, and tribal members; even today, American Indian families often include several generations (Red Horse et al., 2000). Despite this emphasis, Native American children were separated from their parents, extended family, and tribal communities through placement of children in church and state-run boarding schools and later through the Indian Adoption Project, which led to the placement of Native American children in white families. These practices were based on ethnocentric perceptions that favored Anglo assimilation and deemed Native American parents unable to properly care for their children (Palmiste, 2011).

In response, the Indian Children Welfare Act of 1978 sought to prevent such separations from happening and explicitly to establish "minimum Federal standards for the removal of Indian children from their families and the placement of such children in foster or adoptive homes which will reflect the unique values of Indian culture." These standards mandate that for both foster and adoptive placements of Native American children, preference should be given first to extended family, then to tribal members, and finally, other Indian families. Similarly, the Aboriginal and Torres Strait Islander Child Placement Principle, which influences child welfare policy throughout Australian states and territories, promotes the placement of indigenous children first with kin, then indigenous community members, and finally other indigenous caregivers to preserve the children's culture and identity (Boetto, 2010).

These placement preferences and policies highlight a perceived beneficial outcome of kinship care—cultural socialization. Because the current understanding of kinship care includes all caregivers who are emotionally close to a child, a kinship placement does not guarantee that a child will have a similar racial–ethnic background as his or her caregiver, but it certainly increases that likelihood. In contrast to those in nonkinship placements, those in kinship care may have a greater awareness of their genetic and ethnic heritage because of their connections to their birth family. Researchers have shown that children in kinship placements maintain more connections with family and community than those in nonkinship placements (Berrick, Barth, & Needell, 1994; Chapman, Wall, & Barth, 2004; Messing, 2006; Testa & Slack, 2002).

Do these connections actually translate into different outcomes when it comes to a child's understanding and embracing of his or her cultural background? In a study of youth living in relative placements in a London borough, many expressed that they had been able to preserve their ethnic heritage while in care (Broad, Hayes, & Rushforth, 2001). Specifically, many kinship caregivers are grandparents, and a central function of the grandparenting role is the sharing of culture. Findings from the National Survey of Child and Adolescent Well-Being (NSCAW, 2010) show that the majority of the kinship caregivers (60.9 percent) in the sample were grandmothers. Recent research finds that 1 child in 10 in the United States lives with a grandparent and that it is more common for grandparents to serve as primary caregivers among African Americans and Hispanics than among whites, although the greatest increase in caregiving by grandparents, since the start of the Great Recession, has been among whites (Livingston, 2010).

Using a convenience sample of diverse college students, Wiscott and Kopera-Frye (2000) found that ethnic minority students engage in more culturally related activities with their grandparents than do white students, highlighting the role of custodial grandparents in the transmission of a sense of ethnic identity from adults to children. A qualitative study by Cross, Day, and Byers (2010) revealed that in asking grandparents reasons why they became the sole caregivers for their grandchildren, they feared the "loss of traditional values and cultural norms for the children" were they to end up in a nonkinship placement (p. 377). In a study of grandmothers raising grandchildren in Manitoba, Eni, Harvey, and Phillips-Beck (2009) found that the grandmother participants saw the transmission of culture to their grandchildren as a critical function.

Both theorists and researchers have focused much attention on identity development among children, including ethnic identity, but in most cases, they have studied children residing with biological parents, often middle class and white. Not only have identity issues facing foster children been minimally studied, but the effects of kinship foster care on identity have been largely ignored as well (Gibbs & Muller, 2000).

Schwartz (2007), in one of the few studies to examine how the element of living with a relative might influence the development of a child's ethnic identity, found that being with caregivers who share *both* an adolescent's ethnic and family background enhanced the adolescent's sense of ethnic identity. This qualitative study compared the experiences of 18 African American early adolescents, between the ages of 11 and 14 years old, in both kinship and nonkinship same-race placements. Overall, those adolescents in kinship placements interpreted their ethnic identity in a more positive light than did those in nonkinship settings, and for kinship youth, ethnic socialization was less intentional but more natural, relational, practical, and community-based than it was for nonkinship participants. Nonkinship foster parents either did little in the way of socializing or deliberately exposed the adolescents to African American history and culture; by contrast, for kinship participants, their ethnic identity was "caught, not taught"— simply picked up through interactions with their caregivers, birth family, and others in their community, as they learned what it means to be African American and, in particular, how to survive and be viewed in a positive way in a majority-dominated society.

The differences in ethnic socialization by placement type may stem from a number of different factors. The kinship participants were living in areas with a heavily African American population, whereas the nonkinship participants resided in more ethnically diverse communities. As McRoy and Zurcher (1983) concluded in their study of transracial and inracial adolescent African American adoptees, "the opportunity for establishing positive relationships with blacks on an everyday basis was a key factor in the child's development of a positive black racial identity and a corresponding feeling about other blacks" (p. 134).

Additionally, in the Schwartz (2007) study, on average, the nonkinship caregivers had higher socioeconomic status and thus, likely greater education, giving them greater knowledge and access to resources about African American history and culture. With this sort of background, they would have more experience with intentional, topical discussions as a means to communicate information to those in their care. Furthermore, because all of the nonkinship caregivers were licensed foster parents but none of the kinship caregivers were, the nonrelative caregivers had completed child welfare training that specifically addresses ways to help children in foster care maintain their culture identity.

Not only because kinship caregivers have less knowledge about or familiarity with these forms of socialization, but also because of their often-disadvantaged economic situation, passing on survival skills would be viewed as critical. For example, although African American adolescents are at risk of being stopped by a police officer in any neighborhood, they would likely have a greater chance of being stopped in a low-income neighborhood than in another area, where police patrols are less common.

Another factor in the difference in socialization may simply be that, because of their familial connection, kinship caregivers view themselves as more responsible for the upbringing of adolescents in their care and accountable to do what the adolescents' birth parents should be doing (Crumbley, 2015). Denby and Alford (1996) reported that compared with Caucasian parents, African American parents "expressed (an) added socialization factor by stating that they teach their children the following: 'they (European Americans) don't have to worry about some of the things that we have to worry about'" (p. 80). They felt it was important to teach their children how to function in a society as a member of a minority group.

These preliminary findings regarding the relationship between kinship care and ethnic identity suggest some implications for practice and future research. The finding that children in kinship placements experience positive outcomes by maintaining family connections—both within and outside the household—supports the importance of family group decision-making programs, which bring together members of a child's kinship network (Scannapieco & Hegar, 2002). This approach involves convening members of a child's kinship network, including extended family members, close friends, and godparents, to discuss the care and protection of the child as well as assess the needs of the kinship caregiver. Efforts to involve family members require child welfare workers to be familiar with the cultural background and conceptions of family held by those involved in the placement or adoption and for workers to be equipped, in particular, to assist children with ethnic identity formation. Because not all children in care can be placed with kin, practice also should focus on enabling nonrelative foster and adoptive parents to engage in ethnic socialization that is more embedded in daily interactions and connected to children's immediate challenges.

Ethnic identity outcomes for children in kinship settings remain an understudied area. Future research should continue to explore what mechanisms and approaches to ethnic socialization result in the most favorable outcomes for children in different placement settings, including investigation of what community figures and organizations play important roles in ethnic socialization for children in both kinship and nonkinship placements. Research into what contexts encourage involvement that translates into positive ethnic identity formation, also may result in new practices.

## ETHNIC IDENTITY FORMATION IN TRANSRACIAL AND INTERCOUNTRY ADOPTIONS

A positive ethnic identity formation, whether it is promoted by kinship care and biological family members in TRAs or adoptive family members in ICAs, is an important goal to achieve for positive functioning in a child–youth–adult's life. In a study conducted by the Evan B. Donaldson Institute, entitled *Beyond Culture Camp: Promoting Health Identity Formation in Adoption* (McGinnis, Smith, Ryan, & Howard, 2009), the authors did an extensive examination of the identity development in adopted adults and found the following:

1. Adoption is an increasingly significant aspect of identity for adopted people as they age, and it remains so even when they are adults.
2. Race–ethnicity is an increasingly significant aspect of identity for those adopted across color and culture.
3. Coping with discrimination is an important aspect of coming to terms with racial–ethnic identity for adoptees of color.
4. Discrimination based on adoption is a reality, but more so for white adoptees—who also report being somewhat less comfortable with their adoptive identity as adults than their Korean counterparts.
5. Most transracial adoptees consider themselves white or want to be white as children.
6. Positive racial–ethnic identity development is most effectively facilitated by "lived" experiences, such as travel to native country, attending racially diverse schools, and having role models of their own race–ethnicity.
7. Contact with birth relatives, according to white respondents, is the most helpful factor in achieving a positive adoptive identity.
8. Different factors predict comfort with adoptive and racial–ethnic identity for Korean and white adoptees (pp. 4–6).

Adoption, whether it is transracial or intercountry, is a lifelong journey, as reinforced by the findings of the *Beyond Culture Camp* study. TRAs and ICAs have a continuum of needs, and these adoptions involve all triad members: birth parents, adopted persons, and adoptive parents. This continuum of needs begins even before the preplacement procedures when adoption workers are making arrangements for meetings between agency workers and adoptive parents. Neurodevelopmental research focuses on the neonatal development of the infant before it is born and becomes a part of an adoptive family. Adoption-competent mental health training is needed for workers in child protective services and in mental health services to prepare adoptive family members, especially for issues related to racism or adoptism in TRAs and ICAs. Postadoption services are needed to help adoptive families, adopted persons, and birth parents in both open and closed adoptions to address issues related to race and ethnic identity formation. Culturally competent practice and theoretical frameworks that address the intersections of race, ethnicity, gender, sexual orientation, religion, and abilities are needed to guide adoption-competent practice with members of the triad.

### THEORETICAL FRAMEWORKS

Adoptism, according to contributing authors JaeRan Kim and Beth Hall in chapter 9, refers to "the bias that exists in society to privilege families that are genetically connected over those made through adoption." According to Kim and Hall, "racism, sexism, heterosexism, ableism, and adoptism are all enforced and maintained by a society's institutions." These sentiments of institutions contributing to the –isms that affect individuals and families are the foundation of writing this book from a social systems framework and an ecological perspective of understanding human behaviors in social environments from macro-, mezzo-, and microsystems lenses (Zastrow & Kirst-Ashman, 2012). Adopted individuals and adoptive families face problems with systems. In each single system of school or mental health or health or legal settings, recurrent themes seem to emerge of professionals not understanding or accepting the difficult situations that face adopted individuals and adoptive families. Lack of information is a repetitive problem for triad members that systems seem unable to accept. The inconvenience or annoyance of systems lacking information seems to cause services offered to be rude, strife ridden, and full of tension. Adoption-competent professionals are needed across systems to address this problem.

Yet the knowledge of understanding TRAs and ICAs has to be in the context of using an intersectionality theoretical framework because of the complexities in the development and the establishment of identity development.

For individuals and families involved in TRAs and ICAs, it is the intersectionality process of determining the integration of facets of race and ethnicity, sexual orientation, age, social class, religion, and abilities that affirms identity. Adoptive identity is a biculturalization or even multiculturalization process that is based on a strengths and resiliency process. Ellen E. Pinderhughes, Jessica A. K. Matthews, and Xian Zhang in chapter 6 refer to "intersecting identities" and the "scaffolding of identity" in ethnic identity formation of the child or youth in TRAs and ICAs. Yet, in chapter 5, coauthors Bruce Perry, Erin Hambrick, and Robert Perry warn about heeding the impact of trauma on the physical development of the infant, child, or youth, which ultimately would affect the whole identity of the child or youth.

Identity formation is not limited to the child. When an adopted child from an ethnic culture enters the adoptive family of another ethnic culture, the transformation of that family's multicultural ethnic identity has to occur. Becoming a transracial family is a process that reflects the acknowledgment and the acquiring of cultural competence in operating from a stance of competency, not mediocrity, of understanding and knowing culturally different values, beliefs, and norms.

To understand ICAs and TRAs, it is important to focus from a multisystems orientation on national and international laws and policies that affect triad members. Federal legislation such as the MEPA and the ICWA and international legislation such as the Hague Convention on Protection of Children and Co-operation in Respect of Intercountry Adoption (HCIA) have a big impact on all triad members. Systems theory promotes the analysis and understanding of the dynamics of the interactions of individuals, families, communities, organizations, and agencies at micro-, mezzo-, and macrolevel systems as it affects practices and interactions among professionals and triad members.

Systems theory assumes that the interactions among triad members and systems are to be viewed simultaneously rather than sequentially. Thus, in adoptions, whether it is transracial or intercountry, the adopted person is dealt with in the context of simultaneously understanding people and families in their social environments at the individual, family, organizational, and societal levels.

Other theories relevant to TRAs and ICAs are discussed in several chapters. In chapter 4, intersectionality theory and extended family lifecycle theory are discussed in reference to gay, lesbian, bisexual, and transgender families. In chapter 5, trauma and developmental theory are used to explain the neurodevelopmental perspective about TRAs and ICAs. In chapter 6 on ethnic identity formation, racial identity developmental theory is discussed. In chapter 10, family systems theory and attachment theories are presented. All chapters have theoretical references to culturally competent practice and cultural humility.

### CULTURALLY COMPETENT PRACTICE AND CULTURAL HUMILITY

Culturally competent practice is another theoretical framework that guides the practice in working with individuals and families in TRA and ICA situations. Culturally competent practice refers to the understanding of knowledge, values and skills (Fong, 2006; Fong & Furuto, 2001; Lum, 2011) in the context of doing social work practice with ethnic minority and international populations.

Culturally competent practice is the foundation of interpersonal relationships acknowledging cultural differences and working toward competent practice. The National Association of Social Workers (NASW, 2006) has established the following 10 Standards for Cultural Competence in Social Work Practice:

- Standard 1: Ethics and Values
- Standard 2: Self-Awareness
- Standard 3: Cross-Cultural Knowledge
- Standard 4: Cross-Cultural Skills
- Standard 5: Service Delivery
- Standard 6: Empowerment and Advocacy
- Standard 7: Diverse Workforce
- Standard 8: Professional Education
- Standard 9: Language Diversity
- Standard 10: Cross-Cultural Leadership

In applying the NASW Standards for Cultural Competence in working with TRAs and ICAs, it is important for professionals to be aware of and to use culturally competent practice in the arenas of service delivery, language diversity, and workforce and leadership development. But the most important point is for professionals to acknowledge that different ethnic cultures, other than just the white European culture, have cultural values, belief systems, and religious practices. This is a practice that considers the knowledge, values, and skills relevant to the race, ethnicity, and immigration status of the adopted child from international countries.

Also important to culturally competent practice is the concept of cultural humility (Gallardo, 2014; Ortega & Faller, 2011), which is a stylistic way for the practitioner to have an attitude, approach, and personal style of humility in working with clients from different backgrounds and who behave differently because of the contexts of their social environments (Tervalon & Murray-Garcia, 1998). Because the definition of TRA includes the placement of a child of one race into a family of another race, as is often the case in ICAs in which the adoptive parents are of a different race, culturally competent practice promotes the understanding of ICAs in the context of understanding the knowledge, values, and beliefs as well as policies of the sending country and honoring those cultural values and beliefs in the upbringing of the adopted child in the United States. Cultural socialization acknowledges the understanding of human behavior in the social environment and the culturally competency accompanying the knowledge, values, and skills.

This book is designed to help practitioners and educators to gain specific knowledge and skills as well as cultural competence and humility, as they work with TRA and ICA families. With this background and knowledge, these professionals will have an even greater positive impact on children and families experiencing these types of adoption.

### DISCUSSION QUESTIONS

1. Define the terms "transracial adoption" and "intercountry adoption."
2. Explain why the numbers in transracial adoptions have increased and the numbers in intercountry adoptions have decreased.
3. Why is it important to apply culturally competent practice and cultural humility in working with transracial and intercountry adoption children and families?
4. Why is it important to have a multisystem approach in working with children and families in transracial and international adoptions?
5. What does it mean that adoption is a lifelong journey?

**REFERENCES**

Berrick, J. D., Barth, R., & Needell, B. (1994). A comparison of kinship foster homes and foster family homes: Implications for kinship foster care as family preservation. *Children and Youth Services Review, 16,* 33–63.

Billingsley, A., & Giovannoni, J. (1972). *Children of the storm.* New York: Harcourt Brace Jovanovich.

Boetto, H. (2010). Kinship care: A review of issues. *Family Matters, 85,* 60–67.

Broad, B., Hayes, R., & Rushforth, C. (2001). *Kith and kin: Kinship care for vulnerable young people.* London: JRF/NCB.

Chapman, M. V., Wall, A., & Barth, R. P. (2004). Children's voices: The perceptions of children in foster care. *American Journal of Orthopsychiatry, 74,* 293–304.

Child Welfare Information Gateway. (2013). Adoption USA. Washington, DC: Children's Bureau/ACYF.

Children in Kinship Care. (2002). *Assessing the new federalism.* Washington, DC: Urban Institute. Retrieved from www.urban.org_UploadedPDF_900661

Coakley, J. F. (2005). *Finalized adoption disruption: A family perspective* (Unpublished doctoral dissertation). Berkeley: University of California at Berkeley.

Cross, S. L., Day, A. G., & Byers, L. G. (2010). American Indian grand families: A qualitative study conducted with grandmothers and grandfathers who provide sole care for their grandchildren. *Journal of Cross Cultural Gerontology, 25,* 371–383. doi:10.1007/s10823-010-9127-5

Crumbley, J. (2015). Engaging relative caregivers: Managing risk factors in kinship care. Invited presentation given at the National Quality Improvement Center on Adoption and Guardianship Support and Preservation Advisory Board meeting, March 4, Baltimore, MD.

Denby, R., & Alford, K. (1996). Understanding African American discipline styles: Suggestions for effective social work intervention. *Journal of Multicultural Social Work, 4,* 81–97.

Eni, R., Harvey, C. D. H., & Phillips-Beck, W. (2009). In consideration of the needs of caregivers: Grandparenting experiences in Manitoba First Nation communities. *First Peoples Child and Family Review, 4,* 85–98.

Fong, R. (Ed.). (2006). *Culturally competent practices with immigrant and refugee children and families.* New York: Guilford Press.

Fong, R., Dettlaff, A., James, J., & Rodriguez, C. (2015). *Addressing racial disproportionality and disparities in human services: Multisystemic approaches*. New York: Columbia University Press.

Fong, R., & Furuto, S. (Eds.). (2001). *Culturally competent practice: Skills, interventions and evaluations*. Boston: Pearson.

Gallardo, M. (Ed.). (2014). *Developing cultural humility: Embracing race, privilege and power*. Los Angeles, CA: Sage.

Geen, R. (2003). Kinship foster care: An ongoing, yet largely uninformed debate. In R. Geen (Ed.), *Kinship care: Making the most of a valuable resource* (pp. 1–23). Washington DC: Urban Institute.

Gibbons, J., & Rotabi, K. (Eds.). (2012). *Intercountry adoptions: Policies, practices, and outcomes*. Surrey, England: Ashgate Press.

Gibbs, P., & Muller, U. (2000). Kinship foster care moving to the mainstream: Controversy, policy, and outcomes. *Adoption Quarterly, 4*, 57–87.

Groza, V., & Bunkers, K. (2014). Adoption policy and evidence-based domestic adoption practice: A comparison of Romania, Ukraine, India, Guatemala, and Ethiopia. *Infant Mental Health Journal, 35*(2), 160–171.

Gutman, H. (1976). *The black family in slavery and freedom, 1750–1925*. New York: Vintage.

Hegar, R. L. (1999). The cultural roots of kinship care. In R. L. Hegar & M. Scannapieco (Eds.), *Kinship foster care: Policy, practice, and research* (pp. 17–27). New York: Oxford University Press.

Hong, J. S., Algood, C. L., Chiu, Y., & Lee, S. A. (2011). An ecological understanding of kinship foster care in the United States. *Journal of Child and Family Studies, 20*, 863–872. doi:10.1007/s10826-9454-3

Leos-Urbel, J., Bess, R., & Geen, R. (1999*). State policies for assessing and supporting kinship foster parents*. Washington, DC: Urban Institute. Retrieved from http://www.urban.org/url.cfm?ID=409609

Livingston, G. (2010). *Since the start of the Great Recession, more children raised by grandparents*. Pew Research Social & Demographic Trends. Retrieved from http://www.pewsocialtrends.org/2010/09/09/since-the-start-of-the-great-recession-more-children-raised-by-grandparents/

Lum, D. (Ed.). (2011). *Culturally competent practice: A framework for understanding diverse groups and justice issues*. Belmont, CA: Brooks Cole.

Maza, P. (2006). Patterns of relative adoption. *The Roundtable*. Retrieved from http://www.nrcadoption.org/pdfs/roundtable/V20N1-2006.pdf

McGinnis, H., Smith, S. L., Ryan, S., & Howard, J. A. (2009). *Beyond culture camp: Promoting healthy identity formation in adoption*. New York: Donaldson Adoption Institute.

McRoy, R. G., & Zurcher, L. A. (1983). *Transracial and inracial adoptees: The adolescent years*. Springfield, IL: Charles C Thomas.

Messing, J. T. (2006). From the child's perspective: A qualitative analysis of kinship care placements. *Children and Youth Services Review, 28,* 1415–1434.

National Association of Social Work (NASW). (2006). *Cultural competent standards for social work practice*. Washington, DC: Author.

National Survey of Child and Adolescent Well-Being (NSCAW). (2010). *Findings from the NSCAW study* (Research Report No. 15: Kinship Caregivers in the Child Welfare System). Retrieved from http://www.acf.hhs.gov/programs/opre/resource/national-survey-of-child-and-adolescent-well-being-no-15-kinship-caregivers

Ortega, R., & Faller, K. (2011). Training child welfare workers from an intersectional cultural humility perspective: A paradigm shift. *Child Welfare, 90*(5), 27–49.

Palmiste, C. (2011). From the Indian Adoption Project to the Indian Child Welfare Act: The resistance of Native American communities. *Indigenous Policy Journal, 12*(1), 1–10.

Pinderhughes, E., Matthews, J., Deoudes, G., & Pertman, A. (2013). *A changing world: Shaping best practices through understanding of the new realities of intercountry adoption*. New York: Donaldson Adoption Institute.

Punaks, M., & Feit, K. (2014). *The paradox of orphanage laundering: Combating child trafficking through ethical voluntourism*. Portland, OR: Next Generation Nepal.

Red Horse, J. G., Martinez, C., Day, P., Day, D., Poupart, J., & Scharnberg, D. (2000, December). *Family preservation concepts in American Indian communities*. Seattle, WA: Casey Family Programs.

Roby, J. L., & Maskew, T. (2012). Human rights considerations in intercountry adoption: The children and families of Cambodia and the Marshall Islands. In J. L. Gibbons & K. S. Rotabi (Eds.), *Intercountry adoption: Policies, practices, and outcomes* (pp. 55–66). Surrey, England: Ashgate Press.

Scannapieco, M., & Hegar, R. (2002). Kinship care providers: Designing an array of supportive services. *Child and Adolescent Social Work Journal, 19,* 315–327.

Schwartz, A. (2007). "Caught" vs. "taught": Ethnic identity and the ethnic socialization experiences of African American adolescents in kinship and non-kinship foster placements. *Children and Youth Services Review, 29,* 1201–1219.

Selman, P. (2012). Global trends in intercountry adoption: 2001–2010. *Adoption Advocate, 44*(February), 1–15.

Stack, C. (1985). *Foster care: Current issues, policies, and practices.* Norwood, NJ: Ablex.

Tervalon, M., & Murray-Garcia, J. (1998). Cultural humility versus cultural competence: A critical distinction in defining physician training outcomes in multicultural education. *Journal for the Health Care for the Poor and Underserved, 9*(2), 117–125.

Testa, M. F., & Slack, K. S. (2002). The gift of kinship foster care. *Children and Youth Services Review, 24,* 79–108.

U.S. Department of Health and Human Services (HHS). (2014). *Adoption and Foster Care Analysis and Reporting System (AFCARS) report: Preliminary FY 2013 estimates as of July 2014 (No.21).* Retrieved from http://www.acf.hhs.gov/sites/default/files/cb/afcarsreport21.pdf

Vandivere, S., Malm, K. & Radel, L. (2009). *Adoption USA, A Chartbook Based on the 2007 National Survey of Adoptive Parents.* Washington, DC: U.S. Department of Health and Human Services, Office of Assessment Secretary for Planning and Evaluation.

Wells, S. (2011). Disproportionality and disparity in child welfare: An overview of definitions and methods of measurement. In D. Greene, K. Belanger, R. McRoy & L. Bullard (Eds.), *Challenging racial disproportionality in child welfare: Research, policy and practice* (pp 4–12). Washington, DC: Child Welfare League of America.

Wells, S., & Girling, S. (2014). Disproportionality and disparity in child welfare: An overview of definitions and methods of measurement. In R. McRoy & K. Belanger (Eds.), *Examining racial disproportionality through research* (p). Washington, DC: Child Welfare League of America.

Wiscott, R., & Kopera-Frye, K. (2000). Sharing of culture: Adult grandchildren's perceptions of intergenerational relations. *International Journal of Aging & Human Development, 51,* 199–215.

Zastrow, C., & Kirst-Ashman, K. (2012). *Understanding human behavior and the social environment.* 9th ed. Belmont, California: Brooks Cole.

# 1

# Overview of Intercountry Adoptions

▸ ROWENA FONG, RUTH G. McROY,
  AND HOLLEE McGINNIS

### INTRODUCTION AND DEMOGRAPHIC OVERVIEW

THE TERM INTERCOUNTRY ADOPTIONS (ICA) refers to the process by which a family adopts a child from a country other than their own through permanent legal means and the family brings that child to live with them permanently in their country of residence (Bureau of Consular Affairs, 2014). The U.S. Department of State (2009) reports that U.S. parents have adopted approximately 500,000 children from other countries since 1971. The annual number of ICAs peaked in 2004 at 22,991 and has steadily declined to 9,319 in 2011 (U.S. Department of State, 2009). Most children are adopted from Asia, Eastern Europe, Latin America, and more recently from Africa (Zhang & Lee, 2011). China has remained the largest source of children for U.S. ICA over the past decade (Suter, 2008), and the U.S. receives the largest number of children for ICA than any other country (DOS-n.d.-a).

It is clear that the flow of children entering the U.S. from overseas for adoption has been in flux, and part of the reason are changes in regulations among sending and receiving countries. The most significant change to ICA practice in the past decade has been the growing number of countries who are now party to the Hague Convention on Intercountry Adoption. After discussing some of the requirements of the top sending countries to the U.S., the subsequent sections will focus on how the Hague Convention on Intercountry Adoption has changed ICA practice in the U.S. and its impact on adoption practitioners, birth parents, adoptive parents and adoptees.

First, to understand the fluctuation in the flow of children for ICA to the U.S., consider this list from the Bureau of Consular Affairs, of the number of ICAs from the top sending countries in the 2013 fiscal year:

China: 2,306
Ethiopia: 993
Russia: 250
Republic of Korea: 138
India: 119
Guatemala: 23

During fiscal year 2013, a total of 2,306 ICAs took place originating in China, with 5 of those being finalized in the United States (Bureau of Consular Affairs, 2014). This is a decrease from fiscal year 2012, during which 2,697 ICAs took place originating from China, 21 of which were to be finalized in the United States (Bureau of Consular Affairs, 2013).

In 2003 there were 854 ICAs originating in Ethiopia, this number increased each year until it peaked in 2009 with 4,596 ICAs, and it decreased to 4,396 ICAs in 2010 (Selman, 2012). During fiscal year 2013, a total of 993 ICAs took place originating in Ethiopia, 43 of which were to be finalized in the United States (Bureau of Consular Affairs, 2014). This is a decrease from fiscal year 2012, during which 1,568 ICAs originated from Ethiopia, 114 of which were to be finalized in the United States (Bureau of Consular Affairs, 2013).

In 2003, there were 7,743 ICAs originating in Russia; in 2004 ICAs from Russia increased to 9,417 and then decreased steadily until 2010 during which 3,387 ICAs originating from Russia took place (Selman, 2012). During fiscal year 2013, a total of 250 ICAs originated in Russia, 1 of which was to be finalized in the United States (Bureau of Consular Affairs, 2014). This is a decrease from fiscal year 2012, during which 748 ICAs originated in Russia, 2 of which were to be finalized in the United States (Bureau of Consular Affairs, 2013).

During fiscal year 2013, a total of 138 ICAs originated from the Republic of Korea; 67 of these were to be finalized in the United States (Bureau of Consular Affairs, 2014). This is a decrease from fiscal year 2012, during which 627 ICAs originated in the Republic of Korea, 626 of which were to be finalized in the United States (Bureau of Consular Affairs, 2013).

During fiscal year 2013, a total of 119 ICAs took place originating in India, 22 of which were to be finalized in the United States (Bureau of Consular Affairs, 2014). This is a decrease from fiscal year 2012, during which 159 ICAs originated from India, 83 of which were to be finalized in the United States (Bureau of Consular Affairs, 2013).

ICAs originating from Guatemala have also fluctuated greatly. There were 2,677 adoptions in 2003, and the number increased to 4,232 in 2006 (Selman, 2012). In 2008, 4,186 ICAs originated from Guatemala; in 2009, 799 ICAs originated from Guatemala, and by 2010 this decreased to 58 ICAs (Selman, 2012). During fiscal year 2013, a total of twenty-three ICAs took place originating in Guatemala, none of which were finalized in the United States (Bureau of Consular Affairs, 2014). This is an increase from fiscal year 2012, during which seven ICAs originated from Guatemala, two of which were to be finalized in the United States (Bureau of Consular Affairs, 2013).

## THE HAGUE CONVENTION AND INTERCOUNTRY ADOPTION ACT

The Hague Convention on Intercountry Adoption sets minimum intercountry adoption standards and a system of cooperation among countries party to the Hague Convention to establish safeguards to prevent the abduction, sale, or trafficking in children and to ensure that ICAs take place in the best interest of the children involved (Hague Conference on Private Intercountry Law, 1993). To facilitate cooperation among contracting nations, the Hague Convention requires a central authority be established to oversee the obligations of the Convention and provide oversight of activities related to ICA procedures. In addition, the Hague Convention requires adoption service providers to be accredited and approved to provide such services. As of 2014, ninety-three countries are party to the Hague Convention. (For more on The Hague Convention, see chapter 2.)

## INTERCOUNTRY ADOPTIONS REQUIREMENTS BY SENDING COUNTRY

### China

China, a party to the Hague Convention, does not have residency requirements for prospective adoptive parents, but one of the prospective parents must travel to China to finalize the adoption; if only one prospective parent travels to China, then they must have a power of attorney from the other parent that has been approved and notarized by the Chinese Embassy in Washington, DC or by a Chinese Consulate General in the United States (Bureau of Consular Affairs, n.d.-a). China requires that prospective adoptive parents must be between the ages of 30 and 50 years old; couples adopting special needs children may be between 30 and 55 years of age (Bureau of Consular Affairs, n.d.-a). Health requirements for prospective adoptive parents include absence of the following conditions: AIDS; mental disability; actively contagious infectious disease; blindness in either eye; hearing loss in both ears or loss of language (with the exception adoption of children with hearing or language loss); nonfunction or dysfunction of limbs or trunk; incomplete limbs or paralysis; severe facial deformation; severe diseases affecting life expectancy, including malignant tumors, lupus, nephrosis, and epilepsy; major organ transplant within 10 years; schizophrenia; severe mental disorders requiring medication for more than 2 years, including depression, anxiety neurosis, or mania; and a body mass index (BMI) of 40 or greater (Bureau of Consular Affairs, n.d.-a). Neither parent may have a significant criminal record, nor any history of the following: domestic violence, sexual abuse, abandonment or abuse of children, use of narcotics or other potentially addictive drugs used to treat psychiatric illness, or alcoholism, unless the potential parent has been sober for a minimum of 10 years (Bureau of Consular Affairs, n.d.-a). Additionally, prospective adoptive families must have fewer than five children under 18 years of age, and the youngest child must be at least 1 year old (Bureau of Consular Affairs, n.d.-a).

### Ethiopia

Ethiopia is not currently party to the Hague Adoption Convention (Bureau of Consular Affairs, n.d.-b). But Ethiopia does participate in a Pre-Adoption Immigration Review (PAIR) program, which requires prospective adoptive parents to receive a predetermination on the child's likelihood of immigration eligibility (Bureau of Consular Affairs, n.d.-b). This is done before filing an adoption case with a court, which provides the foreign courts and relevant government authorities with information regarding a child's likely permanent legal relationship between the U.S. citizen parent(s) and the child (Bureau of Consular Affairs, n.d.-b). Beginning September 1, 2013, the Ethiopian government required a PAIR letter from United States Citizenship and Immigration Services (USCIS) in all U.S. adoption cases (Bureau of Consular Affairs, n.d.-b).

### Russia

Adoptions in Russia are overseen by the Ministry of Education and Science of the Russian Federation (Bureau of Consular Affairs, 2008). Russia is not party to the Hague Adoption Convention (Bureau of Consular Affairs, n.d.-e). Russia allows ICA by both married couples and single individuals; single individuals must be at least 16 years older than the prospective adoptee (Bureau of Consular Affairs, n.d.-e). Although there are no residency requirements for adoptive parents, the adoption process requires that prospective parents travel to Russia twice (Bureau of Consular Affairs, n.d.-e). Russia also requires that prospective adoptive parents be free of the following medical conditions: tuberculosis (active and chronic), illness of internal organs or nervous system, dysfunction of the limbs, infectious disease, drug or alcohol addiction, psychiatric disorders, and any disability preventing the prospective adoptive parents from working (Bureau of Consular Affairs, n.d.-e). For ICAs from Russia, children must be eligible for adoption by both the destination country and Russian standards. During the requisite waiting period for child eligibility, the child must be registered on a local databank of children without parental care for 1 month, then on a regional databank for 1 month, and finally on a federal databank for 6 months before eligibility for ICA (Bureau of Consular Affairs, n.d.-e). Following adoption, Russia requires registration of the adopted child with the Government of Russia through the Ministry of Foreign Affairs and periodic postadoption placement reports at 6 months following the formal court decision finalizing adoption, another report 6–12 months following, a third report 24 months following the formal decision, and a fourth report after 36 months (Bureau of Consular Affairs, n.d.-e).

As of January 1, 2013, Russian Federal law No. 727-FZ banned the adoption of Russian children by U.S. citizens and terminated the U.S.–Russia Adoption Agreement of 2012, formally terminated on January 1, 2014

(Bureau of Consular Affairs, n.d.-e). Only adoptions that were in progress before January 1, 2013, may continue to be processed, including those adoptions that were in the 30-day waiting period at that time (Bureau of Consular Affairs, n.d.-e). As of July 2, 2013, Russian Federal Law No. 167-FZ banned the adoption, custody, and patronage of all Russian children by same-sex couples and single individuals in countries where same-sex unions are legal (Bureau of Consular Affairs, n.d.-e).

### Republic of Korea

The Republic of Korea (hereafter South Korea) is not currently party to the Hague Adoption Convention. By South Korean law, ICA requires use of an adoption agency authorized by the Ministry for Health, Welfare and Family Affairs (Bureau of Consular Affairs, n.d.-f). Furthermore, the Korean government intends to reduce need for ICA by encouraging domestic adoption and has implemented ICA quotas for adoption agencies that decrease each year (Bureau of Consular Affairs, n.d.-f). Additionally, children are not eligible for ICA until after a five-month waiting period during which time preference is given to domestic adoption (Bureau of Consular Affairs, n.d.-f). All adoptive parents must reside in South Korea at the time of the adoption, but there are no residency requirements for adoptive parents (Bureau of Consular Affairs, n.d.-f). Adoptive parents wishing to adopt from South Korea must be between 25 and 44 years old and be married, with an age difference of no more than 15 years; neither adoptive parent is to be older than 45 years of age (Bureau of Consular Affairs, n.d.-f). Some exceptions exist with regard to age limit if the parents previously adopted a Korean child, or if they are willing to adopt a child with medical problems (Bureau of Consular Affairs, n.d.-f). Couples must have been married at least 3 years; South Korea does not allow adoption by single individuals (Bureau of Consular Affairs, n.d.-f). Financially, prospective adoptive parents should have an income sufficient to support the child, and higher than the U.S. national average (Bureau of Consular Affairs, n.d.-f). Additionally, to be eligible for ICA, children must qualify as an orphan based on the U.S. criteria (Bureau of Consular Affairs, n.d.-f). Timeframes on ICA from South Korea vary from 1 to 4 years, with special needs adoptions being processed in about a year, and adoption of healthy infants taking about 3 years (Bureau of Consular Affairs, n.d.-f).

### India

ICA in India is regulated by the Hague Convention of Protection of Children and Cooperation in Respect of Intercountry Adoption (Bureau of Consular Affairs, n.d.-d). Requirements for prospective adoptive parents from the United States include eligibility and suitability requirements from the U.S. Department of Homeland Security, U.S. Citizenship and Immigration Services based on U.S. immigration law (Bureau of Consular Affairs, n.d.-d). India's requirements for ICA include that prospective parents should be between 25 and 50 years of age if adopting a child who is 3 years old or younger (Bureau of Consular Affairs, n.d.-d). Married couples should have a combined age of less than 90 years (Bureau of Consular Affairs, n.d.-d). For adoption of children older than 3 years of age, prospective adoptive parents may be 25 to 55 years old, with a combined age of 105 years or less for married couples (Bureau of Consular Affairs, n.d.-d). Single prospective adoptive parents may be 30 to 50 years old, for children younger than 3 years old, prospective parents should be 45 years old or younger, and for children older than 3 years of age, prospective parents may be 50 years of age (Bureau of Consular Affairs, n.d.-d). Married couples must have a stable marriage for the 5 years prior to adoption; India does not recognize same-sex couples as eligible for ICA (Bureau of Consular Affairs, n.d.-d).

### Guatemala

Of note, Guatemala is one of the top sending countries for ICAs to the United States, but not to any other country (Selman, 2012). Guatemala is party to the Hague Adoption Convention, but is not a U.S. Hague Partner (Bureau of Consular Affairs, n.d.-c). Because of a determination by the DOS that Guatemala is not fully in accordance with the Hague Convention, all new ICAs to be finalized in the United States are suspended, and only applications filed before December 31, 2007, are being processed (Bureau of Consular Affairs, n.d.-c). In September 2008, the Guatemalan National Adoption Council (CNA) began working to establish guidelines for accreditation of adoption agencies; in August of 2011, the CNA began the "Acuerdo" to guide processing of pending adoption cases under the CNA (Bureau of Consular Affairs, n.d.-c). The Acuerdo differentiates between cases pending with the CNA and cases pending with the Procuraduría General de la Nación; the Acuerdo only applies to those with CNA filed before December 31, 2007 (Bureau of Consular Affairs, n.d.-c).

### IMPACT OF THE HAGUE CONVENTION ON U.S. AGENCIES AND PROFESSIONALS

The United States was signatory to the Hague Convention in 1993 and passed the Intercountry Adoption Act of 2000 (IAA; Pub. L. No. 106-279, 114 Stat. 825) to implement the mandates of the convention. The legislation designated the Office of Children's Issues in the U.S. Department of State (DOS) as the central authority responsible for the administration of ICAs procedures as specified by the convention. In 2003, the DOS issued the Proposed Rules for implementing IAA for public comment. The Final Rules were published in 2006 and the law went into effect in April 2008 (DOS, 2009). Under the Final Rules, the Colorado Department of Human Services (CDHS) and the Council on Accreditation (COA) were designated as the accrediting entities responsible for the approval of adoption service providers (Schmit, 2008); however, COA is now the sole accrediting entity responsible for the approval, monitoring, and oversight of accredited ICA service providers since 2013 (DOS, 2013). In July 2014, the Intercountry Adoption Universal Accreditation Act of 2012 (UAA; Pub. L. No. 112-276) was passed and went into effect (DOS, n.d.-b). This legislation extends IAA accreditation and approval requirements to all agencies and individuals (i.e., for-profit individuals or entities) providing ICA services irrespective of whether a child is being adopted from or emigrating to a country that is party to the Hague Convention.

The implementation of the IAA regulations in 2008 and subsequent passage of the UAA in 2012 marked a significant change in ICA practice for agencies and practitioners in the United States. State laws, state licensing standards, and agency guidelines had regulated the practice of ICA in the past, but they were limited in their ability to hold service providers accountable for unlawful practices in ICA cases (Bailey, 2009). With the implementation of UAA in 2014, ICA has become the only adoption area with national standards for adoption service providers, regulated through federally established accreditation standards. Hence, any agency or person providing ICA services must be accredited or approved, or they may be a supervised or an exempted provider whose work is overseen by a primary provider who is accredited or approved (DOS, n.d.-b). The IAA stipulates civil and criminal penalties for agencies that or individuals who provide ICA services without obtaining accreditation; civil penalties include fines up to $100,000 and criminal penalties include fines up to $250,00 or imprisonment up to 5 years or both (IAA Section 404).

On the one hand, accreditation has been welcomed because it establishes greater transparency, oversight, and monitoring of adoption service providers. According to COA guidelines, adoption service providers are evaluated on the following:

> licensing and corporate governance, financial and risk management, ethical practices and responsibilities, professional qualifications and training for employees, information disclosure, fee practices, quality control policies and practices, responding to complaints, records and reports management, service planning and delivery, standards for cases in which a child is immigrating to the United States (incoming cases) and cases where a child is emigrating from the United States (outgoing cases). (COA, 2014)

Specifically, IAA regulations require accredited adoption service providers to employ supervisors who have a master's degree in social work or related human service field, and clinical workers who have a bachelor's or master's degree in social work or related field and a minimum of 20 hours of training in the field (Bailey, 2009).

On the other hand, to meet these accreditation standards, adoption service providers face greater financial and resource burdens. For instance, adoption service providers must pay the cost of obtaining accreditation. DOS sets the fee that can be charged by COA, the national accrediting entity, and in the 2013 fiscal year, the cost of accreditation ranged from $5,000 to $23,000 (DOS, 2014). Primary adoption service providers must also carry $1 million per aggregate of liability insurance to guarantee an agency is financially solvent. An additional resource burden, particularly for primary adoption service providers, is the requirement of postplacement monitoring and responsibility for finding a new placement should an adoption disrupt (COA, 2014, Standards IC 96.50). Despite IAA's effort to regulate and provide oversight of ICA service providers, some scholars argue the law does not go far enough. For example, Rotabi and Gibbons

(2012) outline several limitations with current standards that undermine the intention of the law. Some of these limitations include lack of standards and guidelines for salaries and compensation paid to U.S. agencies and their employees, limited oversight of foreign service providers, and ability for agencies to operate without a full-time clinical supervisor (Rotabi & Gibbons, 2012).

One potential implication has been the concern that smaller adoption agencies would close because they could not meet the standards to gain accreditation (Bailey, 2009). Although some of the smaller adoption service agencies might be able to continue to provide services if they are overseen by an accredited primary agency, their closure could mean fewer service providers for adoptive families (Bailey, 2009). Currently, no empirical studies have examined the impact of IAA on the closure of adoption service providers or whether the burden of obtaining accreditation has dissuaded individuals from providing new adoption services. What is known is that some adoption service providers have been denied accreditation. The IAA requires DOS to make this information available to the public; since its implementation in 2008, fifteen service providers failed to demonstrate substantial compliance with applicable standards and were denied accreditation or approval to provide adoption services (DOS, 2013).

### IMPACT ON BIRTH FAMILIES

As noted, the purpose of IAA and the Hague Convention is to protect the interests of children and families, both biological and adoptive, and to lessen the risk of exploitation of children involved in ICAs. Specifically, the IAA seeks to protect birthparents and their children by ensuring that a child is not being fraudulently bought or sold for the purposes of adoption (Schmit, 2008). In countries that are party to the Hague Convention, the determination of whether a child is legally adoptable is the responsibility of a child's country of origin (i.e., the sending country) and includes necessary counseling and consent to the adoption by birth parents. In countries that are not party to the Hague Convention, both the DOS and the U.S. Citizenship and Immigration Services (USCIS) work together to ensure that a child is eligible for adoption and meet the criteria of "orphan" as defined by U.S. immigration law. To make this determination, USCIS or DOS may visit the biological mother or orphanage to verify a child's eligibility for adoption (Schmit, 2008). One criticism, however, is that oversight of foreign service providers actions is limited (Rotabi & Gibbons, 2012).

Although IAA primarily outlines regulations for children born overseas and brought to the United States for adoption, it also affects a small group of American children who emigrate and are adopted by foreign parents. According to Groza and McCreery Bunkers (2014), the first reports of U.S. children being adopted abroad appeared in 2004, first in a scholarly article by Sargent (2004) and then in a news story published in the *Christian Science Monitor* (Davenport, 2004).

Although these reports were based on limited data, these adoptions have been reported to be primarily transracial, involving African American infants whose birth parents voluntarily relinquished their parental rights and choose to place their child with white adoptive parents abroad, primarily in Canada and Europe (see also Groza, Houlihan, & Rosenberg, 2001). The IAA requires the DOS to track all incoming and outgoing ICA cases involving the United States, regardless of whether the adoption involves a Hague contracting nation. In the 2013 fiscal year, eighty-four U.S. children were adopted overseas with more than half joining families in Canada and the Netherlands (DOS, 2014); however, information about the age and race of the children emigrating is not available from these reports.

These independent adoptions, in which a birth parent chooses the adoptive parent(s), typically facilitated by an attorney or private agency, has raised some concerns. Although independent adoption is well established in the United States and is permitted by the Hague Convention (Hayes, 2011), other scholars point out the practice compromises the Hague Convention's recruitment guidelines and principle of subsidiary. Groza and McCreery Bunker (2014) note that the *Guide to Good Practice* published by the Hague Conference on Private Intercountry Law (2008) to assist countries in developing Hague Convention–compliant legislation, implies that matching between a child and prospective adoptive parents should be done by professionals with no contact between members of the adoptive and biological family before the legal completion of the adoption.

Furthermore, the principle of subsidiary as articulated in the Hague Convention might be applied to deny a birth parent's choice to place a child overseas first. The concept of subsidiary recognizes the importance of a family for a child's development and recognizes ICA as a viable option; however, the principle recommends a continuum of care options, based on the individual circumstance of the child and his or her best interests. This continuum of care recommends first that national options be pursued, such as placement with extended kin or domestic adoption, followed by intercountry options, such as ICA (Rotabi & Gibbons, 2012). In the United States, the IAA mandates adoption service providers make "sufficient reasonable efforts" to find a placement with U.S. families before placing a child overseas (Avitan, 2007). These "diligent recruitment" efforts to place a child domestically first are specified in the legislation and require agencies to (1) disseminate information about the availability of a child through print, media and internet sources; (2) list the child on a national or state adoption exchange for at least sixty days after the child's birth; (3) respond to inquiries about the adoption of the child; and (4) provide information about a child's background to prospective adoptive parents (Avitan, 2007).

Although IAA provides an exemption to diligent recruitment efforts in the case of independent adoptions and requires adoption service providers to give "significant weight" to birth parent's placement preferences, it does not require the same of state courts who finalize outgoing adoption cases. One scholar has argued that because judges are not required to meet the same standards, in some independent adoption cases, a judge may determine the best interest of a child would be to require the agency to recruit U.S. parents (Avitan, 2007). Hence, ongoing discussions are needed to determine whether a birth parent's right to make a plan for his or her child takes precedence over the principle of subsidiarity as articulated in the Hague Convention (Groza & McCreery Bunkers, 2014).

Finally, the IAA provides little guidance on the content of counseling that U.S. birth parents receive to make an informed consent to an overseas adoption. COA accreditation standards require adoption service providers to ensure that birth parents are informed of the effects of their consent and that such consent be obtained freely and not induced by payments or compensations of any kind (COA 2014, Standards OC 96.53.c). However, the specific components of an informed consent in adoption are not fully spelled out in legal statutes (Smith, 2006). According to a report published by the Donaldson Adoption Institute on contemporary U.S. birth parents, in order "for a woman to make an informed decision about placing her child for adoption, she must be aware of its realities and implications, and must be able to consider them with full and accurate knowledge" (Smith, 2006, p. 29). Research on the motivation of U.S. birth parent(s) who place their children overseas is understudied; however, anecdotal evidence suggests one reason may be the perception that their child will experience less racism abroad than in the United States (Avitan, 2007). As noted earlier, evidence suggests many of these U.S. birth parents are African American, and they may not be fully informed of the social, political, and cultural context of prospective adoptive parents' countries they are choosing for placement of their child for adoption.

#### IMPACT ON ADOPTIVE PARENTS

The Hague Convention and the IAA implementing legislation also provide important protections for prospective adoptive parents that previously did not exist in ICA practice. The IAA rules mandate adoption service providers disclose fees for services rendered to prospective families. The DOS publishes the fees charged by adoption services in their annual report on ICA. In fiscal year 2013, the median fee charged for adoption services was $28,845.85 (DOS, 2014). In addition, the IAA regulations establish a mechanism for adoptive parents to file complaints about services received and requires accredited agencies to be responsive (DOS, n.d.-b). Complaints relating to the Hague Convention, IAA, or UAA can be submitted via the DOS website through the Hague Complaint Registry (HCR). Complaints are given to COA, the national accrediting agency, who investigates whether the agency is in compliance with accreditation standards and acts accordingly (DOS, n.d.-c).

Adoption service providers must disclose to prospective adoptive parent(s) a child's available medical and social information provided by the sending country (COA, 2014, IC 96.49). Accreditation standards specify that medical information should include the date when a child entered a child welfare institution and condition at entry, history of significant illnesses, developmental information (including prenatal and birth history), and any known health risks in the specific region or country where the child resides (COA, 2014, Standards IC 96.49.d). This medical information must be provided no later than 2 weeks before either the adoption or placement for adoption, or the date on which the prospective adoptive parent(s) travel to the foreign country to complete the adoption. In terms of social information, COA accreditation standards also require reasonable efforts be made to obtain information about a child's birth family and "cultural, racial, religious, ethnic, and linguistic background," as well as information about siblings (COA 2014, Standards IC 96.49.f).

One of the most important differences in the IAA regulations compared with other transracial adoption legislation is the requirement that prospective adoptive parent(s) complete a minimum of 10 hours of training that "allows them to be as fully prepared as possible for the adoption of a particular child" and "promote a successful ICA" (COA, 2014, IC 96.48). The accreditation standards specify eight topics that must be covered in the training: (1) the ICA process and conditions in the country of the child where parent(s) plan to adopt, (2) the effects of known environmental and developmental risk factors specific to a child's country of origin, (3) the impact of separating from caregivers and familiar surroundings on a child, (4) research on the impact of institutional care on children's development, (5) risk of attachment disorders and other emotional problems of institutionalized and traumatized children, (6) relevant laws and adoption processes of the sending country and potential delays that may impede the finalization of an adoption, (7) long-term implications of being a multicultural family, and (8) information on postadoption reporting requirements of the sending country. In addition, the home study assessing the suitability of prospective parents to adopt should include information on the "characteristics of the children for whom the prospective adoptive parent(s) would be qualified to care" (COA, 2014, 96.47.a).

Currently, little empirical evidence has explored the impact of these trainings on prospective adoptive parents' preparation and decision to adopt or on the long-term stability of the adoption. Some scholars have pointed out these trainings are not based on evidence or outcomes (Rotabi & Gibbons, 2012). Another concern that has been raised is that the IAA regulations would increase the cost and waiting times to complete an ICA, which in turn could discourage some families from pursuing these adoptions (Bailey, 2009); however, to date, no empirical studies support whether this has in fact happened. The number of ICAs worldwide has been in decline since 2004 (Selman, 2012), but this decline began 4 years before the IAA rules came into effect in the United States.

## IMPACT ON CHILD DEVELOPMENT

The Hague Convention and IAA regulations recognize the importance of preserving an adopted person's identity, including background and medical information. The IAA rules specify medical and social information be given to prospective adoptive parents, which then could be shared with the adopted child. In addition, the implementing regulations require adoption service providers to preserve adoption records and make available nonidentifying information to adoptees and adoptive parent(s) when requested (IAA, Section 96.42). However, while the standards require that preadoption training address the long-term impact of becoming a multicultural family, they do not specifically mention the importance of addressing the cultural and racial identity concerns of the adopted child over his or her lifetime. Another concern has been that the regulations would significantly delay the adoption process because of additional paperwork, procedural requirements, and possibly fewer families seeking an ICA (Bailey, 2009). These delays in adoption procedures would have a direct impact on increasing the length of institutional stays for children, which also would affect their development and result in potentially fewer adoptive families for children.

## CONCLUSION

The preamble to the Hague Adoption Convention states the following:

> The child, for the full and harmonious development of his or her personality, should grow up in a family environment, in an atmosphere of happiness, love and understanding... Intercountry adoption may offer the advantage of a permanent family to a child for whom a suitable family cannot be found in his or her State of origin. (Bureau of Consular Affairs, n.d.-g)

As stated in this preamble, in cases in which a child cannot remain in his or her own country and with his or her biological family, ICA can be an option. It is essential, however, that agencies place the child's best interests first and preserve adoption records as well as provide culturally appropriate training to families in preparation for the placement as well as culturally appropriate postadoption services to adopted children and their families.

As adopted children reach their teen years and emerging adulthood, they often choose to seek their birth families and search for others with whom they can identify. They may want to learn about their country of origin and the culture from which they came, and often they just want to know others who look like themselves. Children adopted from other countries need to be supported by child welfare systems, practitioners, and families that will believe in and support them not only in cultural awareness and sensitivity but also in cultural safety and cultural security (Carriere, 2010). By providing this support, practitioners and families can build resilience among children who are growing up in an environment far from their birth countries and cultures of origin.

### DISCUSSION QUESTIONS

1. What is the Hague Convention and what is the Intercountry Adoption Act (IAA)?
2. The Hague Convention on Intercountry Adoption (HCIA) has intercountry standards to protect the child and his or her rights. What are these standards of HCIA?
3. What are some common misconceptions of the Hague Convention?

### REFERENCES

Avitan, G. (2007). Protecting our children or our pride? Regulating the intercountry adoption of American children. *Cornell International Law Journal, 40*(2), 489–519.

Bailey, J. D. (2009). Expectations of the consequences of new international adoption policy in the U.S. *Journal of Sociology and Social Welfare, 36*(2), 169–184.

Bureau of Consular Affairs. (n.d.-a). *Country information: China.* Washington, DC: U.S. State Department. Retrieved from http://travel.state.gov/content/adoptionsabroad/en/country-information/learn-about-a-country/china.html

Bureau of Consular Affairs. (n.d.-b). *Country information: Ethiopia.* Washington, DC: U.S. State Department. Retrieved from http://travel.state.gov/content/adoptionsabroad/en/country-information/learn-about-a-country/ethiopia.html

Bureau of Consular Affairs. (n.d.-c). *Country information: Guatemala.* Washington, DC: U.S. State Department. Retrieved from http://travel.state.gov/content/adoptionsabroad/en/country-information/learn-about-a-country/guatemala.html

Bureau of Consular Affairs. (n.d.-d). *Country information: India.* Washington, DC: U.S. State Department. Retrieved from http://travel.state.gov/content/adoptionsabroad/en/country-information/learn-about-a-country/china.html

Bureau of Consular Affairs. (n.d.-e). *Country information: Russia.* Washington, DC: U.S. State Department. Retrieved from http://travel.state.gov/content/adoptionsabroad/en/country-information/learn-about-a-country/russia.html

Bureau of Consular Affairs. (n.d.-f). *Country information: South Korea.* Washington, DC: U.S. State Department. Retrieved from http://travel.state.gov/content/adoptionsabroad/en/country-information/learn-about-a-country/south-korea.html

Bureau of Consular Affairs. (n.d.-g). *What is intercountry adoption?* Washington, DC: U.S. State Department. Retrieved from http://travel.state.gov/content/adoptionsabroad/en/adoption-process/what-is-intercountry adoption.html

Bureau of Consular Affairs. (2008). *Country information: Russia.* Washington, DC: U.S. State Department. Retrieved from http://travel.state.gov/content/adoptionsabroad/en/country-information/learn-about-a-country/russia.html

Bureau of Consular Affairs. (2013). *FY 2012 annual report on intercountry adoption.* U.S. Department of State IAA §104(b). Washington, DC: U.S. State Department.

Bureau of Consular Affairs. (2014). *FY 2013 annual report on intercountry adoption.* U.S. Department of State IAA §104(b). Washington, DC: U.S. State Department.

Carriere, J. (Ed.). (2010). *Maintaining identities: The soul work of adoption and aboriginal children in Aski Awasis/children of the Earth First Peoples speaking on adoption.* Halifax and Winnipeg: Fernwood Publishing.

Council on Accreditation (COA). (2014). *Hague accreditation and approval standards.* Retrieved September 22, 2014, from http://coanet.org/standards/standards-for-hague-agencies/

Davenport, D. (2004, October 27). Born in America, adopted abroad. *Christian Science Monitor.* Retrieved from www.csmonitor.com/2004/1027/p11s01-lifp.html

Hague Conference on Private Intercountry Law. (1993). The Hague Convention on protection of children and co-operation in respect of Intercountry Adoption

(1993). Retrieved from www.hcch.net/index_en.php?act=conventions.pdf&cid=69.

Hayes. (2011). The legality of independent intercountry adoption under the Hague Convention. *International Journal of Law, Policy, and the Family*, 25(3), 288–317.

Groza, Houlihan, & Rosenberg. (2001). International adoptions. In V. Groza & K. Rosenberg (Eds.), *Clinical and practice issues in adoption–revised and updated: Bridging the gap between adoptees placed as infants and as older children*. (pp. 187–206). New York: Praeger.

Groza, V., & McCreery Bunkers, K. (2014). The United States as a sending country for intercountry adoption: Birth parents' rights versus the 1993 Hague Convention on Intercountry Adoption. *Adoption Quarterly, 17*(1), 44–64. doi:10.1080/10926755.2014.875089

Rotabi, K. S., & Gibbons, J. L. (2012). Does the Hague Convention on Intercountry Adoption adequately protect orphaned and vulnerable children and their families? *Journal of Child and Family Studies, 21,* 106–119. doi:10.1007/s10826-011-9508-6

Sargent. (2004). Suspended animation: The implementation of the Hague Convention on Intercountry Adoption in Romania and the United States. *Texas Wesleyan Law Review, 10*, 351–380.

Schmit. (2008). The Hague Convention: The problems with accession and implementation. *Indiana Journal of Global Legal Studies*, 15 (1), 375–395.

Selman, P. (2012). Global trends in intercountry adoption: 2001–2010. *Adoption Advocate 44*. Callahan, N. M., & Johnson, C. (Eds.). National Council for Adoption.

Smith, S. L. (2006). *Safeguarding the rights and well-being of birthparents in the adoption process*. New York: Donaldson Adoption Institute. Retrieved from http://www.adoptioninstitute.org/old/publications/2006_11_Birthparent_Study_All.pdf

Suter, E. (2008). Discursive negotiation of family identity: A study of U.S. families with adopted children from China. *Journal of Family Communication*, vol.8, issue 2, 126–147.

U.S. Department of State (DOS). (n.d.-a). Intercountry adoption statistics. Retrieved from http://adoption.state.gov/about_us/statistics.php

U.S. Department of State (n.d.-b). Universal Accreditation Act of 2012. Retrieved from http://adoption.state.gov/hague_convention/agency_accreditation/universal_accreditation_act.php

U.S. Department of State (n.d.-c). Hague Complaint Registry. Retrieved from http://travel.state.gov/content/adoptionsabroad/en/hague-convention/agency-accreditation/hague-complaint-registry.html

U.S. Department of State. (2009). Overview. Retrieved from http://adoption.state.gov/hague_convention.php

U.S. Department of State. (2013). Agencies denied accreditation. Retrieved from http://adoption.state.gov/hague_convention/agency_accreditation/deniedagencies.php

U.S. Department of State. (2014, March). FY 2013 Annual report on intercountry adoption. Retrieved from http://adoption.state.gov/content/pdf/fy2013_annual_report.pdf

Zhang, Y. & & Lee, G. (2011). Intercountry versus transracial adoption: An analysis of adoptive parents' motivation and preferences in adoption. *Journal of Family Issues, 32*, 1. 75–98.

# Legal and Policy Issues Affecting Intercountry Adoption Practices

▸ KAREN SMITH ROTABI AND CARMEN MÓNICO

THE END OF WORLD WAR II in the late forties marked the beginning of the practice of formally adopting children internationally on a large scale. The practice is called intercountry adoption (ICA) and at least one million children have been adopted internationally since the early days, as the practice truly took off in South Korea in the mid-fifties. Half of all international adoptees have joined U.S. families (Selman, 2012). For children, the impact of ICA has been profound; the research on improvements in child development and health alone, make a strong case for the practice of ICA (Juffer & van IJzendoorn, 2012; Miller, 2012). For individuals and couples who build their families through ICA, the opportunity to be matched with a child from another country is frequently a deeply satisfying experience in which their family life goal is realized. However, there have been problems in the actual ICA adoption process, including serious persistent problems in illicit adoptions (Ballard, Goodono, Cochran, & Milbrandt, in press; Gibbons & Rotabi, 2012). When this is the case, birth families are exploited; their circumstances of poverty typically leave them vulnerable and the emotional aftermath of an illicit adoption is profound.

### PROTECTING VULNERABLE PEOPLE: INTERNATIONAL PRIVATE LAW AND A CHILD RIGHTS APPROACH

Attempts at reform are under way globally to regulate the market forces in ICA (Ballard et al., in press; Rotabi & Gibbons, 2012). Most notably, the Hague Convention of May 29, 1993, on Protection of Children and

Co-operation in Respect of Intercountry Adoption (hereafter referred to as the Hague Convention or simply the HCIA), as of June 1, 2014, had ninety-three contracting states, including the United States. As international private law, the Hague Convention was developed to prevent the sales and abduction of children under the guise of ICA (Hague Conference on International Private Law [HCCH], 1993). The "best interests of the child" is the central value (McKinney, 2007). Recognized by adoption experts to be an important step forward (Gibbons & Rotabi, 2012; Roby & Maskew, 2012; Rotabi & Gibbons, 2012), the HCIA has been critical in reform efforts because of an unfortunate pattern of force, fraud, and coercion (Ballard et al., in press; Freundlich, 2000; Gibbons & Rotabi, 2012; Hollingsworth, 2003; Rotabi, 2012c; Rotabi & Gibbons, 2012).

Fundamentally, the primary purpose of the Convention is the protection of the child within his or her biological family and community. Consistent with the HCIA is a continuum of care—called the subsidiarity principle—oriented to preserving biological and kinship family life with child rights–best interests focus. Roby (2007) presents a child rights approach to ICA that is consistent with principles of the HCIA. Before adoption, children's rights include (1) the right to life, maternal, prenatal care, and health care; (2) the right to grow up in a family; and (3) the right to grow up in his or her own culture. During adoption, children's rights include (1) the right to a determination of adoptability, (2) the right to be placed with a properly prepared adoptive family, (3) the right to be matched with families who can and will provide for special needs, (4) the right of protection from becoming a commodity, (5) the right to competent and ethical professional care, and (6) the right to give consent or express own opinion. After adoption, children's rights include (1) the right to full family membership, (2) the right to social acceptance, and (3) the right to have access to birth and identity records.

Importantly, children's right to adoption by extended family, kinship, or other nationals is fundamental. Then, the possibility of ICA may be determined to be appropriate after these in-country options have been explored by professional social workers. Roby (2007) further identifies that countries should provide family support services and also adopt regulations aimed at eliminating unethical practices on the part of public servants, as well as private adoption agencies, and others involved in the ICA chain. The elements in Roby's framework are useful when considering the practical implementation of the HCIA. Presented next are examples of adoption fraud that illustrate both the need for regulation as well as the points of fraud that must be addressed by the HCIA, and related laws. These cases serve as a backdrop—answering the obvious question of *how* illicit adoptions are carried out and thereby pointing to the directions of reform and greater accountability of ICA practices.

**CASE EXAMPLES OF ADOPTION FRAUD**

Child sales and abduction have been orchestrated in a variety of ways in numerous countries around the world. Contextual factors shape *how* illicit adoptions are orchestrated. Cambodia, Guatemala, Haiti, and Chad are presented as illustrative examples.

### Cambodia

In Cambodia an adoption facilitator, employed by Seattle Adoptions International, orchestrated child sales into an adoption scheme in a systematic manner from 1997 to 2001 with an estimated $8 million in profit (Maskew, 2004; Roby & Maskew, 2012; Smolin, 2004, 2006). The investigating U.S. Federal Marshall reported the illegal activities to be consistent with organized crime, including such dynamics as money laundering (Cross, 2005). Law enforcement investigation as well as legal proceedings in the United States uncovered a chain of events related to child sales; impoverished families were approached in villages with bags of rice and relatively small sums of money given upon signature of child relinquishment documents. Once secured, the child then entered into a chain of falsehoods required to establish that the child was an "orphan." Upon investigation, it was found that not only were the vast majority of the children *not* orphans, but many Cambodian families expected to stay in touch with their child. Some families reported that they thought their child was going to boarding school, whereas others understood that their child was going to a family in another country. They, however, expected visits with their child and that the child would return to Cambodia once he or she was a young adult. When it was understood the child would be living with another family, the concept of a legal severance of parental rights was most often not understood by Cambodian families (Cross, 2005).

In this particular case of Cambodia, the adoption facilitator served a relatively short jail sentence related to tax evasion because the laws were not sufficient, at that time, to prosecute on the grounds of child trafficking. After conducting an extensive analysis of the adoption fraud in Cambodia, Smolin (2006) concluded that this chain of illicit activities was orchestrated as "child laundering," a practice similar to money laundering, whereby the money's origin and the resulting illicit gain cannot be identified easily. Child laundering involves a chain of organized crime to change a child's identity by issuing or altering a child's birth certificate and deceitfully representing the child's social history, as well as other falsehoods to obtain the child's adoptability determination—that is the determination that the child is free and clear to be adopted internationally. As in money laundering, illegal transfers of money for child buying occurred; off-shore bank accounts were established and tax evasion transpired along with graft and corruption on the ground in Cambodia (Cross 2005; Maskew 2004; Smolin 2006).

Smolin (2006) asserts that fraudulent practices are orchestrated as part of a system that legitimizes and incentivizes practices of buying—trafficking—children under the guise of appropriate and ethical practices of adoption agencies. Smolin and others have scrutinized different illicit and unethical adoption practices used in other countries (Ballard et al., in press). Next, we look at so-called child rescue during the disaster in Haiti and Chad, and then we turn to Guatemala.

### Haiti and Chad

An important case that further illustrates force, fraud, and coercion occurred in mid-January 2010 during the postearthquake period in Haiti, when a U.S.-based Christian group attempted to transport thirty-three Haitian children to the Dominican Republic for placement in a home, while they waited to be adopted (*The Economist*, 2010; New Life Children's Refuge, n.d.). Once it became clear that the group was engaged in illegal removal of children from their families and community, members of the Idaho-based New Life Children's Refuge were detained in Haiti for child trafficking; the missionaries were charged with child abduction and held in prison for several months (Rotabi & Bergquist, 2010). Members of the group eventually were released from prison, and this event reminded many adoption practitioners and scholars of similar attempts to "rescue" children during emergencies (Bergquist, 2012; Rotabi, Armistead, & Mónico, in press).

For example, in 2007, staff members of the French charity, Zoé's Ark, were detained trying to airlift 103 children from Chad; they were charged with child kidnapping and six of them were jailed (Bergquist, 2012; *The Economist,* 2010; Rotabi & Bergquist, 2010). This particular case, like the Haitian case, received considerable media attention when the fraudulent chain was discovered. The child evacuation plan was disguised as an attempt to rescue children from the war in neighboring Sudan. Although the individuals involved in this "rescue" attempt were incarcerated in Chad, they eventually were pardoned after diplomatic intervention from France (Bergquist, 2012).

### Guatemala

In recent history, Guatemala has the most notorious record of pervasive force, fraud, and coercion as related to ICA on a large scale. In this particular country, the complexity of fraud was rooted in a weak state as a result of a 36-year civil war (1960–1996). Also, Guatemala is one of the poorest countries in the Western Hemisphere where human trafficking, in general, is recognized to be common in the twenty-first century (Estrada Zepeda, 2009). Furthermore, violence against women is so extreme at a societal and familial level that it is considered to be an endemic social problem (Estrada Zepeda, 2009).

These facts coincided with the country's child adoption laws and other social protection regulations that were inadequate during the adoption boom years. An unknown, but significant, number of approximately 30,000 adoptions that took place between 2000 and 2009, were unethical at best and illicit at worst. The problems were such that the United Nations intervened with an investigation that resulted in an explosive report in the year 2000, when attempts were first made to regulate the system (United Nations, 2000).

Regardless of human rights reports and criticism, the ICA system persisted and by 2010 an extensive investigation by the *Comision Internacional contra la Impunidad* (International Commission Against Impunity in Guatemala [CICIG], 2010) found evidence of the participation of members of state institutions in irregular adoptions, including "child laundering" activities by the Court for Children and Adolescents, which declared stolen and purchased children as "abandoned" to begin the adoption process. According to the CICIG report, the U.S. Embassy in 2005 conducted a study of prospective adoptive parents and found that they were paying exorbitant amounts for the adoptions (i.e., US$17,300 to $45,000 in adoption fees). The CICIG (2010) also found that the Office of the Attorney General authorities recognized that some of the birth mothers were being paid to relinquish their children. Family Court judges denied direct responsibility for making final decisions about the adoptions, and social workers handling those cases were *not* conducting home visits or field investigations to verify cases. They relied only on information provided by the lawyers processing the adoption. With Guatemalan lawyers in the main position of power, the adoption of children became a distorted process in which a small group of corrupt lawyers profited from illicit adoptions.

### GUATEMALAN HUMAN RIGHTS DEFENDERS STEP IN TO PROTECT WOMEN AND CHILDREN

Under these conditions the human rights abuses were profound—a failure of the state to protect its children and families. In time, human rights defenders in Guatemala took up the cause to demand change, including filing critical legal cases. For example, Fundación Sobrevivientes or Survivors Foundation (Estrada Zepeda, 2009), provided legal assistance to a group of mothers experiencing child abduction in Guatemala (Mónico, 2013). One of the women is Ana Escobar.

Escobar's case became known when the Associated Press reported about her child's abduction (Associated Press, 2008a, 2008b). Escobar's terrifying story of a child kidnapping unfolded in her workplace, a shoe store in Guatemala City. After her assault, Escobar sought help from the police only to be chastised by the officials as being a birth mother who had changed her mind—accused of already having profited from child sales. She searched and searched for her daughter. Then, upon a chance sighting of the young child when passing an official's office where she was lodging a complaint, Escobar was finally able to plead with officials to DNA test the child that she claimed to be her daughter (Personal communication, A. Escobar, August 9, 2009). That test was positive and the ICA process was suspended for this particular child. It was, at this point in Guatemalan adoption history, the clearest single proven case of child abduction into adoption through organized criminal networks to carry out ICA fraud, which included judges, lawyers, care providers, and adoption agencies. This is evidenced, in part, by the fact that a previous DNA test linked Ana's daughter to the woman who falsely claimed to be the child's birth mother. Furthermore, during the required interview by the U.S. Embassy, this woman falsely claimed to be the birth mother as she verified her consent to the adoption. With such a backdrop of evidence, the world learned that DNA tests were false in Escobar's case. Other cases of DNA fraud also have been documented as the media reported on the failings of Guatemala's ICA system . For example, in another high-profile case, Guatemalan courts found a child to be abducted into adoption. A standing court order for the child's return continues to be ignored by the U.S. family, with no resolution of the case (Rotabi, 2012a).

Legal claims have been observed in other countries to include Vietnam, India, the Marshall Islands, Samoa Islands, El Salvador, and elsewhere (Ballard et al., in press; Bergquist, 2012; Gibbons & Rotabi, 2012). The problem has been so pervasive that long-term attempts to truly regulate illicit adoption practices have been under way in earnest for well over a decade in the United States. Guatemala, too, has undertaken reform. Both countries are presented as case examples of HCIA implementation.

### PRACTICAL IMPLEMENTATION OF THE HAGUE CONVENTION: THE UNITED STATES AND GUATEMALA

To combat illicit practices—child sales and abduction—each HCIA signatory country agrees upon principles and standards, with the "best interests of the child" and the "principle of subsidiarity" being core to HCIA implementation. Each country implements the HCIA as per their context and resources; domestic adoption laws in each country are an important and integral component to effective application of the HCIA.

#### U.S. Implementation of the Hague Convention

In the United States, the Hague Convention entered into full force in April 2008. Part of U.S. implementation of the HCIA was the passage of the U.S. Intercountry Adoption Act of 2000 (IAA, P.L. 106–279 [2000];

Smolin, 2004, 2006). This particular law domesticates principles of the Hague Convention into U.S. legal code, and it creates regulatory mechanisms, including the possibility to effectively prosecute individuals involved in this form of child trafficking (Rotabi, 2008). Other countries that have ratified the Hague Convention and have undertaken the same process of domesticating the HCIA with congruent local legislation. This ensures that ICA laws are harmonized globally—thereby providing a uniform system and procedures that ideally enable and enhance the collaboration between interacting governments (Boéchat, 2013).

U.S. implementation of the HCIA has required substantial institutional changes, and in the twenty-first century, the new policies and procedures have affected practice considerably. Transformation of legal frameworks and policies interface with improved adoption agency systems. As such, greater professionalism within agencies and higher standards on the part of civil servants has improved the ICA system. Implications for practice, related to adoption agencies and professionals will be discussed later in the chapter, and we now turn to the implementation of the HCIA in a low-resource country with significant challenges in terms of regulatory and procedural change.

### Guatemala's Hague Convention Implementation

Guatemala ratified the Hague Convention and a domestic law was passed by Guatemala's Congress at the end of 2007 (Bunkers & Groza, 2012). The Guatemalan law focuses on the subsidiarity principle, which requires that

---

The Hague Convention on Intercountry Adoption (HCIA) requires that a country develop their congruent domestic laws on adoption. For example, in the United States, the Intercountry Adoption Act was passed in 2000, and this legislation identifies the U.S. Department of State (DOS) as the central adoption authority and the DOS Office of Children's Issues provides oversight of U.S. implementation of the HCIA. This regulatory role includes accreditation of adoption agencies as well as responding to illegal activities with powers to initiate investigations in collaboration with the Department of Justice. The Office of Children's Issues may determine that another country is not within convention compliance and deem the country closed for child adoption by U.S. citizens.

a concerted effort is made to support the child's welfare within his or her own community and country. In other words, when a child is orphaned or vulnerable, she must receive appropriate child welfare services before ICA (Rotabi & Gibbons, 2012). When that is not possible, a child can be made available by appropriate government authorities, called the Central Authority in the HCIA.

Fundamentally, this idea of subsidiarity translates into a continuum of care in which a child identified to be at risk of an out-of-home placement ideally would receive family support services to prevent her permanent removal from biological family and community life (HCCH, 2008). Biological family support is fundamental to promote the child's care within the family system, and when that fails, alternative care in the community is the first step for social service authorities to take. This community care may include guardianship and other forms of care, and foster care is appropriate in some countries. Then, when this option is not possible and adoption is identified as a plan, domestic adoption is the priority (HCCH, 2008). Only when a domestic adoption has been ruled out, may a child be identified as appropriate for ICA as per the subsidiarity principle; institutional childcare is not a priority over ICA (HCCH, 2008).

A thorough investigation of the child's social history is necessary when possible, and other case management strategies are required to engage the family to explore all options to preserve the family system, including kinship care. Such an approach, when done well, is time-consuming and often results in delays in child ICA placement. As a result, criticism has been lodged, and the debates about this issue are quite compelling (Bartholet & Smolin, 2012) when one considers the developmental and emotional problems experienced by a child when she must *wait* and languish in care in a residential institution (Juffer & van IJzendoorn, 2012).

## COMMON MISCONCEPTIONS OF THE HAGUE CONVENTION

Even with many positive steps forward to ensure ethical practices, the HCIA has been criticized for a significant downturn in ICAs to the United States and elsewhere. When one examines the facts, however, the HCIA is only one part of the radical decline in the practice. Figure 2.1a depicts the downturn of ICAs to the United States in recent history.

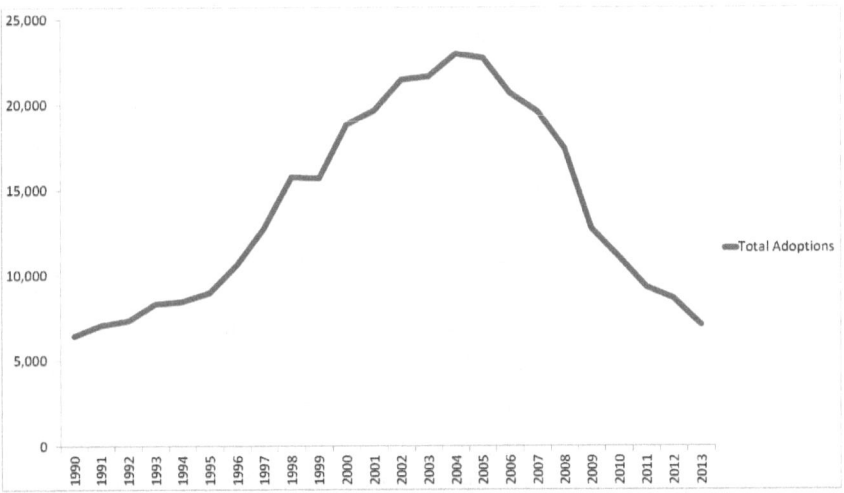

FIGURE 2.1A  **Transnational Adoptions to the United States, 1999–2013**
*Source:* U.S. Department of State, 2014.

One fact is indisputable, ICA to the United States was at an all-time high in 2004 with 22,884 adoptions, and then a free fall in ICA began, with a more than 60 percent decrease overall by 2013. This fact alone underscores that the Hague Convention is not the sole factor in the decrease because the related regulations did not enter into full force in the United States until 2008—some 4 years after the major decrease began (Rotabi, 2008). When looking at the top-three countries of origin in recent times, unique dynamics in Russia, China, and Guatemala help explain the story of the decrease.

The Russian ICA moratorium with the United States is the result of multiple international incidents that enraged both the general public in Russia as well as the political sector (Rotabi & Heine, 2010). Multiple political forces were at play in terms of U.S.–Russia foreign relations, including a completely unrelated human rights abuse incident in Russia that resulted in the death of a relatively prominent individual in a Russian prison. When the United States publicly condemned Russia for its treatment of this particular prisoner, Russian Parliament swiftly instituted an adoption moratorium, and this particular bitter moment between the two governments most certainly contributed to the final moratorium. A moratorium, however, had been debated for several years in Russian Parliament, and it is fair to say that multiple factors contributed to the cessation of ICAs to the United States. Russian Parliament voted to end ICAs to the United States in late 2012 as a result of child abuse and neglect at the hands of U.S. adoptive parents. By mid-2012, Russia counted nineteen deaths of Russian adoptees in the United States, and there were other instances of child maltreatment, including a high-profile child sexual abuse and pornography case (Rotabi, 2012b). Notably, Russia has not signed the Hague Convention, and thus this international private law has had little impact on Russian adoptions. These problems, however, most certainly have been associated with the decline in practice.

In the case of China, a Hague Convention country, the slowdown is related to a number of factors, including a shift to children who are called "special needs" because of medical and emotional challenges (Dowling & Brown, 2009). This is a change from the previous China programming that was consider highly efficient—translating into relatively expedient adoptions of largely healthy and relatively young girl children who were reported to be abandoned (Johnson, 2012; Johnson, Banghan, & Liyao, 1998; Vich, 2013). That now has changed, however, as child abandonment is far less frequent and child placement wait times for China are now more than 5 years. Other factors include more domestic adoptions taking place in China and shifts in the one-child policy and greater flexibility for citizens of China in their family-building options. With an improvement of economic circumstances, some Chinese families simply decide to pay a fine for their second child rather than abandon daughters (Vich, 2013).

The case of Guatemala has been explored, but it is important to note that this small Central American nation was the only country of origin that continued to have a truly significant increase in adoption after 2004 (Selman, 2012). The slowdowns in other countries actually put increasing pressure on Guatemala as a country of origin. This pressure combined with the fact that approximately 90 percent of the children were infants or toddlers who were relatively healthy (Casa Alianza et al., 2007). Also, adoptions were processed quickly, many families experienced a year or less of wait time for child placement, which is an exceptionally short waiting period as compared with other countries (Bunkers & Groza, 2012). As a result, Guatemala was a popular country for U.S. families. The extremely positive reputation among prospective families endured even though most other countries, like Canada and the United Kingdom, entered into adoption moratoriums with Guatemala before 2004 (CICIG, 2010; Rotabi, 2012b). In time, some families who have adopted from Guatemala have come to realize that the expedient process was actually indicative of a loose process that did not safeguard the rights of the child or their families of origin. Some adoptive parents have come to wonder about the ethics of their own cases (Larsen, 2007; Seigal, 2011).

Once Guatemala finally entered into adoption moratorium, there was a shift elsewhere and most notably to Africa and specifically Ethiopia (Rotabi, 2010), an often-cited country to have a noted increase in ICAs in recent times. The number of Ethiopian children adopted by U.S. families is still relatively small in the overall picture, as indicated in figure 2.1b. Dynamics of corruption in Ethiopia have gained attention in the international press, and procedures are of concern there and in other African countries (Bunkers, Rotabi, & Mezmur, 2012; Mezmur, 2010).

Even with the obvious need for greater regulation of ICAs from Africa, many countries such as Ethiopia have not yet signed the Hague Convention. Although there have been attempts to encourage African countries to

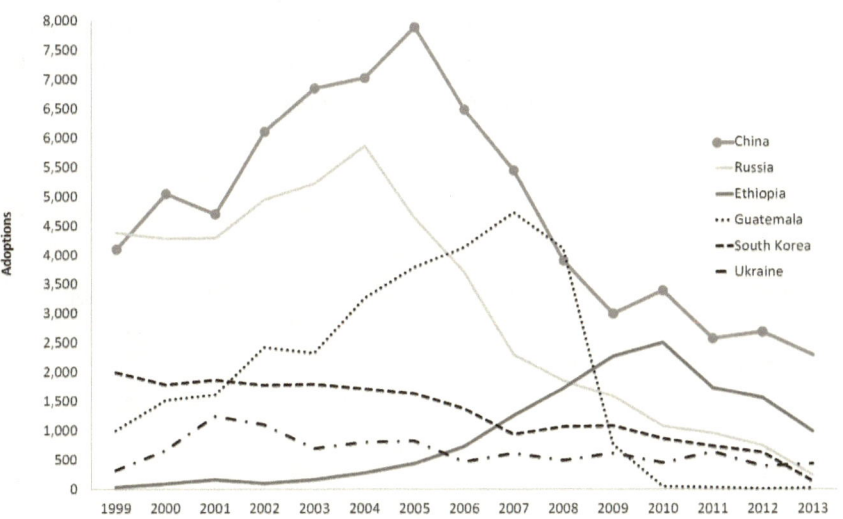

FIGURE 2.1B **U.S. Visas Issued to Orphans, 1990–2013**
Source: U.S. Department of State, 2014.

join this international private law, progress has been slow. Some countries, however, appear to be seeking technical assistance from the Hague Conference on International Law Permanent Bureau and are making steps toward contracting the HCIA. The Hague Permanent Bureau has no ability to *fund* reform initiatives. Humanitarian assistance organizations are poised to assist in this particular aspect of change. Technical assistance, on the other hand, is available from the Hague Permanent Bureau for suggested systems improvement to better meet the obligations of subsidiarity according to the HCIA. Countries moving in that direction are reported to be Mozambique, Rwanda, Namibia, and the Seychelles (Africa Child Policy Forum, 2012). Notably, Uganda has also shown early signs of movement toward the HCIA, and this move is welcome by those making investments in child protection in this particular country, which has seen a remarkable increase in ICA in the past few years (Personal communication, Sylvia Namubiru, August 11, 2014).

Other countries have been on a steady decline, most notably South Korea, which has sent well over 100,000 children worldwide since the mid-fifties. Changes include a vibrant twenty-first-century economy and increasingly less stigmatized circumstances for illegitimate births. Also, in parallel, domestic adoptions are now outnumbering ICAs in South Korea. As such, these social conditions, as well as other factors, like birth control and women's rights have an accumulative effect on ICA downturns. In the case of increased domestic adoptions South Korea is a success story. The country was previously criticized for ignoring their child protection problems and simply sending their orphaned and vulnerable children elsewhere (Fronek, 2006). Systems of care, however, have been built and social services are far more responsive to the needs of children and their families. South Korean adoption declines are an example of global changes in ICA that are not related to moratorium of the practice, but rather to a decrease resulting from social change. This trend is expected to continue globally as systems of childcare are strengthened and economic conditions improve around the world.

### PRACTICAL APPLICATION OF THE HAGUE CONVENTION AND IMPACT

In this era of reform, we now turn to the impact of the HCIA on (1) adoption agencies and professionals, (2) birth families, (3) adoptive families, and (4) child development.

## Impact of the Hague Convention on Adoption Agencies and Professionals

Given the problems outlined thus far, the process and procedures for ICA have been strengthened considerably in the United States and Western Europe where most children are adopted. The most predominant changes have been at the adoption agency level. Improvements include the policies and procedures that do not allow adoption agencies to intervene before attempts to support children and families prior to adoption, as per the subsidiarity principle. Furthermore, adoption agencies and their professionals must be vigilant to prevent child sales and abduction.

Among the Hague Convention–related requirements is greater financial transparency in adoption agency transactions. In practical terms, this translates to adoption agency accountability for how money is handled—for example, salaries based on ordinary professional compensation without opportunity for bonuses or contingency fees based on the number of children placed into adoption. In the United States, a set fee schedule also must be provided for prospective families in their earliest contact with the agency (Council on Accreditation [COA], 2007). This particular area of regulation is important to prevent a bait-and-switch scheme in which families have an expectation for adoption fees and then those costs escalate over time in a leveraging of prospective parents as they become attached to a particular child.

Other areas of improvement, at the agency level, include child placement standards for case planning (a case management requirement), preadoption training of families (with 10 verified educational hours), ICA adoption training of agency personnel (high-quality staff development and training activities), and ethics in general. In the United States, these areas are covered in agency accreditation standards with clear obligations to provide evidence (e.g., training certificates and case plans; COA, 2007).

Another practice area is the preparation of individuals and couples to be culturally aware and ready to integrate culture into adoptive family life. Although some agencies are more committed to this aspect of care than others, Bailey (2006) identifies a practice model that "promotes assessment of parents' cultural understanding, education of children's identity needs, and provision of resources and support for their education of the child's birth culture" (7). In this model, adoption agency staff become knowledgeable and deliver culturally competent services. In addition, in the best cases, adoption agency staff members provide support for parents as "cultural vanguards for their internationally adopted children" (7), and they perform their professional work based on standards promoting (not undermining) the best interest of the child.

Some agencies have transformed into far more effective and ethical organizations than others; however, fundamentally, agency accreditation has been the most important practical change in the United States as a result of the HCIA. Under this new system, financial transparency requirements not only protect children from being sold into ICA but also provide prospective adoptive families greater protections, too. For example, one family's fees may not be used to pay for services related to another family's adoption (COA, 2007). This safeguards application fees on a per-case basis so that if an agency is suffering mismanagement or some other crisis, money cannot be moved from one case to another without accountability. Even with greater financial transparency, there is no actual official documentation of average ICA costs, but it is known that commonly prospective families pay as much as US$25,000–40,000. Costs vary depending on the sending country and circumstances as well as agency operating procedures.

Another critical requirement is that agencies must have funds set aside for the operational budget (several months of monthly expenses) for unforeseen problems and difficult financial times. Furthermore, agencies now must have appropriate insurance and bonding (COA, 2007). All of these steps help to ensure that agencies are managing financial resources in a manner that protects individuals and families, including the children identified for adoption.

Additionally, professional standards include oversight and supervision by qualified professionals, most often master's level social workers (MSWs) with both credentials and appropriate experience. Also, when an agency is evaluated for accreditation, complaints against the agency are reviewed, including complaint documentation, held by state child placement licensing authorities (COA, 2007). This is a particularly important element of agency evaluation as complaints are reviewed and queried as appropriate.

Finally, under the IAA (2000), adoption service providers and professionals can be prosecuted for child trafficking. Although no such convictions under this particular law have been made to date, the message is clear for all of those engaged in ICA. Adoption agency directors and their boards of directors now may be held accountable for the practices taking place under their administration (Rotabi, 2008). As a result, the obligation to supervise those working both in the United States as well as the second country is taken more seriously with regulatory controls. This is particularly true in terms of supervising those providers in a low-resource area where graft and corruption often is pronounced (COA, 2007). As a result, there are multiple agency vulnerabilities in terms of force, fraud, and coercion (Smolin 2004, 2006).

Although the HCIA is an important step forward, concerns about the implications, at the agency level, have been raised. Bailey (2009) conducted a study with agency personnel providing adoption and ICA services; the study analyzed both the intended and unintended consequences of ICA practices during HCIA implementation in the United States. Most participants considered that the new regulations would provide safer and better adoption practices for families and children, particularly through the standardization of procedures and agency transparency, and the reduction of fraud and corruption. Some expressed concerns over the increased costs of insurance and administrative burden adoption agencies would be required to assume, and the danger of displacing small agencies out of ICA operations, regardless of their ethical performance. In addition, the increased paperwork required from prospective adoptive parents could make the adoption process more costly and cumbersome for everyone involved, possibly making the wait for legitimately adoptable children even longer than before (Bailey, 2009). This concern about a child waiting longer for adoptive placement, in the post-HCIA era, is a legitimate concern and it will be addressed later in the chapter.

### Impact of the Hague Convention on Birth Families

Social protection of the most vulnerable is the goal of the HCIA and birth family rights are considered and preserved throughout the international private law. Protections are oriented to appropriate social casework and family support taking place before a child's departure from his or her country of origin. The idea of a continuum of care—oriented to preserving the child's social and cultural life in their family and community of origin—was discussed earlier when considering the implementation of the Hague Convention in Guatemala. And, although this approach may seem straightforward, there are many challenges at the practical level, when one accounts for the vast differences among the countries of origin.

As a result, the Hague Permanent Bureau has also provided a *Guide to Good Practice* (HCCH, 2008), which was developed by adoption and legal experts. Practical recommendations are presented, including a macro-orientation to the bureaucratic structures and policies necessary for regulation to prevent improper financial gain. The requirement for a Central Authority in each country is given consideration as an oversight body; a collaborative relationship between the two Central Authorities involved in one child's case is included in this process. Additionally, direct practice implementation guidance is provided, including ethical consent and relinquishment processes (obtaining consents without inducements), unbiased counseling, the prevention of improper financial gain, legal processes (including necessary documentation of identity and preservation of child and family social history), and so forth.

### Impact of the Hague Convention on Adoptive Families

The HCIA has affected adoptive families in various ways. Improved practices include training of families in the necessary knowledge about the medical and emotional needs of children. Furthermore, cross-cultural considerations are presented to families. With appropriate training as well as enhanced support of adoption agencies—as required by accreditation standards (COA, 2007)—families are now more likely to identify special needs earlier and to seek help from relevant professionals. For example, families now receive detailed information about attachment disorders and medical risks. Also, supportive resources and referrals to services, when necessary, are now an expectation as a clear and reliable service area of adoption agencies. This is an area of system strengthening that supports adoptive families as well as holds them accountable for seeking social care, when necessary.

Another area of impact on adoptive families is the prerequisite home studies (Crea, 2012). Standards for home studies have improved considerably with far greater controls in place to verify backgrounds; financial ability to adopt, including appropriate health insurance; and other critical areas of adoption readiness (COA, 2007). Motivational factors for the individual's or the couple's desire to adopt are considered to ensure that the adoption placement is truly appropriate in terms of a child's permanency in their new family system. Improvements in home studies is one of the most obvious areas of impact in terms of interface with adoptive families—completing a HCIA-compliant home study is not an insignificant task and the individual's or the couple's motivation to adopt inevitably is tested during this intensive assessment process. Now, the process is far more holistic and detailed, and the home study is even worded with legal language not unlike a legal affidavit.

Finally, individuals and couples involved in ICA are now far more knowledgeable about their roles and responsibilities in the prevention of child buying. Although it may be argued that knowledge alone does not prevent corruption, the reality is that roles and responsibilities are now outlined by adoption agencies. Any family that engages in graft and corruption, such as offering a bribe, now does so with full knowledge that they are in violation of the law. This is an enhancement of previous practices, before HCIA implementation, in which families were largely unaware of the dark side of ICA in impoverished countries. When families found themselves navigating difficult ethical terrain in the past, in the pre-HCIA era, they were not armed with the necessary knowledge to manage their behavior in the context of a low-resource nation. It is an overreach to say that knowledge alone is enough, but families now enter into the ICA transaction with enough information to be held appropriately accountable if and when a problem arises.

### IMPACT OF THE HAGUE CONVENTION ON CHILD DEVELOPMENT

In academic literature, child development has received considerable attention, and the developmental gains and health recovery of most adoptees, after placement into their adoptive families, is astounding (Dalen, 2012; Juffer & van IJzendoorn, 2012; Miller, 2012). Note, however, that the Hague Convention does not specifically address child development outcomes; rather, it sets forth regulatory approaches to ethical adoptions as necessary to secure human rights and set forth a positive trajectory of growth and development, in cases in which the child is appropriate for ICA. As such, targets for child development and healthy growth in general are not explicitly outlined in the HCIA. At least two areas of concern, however, are worthy of a closer look: issues of child attachment and attachment disorders in addition to transracial and transcultural dimensions.

### Child Attachment and Attachment Disorders

Attachment disorders are a pronounced area of concern that occurs more frequently for children who have experienced child abuse, neglect, and institutionalization. As touched on earlier, one of the major critiques of the HCIA is bureaucratic delays in processing of children who meet the criteria of an ethical ICA, thereby exposing them to further damage associated with institutional care, including attachment disorders (Bartholet & Smolin, 2012).

Howe (2006) has defined attachment as a "system of protection at times of danger," adding that attachment behaviors are triggered "whenever the highly vulnerable human infant experiences anxiety, fear, confusion, or feelings of abandonment" (p. 128). Attachment disorders and trauma have been found to be associated with long stays in institutions and the abuse and neglect to which children adopted internationally may have been exposed, which can cause antisocial behavior and learning disabilities after adoption (Stelzner, 2003). Even when children are adopted young, trauma and broken attachments may result in serious socioemotional problems related to attachment disorders (Roberson, 2006).

### Transracial and Transcultural Dimensions

The intrinsic nature of ICA as transracial and transcultural became visible in high-resource countries engaged in ICAs, such as the United States. Bailey (2006) asserts that adoption in the United States should be seen as a history of both, interracial and transracial adoption. Historically, the preference of U.S. prospective adoptive parents has been for young, healthy, light-skinned children from foreign countries, with a majority of adopted children being girls (Barrett & Aubin, 1990). One of the major reasons more girls have been adopted historically is China's major role as a country of origin. That country's one-child policy has resulted in more abandoned girl children in the past. More recently, the demand for darker skinned children from countries in Africa has become a dynamic.

Hollingsworth (2008) points out that identity with a cultural group is a critical element of children's developmental outcomes, particularly when physical characteristics of the adoptee differ substantially from their family. Underscoring racial difference is important; the majority of families who adopt are white, whereas most children available for adoption are of color. The presence as a child of color in a white family is remarkable. Research indicates that some internationally adopted children report their "wish to be white like their parents and peers" (Juffer & Tieman, 2012, p. 212).

Often adoptive families and the children receive marked social attention (both positive and negative) as they go about their daily lives. As a result, children adopted internationally, as well as their families, have little ability to just blend in and live with the privacy of their adoption. It is a remarkable feature of the family system and many outsiders respond with comments like "you are so lucky" (referring to an impoverished background or birth family and subsequent rescue) or other remarks may be less direct but indicative of misinformed assumptions about ICA, including ideas like "you must be thankful" (Hopgood, 2010). There are also more subtle experiences of difference and discrimination in the greater society; some problems related to race are profound in terms of identity, self-esteem, and adoptee outcomes.

Hubinette (2012), a Swedish adoptee of color and researcher, asserts that racial issues among transnational adoptees of color tend to become the "elephant in the room" that often adoptive families ignore and do not want to talk about. He asserts that a white colorblindness occurs, excluding the cultural identity of adoptees, while defending and legitimizing the proposition that ICA is "successful." Hubinette (2012) takes a highly critical position when he further points out that this framing parallels a profitable adoption industry, underscoring the utility of such a narrative in further perpetuating a practice that he views as largely exploitative.

Turning to the evidence, Hubinette points out damning evidence in Sweden where international adoptees living in Sweden experience higher rates of substance abuse, criminality, and mental illness, and the statistics for the latter are startling. According to Hubinette (2012), "in fact, no other demographic subgroup in Sweden has a higher suicide rate than adult intercountry adoptees, as completed suicide is four to five times higher among the group than among the Swedish majority population" (p. 224). Poor adoptee child and later adult adoptee adjustment in this largely racially homogenous society of Sweden—where people of color live with great difference and discrimination according to Hubinette—requires critical discourse and social policy considerations in this Nordic country and elsewhere. This is an area for additional transracial adoption research with outcomes oriented toward adult adoptees and their mental health, including morbidity and mortality rates.

## CULTURAL COMPETENCE IN SOCIAL WORK AND ICA PRACTICES

The ecological model, strengths perspective, and empowerment theory are at the heart of culturally competent practice in social work (Browne & Mills, 2011). A truly culturally competent model requires a paradigm shift to "multiculturalization" in social work practice (Fong, 2011). It must include an "intersectional culturally humility perspective" or the ability to embrace diversity, an openness to reflective learning, and the acceptance of cultural differences (Ortega & Faller, 2011). Cultural humility may be the result of systematic self-evaluation and self-critique of the power dynamics inherent in the client–patient relationship (Tervalon & Murray-Garcia, 1998), and this humility may be obtained through a variety of cross-cultural exposures, including international voluntary experiences (e.g., Schuldberg et al., 2012) or work with immigrant and refugees in the United States. A cultural competence model for ICA must aim at enhancing cultural awareness, enabling knowledge acquisition, developing critical skills, and inducing learning; it must promote biculturalization of interventions with adoptees and their families, and it must include constant monitoring of personal and organizational progress toward aiming that competence (Fong, 2011). In fact, cultural competence is considered a "relational, dialogical process (a dialogue rather than an emphasis of worker's competence) between worker and the client, between cultures, and between people and contexts" (Lum, 2011, p. 3). Cultural competency in social work requires the consideration of various functions (practitioner, agency, community levels) as well as the various dimensions (micro, meso, and macro levels) of the model, and ethical standards and competencies must be upheld in the profession to engage in culturally competent practice (Lum, 2011).

Attending to guidelines, two models for ICA practices are considered here. Vonk (2001) argues that although parents have "to transform a particular set of attitudes, knowledge and skills into the ability to meet their children's unique racial and cultural needs . . . [social workers] must engage in a long-term development process towards cultural competence" (p. 248). Racial awareness, multicultural planning, and survival skills are necessary components of that culturally competent parenting practice, which must include pre- and postadoptive training (Vonk, 2001). Baden and Steward (2000) offer a model for understanding and nurturing cultural and identity experiences within transracial and transcultural adoptive families, which takes account of parents, as well as extended families, and their social and environmental contexts. The model identifies sixteen

> identities of transracial adoptees and are made up of the degrees to which they have knowledge of, awareness of, competence within, and comfort with their own racial group's culture, their parents' racial group's culture, and multiple cultures as well as the degree to which they are comfortable with their racial group membership and with those belonging to their own racial group, their parents' racial group, and multiple racial groups of those reared in racially and/or culturally integrated families. (p. 309)

These models exemplify the application of cultural competence principles in ICA practice. Thus, a culturally competent practice in ICA must consider the interaction of transracial and transcultural adoptive parents with their internationally adopted children, as well as the relationships between those families formed through ICA and their agency service providers.

In spite of the importance of developing culturally competent approaches in ICA practices, the Hague Convention, as enacted in the United States, requires only 10 hours of training for prospective adoptive parents, among which cultural competency is only one *of* suggested *and not required* contents (COA, 2007). Furthermore, training of agency personnel has the same ambiguity—cultural competence as a *suggested area* rather than absolute requirement. This area of training obligation in U.S. agency practice is loose as standards lack clear expectations (COA, 2007), allowing for agency discretion to choose from among a range of training topics, rather than an absolute requirement based on best practices in family–child adjustment and adoptee outcomes.

### CONCLUSION

This chapter provided an overview of policy and practical implementation of protective measures for ethical adoption practices, according to the HCIA. The backdrop of illicit adoptions offers illustrative examples, providing a basis from which to focus on *how to* regulate ICA practice. This chapter highlighted some of the major characteristics of adoption practices, using experiences in Guatemala and the U.S. implementation of the Hague Convention as case examples. In doing so, some of the issues of HCIA implementation are highlighted, including the fact that joining the international private law does not guarantee future ICA from a particular country.

Guatemala serves as a reminder that even signing the Hague Convention may result an indefinite moratorium for implementation so that the country can develop a consistent and humane alternative care and domestic adoption system.

We do not present the Hague Convention as a panacea. In fact, as authors, we know of no example of justice being fully served in cases of child sales or abduction gone before a court as a result of HCIA-related laws. This is poignant in regards to the biological family awaiting their daughter's return to Guatemala—there is simply no justice in this case thus far. As a result, we conclude that the HCIA ultimately lacks true and meaningful enforcement in these sorts of cases.

Furthermore, although there are useful theoretical frameworks and practical examples to improve ICA practices, we recognize that the market forces make these improvements difficult to implement, as the unscrupulous entrepreneurs continue to exploit children and their families as orphans are constructed through various means of child laundering. Upon conducting an analysis of the decline in ICA, Selman (2012) lamented that even more creative methods and nefarious practices may emerge as the demand for healthy children continues with even greater pressure from the marketplace. One may argue that the child rescue attempts in post-earthquake Haiti and the war-torn region of Sudan are examples of creative means of child abduction into adoption in this post-HCIA era, as discussed previously.

Although new illicit practices have not yet become apparent in documented trends, the sheer finances behind force, fraud, and coercion are not to be underestimated. This is particularly true across a range of low-resource countries that may have signed and ratified the HCIA, but remain largely lawless in the real or practical application of child protection laws and family support policies and practices. Currently, this is a concern in Cambodia as the United States may soon lift its moratorium.

Extreme poverty and scant child protection systems, however, remain a serious problem in a country that has a notorious history of ICA fraud. Fundamentally, it is difficult for a destination country, like the United States, to truly enforce HCIA policies when a country of origin has limited resources and child protection capacity in terms of a solid partnership in ethical ICA.

Lastly and importantly, concerns about the slowdown of the adoption process are legitimate when one considers children languishing in institutional care or other difficult circumstances as they wait for an adoptive placement. Developing both ethical and efficient systems are imperative to address this problem. Although ICA offers an alternative to less than 1 percent of all orphaned and vulnerable children in the world, the overall positive outcomes of an ethical and successful ICA cannot be underestimated. For it is the right of every child to grow up in a family environment.

### DISCUSSION QUESTIONS

1. What are the core problems with seeking informed consent from an impoverished birth mother who is interfacing with adoption agency representatives from high-resource countries?
2. Corruption is a problem in intercountry adoption (ICA). How may a social worker act in an unethical manner to "push through" an adoption case?
3. How might prospective adoptive parents become victims of fraud during the ICA process, especially as they interface with officials in a low-resource country? How might they become victims of fraud when interfacing with an unethical adoption agency?

### REFERENCES

Africa Child Policy Forum. (2012). *Africa: The new frontier for intercountry adoption.* Addis Ababa: Author.

Associated Press. (2008a, July 24). DNA tests confirm the first stolen baby in troubled Guatemalan adoption system. *Los Angeles Times.* Retrieved from www.msnbc.msn.com/id/25821096/ns/world_news-americas/t/dna=tests-confirm-first-stolen-guatemalan-baby/

Associated Press. (2008b, July 24). Stolen Guatemalan baby found just before adoption by U.S. couple. *Fox News*. Retrieved from http://www.foxnews.com/story/0,2933,390044.html

Baden, A. L., & Steward, R. J. (2000). A framework for use with racially and culturally integrated families: The cultural-racial identity model as applied to transracial adoption. *Journal of Social Distress and the Homeless, 9*(4), 309–336.

Bailey, J. D. (2006). A practice model to protect ethnic identity of international adoptees. *Journal of Family Social Work, 10*(3), 1–11. doi:10.1300/J039v10n03_01

Bailey, J. D. (2009). Expectations of the consequences of new international adoption policy in the U.S. *Journal of Sociology and Social Welfare, 36*(2), 169–182.

Ballard, R., Goodono, N., Cochran, R., & Milbrandt, J. (in press). *The intercountry adoption debate: Dialogues across disciplines*. Newcastle upon Tyne, England: Cambridge Scholars Publishing.

Bartholet, E., & Smolin, D. M. (2012). The debate. In J. L. Gibbons & K. S. Rotabi (Eds.), *Intercountry adoption: Policies, practices, and outcomes* (pp. 233–251). Surrey, England: Ashgate Press.

Barrett, S., & Aubin, C. (1990). Feminist considerations of intercountry adoptions. *Women and Therapy, 10*(1–2), 127. doi:10.1300/J015v10n01_12

Bergquist, K. J. S. (2012). Implications of the Hague Convention on the humanitarian evacuation and "rescue" of children. In J. L. Gibbons & K. S. Rotabi (Eds.), *Intercountry adoption: Policies, practices, and outcomes* (pp. 43–54). Surrey, England: Ashgate Press.

Boéchat, H. (2013, July 6). The grey zones of intercountry adoption: When adoptability rules are circumvented. Paper presented at the Fourth International Conference on Adoption (ICAR4), Bilbao, Spain.

Browne, C., & Mills, C. (2011). Theoretical frameworks: Ecological model, strengths perspective and empowerment theory. In R. Fong & S. B.C.L. Furuto (Eds.), *Cultural competence practice: Skills, intervention and evaluation* (pp. 10–32). Boston: Allyn & Bacon.

Bunkers, K. M., & Groza, V. (2012). Intercountry adoption and child welfare in Guatemala: Lessons learned pre and post ratification of the 1993 Hague Convention on the Protection of Children and Cooperation in Respect of Intercountry Adoption. In J. L. Gibbons & K. S. Rotabi (Eds.), *Intercountry adoption: Policies, practices, and outcomes* (pp. 119–131). Surrey, England: Ashgate Press.

Bunkers, K. M., Rotabi, K. S., & Mezmur, B. (2012). Ethiopia: Intercountry adoption risks and considerations for informal care. In J. L. Gibbons & K. S. Rotabi (Eds.), *Intercountry adoption: Policies, practices, and outcomes* (pp. 131–142). Surrey, England: Ashgate Press.

Casa Alianza, Presidential Commission for Human Rights (COPREDEH), Myrna Mack Foundation, Survivors Foundation, Social Movement for the Rights of Children and Adolescents, Human Rights office of the Archbishop of Guatemala, and the Social Welfare Secretariat. (2007). *Adoptions in Guatemala: Protection or market?* Guatemala City, Guatemala: Casa Alianza Publications.

Council on Accreditation (COA). (2007). *Hague accreditation and approval standards.* New York: Author. Retrieved from http://www.coanet.org/files/Hague_Accreditation_and_Approval_Standards.pdf

Crea, T. M. (2012). Intercountry adoptions and home study assessments: The need for uniformed practices. In J. L. Gibbons & K. S. Rotabi (Eds.), *Intercountry adoption: Policies, practices, and outcomes* (pp. 265–272). Surrey, England: Ashgate Press.

Cross, R. (2005, April 15). *Operation broken hearts: Transcript of Richard Cross video.* Lecture given at Samford University, Birmingham, Alabama. Retrieved from http://cumberland.samford.edu/files/rushton/Richard_Cross_transcript.pdf

Dalen, M. (2012). Cognitive competence, academic achievement, and educational attainment among intercountry adoptees: Research outcomes from the Nordic countries. In J. L. Gibbons & K. S. Rotabi (Eds.), *Intercountry adoption: Policies, practices, and outcomes* (pp. 199–220). Surrey, England: Ashgate Press.

Dowling, M., & Brown, G. (2009). Globalization and international adoption from China. *Child & Family Social Work, 14*(3), 352–361. doi:10.1111/j.1365-2206.2008.00607.x

*The Economist.* (2010, February 4). *Saviours or kidnappers?; International adoption.* Retrieved from http://www.economist.com/node/15469423

Estrada Zepeda, B. E. (2009). *Estudio Jurídico-social sobre trata de personas en Guatemala* [Socio-judicial study on human trafficking in Guatemala]. Guatemala City, Guatemala: Fundación Sobrevivientes [Survivors Foundation].

Fong, R. (2011). Culturally Competent Social Work Practice: Past and Present. In R. Fong & S. B.C.L. Furuto (Eds.), *Cultural competence practice: Skills, intervention and evaluation* (pp. 1–9). Boston: Allyn & Bacon.

Freundlich, M. (2000). Market forces: The issues in international adoption. In M. Freundlich, *Adoption and ethics* (pp. 37–66). Washington, DC: Child Welfare League of America.

Fronek P. (2006). Global perspectives in Korean intercountry adoption. *Asia Pacific Journal of Social Work and Development, 16,* 21–31.

Gibbons, J. L., & Rotabi, K. S. (Eds.). (2012). *Intercountry adoption: Policies, practices, and outcomes.* Surrey, England: Ashgate Press.

Hague Conference on Private International Law. (1993). *Convention of 29 May 1993 on protection of children and co-operation in respect of intercountry adoption.* Retrieved from http://www.hcch.net/index_en.php?act=conventions.text&cid=69

Hague Conference on Private International Law (HCCH). (2008). *The implementation and operation of the 1993 Hague Intercountry Adoption Convention: Guide to good practice.* Retrieved from http://www.hcch.net/upload/wop/ado_pd02e.pdf

Hollingsworth, L. D. (2003). International adoption among families in the United States: Considerations of social justice. *Social Work, 48,* 209–219.

Hollingsworth, L. D. (2008). Commentary: Does the Hague Convention on Intercountry Adoption address the protection of adoptees' cultural identity? And should it? *Social Work, 53,* 377–379.

Hopgood, L. (2010). *Lucky girl.* New York: Algonquin Books.

Howe, D. (2006). Development attachment psychotherapy with fostered and adopted children. *Child and Adolescent Mental Health, 11*(3), 128–134.

Hubinette, T. (2012). Post-racial utopianism: White color-blindness and "the elephant in the room": Racial issues for transnational adoptees of color. In J. L. Gibbons & K. S. Rotabi (Eds.), *Intercountry adoption: Policies, practices, and outcomes* (pp. 221–229). Surrey, England: Ashgate Press.

Intercountry Adoption Act of 2000. (2000). P.L. 106-279. U.S. Government Printing Office. Retrieved from http://www.gpo.gov/fdsys/pkg/BILLS-106hr2909enr/pdf/BILLS-106hr2909enr.pdf

International Commission Against Impunity in Guatemala [CICIF]. (2010). *Report on actors involved in the irregular adoption process in Guatemala after the entry into force of the Adoption Law 77-2007.* Retrieved from http://www.cicig.org/index.php?mact=News,cntnto1,detail,0&cntnto1articleid=547&cntnto1returnid=52

Johnson, K. (2012). Challenging the discourse of intercountry adoption: Perspectives from rural China. In J. L. Gibbons & K. S. Rotabi (Eds.), *Intercountry adoption: Policies, practices, and outcomes* (pp. 103–118). London, England: Ashgate Press.

Johnson, K., Banghan, H., & Liyao, W. (1998). Infant abandonment and adoption in China. *Population and Development Review, 24*(3), 469–510. doi:10.2307/2808152

Juffer, F., & Tieman, W. (2012). Families with intercountry adopted children: Talking about adoption and birth culture. In J. L. Gibbons & K. S. Rotabi (Eds.), *Intercountry adoption: Policies, practices, and outcomes* (pp. 212–220). London, England: Ashgate Press.

Juffer, F., & van IJzendoorn, M. H. (2012). Review of meta-analytical studies on the physical, emotional, and cognitive outcomes of intercountry adoptees. In J. L. Gibbons & K. S. Rotabi (Eds.), *Intercountry adoption: Policies, practices, and outcomes* (pp. 175–186). London, England: Ashgate Press.

Larsen, E. (2007, Nov/Dec). Did I steal my child? *Mother Jones.* Retrieved from http://motherjones.com/politics/2007/10/did-i-steal-my-daughter-tribulations-global-adoption

Lum, D. (2011). *Culturally competent practice: A framework for understanding diverse groups and justice issues* (pp. 3–47). Belmont, CA: Brooks/Cole.

Maskew, T. (2004). Child trafficking and intercountry adoption: The Cambodian experience. *Cumberland Law Review, 35,* 619–638.

McKinney, L. (2007). International adoption and the Hague Convention: Does implementation of the Convention protect the best interests of children? *Whittier Journal of Child and Family Advocacy, 6,* 361–375.

Mezmur, B. N. (2010, June). The Sins of the saviors: Trafficking in the context of intercountry adoption from Africa. Paper presented at the Special Commission of the Hague Conference on International Private Law. The Hague, Netherlands.

Miller, L.C. (2012). Medical status of internationally adopted children. In J. L. Gibbons & K. S. Rotabi (Eds.), *Intercountry adoption: Policies, practices, and outcomes* (pp. 187–198). London, England: Ashgate Press.

Mónico, C. (2013). Implications of Child Abduction for Human Rights and Child Welfare Systems: A Constructivist Inquiry of the Lived Experience of Guatemalan Mothers Publically Reporting Child Abduction for Intercountry Adoption. (Doctoral dissertation). Available from VCU Digital Archives, Electronic Theses and Dissertations, http://hdl.handle.net/10156/4373

New Life Children's Refuge. (n.d.). *Haitian orphan rescue mission.* Retrieved March 20, 2010, from http://www.esbctwinfalls.com/clientimages/24453/pdffiles/ haitnlcrhaitianorphanrescuemission.pdf

Ortega, R. M., & Faller, K. C. (2011). Training child welfare workers from an intersectional cultural humility perspective: A paradigm shift. *Child Welfare, 90*(5), 27–47.

Roberson, K. C. (2006). Attachment and caregiving behavioral systems in intercountry adoption: A literature review. *Children and Youth Services Review, 28*, 727–740. doi:10.1016/j.childyouth.2005.07.008

Roby, J. L. (2007). From rhetoric to best practice: Children's rights in intercountry adoption. *Children's Legal Rights Journal, 27*(3), 48–71.

Roby, J. L., & Maskew, T. (2012). Human rights considerations in intercountry adoption: The children and families of Cambodia and the Marshall Islands. In J. L. Gibbons & K. S. Rotabi (Eds.), *Intercountry adoption: Policies, practices, and outcomes* (pp. 55–66). Surrey, England: Ashgate Press.

Rotabi, K. S. (2008). Intercountry adoption baby boom prompts new U.S. standards. *Immigration Law Today, 27*(1), 12–19.

Rotabi, K. S. (June, 2010). From Guatemala to Ethiopia: Shifts in intercountry adoption leave Ethiopia vulnerable for child sales and other unethical practices. *Social Work and Society News Magazine*. Retrieved from http://www.socmag.net/?p=615

Rotabi, K. S. (2012a, July). *Child abduction, adoption, poverty and privilege clash as a child's return to Guatemala is blocked*. Retrieved from http://rhrealitycheck.org/article/2012/07/26/child-abduction-adoption-poverty-and-privilege-clash-as-child%E2%80%99s-return-to-guatema/

Rotabi, K. S. (2012b). Fraud in intercountry adoption: Child sales and abduction in Vietnam, Cambodia, and Guatemala. In J. L. Gibbons & K. S. Rotabi (Eds.), *Intercountry adoption: Policies, practices, and outcomes* (pp. 67–76). Surrey, England: Ashgate Press.

Rotabi, K. S. (2012c, October). *The Second Russian-American Child Welfare Forum: Opening remarks of the Russian child rights commissioner about intercountry adoption, responses, and the spirit of child protection collaboration between the two nations*. Retrieved from http://www.socmag.net/?p=776

Rotabi, K. S., Armistead, L., & Mónico, C. C. (in press). Sanctioned Government Intervention, "Misguided Kindness," and Child Abduction Activities of U.S. Citizens in the Midst of Disaster: Haiti's Past and its Future as a Nation Subscribed to the Hague Convention on Intercountry Adoption. In R. Ballard, N. Goodno, R. Cochran, & J. Milbrandt, (Eds.), *The Intercountry Adoption Debate: Dialogues Across Disciplines*. Newcastle upon Tyne, England: Cambridge Scholars Publishing.

Rotabi, K. S., & Bergquist, K. J. S. (2010). Vulnerable children in the aftermath of Haiti's earthquake of 2010: A call for sound policy and processes to prevent international child sales and theft. *Journal of Global Social Work Practice*. Retrieved from http://www.globalsocialwork.org/vol3no1/Rotabi.html

Rotabi, K. S., & Gibbons, J. L. (2012). Does the Hague Convention on Intercountry Adoption adequately protect orphaned and vulnerable children and their families? *Journal of Child and Family Studies, 21*(1), 106–119. doi: 10.1007/s10826-011-9508-6

Rotabi, K. S., & Heine, T. M. (2010). Commentary on Russian child adoption incidents: Implications for global policy and practice. *Journal of Global Social Work Practice*. Retrieved from http://www.globalsocialwork.org/vol3no2/Rotabi.html

Schuldberg, J., Jones, C. A., Hunter, P., Bechard, M., Dornon, L., Gotler, S., Shouse, H., & Stratton, M. (2012). Same, same but different: The development of cultural humility through an international volunteer experience. *International Journal of Humanities and Social Sciences, 2*(17), 17–30.

Seigal, E. (2011). *Finding Fernanda: Two mothers, one child, and a cross-border search for truth*. Oakland, CA: Cathexis Press.

Selman, P. (2012). The rise and fall of intercountry adoption in the 21st century: Global trends from 2001 to 2010. In J. L. Gibbons & K. S. Rotabi (Eds.), *Intercountry adoption: Policy, practice, and outcomes* (pp. 7–28). Surrey, England: Ashgate Press.

Smolin, D. M. (2004). Intercountry adoption as child trafficking. *Valparaiso University Law Review, 39*, 281–325.

Smolin, D. M. (2006). Child laundering: How the intercountry adoption system legitimizes and incentivizes the practices of buying, trafficking, kidnapping, and stealing children. *Wayne Law Review 52*(1), 113–200. Retrieved from://works.bepress.com/david_smolin/1

Stelzner, D. M. (2003). Intercountry adoption: Toward a regime that recognizes the "best interests" of adoptive parents. *Case Western Reserve Journal of International Law, 35*(1), 113–152.

Tervalon, M., & Murray-Garcia, J. (1998). Cultural humility versus cultural competency: A critical distinction in defining physical training outcomes in multicultural education. *Journal of Health Care for the Poor and the Underserved, 9*(2), 117–125.

United Nations. (2000). *Rights of the child—report of the special rapporteur on the sale of children, child prostitution and child pornography, Ms Ofelia Calcetas-Santos*. Retrieved from http://poundpuplegacy.org/node/30853

U.S. Department of State. (2014). *Intercountry adoption: Statistics.* Retrieved from http://adoption.state.gov/about_us/statistics.php

Vich, J. (2013, July 8). Realities and imaginaries on the Chinese transnational adoption program. Paper presented at the Fourth International Conference on Adoption (ICAR4), Bilbao, Spain.

Vonk, M. E. (2001). Cultural competence for transracial adoptive parents. *Social Work, 46*(3), 246–255.

# 3

# Legal and Policy Issues Affecting Transracial Adoption Practice

▸ RUTH G. McROY, AMY GRIFFIN, AND HOLLEE McGINNIS

THE U.S. FAMILY IS BECOMING more diverse as parents are choosing more frequently to adopt children not of their same race, through intercountry adoption and domestic transracial adoption (TRA). TRA refers to the legal placement of a child of one racial or ethnic group with adoptive parents of another ethnic group. Often in the United States, these adoptions typically refer to the "placement of children of color either from the U.S. or from another country, with Caucasian families" (Child Welfare Information Gateway, 2013b). According to the findings from the 2007 National Survey of Adoptive Parents, "four out of ten adopted children were in transracial adoptions—that is, their parents reported that both adoptive parents are (or the single adoptive parent is) of a different race, culture, or ethnicity than their child. The majority of adopted children have non-Hispanic white parents, but are not themselves non-Hispanic white" (Vandivere, Malm, & Radel, 2009, pp. 5–6).

Although TRA can apply to both domestic and international adoptions, in this book, TRA refers to domestic adoptions that occur in the United States. Adoptions that occur in international countries are referred to as intercountry adoptions (ICA).

### DEMOGRAPHICS

Domestic TRAs have increased since the passage of the Multiethnic Placement Act (MEPA) in 1994 made it illegal for agencies to refuse to place a child based on the race of the child or the family. Since that time, TRAs from the foster care system have grown from a rate of 10.8 percent in 1995 (20,000 total), to a rate of 15 percent in 2001 (50,000 total; National Adoption Information Clearinghouse, 2008, as cited in Malott & Schmidt 2012). Only a relatively small proportion of domestic private infant adoptions involve parents adopting children of different races; those that do are five times more likely to adopt children of other races, such as Asian, than black children (U.S. Government Accountability Office [GAO], 2007, as cited in Zhang & Lee, 2011). Also, Farr & Patterson (2009) found in their research, that "transracial adoptions occurred more often among lesbian and gay couples than among heterosexual couples and that they occurred more often among interracial than among same-race couples" (p. 187).

### Who Is Affected by Transracial Adoptions?

TRAs rarely involve the adoption of white children by black or other families of color. In 2007, as part of the National Survey of Children's Health, the first ever National Survey of Adoptive Parents was conducted with parents who had adopted 2,089 children from foster care, other domestic sources, and other countries (National Survey of Adoptive Parents, 2007). According to the findings,

> Adopted children are less likely to be of White or Hispanic origin than children in the general U.S. population, and they are more likely to be Black. The racial distribution of children varies by type of adoption, with children adopted from foster care most likely to be Black (35%) and those adopted internationally least likely to be Black (3%). The majority of children adopted internationally are Asian (59%), and the majority of children adopted privately from the United States are most likely to be White (50%). (Vandivere et al., 2009, p. 13)

The study findings revealed that white parents are likely to be adoptive parents of children from the foster care system (63 percent) compared with black parents (27 percent), even though a disproportionately high number (about 24,000) of black children in foster care are in need of adoption (U.S. Department of Health and Human Services [DHHS], 2014; Vandivere et al., 2009). The majority of TRAs occur for those adopting internationally (84 percent), a little more than a quarter of foster care adoptions are transracial (28 percent), and 21 percent of private domestic adoptions are transracial (Vandivere et al., 2009, p. 14).

### History of Transracial Adoptions

In many circles, the practice of TRA continues to be controversial, as it tends to challenge what was once considered "traditional" or inracial adoptions. Traditional or inracial adoptive placements attempt to match phenotypic characteristics (including race) of the parents with those of children (Jennings, 2006). For years, it was assumed that such matching would facilitate bonding of parent and child as similar characteristics would make them indistinguishable from families with biological children (McRoy & McRoy, 1974). Moreover, when adoption agencies were first established in the 1920s, their purpose was to assist white childless couples seeking to adopt healthy white infants, which typically had been relinquished by white unmarried mothers. At that time, black children typically were cared for in the public foster care system, and the option of being adopted was rarely made available to them.

> Historically Blacks have had to develop their own informal networks for foster care and adoption. While the majority of White children born out-of-wedlock were placed for formal adoption, nine out of every ten Black children born out of wedlock were retained by the extended family and only one-tenth placed with formal adoption agencies. (Hill, 1977, p. iv)

Over time, a number of events led to a shift in focus away from these traditional kinship arrangements and preference for inracial adoptions. Placements of children from other countries in the United States very slowly began to affect sentiment toward TRAs. For example, in the 1950s following the end of the Korean War, 2,300 Korean orphans were brought to the United States for the purpose of adoption. Because many of these children were half Korean and half white, it was assumed that such "mixed-race children" would be considered outcasts in Korea and were brought to the United States for placement with white families (Child Welfare League of America [CWLA], 1960).

During this period of the fifties, however, most individuals still rejected the practice of TRAs of black children and, in fact, the CWLA, which sets standards for adoption services, "cautioned that children with the same racial characteristics as their adoptive parents could be integrated more easily into the average family" (McRoy, 1989, p. 149). Between 1958 and 1968, the Bureau of Indian Affairs and the CWLA initiated a joint project involving the transracial placement of about 400 Native American children with white families. Families tended to believe that they were "providing homes for deprived children, who held the social status of the first real or pure Americans" (Benet, 1976; McRoy, 1989, p. 149).

In the 1960s, as the nation focused on racial integration and the civil rights movement, more attention was given to the large numbers of African American children languishing in the foster care system and needing permanency through adoption (McRoy, 1989). Attitudes toward TRA began to change during this period and an increasingly larger proportion of white families began to consider this option. Also, a decrease in white infants being born out of wedlock, and subsequently relinquished and placed for adoption, occurred because of the widespread use of contraceptives, liberalized abortion laws, and increased social acceptance of unwed parenthood (McRoy, 1994).

By the 1970s, approximately 119 white families were approved for adoption per 100 white children waiting to be adopted, whereas approximately 50 non-white adoptive homes were approved per 100 non-white children waiting to be adopted (McRoy & Zurcher 1983; Smith, 1972). This resulted in African American children frequently being labeled as "hard to place" and African American families were designated as being "hard to reach." The "hard-to-reach" label may be a result of the historic discrimination African American families have faced within the child welfare system, which affected the desire of these families to interact with the system. In the past, African American families seeking to adopt children often faced barriers in the approval process of becoming adoptive parents. The lack of African American staff in child welfare agencies, perceived cultural differences, and lack of recruitment strategies, only exacerbated the problem. The growing rate of African American children in need of adoptive homes and the belief that African American families were not interested in adopting, led some agencies to consider transracial placements instead of addressing the barriers that prevented these families from working successfully with the system and examining the reasons African American children were represented disproportionately in the system (Lakin & Whitfield, 1997; McRoy, Oglesby, & Grape, 1997).

In 1968, the CWLA changed its previous position giving preference for inracial placements, and stated that "There are families who have the capacity to adopt a child whose racial background is different from their own and such families should be encouraged to consider such a child" (CWLA 1968, p. 34). This was the first occurrence of the CWLA encouraging TRAs. Additionally, around the same time, the National Association for the Advancement of Colored People (NAACP) and the National Urban League called for consideration of TRAs (Benet, 1976; McRoy, 1989).

This support led to more than 10,000 black children being transracially adopted between 1967 and 1972 (Costin, 1979). This support, however, did incur a backlash from the National Association of Black Social Workers (NABSW) who stated in 1972: "Black children belong physically and psychologically and culturally in black families where they receive the total sense of themselves and develop a sound projection of their future. Only a black family can transmit the emotional and sensitive subtleties of perceptions and reactions essential for a black child's survival in a racist society" (pp. 2–3).

By 1973, the CWLA reversed its position claiming that children should be in same race placements to help facilitate integration within a new family and community, suggesting that state exchanges should be utilized to find inracial placements before considering a transracial placement (McRoy, 1989). This reversal led to a decline in the number of transracial adoptions. In 1981, the North American Council on Adoptable Children (Gilles & Kroll, 1991) issued a position statement: "Placement of children with a family of like ethnic background is desirable because such families are likely to provide the special needs of minority children with the strengths that counter the ill effects of racism.... NACAC supports inclusion of multiethnic adoption as an option for children" (NACAC 1993, p. 37).

In 1994, as the rates of African American children in need of adoption continued to increase (46 percent) the NABSW modified its position and stated that although same-race adoptions were preferred, TRAs should be considered in certain situations (McRoy, 2004).

## POLICIES REGULATING TRANSRACIAL ADOPTIONS

Policies regulating transracial adoptions vary by adoption type and a child's origins. Two federal laws apply to the adoption of children of color who are involved in the public child welfare system. The Multi-Ethnic Placement

Act (MEPA) of 1997, as amended by the Removal of Barriers to Interethnic Adoption Provisions (IEP) of 1996, was designed to

> eliminate race-related barriers to adoption by prohibiting foster care and adoption agencies that receive federal funds from delaying or denying placement decisions on the basis of race, color, or national origin of either the adoptive or foster parent or child. The law also requires states to diligently recruit potential foster and adoptive families that reflect the ethnic and racial diversity of children in the state who need foster care and adoptive homes. (GAO 2007, p. 10)

The Indian Child Welfare Act (ICWA) of 1978 governs cases involving the adoption of Native American children. After legislation is passed, the U.S. Congress delegates give rule-making authority to a federal agency that issues administrative regulations, explaining how the law will be put into effect (Bailey & Delavega, 2011). Different federal agencies oversee the implementation of the three federal laws related to TRA: the Department of the Interior, Bureau of Indian Affairs (BIA), stipulates regulations for the implementation of ICWA; and the Department of Health and Human Services (DHHS), in conjunction with the Office of Civil Rights (OCR), regulates the implementation of MEPA-IEP. Furthermore, state laws and court cases shape state adoption practices, as well as (1) standards of practice issued by accreditation agencies, (2) best practices issued by child welfare organizations and social work associations, and (3) individual agency policies.

### Passage of the Multiethnic Placement Act (MEPA)

In 1994, to help alleviate the barriers to African American children being adopted, Congress passed MEPA (PL-103-382). Two years later, the IEP amended MEPA, which removed the word "solely" in the legislation regarding the refusal or rejection of an adoptive placement "solely on the basis of race." The goals of MEPA were to decrease the length of time a child waits to be adopted; to help prevent discrimination on the basis of race, culture, or national origin; and to identify and recruit foster and adoptive parents that meet the needs of children waiting placement (Chibnall, Dutch, Jones-Harden, Brown & Gourdine, 2003). MEPA-IEP, however, set the policy standard that race could no longer be a factor to deny or delay the placement of the child.

The passage of MEPA resulted from increased attention being given to children aging out of the foster care system without permanent placements and the discrepant rates for minority, especially African American children. By the early 1990s, only 3 percent of white unmarried mothers placed their infants for adoption, compared with 31.7 percent who placed in the sixties. Yet, the desire for couples seeking to adopt children remained: approximately 2 million white couples sought to adopt children (especially infants) by the nineties (McRoy, 1994).

### The Indian Child Welfare Act

In direct contrast to MEPA, which promotes colorblindness, another piece of federal legislation, the ICWA of 1978 (PL-95-608), addresses the disproportionately high rates of Native American children in care. At the same time, it attempts to provide permanence for Native American children, while focusing on the issue of race. ICWA sought to "protect the best interests of Indian children and to promote the stability and security of Indian tribes and families." The ICWA gives Native American communities the ability to make placement decisions of any Native child whose parental rights have been terminated. The Native American courts require higher standards of proof to be provided before a child is removed from their parents. If a removal does happen, however, efforts must be made to place the child with

> a member of the Indian child's extended family first and if not possible, place with an Indian foster home licensed, approved, or specified by the Indian child's tribe, and, if this is not possible, find an Indian foster home licensed or approved by an authorized non-Indian licensing authority, or an institution for children approved by an Indian tribe or operated by an Indian organization which has a program suitable to meet the Indian child's needs. (National Indian Child Welfare Association, 2015)

This decision was made to help children maintain connections to their families and tribes. Although ICWA has effectively handled the sovereignty issue for Native American children, there has never been federal legislation with the same aim for African American children (Dixon, 2013).

Some have suggested that based on the lessons of ICWA we should find ways to empower African American communities and give them a role in the provision of services to children and families (Curtis & Denby, 2011). Clearly, much more needs to be done to support, empower, and preserve African American and Native American birth families to enable them to parent their children within their communities.

### IMPACT OF MEPA ON AFRICAN AMERICAN ADOPTIONS

Has MEPA solved the problem of the child welfare system finding African American children permanent homes? It is relatively impossible to determine the placement patterns for groups of children, as no official recording of racial heritage exists for private or public adoptions (Samuels, 2009). Statistics for FY 2004 on youth placed with public agency involvement, however, suggest that 28 percent of the children were placed transracially (Child Welfare Information Gateway, 2013a). Additionally, of the 2.5 percent of all households that adopt children, less than 24 percent of these adoptions are transracial (Kreider, 2003). Hansen and Pollack (2007) found that between 1996 and 2003, the proportion of black children who were adopted transracially from foster care rose from 17.2 percent in 1996 to 20.1 percent in 2003.

According to the 2007 National Survey of Adoptive Parents, approximately 28 percent of children adopted from the foster care system are categorized as TRAs. Of all adoptions, approximately 63 percent of the children adopted in 2007 from the child welfare system were white, 27 percent were black, and 5 percent were of Hispanic origin (Vandivere et al., 2009).

Despite the passage of the MEPA in 1994, minority children in care remain overrepresented, and African American children are adopted at significantly lower rates than white children. In 2012, of the 399,546 children in foster care, 26 percent or 101,938 were black, and of the 101,719 children awaiting adoption in the foster care system, 26 percent or 26,117 were black. Yet, black children represent just 13.9 percent of the U.S. child population (DHHS, 2013). Also, black children who have had their parental rights terminated and freed for adoption, still have lower rates of adoption (GAO, 2007). According to the GAO, "over the last five years, African American children as well as Native American children have consistently experienced lower rates of adoption than children of other races and ethnicities"

(2007, p. 56). Between 2001 and 2005, the adoption rate for black children was approximately 30 percent compared with other racial and ethnic groups for whom the figures were between 40 and 50 percent (GAO, 2007). African American children in foster care compared with other groups, experience longer waits for permanency, particularly through adoption, than those in other racial and ethnic groups. A number of factors may lead to this outcome, including disproportionate removals of African American children, the need for more successful prevention and family preservation and reunification programs, and insufficient and ineffective recruitment and retention programs for adoptive families for African American children waiting to be adopted.

After a lengthy review of the law's impact, the 2007 U.S. Commission on Civil Rights report concluded that MEPA thus far has failed to remove barriers toward adoption and achieve equity in finding permanent adoption placements for African American children (Donaldson Adoption Institute, 2008). Not only has MEPA-IEP failed to solve the issue of overrepresentation, but it also fails to reduce the time African American children spend in the child welfare system. Black children remain in foster care on average 9 months longer than white children (GAO, 2007). Additionally, black children that are adopted transracially are typically younger than 4 years old (Maza, 2004). Age plays a significant role in TRAs, as younger children are notably more likely to be placed in TRAs, compared with older children in other racial and ethnic groups (Padilla, Vargas, & Chavez, 2010).

Implementation of federal laws require changes in state laws, regulations, and policies at the county level, although federal law takes precedence if state laws are not in compliance. After the enactment of MEPA in 1994, the OCR reviewed each state's statutes, regulations, and policies and found that twenty-eight states and the District of Columbia did not conform to the Act, all of which had made changes to comply with the law (GAO, 1998). Furthermore, OCR continued to investigate complaints of discrimination filed with the agency as part of its ongoing efforts to determine whether agency policies and caseworker actions were in compliance with civil rights laws and MEPA. After the enactment of the 1996 IEP amendment, OCR investigated only case-by-case complaints of violations and in 1997 began reviews in selected locations (GAO, 1998).

Although there is no comprehensive list of all cases that have been brought to OCR for violation of MEPA-IEP, a sample of cases from nine states (Alabama, Arizona, California, Florida, Minnesota, Nevada, Ohio, South Carolina, and Washington) are available online (OCR, n.d.). In most cases, states agreed to corrective actions without paying fines. In two cases, Ohio and South Carolina, penalties were imposed of $1.8 million and $107,000 respectively (Smith et al., 2008). In the case of Ohio, OCR began their investigation in response to allegations contained in newspaper reports and a complaint filed in *John Doe v. Hamilton County Department of Human Services,* Civil Case No. C-1-99-281, in the U.S. District Court for the Southern District of Ohio, in which plaintiffs alleged African American foster children were being denied the opportunity to be placed for adoption with their white foster parents (Simeone, 2003). After their investigation, OCR and DHHS affirmed the state had violated MEPA-IEP regulations because it permitted adoption specialists to consider the race of prospective adoptive parents if they were "not of the same cultural heritage" as the child and required adoption workers to evaluate prospective parents' cultural competency and plan to ensure that a child's cultural identity was preserved in TRAs.

South Carolina was found to violate MEPA-IEP on several counts. In its violation Letter of Findings, OCR found six systematic violations and numerous individual violations (Freeman, 2005). The six systematic violations included the following: (1) treating racial preference differently from all other prospective parent's preferences of the child they hoped to adopt; (2) matching children with adoptive parents based on the racial or ethnic preference of the birth parent; (3) assessing the cultural competency of prospective adoptive parents who are racially or ethnically different from the prospective child; and, for adoption specialists; (4) using race to make adoptive placements (i.e., if the number of prospective parents of the same race as the child is sufficient, then preference would be to place a child with such a family); (5) including a description of the parent's skin color or complexion in the assessment of prospective adoptive parents; and (6) treating a prospective adopted child's racial preference differently from all preferences when the child is old enough to be involved in a placement decision.

### ISSUES AFFECTING TRANSRACIAL ADOPTIONS

Related issues that affect TRAs include disproportionate representation of African American children in foster care and awaiting adoption, the need for effective adoptive parent recruitment strategies, and the need for mandatory training to prepare transracial adoptive families. Each will be discussed in the following sections

### Disproportionality

MEPA did not directly address the reasons why African American youth are disproportionately represented within the child welfare system. The percentage of children of a particular race or ethnicity in foster care varies by state. In 2011, African American children were disproportionately represented in care in thirty-two states, Alaska Native/Native American children were disproportionately represented in seventeen states, and children reported as having "two or more races" were disproportionately represented in twenty states. In no state, however, did the percentage of white children in foster care exceed the percentage of these children in the state's population (DHHS, 2013). Disproportionate poverty is another factor, which often is identified as associated with disproportionate placement in foster care. African Americans are four times more likely to live in poverty and African American children are twice as likely to live in impoverished families compared with white children (GAO, 2007). Poor families will have greater difficulty securing support services compared with nonpoor families (GAO, 2007).

African American children are also the most likely racial or ethnic group to be referred to protective services (Gryzlak, Wells, & Johnson, 2005). Minority children will enter foster care at disproportionately greater rates and also will remain in care longer, will experience a greater number of placement moves, and will be less likely to reunify with their birth parents or be adopted compared with white children (Hill, 2006; Wulczyn, Chen, & Hislop, 2007). Allegations of abuse and neglect are more likely to be substantiated for African American children (Ards, Chung, & Myers, 2003; Fluke, Yuan, Hedderson, & Curtis, 2003). Such disparities led the Casey–Center for the Study of Social Policy Alliance for Racial Equity to conclude "the disparities ... can best be described as a 'chronic crisis'" (Center for Community Partnerships in Child Welfare, 2006). Because poverty is clearly a causal factor leading to disproportionate out-of-home placements for African American children, ongoing advocacy for policies and practices to address these inequities is needed to improve outcomes for all children and families. It is hoped that increasing our understanding of the root causes and solutions to these disparate outcomes will lead to more culturally specific and data-driven practices and policies to be established.

### Parental Recruitment

An important yet often overlooked and under-implemented aspect of MEPA is the requirement of states to actively recruit a diverse population of foster and adoptive parents. The goal of such recruitment is to create a diverse pool of eligible applicant families to meet the diverse needs of children in care. The state agencies' federal funding is tied directly to their efforts in active recruitment as well as adherence to colorblind policies in placement (Hollinger & ABA Center on Children and the Law, 1998). Noncompliance with MEPA-IEP results in an agency's violation of Title VI of the Civil Rights Act of 1964. Noncompliance may result in large financial penalties and lawsuits by individuals who believe that these standards were violated (Howe, 1999).

Because of fear of violating the colorblind policies of MEPA, many child welfare agencies have let the recruitment of diverse families who reflect the racial and ethnic background of children waiting in care to become an afterthought. Such fear may lead to less than perfect placements for children as it could affect jobs and funding for the agency (DHHS, 2003; Smith et al., 2008). However, because of the fact that African American children continue to wait in disproportionately high numbers, there remains a need to push for diligent recruitment of families. Strategies for recruiting and retaining African American prospective adopters need further development. For instance, findings from a study of African American adopters from private African American adoption agencies, revealed that 70 percent of their adopters previously had been unsuccessful in adopting a child through a public adoption agency (Smith-McKeever & McRoy, 2005). Minority-specific placement agencies have had success in recruiting a more diverse pool of adoptive families (e.g., Homes for Black Children; Black Adoption Program and Services; One Church, One Child) and, as such, techniques they use should be modified and followed, including tailoring culturally relevant and specific adoption materials and recruiting and retaining African American families.

Recruitment no longer can be an afterthought for adoption agencies. New ways and techniques should be utilized to reach a greater diversity of people, such as connecting with faith groups and developing better relationships with minority communities as a whole to break down the historic roots of mistrust. Increased postadoption support should be offered in recognition that adoption is a life-long process. These recommendations along with others were made clear in a report focused on MEPA from the Donaldson Adoption Institute (2008) and are supported by a large number of other key stakeholders. The recommendations are based on the belief that acknowledging and addressing the significance of racial and cultural differences with a child will help them to develop and feel more connected to their heritage and identity (Vonk & Angaran, 2003).

**Mandatory Training**

As a result of fears of violating MEPA, agency-sponsored preparation classes for families planning or thinking about raising a child from a different race or culture often do not occur during the placement process (Smith, et al., 2008). Training on the challenges of TRAs may be offered, according to the law's provisions, as long as it is made a requirement for all adoptive families, regardless of the race of the child they adopt (McRoy et al., 2007). Conversely, other child-specific trainings (e.g., adopting a child with HIV or a sexually abused child) legally can be offered to families adopting that specific "type" of child. A study of child welfare agencies suggested that many direct practice workers and supervisors are unaware of MEPA and its intended goals, suggesting that a gap exists between policy and practice (Chibnall et al., 2003).

The lack of mandatory classes or sponsored classes for families seeking to transracially adopt tends to run counter to the empirical research findings on the special issues involved in TRAs. Many studies have demonstrated the importance of cultural and racial socialization to aid in the transracially adopted child's development of positive racial identity, adjustment, and self-esteem (Mohanty, Keokse, & Sales, 2007; Yoon, 2001). There is a need to provide adoptive families with training on racial and ethnic awareness, multiculturalism and coping skills to deal with prejudice (de Haymes & Simon, 2003; Vonk, 2001). Transracially adopted children "must learn how to navigate racialized stigma from parents whose racial status is not stigmatized" (Samuels, 2009, p. 83). Adoptive families should be prepared to handle questions, manage experiences of discrimination, and find connections with other children to address inherent differences. Social workers and those involved in the adoption need to find a way to work within the requirements of MEPA while adequately preparing families to provide cultural and racial socialization skills.

### Practice and Policy Implications

For those who work within child welfare agencies, especially social workers, it is critical that they are knowledgeable and both adoption and are culturally competent. Research suggests that three out of ten parents of adopted children reported not receiving at least one adoption-specific support (including meeting with agency staff, adoption support groups, parent training, and web-based resources; Vandivere et al., 2009). A 2008 nationwide study on the knowledge child welfare social workers had about MEPA and IEP as well as their views on race issues in adoption, revealed that although respondents seemed knowledgeable about the legislation, they "lacked familiarity with the empirical findings on transracial adoptions and specifically on the impact on cultural identity on transracially adopted children" (Mapp, Boutte-Queen, Erich, & Taylor, 2008, p. 383). These authors called for more research on outcomes of TRA as well as the need for social workers to have more training on interpreting the results of empirical studies of TRA and their implications for their work with children and families.

Curtis and Denby (2011) have suggested that a policy reform approach should be taught and modeled under an oppression framework. Curtis and Denby refer to the poor outcomes of African American children as "civilized oppression," a term coined by Young (1990), who stated that "the vast and deep injustices some groups suffer as a consequence of often unconscious assumptions and reactions of well-meaning people in ordinary interactions that are supported by . . . structural features of bureaucratic hierarchies and market mechanisms" (p. 41). This framework would help to enable a deeper understanding of the issues and policy at hand. Moreover, social workers should advocate for culturally sensitive prevention, family preservation, recruitment, and retention programs.

## TRANSRACIAL ADOPTIONS: CONCLUSIONS AND IMPLICATIONS

The belief that race or cultural heritage is central to a child's best interests when making an adoption placement decision has been long held in social work theory and practice (Smith, McRoy, Freundlich, & Kroll, 2008). Social work as a profession has set standards that call for respect of a client's cultural, religious, ethnic identities, and backgrounds. In that respect, the principles of ICWA are consistent with social work values and standards of practice. MEPA-IEP, on the other hand, has been harder to implement in part because the legal principles contradict long-held social work values. A report by the GAO summarized the problem of implementing MEPA-IEP as follows:

> The implementation of this amended act predominantly relies on the understanding and willingness of individual caseworkers to eliminate a historically important factor—race—from the placement decisions they make. While agency officials and caseworkers understand that this legislation prohibits them from delaying or denying placements on the basis of race, not all believe that eliminating race will result in placements that are in the best interests of children, which is a basic criterion for placement decisions. (1998, p. 3)

Before the passage of MEPA-IEP, no federal statute restricted the use of race as a criterion for adoption placements and no federal court decisions prohibited social workers' consideration of race (Banks, 2009). Furthermore, MEPA-IEP's prohibition on addressing racial issues runs counter to contemporary research on TRA. This research has found that although transracial adoptees as a group have few serious behavioral or emotional problems compared with adoptees placed in same-race families, adolescent and young adult transracial adoptees do struggle with various aspects of their racial and ethnic identity and racial discrimination, a fact masked by earlier research because this aspect of identity becomes more salient with age (for a summary of the literature, see McGinnis, Smith, Ryan, & Howard, 2009). Notably, white families tend to adopt children at younger ages, when children have not experienced as much trauma.

The divergent legal mandates regulating TRAs also put unrealistic demands on adoption agencies and prospective adoptive parents. For instance, a private adoption agency may be involved in both domestic and international adoptions, in which case the training of prospective parents seeking to adopt from overseas would have to provide information about becoming a multicultural family, but such information would be in violation of MEPA-IEP for prospective transracial adoptive parents of a child in foster care (Smith et al., 2008). Social work has long been concerned and involved in shaping adoption practice (Bailey & Delavega, 2011); hence, it is critical that the profession continues to advocate for the best interests of children in adoption and contribute to the formation of policies based on practice and research evidence.

For those who work within child welfare agencies, especially social workers, it is critical that they are knowledgeable and operate from a position of cultural humility, in which they are able to work with populations that are culturally different (Ortega & Faller, 2011). A 2008 nationwide study on the knowledge child welfare social workers have about MEPA and IEP, as well as their views on racial issues in adoption, revealed that although respondents seemed knowledgeable about the legislation, they "lacked familiarity with the empirical findings on transracial adoptions and specifically on the impact on cultural identity on transracially adopted children" (Mapp et al., 2008, p. 383). Clearly, more research is needed on outcomes of TRAs and social workers need more training to interpret the results of empirical studies of TRAs and their implications for their work with children and families.

#### DISCUSSION QUESTIONS

1. What were the factors that led to changes in practices around the placement of children transracially?
2. Why do most transracial adoptions involve the placement of African American children with white families?
3. Why are African American and Native American children disproportionately represented in care?
4. What else needs to be done to increase the likelihood of finding permanency for African American children? What other recruitment and retention strategies would you recommend?

**REFERENCES**

Ards, S., Chung, C., & Myers, S. (1999). The effects of sample selection bias on racial differences in child abuse reporting, *Child Abuse & Neglect, 23*(12), 1211–1215.

Bailey, J. D., & Delavega, M.E. (2011). Rules on The Hague and Intercountry Adoption Act: Public comments and the State's responsiveness. *Journal of Policy Practice, 10,* 35–50. doi:10.1080/15588742.2010.521920

Banks, R. R. (2009). The Multiethnic Placement Act and the troubling persistence of race matching. *Capital University Law Review, 38*(2), 271–290.

Benet, M. (1976). *The politics of adoption,* New York: Free Press.

Center for Community Partnerships in Child Welfare. (2006). *Places to watch: Promising practices to address racial disproportionality in child welfare.* Washington, DC: Center for the Study of Social Policy.

Chibnall, S., Dutch, N. M., Jones-Harden, B., Brown, A., & Gourdine, R. (2003). *Children of color in the child welfare system: Perspectives from the child welfare community.* Washington, DC: Child Welfare League of America.

Child Welfare Information Gateway. (2013a). *Transracial adoption.* Retrieved from https://www.childwelfare.gov/adoption/adopt_parenting/foster/transracial.cfm

Child Welfare Information Gateway. (2013b). *Transracial and transcultural adoption.* Retrieved from https://www.childwelfare.gov/pubs/f_trans.cfm

Child Welfare League of America (CWLA). (1960). *Adoption of oriental children by American White families, An interdisciplinary symposium.* New York: Child Welfare League of America.

Child Welfare League of America. (1968). *Standards for adoption service,* New York: CWLA.

Costin, L. (1979). *Child welfare: Policies and practice.* New York: McGraw Hill.

Curtis, C. M., & Denby, R. W. (2011). African American children in the child welfare system: Requiem or reform. *Journal of Public Child Welfare, 5*(1), 111–137.

de Haymes, M. V., & Simon, S. (2003). Transracial adoption: Families identify issues and needed support services. *Child Welfare, 82*(2), 251–272.

Dixon, J. (2013). The African-American child welfare act: A legal redress for African-American disproportionality in child protection cases. *Berkeley Journal of African American Law & Policy, 10*(2), 109–145.

Farr, R. & Patterson, C. (2009). Transracial adoption by lesbian, gay, and heterosexual couples: Who completes transracial adoptions and with what results? *Adoption Quarterly, 12:* 187–204.

Fluke, J. D., Yuan, Y. T., Hedderson, J., & Curtis, P. A. (2003). Disproportionate representation of race and ethnicity in child maltreatment: Investigation and victimization. *Children and Youth Services Review, 25,* 359–373.

Freeman. (2005). Letter from Roosevelt Freeman, Reg'l Manager, Office for Civil Rights, Dep't of Health & Human Servs. to Kim S. Aydlette, State Dir., S.C. Dep't of Soc. Servs. (Oct. 31, 2005), at 10. Retrieved from http://www.hhs.gov/ocr/civilrights/activities/examples/Adoption%20Foster%2OCare/010043810f.pdf

Gilles, T., & Kroll, J. (1991). *Barriers to same race placement.* St. Paul, MN: North American Council on Adoptable Children.

Gryzlak, B. M., Wells, S. J., & Johnson, M. A. (2005). The role of race in child protective services screening decisions. In D. Derezotes, J. Poertner, and M. Testa (Eds.), *Race matters in child welfare: The over-representation of African American children in the system.* Washington, DC: CWLA.

Hansen, M.E., & Pollack, D. (2007). Transracial adoption of Black children: An economic analysis. Retrieved August 23, 2013, from http://law.bepress.com/expresso/eps/1942

Hill, R. (1977). *Informal adoption among black families.* Washington, DC: National Urban League.

Hill, R. (2006). *Synthesis of research on disproportionality in child welfare: An update.* Casey–CSSP Alliance for Racial Equity in the Child Welfare System, Casey Family Programs. Retrieved from http://www.racemattersconsortium.org/docs/BobHillPaper_FINAL.pdf

Hollinger, J. H., & ABA Center on Children and the Law. (1998). *A guide to the Multiethnic Placement Act of 1994 as Amended by the Interethnic Adoption Provisions of 1996.* Washington, DC: American Bar Association.

Howe, R. A. (1999). Adoption laws and practices in 2000: Serving whose interests? *Family Law Quarterly, 33*(3), 677–689.

Jennings, P. (2006). The trouble with the Multiethnic Placement Act: An empirical look at transracial adoption. *Sociological Perspectives, 49*(4), 559–582.

Kreider, R. M. (2003). *Adopted children and stepchildren: 2000. Census 2000 special reports*. Washington, DC: U.S. Department of Commerce.

Lakin, D. S., & Whitfield, L. (1997). Adoption recruitment: Meeting the needs of waiting children. In R. J. Avery (Ed.), *Adoption policy and special needs children.* Westport, CT: Auburn House

Malott, K. & Schmidt, C. (2012). Counseling families formed by transracial adoption: Bridging the gap in the multicultural counseling competencies. *The Family Journal, 20* (4), 384–391.

Mapp, S., Boutte-Queen, N., Erich, S., & Taylor, P. (2008). Evidence-based practice or practice-based evidence: What is happening with MEPA and current adoption practices? *Families in Society: Journal of Contemporary Social Services, 89*(3), 375–384.

Maza, P. L. (2004). *Adoption data update.* Presented at the Child Welfare League of America National Conference and NACA Meeting, Washington, DC.

McGinnis, H., Smith, S., Ryan, S., & Howard, J. (2009). *Beyond culture camp: Promoting healthy identity formation in adoption.* New York: Donaldson Adoption Institute.

McRoy, R. G. (1989). An organizational dilemma: The case of transracial adoptions. *Journal of Applied Behavioral Science, 25*(2), 145–160.

McRoy, R. G. (1994). Attachment and racial identity issues: Implications for child placement decision-making, *Journal of Multicultural Social Work, 3*(3), 59–74.

McRoy, R. G. (2004). African American adoptions. In J. E. Everett, S. P. Chipungu and B. R. Leashore (Eds.), *Child welfare revisited: An Afrocentric perspective.* New Brunswick, NJ: Rutgers University Press.

McRoy, R., & McRoy, M. (1974). *Black homes for black children.* Lawrence, KS: Author's Forum.

McRoy, R., Mica, M., Freundlich, M., & Kroll, J. (2007). Making MEPA-IEP work: Tools for professionals. *Child Welfare, 86*(2), 49–66.

McRoy, R. G., Oglesby, Z., & Grape, H. (1997). Achieving same-race adoptive placements for African American children: Culturally sensitive practice approaches. *Child Welfare, 76*(1), 85–104.

McRoy, R. G., & Zurcher, L. A. (1983). *Transracial and inracial adoptees.* Springfield, IL: Charles C Thomas.

Mohanty, J., Keokse, G., & Sales, E. (2007). Family cultural socialization, ethnic identity, and self-esteem: Web-based survey of international adult adoptees. *Journal of Ethnic & Cultural Diversity in Social Work, 15*(3/4), 153–172.

National Association of Black Social Workers. (1972). *Position statement on transracial adoptions.* Paper presented at the National Association of Black Social Workers Conference, Nashville, TN.

National Indian Child Welfare Association. (2015). *Indian Child Welfare Act.* Retrieved from www.NICWA.org

National Survey of Adoptive Parents. (2007). Retrieved from http://aspe.hhs.gov/hsp/09/NSAP/

North American Council on Adoptable Children (NACAC). (1993). *NACAC policy statement on race and adoption.* St Paul, MN: NACAC.

Office of Civil Rights (OCR). (n.d.). Retrieved from http://www.hhs.gov/ocr/civilrights/activities/examples/Adoption%20Foster%20Care/adoption_case_summaries.html

Ortega, R., & Faller, K. (2011). Training child welfare workers from an intersectional cultural humility perspective: A paradigm shift. *Child Welfare*, 90(5), 27–37.

Padilla, J. B., Vargas, J. H., & Chavez, L. (2010). Influence of age on transracial foster adoptions and its relation to ethnic identity development. *Adoption Quarterly*, 13(1), 50–73.

Samuels, G. M. (2009). "Being raised by white people": Navigating racial difference among adopted multiracial adults. *Journal of Marriage and Family*, 71(1), 80–94.

Simeone. L. (2003). Letter from Lisa M. Simeone, Reg'l Manager, Office for Civil Rights, Dep't of Health & Human Servs., to Suzanne A. Burke, Dir., Hamilton County of Job & Family Servs. and Tom Hayes, Dir., Ohio Dep't of Job & Family Servs. (Oct. 20, 2003), at 7–8, 10, 20, 39. Retrieved from http://www.law.harvard.edu/faculty/bartholet/HHSOCR.pdf

Smith, M. J. (1972). Adoption in the first half of 1972. *Child Welfare*, 51(9), 585.

Smith, S. L., McRoy, R., Freundlich, M., & Kroll, J. (2008). *Finding families for African American Children: The role of race and law in adoption from foster care.* New York: Donaldson Adoption Institute. Retrieved from http://adoptioninstitute.org/old/publications/MEPApaper20080527.pdf

Smith-McKeever, T. C., & McRoy, R. G. (2005). The role of private adoption agencies in facilitating African American adoptions. *Families in Society*, 86, 533–540.

U.S. Commission on Civil Rights. (2010). The Multiethnic Placement Act: Minorities in foster care and adoption. A Briefing Before the United States Commission on Civil Rights Washington, DC.

U.S. Department of Health and Human Services (DHHS). (2003). *Children of color in the child welfare system: Perspectives from the child welfare community,* Retrieved from www.acf.hhs.gov/programs/opre/abuse_neglect/respon_coc/reports/persp_ch_welf/child of_color.pdf

U.S. Department of Health and Human Services. (2010). *Child welfare outcomes 2006–2009: Report to Congress, 2010.* Retrieved from www.acf.hhs.gov/programs/cb/pubs/cwo06-09/cwo06-09.pdf

U.S. Department of Health and Human Services, Administration for Children and Families, Administration on Children, Youth and Families, Children's

Bureau. (2013). *Child welfare outcomes 2008–2011: Report to Congress.* Retrieved from http://www.acf.hhs.gov/programs/cb/resource/cwo-08-11

U.S. Department of Health and Human Services, Administration for Children and Families, Administration on Children, Youth and Families, Children's Bureau. (2013, July). *Preliminary estimates for FY 2012 as of July 2013.* Retrieved from www.acf.hhs.gov/programs/cb

U.S. Department of Health and Human Services, Administration for Children and Families, Administration on Children, Youth and Families, Children's Bureau. (2014, July). *Preliminary estimates for FY 2013 as of July 2014 (No. 21).* Retrieved from www.acf.hhs.gov/programs/cb

U.S. Government Accountability Office (GAO). (1998). Foster care: Implementation of the Multiethnic Placement Act poses difficult challenges. (GAO Publication No. HEHS-98-2204). Washington, DC: U.S. Government Printing Office.

U.S. Government Accountability Office (GAO). (2007, July). African American children in foster care: Additional HHS assistance needed to help states reduce the proportion in care. (GAO Publication No. 07-816). Washington, DC: U.S. Government Printing Office.

Vandivere, S., Malm, K., & Radel, L. (2009). *Adoption USA: A chartbook based on the 2007 National Survey of Adoptive Parents.* Washington, DC: U.S. Department of Health and Human Services, Office of the Assistant Secretary for Planning and Evaluation.

Vonk, M. E. (2001). Cultural competence for transracial adoptive parents. *Social Work, 46*(3), 246–254.

Vonk, M. E., & Angaran, R. (2003). Training for transracial adoptive parents by public and private adoption agencies. *Adoption Quarterly, 6*(3), 53–62.

Wulczyn, F., Chen, L., & Hislop, K. (2007). *Foster care dynamics 2000–2005: A report from the Multistate Foster Care Data Archive.* Chicago: Chapin Hall Center for Children.

Yoon, D. P. (2001). Causal modeling predicting psychological adjustment of Korean-born adolescent adoptees. *Journal of Human Behavior in the Social Environment, 3,* 65–82.

Young, M. I. (1990). *Justice and the politics of difference.* Princeton, NJ: Princeton University Press

Zhang, Y., & Lee, G. (2011). Intercountry versus transracial adoption: An analysis of adoptive parents' motivation and preferences in adoption. *Journal of Family Issues, 32,* 1(1), 75–98.

# 4

# Interculturally Competent Practice with Gay and Lesbian Families

▸ DEVON BROOKS, DONI WHITSETT, AND JEREMY T. GOLDBACH

IN THE UNITED STATES AN estimated 37 percent of adults who identify as lesbian, gay, bisexual, or transgender (LGBT) have had a child at some point in their lives. As many as 6 million U.S. children and adults have an LGBT parent (Gates, 2013). The best available evidence suggests that parents who identify as either lesbian or gay typically have children in the context of heterosexual relationships (Gates, 2011, 2013; Goldberg, Gartrell & Gates, 2014; Tasker, 2013). However, a significant proportion of lesbian and gay parents have children through adoption. Lesbian and gay adoptions (LGAs)—that is, adoptive families headed by lesbians and gay men—are common in most parts of the world where adoptions takes place. Comprehensive and current statistics on the sexual orientation of adoptive parents are not available. Nonetheless, drawing from multiple data sources, including the 2008/2010 General Social Survey, the Gallup Daily Tracking Survey, Census 2010, and the Census Bureau's 2011 American Community Survey, Gates (2013) estimates that 16,000 lesbian and gay U.S. couples are raising more than 22,000 adopted children. He further estimates that lesbian and gay couples are four times more likely than straight couples to be raising adopted children. Among couples with children under the age of 18 years old in the home as of 2010, Gates reports that 13 percent involve lesbian and gay couples compared with just 3 percent for straight couples. He also reports that among all children under the age of 18 years old who were being raised by lesbian and gay couples as of 2010, approximately 10 percent were adopted, compared with just 2 percent of children being raised by straight couples. As best can be told, an estimated 1.4 percent of all adopted

## HOW MANY LESBIAN AND GAY ADOPTIVE FAMILIES ARE THERE?

> It is estimated that 16,000 lesbian and gay U.S. couples are raising more than 22,000 adopted children. Lesbian and gay couples are four times more likely than straight couples to be raising adopted children (Gates, 2013). The number of lesbian and gay adoptions inevitably will grow as lesbian and gay adoptions are becoming increasingly accepted and promoted as a means for creating families and for finding homes for children in need of safe, loving, and permanent families.

children who were living in households with two parents as of 2010 were living in a lesbian or gay household (Gates, 2013). These statistics pertain to *couples*. About one-third of finalized U.S. adoptions involve a single parent (Child Welfare Information Gateway, 2013). Thus, the prevalence of lesbian and gay adoption is almost certainly greater than 1.4 percent as a percentage of single-parent adoptions involve adoptions by single lesbians and gay men. Moreover, it is unclear from available statistics whether and how lesbian and gay couples are included in estimates of the incidence and prevalence of adoption.

The number of lesbian and gay adoptions will inevitably grow as LGAs are becoming increasingly accepted and promoted as a means for creating families and for finding homes for children in need of safe, loving, and permanent families. In 1999 just 38 percent of Americans favored gay adoption, whereas 57 percent opposed it. In 2012, 52 percent of Americans favored gay adoption, whereas 42 percent opposed it (Pew Research Center, 2012). Increased acceptance of LGAs worldwide is due in part to advocacy by and on behalf of lesbians and gay men who maintain that lesbian and gay parents and their children are entitled to the same treatment and legal protections afforded other families (Cooper & Cates, 2006). This acceptance is also in response to a now-sizable body of empirical studies (discussed later) demonstrating that the sexual orientation of parents does not negatively affect children's development and outcomes, although some findings hint that children raised by lesbian and gay parents actually may have better outcomes in some areas of functioning than children raised by straight parents. Furthermore, greater tolerance and acceptance of diverse cultures, values, attitudes, and behaviors has likely contributed to the acceptance

## WORKING WITH LESBIAN AND GAY ADOPTIVE FAMILIES

> Professionals working with lesbian and gay adoptive or prospective adoptive families must have knowledge and skills to assess and screen children for disorders and issues related to the unique circumstances of their experiences. Despite the large and growing numbers of LGAs, however, there are few frameworks to guide professionals who work with lesbian and gay families in general and, more particularly, with lesbian and gay families who adopt transracially or internationally.

of LGAs by the general population, professional organizations, and social institutions.

Professionals working with lesbian and gay adoptive or *prospective* adoptive families, in particular, must have knowledge and skills to assess and screen children for disorders and issues related to the unique circumstances of their experiences. Accurate assessment and screening is essential in the development of matching children with families and in the development of treatment plans. Despite the large and growing numbers of LGAs, there are few frameworks to guide professionals who work with lesbian and gay families in general and, more particularly, with lesbian and gay families who adopt transracially or internationally. As detailed later, compared with their straight counterparts, lesbian and gay families appear more likely to adopt or to be open to adopting children across racial, ethnic, and cultural lines. We aim to enhance professionals' ability to work with culturally diverse lesbian and gay families who adopt children transracially or internationally by introducing the concept of "intersectionality" to the study and practice of adoption and by using an intersectional lens to review existing statistics and empirical findings relevant to lesbian and gay adoptive families.

### INTERSECTIONALITY

Over the past decade, numerous approaches to intersectionality have surfaced in the literature in the United States and especially throughout Europe (Davis, 2008). As suggested by Lev and Sennott (2013), a new generation of lesbian and gay (prospective) parents are looking for clinicians who are able to work competently with the matrix of intersecting identities

## HIGHLIGHTS OF INTERSECTIONALITY

> Numerous frameworks and theories of intersectionality exist. An intersectional perspective is particularly useful for understanding and working with lesbian and gay adoptive families, in part because of the cultural diversity that characterizes these families. An intersectional perspective recognizes the importance (or "salience") of multiple factors related to different aspects of culture, such as sexual orientation, race, and gender. From an intersectional perspective, factors interact with one another to contribute to experiences of disadvantage, oppression, or discrimination, as well as to experiences of advantage, access, and privilege. The salience and intersection of factors, and their consequences, are influenced by contextual factors, including societal, environmental, political, geographic, and historical factors.

that each parent may hold. To the best of our knowledge, however, there have been no applications of intersectionality to professional practice with lesbian and gay adoptive families.

In short, intersectionality frameworks and theories suggest that aspects of identity, such as sexual orientation, gender, and race (1) are socially constructed, (2) interact with one another on multiple levels, and (3) alone and together are associated with oppression and privilege (Crenshaw, 1991, 1995; McCall, 2005). Such perspectives are particularly relevant and useful to clinicians, as well as to other professionals and educators, who work with lesbian and gay families who adopt transracially or internationally because of the cultural diversity that exists among these families. Intersectionality perspectives can be used to illuminate and to better understand issues—both good and bad—stemming from cultural background and identity, including the discrimination, disadvantage, and oppression that can be associated with being a member of a sexual minority group (e.g., being lesbian or gay) or being a member of a minority racial, ethnic, or cultural group.

Intersectionality perspectives recognize that real or perceived group membership can make people vulnerable to various forms of bias. Yet because people are simultaneously members of many groups, complex identities can shape the specific way each person experiences and responds to that bias (Hess, 2012). Those experiences and responses can vary for the same individual depending on the context in which they occur. Instead of summarizing the effects of individual aspects of identity, advocates of intersectionality stress the interwoven nature of the aspects, as well as how different aspects can strengthen or weaken the effects of other aspects (Crenshaw, 1989; Winker & Degele, 2011). Thus, rather than being approached individually and independently, intersectionality perspectives suggest that combining identities (or aspects of identities) does not merely increase one's burden or challenge, but instead produces substantively distinct experiences (Association for Women's Rights in Development [AWID], 2004, p.2). Murphy et al. (2009) suggest that the complexities of cultural diversity demand frameworks and methodologies that capture the breadth and depth of the diverse human experience. Intersectional approaches resist treating all members of a single social group as the same and assuming they share the same experience (Hankivsky et al., 2010). Identities are conceptualized not individually in terms of either sexual orientation, gender, or race, but rather interdependently in terms of their simultaneous, dynamic, and interactive effects (Hess, 2012; Jani et al., 2011). For example, being adopted by a gay parent in and of itself may not result in teasing of an adopted child (an aspect of identity). But being an adopted child who is *both* male and of color (aspects of identity) may result in teasing and that teasing may be different in nature or amount than teasing that might occur when considering only the independent effects of either gender or race. The nature or amount of teasing, for instance, might be different if the adopted child was instead a *female* of color or a *white* male. The nature or amount of teasing might be altogether different for a male of color who is adopted by a *single* gay parent or by a *heterosexual* couple. The effects of any of these examples might vary depending on the historical, geographic, political, or sociocultural context. For example, the nature or amount of teasing of an adopted child who is both male and of color may result in more teasing in the year 2020 than the year 2015. Or the child may experience less teasing if the adoptive family lives in an area that is culturally diverse and known for its high number and acceptance of lesbians and gay men (such as the San Francisco Bay Area of California in the United States) versus a more racially homogenous area with a low number and less acceptance of out (i.e., self-identified) lesbians and gay men.

## ADOPTION THROUGH AN INTERSECTIONAL LENS

Adoptions can take many different forms and be described in a variety of ways. The term "transracial adoption" (also referred to as interracial adoption) refers typically to the adoption of a child into a family of a different racial, ethnic, or cultural background than the child. The term "inracial adoption" conversely, refers to the adoption of a child into a family of the same background of the child. Both transracial and inracial adoptions can involve foreign-born children. The term "intercountry adoption" (also referred to as international and transnational adoption) typically refers to the adoption of a child into a family of a different nationality. That is, the child was adopted from another country and a change in country of residence occurred because of the adoption. The term "domestic adoption," on the other hand, refers to the adoption of a child from the same country in which at least one of the adoptive parents has citizenship. The term transracial is used by some to refer only to domestic adoptions and by others to refer to either domestic or intercountry adoptions, assuming the adoption involves a child of a different race or ethnicity from the adoptive parents. If there is a racial or ethnic match between at least one parent and a child adopted from another country, the adoption may be considered by some as inracial and by others as transracial. None of these terms widely used to describe adoptive families captures the nuances involved when an interracial couple adopts or when the race or nationality of one of the parents matches that of the adopted or child. Also not captured are the nuances of transracial and intercountry adoptions involving a child or parent who is biracial or who has dual citizenship, and the race or nationality of the child and at least one parent matches. Finally, the term does not capture the nuances of families composed of multiple adopted children, at least one of whom is adopted transracially or internationally, and at least one is not.

The remainder of this section of our chapter uses an intersectionality lens to examine statistics, policy, and practices on adoption, particularly those that may have special implications for understanding the development and functioning of transracially or internationally adopted children who are adopted by lesbian and gay parents. We begin with a review of adoption in general, followed by reviews of transracial and international adoptions. We then summarize statistics, policies, and practices related to lesbian and gay adoptions. Finally, we attempt to bring the various aspects of adoption together in our review of cultural diversity within lesbian and gay transracial and international adoptions.

### A LOOK AT GLOBAL ADOPTION

Among the 195 countries in the world, adoption is practiced or allowed in 173. Worldwide, data on the number and characteristics of domestic adoptions are rarely available, and when they are, they tend to be out of date. Similarly, comparable information on trends in international adoptions, that is, adoptions that involve a change of country of residence for the adopted person—often is lacking or is available for just a few countries. Data compiled recently for a United Nations (2009) comprehensive report on child adoption worldwide suggest that about 260,000 children are adopted each year. This represents about 1.5 percent of available children *worldwide* and 12 children adopted each year for every 100,000 people under the age of 18 years old. The United States accounts for about half of the total number of child adoptions (United Nations, 2009). In the United States, an estimated 1,527,020 children under 18 years old were living with one or more adoptive parents as of 2010, the most recent year for which comprehensive data are available. An additional 545,292 adults 18 years and over were living with an adoptive parent. Together, about 2,072,312 U.S. children of any age were living with an adoptive parent. Adopted children thus accounted for 2.3 percent of children living with a parent in 2010.

Globally, 85 percent of all adoptions are domestic. About 220,000 children are adopted domestically each year. About 86 percent of these domestic adoptions take place in just ten out of thirty countries in which adoptions occur. These ten countries include the United States, China, the Russian Federation, the United Kingdom, Ukraine, Brazil, Germany, Uzbekistan, Kazakhstan, and Canada. The United States has more domestic adoptions than all other countries combined (United Nations, 2009).

#### Transracial Adoption

The earliest known case of transracial adoption in the United States occurred in California in 1944 (California Adoption Survey Committee, 1946), and the formal practice of placing large numbers of children transracially began later that decade when thousands of Korean, Japanese and Chinese war orphans were placed with white American families (making them both transracial and intercountry adoptions). The incidence of such adoptions gained momentum in the mid-fifties and decreased somewhat during the early sixties. It increased again in the late sixties—this time with an emphasis on the placement of black children into white homes (Jones & Else, 1979; Simon, Altstein, & Melli, 1994), reflecting a shift from international transracial adoptions to domestic transracial adoptions. Today, about 24 percent of U.S. adoptions of children under 18 years old are transracial (Kreider & Lofquist, 2014). These adoptions involve the adoption of a child either from the United States (i.e., domestic adoption) or another country, that is, intercountry (or international) adoption.

**International Adoption**

About 15 percent of adoptions worldwide are international adoptions. As with domestic adoptions, most international adoptions involve relatively few countries. The United States is the leading location of international adoptions (U.S. Department of State, 2011), adopting nearly more children internationally than the rest of the world combined (United Nations, 2009). Rounding out the ten receiving countries (of twenty-seven) with the largest number of international adoptions are France, Spain, Italy, Germany, Canada, Sweden, the Netherlands, Denmark, and Norway. Together, these nine countries and the United States account for 89 percent of all international adoptions (United Nations, 2009).

In 2013, 7,094 children were adopted internationally—about one-third the number of international adoptions completed a decade prior. Among the children who were internationally adopted children in 2013, ninety-four sending countries were represented. According to the U.S. Department of State (2014), of the sending countries, 77 percent of international adoptions involved children from the following ten countries: China (33 percent), Ethiopia (14 percent), Ukraine (6 percent), Haiti (5 percent), the Democratic Republic of Congo (4 percent), Uganda (4 percent), Russia (4 percent), Nigeria (3 percent), Philippines (3 percent), and Ghana (2 percent). In 2013, 84 U.S. children were adopted outside the U.S., down from a peak of 315 in 2009 and from 105 in 2004 (U.S. Department of State, 2014; Voigt & Brown, 2013). Receiving countries for the 2013 outgoing adoptions were Austria (31 percent), Ireland (27 percent), the Netherlands (24 percent), Canada (12 percent), Switzerland (2 percent), the United Kingdom (2 percent), and Tanzania (1 percent) (U.S. Department of State, 2014).

In the United States, international adoptions accounted for approximately 17 percent of all U.S. adoptions of children under 18 years of age as of 2011. Of all adopted children in the United States who live with a parent—including those 18 years and older—between 17 and 25 percent involved foreign-born children as of 2010 (Kreider & Lofquist, 2014). International adoptions grew in popularity in the United States following World War II. At least 50,000 such adoptions took place between 1948 and 1969. In the eighties, the number of international adoptions was fairly stable at about 20,000 per year. With the opening of China and Russia in the nineties, the number of international adoptions increased dramatically. International adoptions peaked in 2004 at 22,991 (U.S. Department of State, 2011). After decades of steady growth, each year since 2004, the number of international adoptions has decreased. In the past decade, major sending countries, such as China, Korea, Guatemala, and Russia, placed large cohorts of young children for adoption in the United States (Selman, 2009). China is the leading source of adoptive children for the United States. Russia had long been the second-largest provider (Voigt & Brown, 2013), but currently ranks seventh in terms of international adoptions (U.S. Department of State, 2014).

A survey of the top twenty-three nations that adopt children from abroad recorded 23,626 international adoptions in 2011—down from 45,299 in 2004 (Selman, 2012). Both in the United States and abroad, a decline in international adoptions in the past decade has been attributed to economic and political changes that allow or support children remaining with their biological families. The decline also has been attributed to rising regulations and growing sentiment, particularly in China and Russia but also in other major sending countries, against sending orphans abroad and promoting domestic adoptions. The reduction in international adoptions has been attributed to changes in the policies of particular countries and the implementation of the Hague Convention and the Intercountry Adoption Act (IAA). The IAA, which took effect in 2008, requires that adoption agencies be accredited. As the largest sending country since 1995, China's move in the mid-2000s to restrict the eligibility criteria for international adoptive parents had a significant impact on the decline in all international adoptions. These restrictions went along with changes that already had been made to encourage adoption within China (Kreider & Lofquist, 2014). In 2007, China enacted a stricter policy requiring that adoptive parents be married couples for at least 2 years. If either parent previously has been divorced, they are not eligible to adopt until 5 years after their wedding. Adopters are also required to be between the ages of 30 and 50 years old with assets of at least $80,000. They must be in good health, including not being overweight or blind and not having facial deformities. Prohibited are those who have taken antidepressants for serious mental disorders in the previous 2 years, and those who have schizophrenia or a terminal disease. In 2011, China began allowing single women to adopt, but only children with special needs and only after signing an affidavit that they are not homosexual (Voigt & Brown, 2013). In addition to China, other countries, such as Korea, are attempting to promote domestic adoption rather than relying on international adoption (Vandivere, Malm, & Radel, 2009). Some countries (e.g., Ghana, Bhutan, Guatemala, Kazakhstan, Kyrgyzstan, Russia, and Rwanda) have banned international adoptions altogether or have been banned by receiving countries. For example, the United States does not accept adoptions from Cambodia, Montenegro, and Vietnam (Voigt & Brown, 2013). The overall decrease in international adoption was reflected in the number of immigrant visas issued to orphans coming to the United States for adoption (Kreider & Lofquist, 2014).

### Lesbian and Gay Adoption

LGAs are those in which one or both parents are lesbians or gay men. As is the case with adoption in general, statistics on LGAs worldwide are not available. In the United States, it has been estimated that between 3 and 6 percent of adoptions are LGAs (Brodzinsky, Patterson, & Vaziri, 2002; Brooks, Kim, & Wind, 2012). This translates to about 65,500 adopted children being raised by one or two parents who are lesbian or gay men. Another 2 million lesbians and gay men are believed to be interested in pursuing adoption (Gates, Badgett, Macomber & Chambers, 2007).

LGAs typically originate in one of three ways. Individually, as a single parent, lesbians and gay men may adopt children who are biologically unrelated to them. Or, as a married or unmarried couple, lesbians and gay men can adopt jointly. Finally, a same-gendered partner may petition to adopt the related biological or adopted child of her or his partner or spouse (i.e., a second-parent or stepparent adoption; Montero 2014).

Statistics on lesbian and gay foster care placements are relevant to our discussion of LGAs as a percentage of children placed in foster care go on to be adopted by their foster parents. Lesbian and gay couples are six times more likely than straight couples to be raising foster children. Among lesbian and gay couples with children under the age of 18 years old, 2 percent are raising a foster child compared with 0.3 percent of straight couples. Approximately 2,600 lesbian and gay couples are raising an estimated 3,400 foster children in the United States (Gates, 2013). Statistics on the number of single lesbians and gay men who are raising foster children are not available.

Despite growing acceptance of lesbian and gay adoption and foster parenting, barriers to such placements persist (Ryan, Pearlmutter, & Groza, 2004). The most profound examples are laws and statutes that make it illegal for lesbians and gay men who are open about their sexual orientation or for prospective adoptive and foster parents who are suspected of being lesbian or gay to adopt or foster (Baumle & Compton, 2011). For instance, as of December 2013, nineteen U.S. states and the District of Columbia explicitly allowed LGBT individuals and couples the right to adopt without restrictions. Twenty-one states and the District of Columbia allow same-gender couples to adopt jointly. Although intercountry adoption has provided a path to parenthood for thousands of parents (Ishizawa et al., 2006; Selman, 2009), in recent years, new regulations have curtailed the ability of lesbians and gay men to adopt outside their countries. When lesbians and gay men are permitted to adopt internationally, in most instances, they must do so individually rather than as a couple (Goldberg, 2010; Lev & Sennott, 2013). Some countries—such as China, which sends more children annually to the United States than any other country—have a two-tiered system of eligibility requirements that privileges heterosexual married couples and penalizes single parents and same-sex adoptive parents. When adopting from China, only straight married couples are allowed to adopt "high-demand" healthy infant girls, whereas other adopters are allowed to adopt only from the "special needs" program, which places children with known medical conditions. China also requires an affidavit certifying that single applicants are not part of a lesbian or gay couple (U.S. Department of State, 2011).

### Diversity Within Lesbian and Gay Transracial and International Adoptions

There is significant variation in the prevalence of transracial adoption in the United States by the race of the adoptive parent and by the number of parents in the adopting family. Lesbian and gay couples and single parents, compared with straight couples, have higher odds of adopting transracially. This effect is most pronounced for single adoptive parents who have more than three times the odds of adopting transracially compared to straight couples. Transracial adoption is most prevalent among white adoptive parents with 18 percent (about one of every six adoptions) involving white adoptive parents adopting a child of a different race. About 5 percent of black parents adopt transracially, and about 13 percent of Hispanic and Asian parents combined adopt transracially (Ishizawa et al., 2006).

Of all adopters, white adoptive parents who are single are the most likely to adopt transracially, with almost one in three adopting transracially. When they adopt transracially, white parents tend to adopt Hispanic and Asian children. Six percent of white transracial adoptive parents adopt a Hispanic child and 6 percent of white transracial adoptive parents adopt an Asian child. Less than 2 percent of white transracial adoptive parents adopt a black child (Raleigh, 2012). When black children are adopted transracially

### CULTURAL DIVERSITY WITHIN LESBIAN AND GAY ADOPTIVE FAMILIES

> Compared with their straight counterparts, lesbian and gay families appear more likely to adopt or to be open to adopting children across racial, ethnic, and cultural lines. Among lesbian and gay adoptive families, there is variation in the prevalence of transracial adoption by the race, gender, and [dis]abilty status of the adopted child and by characteristics of the adoptive parent(s), including gender and race, the number of parents in the adopting family, whether an adoptive couple is interracial or same race, and income.

by white parents, the parents are more likely to be lesbian and gay couples or single parents. About 6 percent of white lesbian and gay couples and 5 percent of white single parents adopt a black child. By contrast, less than 2 percent of white straight couples adopt a black child.

Apart from race and the number of parents in a family, several other characteristics appear to be associated with the likelihood of adopting transracially or internationally. Research suggests that lesbian and gay couples are more likely than straight couples to be in interracial relationships (Rosenfeld, 2007; Schwartz & Graf, 2009). Parents who are part of an interracial couple have much higher odds of adopting transracially (Farr & Patterson, 2009). White parents with higher incomes are less likely to adopt black children but more likely to adopt Hispanic and Asian children (Krawiec, 2010; Quiroz, 2007). Children adopted transracially (by lesbians and gay men) are more likely to be girls and to have an identified disability (Kreider & Cohen, 2009).

### What the Research Shows

It is difficult to generalize about adoption because adopted children have highly varied characteristics and experiences prenatally, between birth and adoptive placement, and postadoption (Grotevant & McDermott, 2014). Furthermore, the characteristics and experiences of adoptive parents and families vary widely. As lesbian and gay transracial and international adoption is a recent phenomenon (at least in terms of scale and acceptance as a legitimate and even desirable family form), little is known from an empirical standpoint about the intersectional issues faced by these families, above and beyond those faced by lesbian and gay families or by adoptive families. We therefore glean from related bodies of empirical knowledge issues that may portend future challenges for the growing population of lesbian and gay transracial and international adoptive families, as well as for the professionals and educators who work with these families. We begin with a discussion of issues and outcomes experienced by lesbian and gay families in the general population, followed by a discussion of those same issues as experienced by adoptive families. Our review is not meant to be exhaustive. Instead, we highlight results that we believe have particular relevance to lesbian and gay transracial and international adoptive families.

## WHAT THE RESEARCH SHOWS

> It is difficult to generalize about adoption because of the varied characteristics and experiences of adopted children and because of the varied characteristics of adoptive parents and families (Grotevant & McDermott, 2014). Nonetheless, the research generally suggests that most adopted children develop within the typical range, but they are at increased risk for various developmental problems and are overrepresented in mental health services (Juffer & van Ijzendoor, 2005; Palacios & Brodzinsky, 2010). The trajectories of individual children vary greatly depending on the number and nature of pre- and postadoptive risk and protective factors (Grotevant & McDermott, 2014; Ji, Brooks, Barth, & Kim, 2010). Children do not appear to be at risk for adverse outcomes as a result of lesbian or gay adoption, transracial adoption, or international adoption.

### Lesbian and Gay Families

Early studies on lesbian and gay families were largely interested in the potential impact of parents' sexual orientation on their children's sexual orientation. Those studies, along with studies on sexuality and homosexuality, have established that parental homosexuality does not predispose or foster homosexual orientation or gender identity in children and adolescents. Studies that focused more specifically on the correlation between being raised by lesbian or gay parents have found that there is no correlation between children's sexual orientation and the type of family in which they were raised (Bailey, Bobrow, Wolfe, & Mikach, 1995; Golombok & Tasker, 1996; Golombok, Spencer, & Rutter, 1983; Tasker & Golombok, 1995). Although pervasive cross-gender role behavior is not related to being raised by lesbian or gay parents, some studies do reveal less gender-stereotyped behavior among children raised by lesbian or gay parents (e.g., Brewaeys, Ponjaert, Van Hall, & Golombok, 1997; Golombok et al., 2003).

Later studies on lesbian and gay families have examined the impact of parental sexual orientation and of being raised by lesbian or gay parents on children's development, adjustment, and well-being in a numerous spheres of functioning. A now considerably large body of rigorous studies has substantiated that children reared in lesbian- and gay-headed families have similar outcomes to children raised in straight-headed families, and those outcomes tend to be positive. Children and adults raised in lesbian and gay families do not experience any additional negative outcomes in terms of emotional and behavioral adjustment (including internalizing and externalizing behaviors), psychological functioning, and psychiatric problems (Averett, Nalavany, & Ryan, 2009; Flaks, Ficher, Masterpasqua & Joseph, 1995; Goldberg, 2010; Golombok et al., 2003; Golombok, Spencer, & Rutter, 1983; Kirkpatrick, Smith & Roy, 1981; Tasker and Golombok, 1995; Wainright, Russell, & Patterson, 2004; Mallon, 2000).

Studies find that the social functioning outcomes of children and adults raised by lesbian and gay parents are similar to those of their counterparts raised by straight parents (Gartrell et al., 2005; Gartrell & Bos, 2010; Goldberg, 2010; Golombok et al., 2003; Wainright & Patterson, 2008). It appears, however, that although the outcomes are similar, social functioning *trajectories* may be influenced by parental sexual orientation. Some studies find no differences in the experiences of children with lesbian and gay parents, but several indicate higher rates of reported teasing and bullying among children with lesbian and gay parents than among children with straight parents (Kosciw & Diaz, 2008; MacCallum & Golombok, 2004; Rivers et al., 2008). Note that some evidence indicates that children raised by lesbian and gay parents may be subject to teasing at certain developmental stages (Gartrell et al., 2000, 2005; Kuvalanka, Leslie, & Radina, 2013; Leddy, Gartrell, & Bos, 2012; Ray & Gregory, 2001). Although rare among preschool-age children, teasing related to parents' sexual orientation becomes more common for children in middle school (Gartrell et al., 2005; Kosciw & Diaz, 2008; Kosciw, Greytak, & Diaz, 2009). Such teasing appears to be moderated by several factors. Children with lesbian and gay parents who do not encounter teasing related to their parents' sexual orientation attribute it to the geographic region or community in which they reside and to the type of school that they attend (e.g., progressive or private schools; Leddy et al., 2012; Ray & Gregory, 2001). Interestingly, despite the teasing that may be encountered, particularly in middle school, the handful of studies examining academic achievement and educational outcomes find no evidence that children raised by lesbian and gay parents demonstrate more problems than their peers raised by straight parents (Gartrell & Bos, 2010; Potter,

2012; Rosenfeld, 2010; Wainright, Russell & Patterson, 2004). From an intersectional perspective, these findings suggest the salience of two factors: sexual orientation and development stage.

Along with child-level outcomes, studies on lesbian and gay families have investigated development and outcomes at both the parent and family level. Few differences based on parents' sexual orientation have been found in studies that have examined parents' mental health. In terms of parenting competence and parenting stress, studies comparing lesbian and gay parents with straight parents find more similarities than differences (Biblarz & Stacey, 2010; Bos, Van Balen, & Van Den Boom, 2004; Goldberg & Smith, 2009; Golombok et al., 2003; Leung, Erich, & Kanenberg, 2005). Numerous researchers have commented on the positive functioning and outcomes demonstrated by lesbian and gay families despite being vulnerable to nonsupport and alienation from their families of origin; lack of recognition and support in the legal sphere; and confronting stigma, heterosexism, and homophobia in a variety of social contexts (Goldberg, 2010; Goldberg, Gartrell, & Gates, 2014). These findings are somewhat surprising given that parenting stress has been found to be compounded by being a member of a stigmatized group (Armesto, 2002).

**Adoptive Families**

An extensive body of empirical studies has examined adoptive families (for a recent review of the literature on developmental outcomes for children and adolescents, with a focus on the biological and social processes that mediate the connections between adoption and outcomes, see Grotevant & McDermott, 2014). Most adopted children develop within the typical range (Palacios & Brodzinsky, 2010), but children raised in adopted families are at increased risk for various developmental problems. They are overrepresented in mental health services when compared with nonadopted children (Juffer & van Ijzendoorn, 2005). Estimates suggest that the prevalence of psychological disorders in the population ranges from 29 to 96 percent and that at least half have an identified health problem (Lavner, Waterman, & Peplau, 2012). These patterns represent group trends, and the trajectories of individual children vary greatly depending on the number and nature of pre- and postadoptive risk and protective factors (Grotevant & McDermott, 2014; Ji et al., 2010).

Studies indicate that significant early adversity or trauma before adoptive placement is associated with postadoption adjustment and outcomes. For instance, prenatal drug exposure, sexual abuse in childhood, and lack of parental monitoring and supervision have been linked to subsequent substance abuse, high levels of sexual risk taking, externalizing and internalizing behavior problems, and mental health problems (Barnes, Reifman, Farrell, & Dintcheff, 2000; DiClemente, Wingood, Crosby, Sionean et al., 2001; Glantz & Chambers, 2006; Juffer et al., 2011; Putnam, 2003; Rai et al., 2003; Simmel et al., 2001). Even among children who have not experienced early adversity or trauma, patterns of initial positive adjustment are followed by socioemotional and behavioral problems that emerge during middle childhood and adolescence (Grotevant & McDermott, 2014; Hawk & McCall, 2010). These findings suggest that the experience of adoption or the postadoption environment may pose risks for some children.

Over the past decade, numerous studies have examined transracial and intercountry adoptions. Although there is disagreement over the interpretation of the findings from these studies, most have found that the experience of being adopted transracially does not harm children's psychological well-being per se (Alexander & Curtis, 1996; Bagley, 1993; Brooks & Barth, 1999; Feigelman & Silverman, 1984; Rushton & Minnis, 1997; Shireman & Johnson, 1986; Simon, Altstein, & Melli, 1994; Vroegh, 1997; Zastrow, 1977). Rather, it appears that the *experience* of transracial adoption vis-à-vis inracial adoption is qualitatively different (Bagley, 1993; Brooks & Barth 1999). Findings do suggest, however, that transracial adoptees tend to be highly acculturated to the majority Anglo-American culture and to have weak affiliations and identifications with others of their same racial groups (Andujo, 1988; Brooks & Barth, 1999; McRoy, 1994; McRoy, Zurcher, Lauderdale, & Anderson, 1984).

### Lesbian and Gay Adoptive Families

Placement of children into lesbian and gay adoptive families does not appear to be among the postadoption placement risk factors. Studies comparing outcomes of children adopted by lesbian and gay families with those of children adopted by straight families find no differences in levels of attachment between children and their adoptive parents or in children's internalizing and externalizing behaviors (Erich, Hall, Kanenberg & Case, 2009; Erich, Kanenberg, Case, Allen, & Bogdanes 2009). Studies comparing lesbian and gay parents with straight parents show similarities across many domains, including parenting style and skill, emotional adjustment, psychological stability, sensitivity, financial security, resourcefulness, and parenting skill (Brooks & Goldberg, 2001; Flaks et al., 1995; Goldberg & Smith, 2008; Ryan, 2008; Ryan & Cash, 2004). Lesbian couples, however, have been found to exhibit more parenting awareness skills than straight couples (Flaks, Ficher, Masterpasqua & Joseph, 1995). Studies examining family-functioning problems in lesbian or gay and straight adoptive families generally find no differences based on the sexual orientation of parents (Erich, Leung, Kindle, & Carter, 2005; Leung, Erich, & Kanenberg, 2005).

The extent to which lesbian and gay adopters were included in studies on transracial adoption is unknown. It is likely however, that the studies included largely samples of heterosexual adopters. Only one study to date (Farr & Patterson, 2009) has addressed child development and family outcomes in transracial adoptive families that included lesbian, gay, and straight adopters. The study included 106 families with a total of 212 parents and 106 children and 50 heterosexual families. Forty-three percent of the sample consisted of transracial adoptive families; the remaining 57 percent consisted of inracial adoptive families. Parents were well educated and had high family incomes. Among the lesbian and gay families who adopted transracially, 55 percent had a graduate degree and an average family income of $149,000. Among the lesbian and gay families who adopted inracially, 51 percent had a graduate degree and an average family income of $179,000. Children in the sample were adopted at birth or during the first few weeks of life. At the time of the study, the adopted children had an average age of 3 years. Assessments of child development and parenting revealed no significant differences between transracial and inracial adoptive lesbian and gay families. Children in both family types were functioning well; average scores for externalizing and internalizing behaviors, and total behavior problems were significantly lower than clinical cutoff scores. Transracial and inracial adoptive lesbian and gay parents reported similar parenting approaches and similar levels of parenting stress, which were relatively low. Parents also were found to use effective parenting techniques and were well adjusted, regardless of type of adoption.

## IMPLICATIONS FOR PROFESSIONALS WORKING WITH LESBIAN AND GAY FAMILIES WHO ADOPT TRANSRACIALLY OR INTERNATIONALLY

Although no practice models exist for professionals and educators working with lesbian and gay transracial and international adoptions, myriad theories and frameworks do exist from which professionals and educators can draw. Most of them rely on a strengths approach that attempts to identify the positive foundation of a person's resources (or what may need to be added) and strengths that will lay the basis to address the challenges resulting from the "problems" (Hammond, 2010). Next, we provide a quick overview of some of the theoretical and practice approaches that have been used widely in the past in work with LGBT families and with adoptive families.

### Traditional Approaches

Among the approaches directly relevant to our discussion of lesbian and gay transracial and international adoption are culturally responsive approaches to working with lesbian and gay families, often referred to as "gay-affirmative" or "lesbian- and gay-affirmative" practice models. One such model is the Expanded Family Life Cycle model developed by McGoldrick, Carter, and Garcia-Preto (2010). This model integrates lesbian, gay, bisexual, transgender, and queer people within the larger issues of family processes, highlighting the unique issues of sexual orientation and gender identity. The model also highlights the complex matrix of other cultural factors, including race, ethnicity, class, ability status, and religion. Furthermore, the model approaches the various issues, processes and factors within a larger context of the historical, economic, and political influences embedded within a social justice perspective (Lev & Sennott, 2013). Although affirmative models like the Expanded Family Life Cycle model acknowledge complexity within families stemming from cultural diversity, including LGBT families and racially or ethnically diverse families, these models do not explicitly address the unique circumstances, strengths, and challenges that often are associated with adoption.

Complementing the affirmative approaches are those designed to provide guidance or training on working with families in general, or particularly with adoptive families. Several notable approaches include the family life cycle (Carter & McGoldrick, 1989), the adoptive family life cycle (Brodzinsky, 1993; Brodzinsky & Schechter, 1990; Hajal & Rosenberg, 1991), the Lifelong Families Model (which focuses on preparing for permanency), the Permanency and Adoption Competency Certificate, the Training on Adoption Competency, and the National Adoption Competency Mental Health Training Initiative. Still other approaches are designed to explain and address particular characteristics or issues commonly experienced by adopted children or adoptive families. These include theories related to grief and loss, attachment and reactive attachment disorder, identity development, stress and coping, resiliency, and trauma-informed care. Although adoptive family approaches acknowledge complexity and diversity within adoptive families, the approaches are not yet guided by a coherent framework for explaining development and functioning through a nonadoptive lens when called for.

Existing approaches to working with increasingly diverse families and family members have come under great scrutiny in the past few decades because of concerns that they ignore the unique experiences and developmental processes of particular groups (Gilligan, 1993; Jordan, Kaplan, Miller, Stiver, & Surrey, 1991). Other concerns relate to the sense that the complex multidimensionality of race, ethnicity, class, and religion is minimized and ignored (Lev & Sennott, 2013; McGoldrick & Hardy, 2008). Specifically with respect to working with culturally diverse lesbian and gay populations, emphasis has grown over the past decade on using contextual approaches (Lebow, 2005; McDowell, 2005; Nichols & Schwartz, 2009; Walsh, 2003). Working with lesbian and gay populations requires an understanding of both the "normative" developmental and life-cycle issues that individuals, couples, and families face, as well as the unique issues experienced by those with diverse orientations, identities, and expressions. Contextual approaches are lauded for their focus on client's strengths through the exploration and emergence of the client's intersecting identities (Sennott & Smith, 2011). Existing approaches often are organized as though these risk factors are mutually exclusive and separable. As a consequence, many interventions and policies fail to capture

## PRACTICE HIGHLIGHTS

> No practice models exist for professionals and educators working specifically with lesbian and gay transracial and international adoptions. Yet professionals and educators can draw from myriad theories and frameworks. Many of the existing approaches are limited in that they do not capture the interactive effects of multiple factors (such as sexual orientation, race, gender, class, and other aspects of cultural diversity) or the influencing role of context. Lack of emphasis on the life-span and family-cycle perspectives further limit existing approaches.
>
> For lesbian and gay families that adopt transracially or internationally, an intersectional perspective highlights the importance of considering multiple and intersecting cultural factors in relation to a particular context. Such a perspective should be applied to each member of the adoptive family, as well as the adoptive family unit, to better understand development and functioning and potential practice responses. Practitioners should be mindful that the salience and interaction of factors that influence the development of problems or challenges may be entirely different than those that are incorporated into a treatment response.

the *interactive* effects of sexual orientation, race, gender, class, and other aspects of cultural diversity, such as those depicted in the following case study. Additionally, they fail to provide direction on how to approach diversity within particular contexts—contexts that are often invisible or changing.

### CASE ILLUSTRATION: MARIA, CHRISTINE, AND AVA

#### Background

Maria and Christine are a middle-age, interracial lesbian couple living with their adopted daughter Ava in San Francisco's Castro district, which is known for being one of the first and most lively gay neighborhoods in the United States. Maria immigrated to the United States from San Salvador with her first spouse— husband Alejandro— when they were both 18 years old. Within 1 year of arriving in the United States Maria got pregnant with their child, Luis. Maria met Christine at a diner they both frequented often for breakfast. Christine was an "out" lesbian and previously had had numerous romantic partners. Maria had never really questioned her sexual orientation but when she met Christine she knew "this was different." Soon after meeting Christine, Maria felt a passion she had never felt. Eventually the marriage between Maria and Alejandro was dissolved, and they both agreed that Alejandro should have primary custody over Luis. Maria and Christine have been a couple now for 17 years and have been married for the past 7 years.

While in their early 40s, Maria and Christine decided to adopt so that they could have their "own family." The couple worked with a private adoption agency known for placing children with lesbians and gay men. The agency offered a variety of both pre- and postplacement services, such as counseling, legal, education, and supportive services. Within weeks of finishing their home study, Maria and Christine were contacted about a baby living in an orphanage in Korea. From what the agency told the couple, the baby was the product of a short-lived romance between a Korean schoolgirl in her late teens and an African American soldier. Because her father was also a soldier, Christine felt that "this was meant to be" and began developing a strong bond with the baby even before they met. After several trips to Korea, Maria and Christine brought their new daughter, Ava, home. By all accounts, the adoption went fairly smoothly; it was finalized in just over a year when Ava was about 18 months old. During the finalization of the adoption and for a few years later, the adoption agency kept in contact with the couple and offered services to help them navigate their new life as a same-sex transracial and international adoptive family. Both mothers attached quickly to Ava and as Ava grew up, she remained close to her mothers. Conversely, Maria's other child, Luis, from her first marriage, developed a strained relationship with Maria and Christine. Over time, however, Luis developed a warm and caring relationship with Ava, although he never quite viewed or accepted her as his "real sister."

### The Family Through an Intersectional Lens

Because her family lived in an area where same-sex couples were common, as a young child, Ava did not experience the stigma other children with lesbian or gay

**CASE ILLUSTRATION: MARIA, CHRISTINE, AND AVA** (CONTINUED)

parents might experience growing up in a more conservative or traditional region. Adolescence, however, brought new challenges for Ava, who went into puberty earlier than average at around 10 years old. Her secondary sexual characteristics (breast development and pubic hair) made her self-conscious about her appearance; she tried to minimize her breasts with baggy sweaters and avoided the locker room. Luis, now a young man, avoided his sister as her budding sexuality was too stimulating for him. As siblings who were not related "by blood," in which case the incest taboo would have kicked in and dampened his feelings, he unconsciously withdrew from Ava to protect himself. Ava felt rejected by her brother, which only added to her growing insecurity about her appearance and now about being adopted.

Although Ava loved her parents she realized early on that she was "different" from them in terms of her racial appearance, as well as in her burgeoning identifications and orientations. For the most part, the racial and transracial aspects of Ava's experience were not salient in her younger years. When Ava was in elementary school, her family attended a summer camp for transracial adoptive families, and they all found this to be an enjoyable experience. But the family did not return to the camp, largely because Ava preferred other types of camps that nurtured her artistic and athletic interests. Maria and Christine mostly avoided the topic of race and ethnicity in their family, and Ava grew up to rarely speak about it. Later, this caused some frustration for Ava; although she "appeared" black and Asian on the outside, she felt disconnected from this part of herself, and she longed to understand her biological and cultural heritage. Not only did Ava look different from her family but also her romantic and erotic feelings leaned in the direction of boys, not girls. Growing up and now as a preteen, Ava had no attraction to other girls or desire to be physical with them. Nevertheless, as the child of lesbian parents who fairly strongly identified as lesbians and as part of the gay community, Ava was open to the possibility of being lesbian or bisexual. Once or twice Ava kissed other girls on the lips "just to see what it was like." She concluded that it was "kinda gross . . . like kissing one of my moms."

Despite her surroundings and her openness about her parents' relationship, Ava became self-conscious about them during her adolescence and was reluctant to bring friends and potential boyfriends home. This created some tension at home as her parents wanted to know who their daughter was spending time with and to provide some appropriate supervision. Ava's recognition of her "differentness" was generally a source of stress for her. Peers often asked where her father was or why she looked so different from her mothers. Both Maria and Christine helped Ava field these questions the best they could, but Maria and Christine struggled as the questions seemed to "always change." Sometimes the questions had to do with being part of a lesbian or gay family; other times they had to do with race, ethnicity, or culture. Still other times, the questions had to do with adoption, in general, or more specifically with transracial adoption or international adoption. Over time, Christine tended to view and answer questions through a lens that was largely about sexual orientation or gender. Maria grew impatient with Christine, admonishing her that "not everything is about being gay," to which Christine typically responded, "at least I'm proud of who I am." Issues related to adoption, for the most part, were minimized or dismissed altogether by both Maria and Christine.

It seemed that members of the family increasingly were either arguing with or withdrawing from one another. Maria and Christine felt they had grown apart and that they might get along better if they were no longer married to one another, a prospect they shared with Ava who was devastated by the news. Ava began exhibiting signs of depression, was losing sleep, and stopped eating, and her grades began to suffer. She also began smoking pot with her friends, something she previously had declined to do despite the peer pressure. Her depression worsened and she spent many days in her room, sleeping and playing video games. She eventually withdrew from her friends and lashed out at Christine, saying the (impending) divorce was her fault. But internally, Ava felt it was really her fault—that somehow she was to blame. She felt more alone than she ever had.

Alone in her room Ava searched the Internet for her biological family. She wanted to know the "real story" surrounding her adoption. Secretly, she hoped to connect with her biological family out of fear that she was about to be rejected by the only family she had ever known—Maria and Christine, and her brother Luis. In her searching, Ava stumbled onto a free, online support group for children of LGBT parents who had divorced. The group was led by a professional social worker and met once each week on Sunday. At first Ava was reluctant to share her feelings with the group. Interestingly, the physical distance of the online group allowed Ava to feel less exposed and to go at her own pace. As she gradually

CASE ILLUSTRATION: MARIA, CHRISTINE, AND AVA (CONTINUED)

felt more comfortable her story poured out. To the group Ava revealed feelings of hurt at being "given up" by her "real mom." She began to grieve the biological mother she never knew and a homeland she had never visited. Now Ava worried that one or both of her adoptive mothers wouldn't "want her." The online support group proved to be a balm for her wounds as Ava saw her own pain reflected in the faces and stories of the others.

Acutely aware of Ava's pain, Maria and Christine decided to seek out a family therapist to help them address the conflict the family was experiencing (which they referred to as "chaos"), as well as to prepare Ava for the divorce that they considered almost inevitable. Christine found a gay-affirmative therapist through friends. In a neutral atmosphere with their empathic therapist, the family was able to discuss emotionally laden topics related to being an adoptive family, such as Ava's desire to search for members of her biological families, as well as topics related to the impending divorce, such as custody issues, financial arrangements, and who would spend what holidays with Ava. In addition to his affirmative stance, the family's therapist utilized a solution-focused therapy approach. Such an approach emphasizes the notion that solutions come from the family and that the family has within it the resilience, strength, and wisdom to affect the changes they seek. In their most recent session, the therapist asked Ava, Maria, and Christine what is known as the "miracle question": *If you could wake up tomorrow morning and realize that a miracle had taken place overnight and something had changed what would you notice?* (Berg, 1994). As Maria and Christine envisioned their "miracle," they began to have hope and to question whether their decision to divorce might have been premature.

## CONCLUSION

Families in previous studies on lesbian and gay families have been found to do well despite experiencing numerous barriers and assaults related to their sexual orientation. It is possible that the families who were studied do not reflect the larger population of lesbian and gay families. As lesbian and gay adoptions become more common, it is possible that we will see an increasing number of parents who are not as resourceful or effective in their parenting as parents in samples of past studies. From an intersectional perspective, we should not be surprised if future studies reveal altogether new issues or worsening of some already empirically established issues that stem directly from the intersectional aspects of LGAs. As more "typical" lesbian and gay families adopt, professionals and educators may encounter more families struggling to address the multiple and dynamic challenges of lesbian and gay transracial and intercountry adoption.

By all accounts, lesbian and gay adoptive families, especially those consisting of children who are adopted transracially or internationally, should be expected to encounter numerous challenges over the life span of the family. Those challenges sometimes stem from the experience of adoption and the circumstances leading to adopt. Other times, the challenges may relate to the individual or combined effects of having a family member who is a member of a sexual, racial, or cultural minority group. An intersectionality perspective, however, suggests that an alternative explanation for the positive outcomes experienced by transracially and internationally adopted children raised in lesbian and gay families may be related to an enhanced ability to negotiate different aspects of identity. Moreover, it is possible that the experience of encountering and addressing multiple forms of oppression, discrimination, and disadvantage provide children with special strengths that enhance their development and resiliency. To this end, the unique strengths and experiences of transracially and international adopted children raised in lesbian and gay families may make them particularly adept at navigating in an increasingly diverse and global world.

### DISCUSSION QUESTIONS

1. From a life-span perspective, which cultural factors were salient for Ava and her family and how did they intersect with one another?
2. What value—negative, neutral, or positive— did each of the following cultural factors have for Ava?
    a. Race
    b. Nationality
    c. Gender
    d. Sexual orientation
    e. Being adopted

f. Being transracially adopted
   g. Being internationally adopted
   h. Being adopted by a lesbian couple
3. In terms of Ava's development and functioning, how did environmental and developmental factors influence the cultural factors presented in question 2, as well as their salience and impact?
4. From an intersectional perspective, how might divorce have affected Ava similarly and differently than it would have had she been raised by her biological parents? By a heterosexual adoptive couple? By an inracially adoptive couple?
5. What factors contributed to Ava's sense of identity and her feelings of being different at various developmental stages?

**REFERENCES**

Alexander, R., & Curtis, C. M. (1996). A review of empirical research involving the transracial adoption of African American children. *Journal of Black Psychology, 22*(2), 223–235.

Andujo, E. (1988). Ethnic identity of transethnically adopted Hispanic adolescents. *Social Work, 33*(6), 531–535.

Armesto, J. C. (2002). Developmental and contextual factors that influence gay fathers' parental competence: A review of the literature. *Psychology of Men & Masculinity, 3*(2), 67–78.

Association for Women's Rights in Development (AWID). (2004). Intersectionality: A tool for gender and economic justice. *Women's Rights and Economic Change, 9*.

Averett, P., Nalavany, B., & Ryan, S. (2009). An evaluation of gay/lesbian and heterosexual adoption. *Adoption Quarterly, 12*(3–4), 129–151.

Bagley, C. (1993). Transracial adoption in Britain: A follow-up study, with policy considerations. *Child Welfare: Journal of Policy, Practice, and Program, 72*(3), 285–299.

Bailey, J. M., Bobrow, D., Wolfe, M., & Mikach, S. (1995). Sexual orientation of adult sons of gay fathers. *Developmental psychology, 31*(1), 124–129.

Barnes, G. M., Reifman, A. S., Farrell, M. P., & Dintcheff, B. A. (2000). The effects of parenting on the development of adolescent alcohol misuse: A six-wave latent growth model. *Journal of Marriage and Family, 62*(1), 175–186.

Baumle, A. K., & Compton, D. L. R. (2011). Legislating the family: The effect of state family laws on the presence of children in same-sex households. *Law & Policy, 33*(1), 82–115.

Berg, I. K. (1994). *Family based services: A solution-focused approach*. New York: Norton.

Biblarz, T. J., & Stacey, J. (2010). How does the gender of parents matter? *Journal of Marriage and Family, 72*(1), 3–22.

Bos, H. M., Van Balen, F., & Van den Boom, D.C. (2004). Experience of parenthood, couple relationship, social support, and child-rearing goals in planned lesbian mother families. *Journal of Child Psychology and Psychiatry, 45*(4), 755–764.

Brewaeys, A., Ponjaert, I., Van Hall, E. V., & Golombok, S. (1997). Donor insemination: Child development and family functioning in lesbian mother families. *Human reproduction, 12*(6), 1349–1359.

Brodzinsky, D. M. (1993). Long-term outcomes in adoption. *The Future of Children, 3*(1), 153–166.

Brodzinsky, D. M., & Schechter, M. D. (1990). *The psychology of adoption*. Oxford, England: Oxford University Press.

Brodzinsky, D. M., Patterson, C. J., & Vaziri, M. (2002). Adoption agency perspectives on lesbian and gay prospective parents: A national study. *Adoption Quarterly, 5(3)*, 5–23.

Brooks, D., & Barth, R. P. (1999). Adult transracial and inracial adoptees: Effects of race, gender, adoptive family structure, and placement history on adjustment outcomes. *American Journal of Orthopsychiatry, 69*(1), 87–99.

Brooks, D., & Goldberg, S. (2001). Gay and lesbian adoptive and foster care placements: Can they meet the needs of waiting children? *Social Work, 46*(2), 147–157.

Brooks, D., Kim, H., & Wind, L. (2012). Supporting gay and lesbian adoptive families before and after adoption. In D.M. Brodzinsky & A. Pertman (Eds.), *Adoption by lesbians and gay men: A new dimension in family diversity* (pp. 150–183). New York: Oxford University Press.

California Adoption Survey Committee. (1946). *Report of the California Adoption Survey Committee*. Author. Sacramento: Department of Social Welfare.

Carter, B., & McGoldrick, M. (1989). *The changing family life cycle: A framework for family therapy*, 2nd ed. Boston: Allyn and Bacon.

Child Welfare Information Gateway. (2013, October). *Adopting as a single parent*. Retrieved from https://www.childwelfare.gov/pubs/single_parent.cfm

Cooper, L., & Cates, P. (2006). *Too high a price: The case against restricting gay parenting*. New York: American Civil Liberties Union Foundation.

Crenshaw, K. (1989). Demarginalizing the intersection of race and sex: A black feminist critique of antidiscrimination doctrine, feminist theory and antiracist politics. *The University of Chicago Legal Forum, 140*, 139–167.

Crenshaw, K. (1991). Mapping the margins: Intersectionality, identity politics, and violence against women of color. *Stanford Law Review, 43*(6), 1241–1299.

Crenshaw, K. W. (1995). The intersection of race and gender. In K. W. Crenshaw, N. Gotanda, G. Peller, & K. Thomas (Eds.), *Critical race theory: The key writings that formed the movement* (pp. 357–383). New York: New Press.

Davis, K. (2008). Intersectionality as buzzword A sociology of science perspective on what makes a feminist theory successful. *Feminist theory, 9*(1), 67–85.

DiClemente, R. J., Wingood, G. M., Crosby, R., Sionean, C., Cobb, B. K., Harrington, K., Davies, S. & Oh, M. K. (2001). Parental monitoring: Association with adolescents' risk behaviors. *Pediatrics, 107*(6), 1363–1368.

Erich, S., Hall, S. K., Kanenberg, H., & Case, K. (2009). Early and late stage adolescence: Adopted adolescents' attachment to their heterosexual and lesbian/gay parents. *Adoption Quarterly, 12*(3–4), 152–170.

Erich, S., Kanenberg, H., Case, K., Allen, T., & Bogdanos, T. (2009). An empirical analysis of factors affecting adolescent attachment in adoptive families with homosexual and straight parents. *Children and Youth Services Review, 31*, 398–404.

Erich, S., Leung, P., Kindle, P., & Carter, S. (2005). Gay and lesbian adoptive families: An exploratory study of family functioning, adoptive child's behavior, and familial support networks. *Journal of Family Social Work, 9*, 17–32.

Farr, R. H., & Patterson, C. J. (2009). Transracial adoption by lesbian, gay, and heterosexual couples: Who completes transracial adoptions and with what results? *Adoption Quarterly, 12*(3–4), 187–204.

Feigelman, W., & Silverman, A. R. (1984). The long-term effects of transracial adoption. *Social Service Review*, 588–602.

Flaks, D. K., Ficher, I., Masterpasqua, F., & Joseph, G. (1995). Lesbians choosing motherhood: A comparative study of lesbian and heterosexual parents and their children. *Developmental Psychology, 31*(1), 105–114.

Gartrell, N., Banks, A., Reed, N., Hamilton, J., Rodas, C., & Deck, A. (2000). The National Lesbian Family Study: 3. Interviews with mothers of five-year-olds. *American Journal of Orthopsychiatry, 70*(4), 542–548.

Gartrell, N., & Bos, H. (2010). US national longitudinal lesbian family study: Psychological adjustment of 17-year-old adolescents. *Pediatrics, 126*(1), 28–36.

Gartrell, N., Deck, A., Rodas, C., Peyser, H., & Banks, A. (2005). The National Lesbian Family Study: 4. Interviews with the 10-year-old children. *American Journal of Orthopsychiatry, 75*(4), 518–524.

Gates, G. J. (2011). *How many people are lesbian, gay, bisexual, and transgender?* Williams Institute, University of California School of Law.

Gates, G. J. (2013, February). *LGBT parenting in the United States.* Williams Institute, University of California School of Law.

Gates, G. J., Badgett, M. V., Macomber, J. E., & Chambers, K. (2007). *Adoption and foster care by gay and lesbian parents in the United States.* Williams Institute, University of California School of Law.

Gilligan, C. (1993). *In a different voice: Psychological theory and women's development.* New York: Harvard University Press.

Glantz, M. D., & Chambers, J. C. (2006). Prenatal drug exposure effects on subsequent vulnerability to drug abuse. *Development and Psychopathology, 18*(03), 893–922.

Goldberg, A. E. (2010). Studying complex families in context. *Journal of Marriage and Family, 72*(1), 29–34.

Goldberg, A.E., Gartrell, N.K., & Gates, G. (2014). Research Report on LGB-Parent Families. Los Angeles, CA: The Williams Institute, UCLA School of Law. Retrieved from http://williamsinstitute.law.ucla.edu/wp-content/uploads/lgb-parent-familiesjuly-2014.pdf

Goldberg, A. E., & Smith, J. Z. (2008). Social support and psychological well-being in lesbian and heterosexual preadoptive couples. *Family Relations, 57*(3), 281–294.

Goldberg, A. E., & Smith, J. Z. (2009). Perceived parenting skill across the transition to adoptive parenthood among lesbian, gay, and heterosexual couples. *Journal of Family Psychology, 23*(6), 861–870.

Golombok, S., Perry, B., Burston, A., Murray, C., Mooney-Somers, J., Stevens, M., & Golding, J. (2003). Children with lesbian parents: A community study. *Developmental psychology, 39*(1), 20–33.

Golombok, S., Spencer, A., & Rutter, M. (1983). Children in lesbian and single-parent households: Psychosexual and psychiatric appraisal. *Journal of Child Psychology and psychiatry, 24*(4), 551–572.

Golombok, S., & Tasker, F. (1996). Do parents influence the sexual orientation of their children? Findings from a longitudinal study of lesbian families. *Developmental Psychology, 32*(1), 3–11.

Grotevant, H. D., & McDermott, J. M. (2014). Adoption: Biological and social processes linked to adaptation. *Annual Review of Psychology, 65*, 235–265.

Hajal, F., & Rosenberg, E. B. (1991). The family life cycle in adoptive families. *American Journal of Orthopsychiatry, 61*(1), 78–85.

Hammond, W. (2010). *Principles of strength based practice.* Resiliency Initiatives: Calgary, Alberta, Canada. Retrieved from www.resil.ca

Hankivsky, O., Reid, C., Cormier, R., Varcoe, C., Clark, N., Benoit, C., & Brotman, S. (2010). Exploring the promises of intersectionality for advancing women's health research. *International Journal for Equity in Health, 9*(5), 1–15.

Hawk, B., & McCall, R. B. (2010). CBCL behavior problems of post-institutionalized international adoptees. *Clinical Child and Family Psychology Review, 13*(2), 199–211.

Hess, L. (2012). *Intersectionality: A systematic review and application to explore the complexity of teen pregnancy involvement* (Doctoral Columbia University).

Ishizawa, H., Kenney, C. T., Kubo, K., & Stevens, G. (2006). Constructing interracial families through intercountry adoption. *Social Science Quarterly, 87*(5), 1207–1224.

Jani, J. S., Pierce, D., Ortiz, L., & Sowbel, L. (2011). Access to intersectionality, content to competence: Deconstructing social work education diversity standards. *Journal of Social Work Education, 47*(2), 283–301.

Ji, J., Brooks, D., Barth, R. P., & Kim, H. (2010). Beyond preadoptive risk: The impact of adoptive family environment on adopted youth's psychosocial adjustment. *American Journal of Orthopsychiatry, 80*(3), 432–442.

Jones, C., & Else, J. (1979). Racial and cultural issues in adoption. *Child Welfare, 58,* 373–382

Jordan, J. V., Kaplan, A. G., Miller, J. B., Stiver, J. L., & Surrey, L. P. (Eds.). (1991). *Women's growth in connection.* New York: Guilford Press.

Juffer, F., Palacios, J., Le Mare, L., Sonuga-Barke, E. J., Tieman, W., Bakermans-Kranenburg, M. J., Vorria, P., van IJzendoorn, M. H., & Verhulst, F. C. (2011). II. Development of adopted children with histories of early adversity. *Monographs of the Society for Research in Child Development, 76*(4), 31–61.

Juffer, F., & van IJzendoorn, M. H. (2005). Behavior problems and mental health referrals of international adoptees: A meta-analysis. *JAMA, 293*(20), 2501–2515.

Kirkpatrick, M., Smith, C., & Roy, R. (1981). Lesbian mothers and their children: A comparative survey. *American Journal of Orthopsychiatry, 51*(3), 545–551.

Kosciw, J. G., & Diaz, E. M. (2008). *Involved, invisible, ignored: The experiences of lesbian, gay, bisexual and transgender parents and their children in our nation's k-12 schools.* Gay, Lesbian and Straight Education Network (GLSEN), New York, NY.

Kosciw, J. G., Greytak, E. A., & Diaz, E. M. (2009). Who, what, where, when, and why: Demographic and ecological factors contributing to hostile school climate for lesbian, gay, bisexual, and transgender youth. *Journal of Youth and Adolescence, 38*(7), 976–988.

Krawiec, K. (2010). Price and pretense in the baby market. In M. Goodwin (Ed.), *Baby markets: Money and the new politics of creating families* (pp. 41–55). Cambridge, England: Cambridge University Press.

Kreider, R. M., & Cohen, P. N. (2009). Disability among internationally adopted children in the United States. *Pediatrics, 124*(5), 1311–1318.

Kreider, R. M., & Lofquist, D. A. (2014). Adopted children and stepchildren: 2010. *Adoption Quarterly, 13*, 268–291.

Kuvalanka, K. A., Leslie, L. A., & Radina, R. (2013). Coping with sexual stigma: Emerging adults with lesbian parents reflect on the impact of heterosexism and homophobia during their adolescence. *Journal of Adolescent Research, 29*(2), 241–270.

Lavner, J. A., Waterman, J., & Peplau, L. A. (2012). Can gay and lesbian parents promote healthy development in high-risk children adopted from foster care? *American Journal of Orthopsychiatry, 82*(4), 465–472.

Lebow, J. L. (Ed.). (2005). *Handbook of clinical family therapy*. Hoboken, NJ: Wiley.

Leddy, A., Gartrell, N., & Bos, H. (2012). Growing up in a lesbian family: The life experiences of the adult daughters and sons of lesbian mothers. *Journal of GLBT Family Studies, 8*(3), 243–257.

Leung, P., Erich, S., & Kanenberg, H. (2005). A comparison of family functioning in gay/lesbian, heterosexual and special needs adoptions. *Children and Youth Services Review, 27*(9), 1031–1044.

Lev, A. I., & Sennott, S. L. (2013). Clinical work with LGBTQ parents and prospective parents. In A. E. Goldberg & K. R. Allen (Eds.), *LGBT-parent families* (pp. 241–260). New York: Springer.

MacCallum, F., & Golombok, S. (2004). Children raised in fatherless families from infancy: A follow-up of children of lesbian and single heterosexual mothers at early adolescence. *Journal of Psychology and Psychiatry, 45*, 1407–1419.

Mallon, G. P. (2000). Gay men and lesbians as adoptive parents. *Journal of Gay & Lesbian Social Services, 11*(4), 1–22.

McCall, L. (2005). The complexity of intersectionality. *Signs, 30*(3), 1771–1800.

McDowell, T. (2005). Practicing a relational therapy with a critical multicultural lens. Introduction to a special section. *Journal of Systemic Therapies, 24*, 1–4.

McGoldrick, M., Carter, B. & Garcia-Preto, N. (2010). *The expanded family life cycle: Individual, family, and social perspectives* (4th ed.). Boston: Allyn and Bacon.

McGoldrick, M., & Hardy, K. V. (Eds.). (2008). *Re-visioning family therapy: Race, culture, and gender in clinical practice.* New York: Guilford Press.

McRoy, R. G. (1994). Attachment and racial identity issues: Implications for child placement decision making. *Journal of Multicultural Social Work, 3*(3), 59–74.

McRoy, R. G., Zurcher, L. A., Lauderdale, M. L., & Anderson, R. E. (1984). The identity of transracial adoptees. *Social Casework, 65*(1), 34–39.

Montero, D. (2014). Attitudes toward same-gender adoption and parenting: An analysis of surveys from 16 countries. *Advances in Social Work, 15*(2), 444–459.

Murphy, Y., Hunt, V., Zajicek, A.M., Norris, A. N., & Hamilton, L. (2009). *Incorporating intersectionality in social work practice, research, policy, and education.* NASW Press, National Association of Social Workers.

Nichols, M. P., & Schwartz, R. C. (Eds.). (2009). *Family therapy: Concepts and methods* (7th ed.). Boston: Pearson/Allyn & Bacon.

Palacios, J., & Brodzinsky, D. (2010). Review: Adoption research: Trends, topics, outcomes. *International Journal of Behavioral Development, 34*(3), 270–284.

Pew Research Center. (2012, July 31). *Obama Endorsement Has Limited Impact.* Retrieved from http://www.pewforum.org/files/2012/07/Democrats-Gay-Marriage-Support-full.pdf

Potter, D. (2012). Same-sex parent families and children's academic achievement. *Journal of Marriage and Family, 74*(3), 556–571.

Putnam, F. W. (2003). Ten-year research update review: Child sexual abuse. *Journal of the American Academy of Child & Adolescent Psychiatry, 42*(3), 269–278.

Quiroz, P. A. (2007). *Adoption in a color-blind society.* Lanham, MD: Rowman & Littlefield.

Rai, A. A., Stanton, B., Wu, Y., Li, X., Galbraith, J., Cottrell, L., Pack, R., Harris, C., D'Alessandri, D., & Burns, J. (2003). Relative influences of perceived parental monitoring and perceived peer involvement on adolescent risk behaviors: An analysis of six cross-sectional data sets. *Journal of Adolescent Health, 33*(2), 108–118.

Raleigh, E. (2012). Are same-sex and single adoptive parents more likely to adopt transracially? A national analysis of race, family structure, and the adoption marketplace. *Sociological Perspectives, 55*(3), 449–471.

Ray, V., & Gregory, R. (2001). School experiences of the children of lesbian and gay parents. *Family Matters, 59*, 28–34.

Rivers, I., Poteat, V. P., & Noret, N. (2008). Victimization, Social Support, and Psychosocial Functioning Among Children of Same-Sex and Opposite-Sex Couples in the United Kingdom. *Developmental Psychology, 44*(1), 127–134.

Rosenfeld, M. J. (2007). *The age of independence: Interracial unions, same-sex unions, and the changing American family.* Cambridge, MA: Harvard University Press.

Rosenfeld, M. J. (2010). Nontraditional families and childhood progress through school. *Demography, 47*(3), 755–775.

Rushton, A., & Minnis, H. (1997). Annotation: Transracial family placements. *Journal of Child Psychology and Psychiatry, 38*(2), 147–159.

Ryan, S. (2008). Parent-child interaction styles between gay and lesbian parents and their adopted children. *Journal of GLBT Family Studies, 3*(2–3), 105–132.

Ryan, S. D., & Cash, S. (2004). Adoptive families headed by gay or lesbian parents: A threat ... or hidden resource. *University of Florida Journal of Law & Public Policy, 15*(3), 443–465.

Ryan, S. D., Pearlmutter, S., & Groza, V. (2004). Coming out of the closet: Opening agencies to gay and lesbian adoptive parents. *Social Work, 49*(1), 85–95.

Schwartz, C. R., & Graf, N. L. (2009). Assortative matching among same-sex and different-sex couples in the United States, 1990–2000. *Demographic Research, 21*, 843–878.

Selman, P. (2009). The rise and fall of intercountry adoption in the 21st century. *International Social Work, 52*(5), 575–594.

Selman, P. (2012). The global decline of intercountry adoption: What lies ahead? *Social Policy and Society, 11*(03), 381–397.

Sennott, S., & Smith, T. (2011). Translating the sex and gender continuums in mental health: A transfeminist approach to client and clinician fears. *Journal of Gay & Lesbian Mental Health, 15*(2), 218–234.

Shireman, J. F., & Johnson, P. R. (1986). A longitudinal study of black adoptions: Single parent, transracial, and traditional. *Social Work, 31*(3), 172–176.

Simmel, C., Brooks, D., Barth, R. P., & Hinshaw, S. P. (2001). Externalizing symptomatology among adoptive youth: Prevalence and preadoption risk factors. *Journal of Abnormal Child Psychology, 29*(1), 57–69.

Simon, R. J., Altstein, H., & Melli, M. S. (1994). *The case for transracial adoption.* Washington, DC: American University Press.

Tasker, F. (2013). Lesbian and gay parenting post-heterosexual divorce and separation. In A. E. Goldberg & K. R. Allen (Eds.), *LGBT-Parent Families* (pp. 3–20). New York: Springer.

Tasker, F., & Golombok, S. (1995). Adults raised as children in lesbian families. *American Journal of Orthopsychiatry, 65*(2), 203–215.

United Nations, Department of Economics. (2009). *Child adoption: Trends and policies* (No. 292). United Nations Publications.

U.S. Department of State. (2011). *Total Adoptions to the United States.* Washington, DC: Author

U.S. Department of State. (2014). *FY 2013 Annual Report on Intercountry Adoption.* Retrieved from http://travel.state.gov/content/dam/aa/pdfs/fy2013_annual_report.pdf

Vandivere, S., Malm, K., and Radel, L. (2009). *Adoption USA: A Chartbook Based on the 2007 National Survey of Adoptive Parents.* Washington, DC: U.S. Department of Health and Human Services, Office of the Assistant Secretary for Planning and Evaluation.

Voigt, K., & Brown, S. (2013, September 17). *International adoptions in decline as number of orphans grows.* Retrieved from http://www.cnn.com/2013/09/16/world/international-adoption-main-story-decline/index.html?iref=allsearch

Vroegh, K. S. (1997). Transracial adoptees: Developmental status after 17 years. *American Journal of Orthopsychiatry, 67*(4), 568–575.

Wainright, J. L., & Patterson, C. J. (2008). Peer relations among adolescents with female same-sex parents. *Developmental Psychology, 44*(1), 117–126.

Wainright, J. L., Russell, S. T., & Patterson, C. J. (2004). Psychosocial adjustment, school outcomes, and romantic relationships of adolescents with same-sex parents. *Child development, 75*(6), 1886–1898.

Walsh, F. (Ed.). (2003). *Normal family processes: Growing diversity and complexity.* New York: Guilford Press.

Winker, G., & Degele, N. (2011). Intersectionality as multi-level analysis: Dealing with social inequality. *European Journal of Women's Studies, 18*(1), 51–66.

Zastrow, CH. (1977). *Outcome of Black Children–White Parent Transracial Adoptions.* San Francisco, CA: R & E Research Associates.

### RECOMMENDED RESOURCES

Adopt USKids. (n.d.). *Adoption laws and resources for LGBT families.* Retrieved from http://www.adoptuskids.org/for-families/who-can-foster-and-adopt/adoption-laws-and-resources-for-lgbt-families

Brodzinsky, D. M., & Schechter, M. D. (1990). *The psychology of adoption.* Oxford, England: Oxford University Press.

Crenshaw, K. W. (1995). The intersection of race and gender. In K. W. Crenshaw, N. Gotanda, G. Peller, & K. Thomas (Eds.), *Critical race theory: The key writings that formed the movement* (pp. 357–383). New York: New Press.

Grotevant, H. D., & McDermott, J. M. (2014). Adoption: Biological and social processes linked to adaptation. *Annual Review of Psychology, 65*, 235–265.

Human Rights Campaign. (n.d.). *Resources: Professional organizations on LGBT parenting.* Retrieved from http://www.hrc.org/resources/entry/professional-organizations-on-lgbt-parenting

National Clearinghouse on Child Abuse and Neglect Information, National Adoption Information Clearinghouse. (n.d.). *Gay and lesbian adoptive parents: Resources for professionals and parents.* Retrieved from https://www.childwelfare.gov/pubPDFs/f_gay.pdf

PACT: An Adoption Alliance. (n.d.). *Pact family camp.* Retrieved from http://www.pactadopt.org/adoptive/services/education/pact_camp.html

# 5

# A Neurodevelopmental Perspective and Clinical Challenges

▸ BRUCE D. PERRY, ERIN HAMBRICK,
   AND ROBERT D. PERRY

THROUGHOUT HISTORY, HUMANKIND HAS USED adoption—both "legal" and informal—to maintain and sustain family, community, and culture. Many factors contribute to the choice to adopt but, in its current manifestations, a primary factor remains the powerful positive emotional and social features, including empathy. The act of "adopting"—caring for the child (or offspring) of another parent as if they are your own—is a remarkable manifestation of love and empathy. Other species adopt; indeed, there are examples of cross-species adoption in the natural world (Holland, 2011). A central feature of adoption—in humans and other animals—is the expression of mutual, reciprocal affection. The adopter and adoptee both give and receive pleasure from the relational interactions. The mutual capacity to envision, manifest and grow a powerful emotional connection is at the heart of the successful adoption. This process—forming and growing a sustaining love—can be challenged by many trauma- and neglect-related effects on the development of the adopted child. Unfortunately, children who are adopted often have experienced maltreatment and other developmental adversities that affect the child's relational capacities. This chapter will examine the impact of these developmental adversities on the child's neurobiological development and explore the clinical implications of these adverse experiences in context of intercountry and transracial adoption.

### SCOPE AND CONTEXT

Between 1999 and 2005, intercountry adoption became increasingly common in the United States, with 142,409 children identified as internationally adopted by the U.S. Department of State (n.d.). It is estimated that 70 to 90 percent of internationally adopted children are transracial adoptions (Lee, 2003). As will be discussed, earlier adoption is associated with better outcomes; unfortunately fewer than 20 percent of intercountry adoptions take place before the age of 1 year old (Johnson, 2002). Between 2006 and 2012, rates of intercountry adoption slowly decreased with only 99,530 children adopted within this seven-year span. This decrease in rates may be related to increased regulatory hurdles, such as intercountry adoption regulations fees; and, in part, to an increased awareness of the difficulties faced by families who have adopted internationally.

**Preadoption Adversity**

The majority of intercountry adoptees have experienced some form of adversity during development. An estimated 85 percent of internationally adopted children were institutionalized at some point (Loman, Wiik, Frenn, Pollak, & Gunnar, 2009). Early studies of institutionalized children documented less-than-ideal developmental environments (Mason & Narad, 2005; Spitz, 1945, 1946). Although each institution was somewhat different, well-intended but developmentally destructive practices were common, and in some settings remain so. Historically, orphanages were disease ridden and to minimize the spreading of disease, children were kept from playing with one another and frequently left alone in cribs, rarely handled by caregivers except for during feeding and changing. Rocking, touching, and speaking to the children rarely occurred. Institutions tended to be devoid of social interactions, relying on consistent routines with low ratios of caregiver to child (e.g., one caregiver for thirty or more infants). These practices persist in many settings. A recent study by Groark, McCall, and Fish (2011) evaluated the characteristics of several Central American orphanages. Most were found to be clean but had minimal staff–child interactions. The interactions that did occur lacked emotional responsiveness to the individual needs of the children. Staff worked long hours and frequently rotated between wards, leading to a lack of consistency in caregiving, all with minimal physical and sensory input. Children were not encouraged to play together, further decreasing social interactions.

Although not a certainty, many institutionalized children have had other developmental challenges—such as prenatal exposure to alcohol, neglect, traumatic stress, and attachment disruptions—all of which are known to impact the development of the brain and lead to a range of complex cognitive, emotional, behavioral, social, and physiological problems (Anda et al., 2006; Perry, 2008) that appear to be overrepresented in samples of international adoptees (Bakermans-Kranenburg, van IJzendoorn, & Juffer, 2008; Johnson, n.d.; Juffer & van Ijzendoorn, 2005; Loman et al., 2009). The risk of in-utero exposure to stress hormones and teratogens, such as alcohol and drugs, is estimated to be close to 60 percent (McCarthy, 2005). Furthermore, the probability that the immediate perinatal period before institutionalization was in chaotic, higher risk environment with less-than-ideal attachment experiences remains high. These early risks for attachment development are compounded in children who spent their first months or years in institutions with poor staff-to-child ratios and socially sterile environments.

### Functional Consequences of Developmental Adversity

The emotional, social, cognitive, and physiological consequences of this kind of complex and multidimensional developmental trauma are significant and heterogeneous (De Bellis, 2005; Nelson, Bos, Gunnar, & Sonuga-Barke, 2011; Perry, 2002). When examining "international" adoptees as a group, statistically significant risks are seen for a host of problems. It is difficult to take general findings from grouped data, however, and apply to the individual child. Each child has a unique set of genetic gifts (or challenges) and epigenetic, prenatal, perinatal, and early childhood experiences; the behaviors of one institutionalized child may greatly differ from that of another. Following adoption from an international institutional setting, a child may have problems with attention, but many will not; a child may have problems with learning, but many will not; a child may have difficulties with relationships, but many do not. This complexity requires a careful examination of the individual's developmental history (as well as it can be determined) and current set of strengths and vulnerabilities (Perry, 2009).

With this caveat, taken as "group," a range of behavior problems and social skills deficits has been found in this population. These behavior problems are interrelated with cognitive challenges (Groark et al., 2011; Loman et al., 2009). Cognitive flexibility often is undeveloped in these children. These executive functioning impairments are common in maltreated children (Moffit et al., 2011; Piquero, Jennings, & Farrington, 2010). Some institutionalized children have been described as having "institutional autism" due to their difficulties reading and interpreting social nuances, mimicking the emotional responses of others, and demonstrating primitive self-soothing (O'Connor, Rutter, & English and Romanian Adoptees Study Team, 2000; Rutter et al., 1998). Many issues may not become evident until adolescence (Johnson & Gunnar, 2011) and can be confusing to caregivers who generally have seen typical development in their adopted child before this time.

Many institutionalized children may exhibit behavioral paradoxes (see "The Clinical Challenge"). In one moment, the child may demonstrate independent or even "parentified" behaviors and prefer to self-soothe, feed himself (or hoard food), and avoid physical affection, while in the next moment he may act completely infantile and seek physical comfort, rocking or even bottle-feeding. Others may seem to require affection at all times and exhibit separation fears as well as the inability to complete tasks independently. Impairments in self-regulation, or the ability to self-soothe when stressed, transition between novel tasks, persevere when challenged, and make adaptive behavioral choices likely will exist but will differ depending on the task and the context. For example, many children may find situations with high-intimacy expectations (such as family time) to be highly dysregulating and thus may exhibit poor self-regulation in the home, even though they are able to excel in less intimate school or daycare environments (see "The Clinical Challenge"; MacLean, 2003).

### Neurodevelopmental Consequences of Developmental Adversity

One of the fundamental principles of neurodevelopment is "activity dependence"—basically, neural networks (and the functions that they mediate) develop, organize, and function optimally when they receive "appropriate" nature, timing, and pattern of experience. Although there is much to learn about the timing and nature of optimal versus necessary experiences required to express functional potential, it is clear that extremes of neglect, chaos, distress, and traumatic experiences can lead to a range of neurodevelopmental problems (Anda et al., 2006; Perry, 2008).

The mechanisms by which experience influences development takes place at multiple, often parallel, interactive systems, ranging from genome to neural network to whole-organ systems to a family and community. For example, (1) an overwhelming traumatic experience can alter immediate release of neurotransmitter at a range of neural networks associated with the stress response and influence synaptic dynamics leading to changes in local synaptic density and structure; (2) these immediate "adaptive" changes resulting from sensing and processing threat, in turn, working at a micro level, can alter gene expression via a variety of epigenetic mechanisms and lead to long-term changes in gene expression; and (3) working at a macro level will alter widespread neural systems in complex ways (e.g., by creating new "associations" between sensory cues simultaneously present during the traumatic experience). Collectively, these complex mechanisms can mediate long-term alterations at the level of the epigenome, neuron, neural network, broader stress-response systems, multiple organs, and, ultimately, the individual, family, community, and culture. Experiences—both good and bad—have echoes deep, wide, and long and are found deep into our biological core, and so it is with intercountry adoptees.

With the heterogeneous nature of the developmental experiences of the intercountry adoptees, it is not surprising that the few studies examining neurodevelopmental functioning in this population have found significant (but varied) differences from comparison populations (e.g., O'Connor et al., 2000; Rutter et al., 1998; Rutter & English and Romanian Adoptees Studies Team, 1999). Among the findings are altered local brain activity in various cortical areas (Chugani et al., 2001); decreases in brain size (and head circumference) in extreme total global neglect (Perry, 2002); altered connectivity between key brain regions (Eluvanthingal et al., 2006); neuroendocrine regulation differences (Bruce, Fisher, Pears, & Levine, 2009); altered hippocampal, amygdala, and corpus callosum size (Mehta et al., 2009); and various measures of brain electrical activity (Vanderwert, Marshall, Nelson, Zeanah, & Fox, 2010). De Bellis (2005) and Nelson et al. (2011) provide reviews of this small but growing body of research.

### THE CLINICAL CHALLENGE

Twenty-five years ago many adoptive parents and their consulting medical teams had minimal understanding of the complex effects of these early life adversities on development. Although landmark studies describing some of the adverse effects of neglect, institutionalization, "psychosocial dwarfism," and adoption existed (Dennis, 1973; Spitz, 1945, 1946; and, especially, Money's excellent book from 1994), these were not widely incorporated into routine medical or psychological training. Indeed, the dissemination of these important learnings continues.

These early learnings about the potential challenges of intercountry adoption certainly were not part of the common understanding and awareness of the majority of adoptive parents. Over the ensuing years, the emotional, behavioral, learning, and physical health problems seen in adopted children and youth have stimulated more research and an increase in public awareness of these issues. Again, with the caveat against overgeneralizing to all intercountry adoptees, in several key clinical areas, a neurodevelopmental perspective can be helpful.

### Altered Stress-Response Systems

There are two major and interactive adaptive response patterns to significant threat: the arousal response and dissociation. The arousal response activates the individual and prepares them to flee or fight (Perry, 2008; Perry, Pollard, Blakley, Baker, & Vigilante, 1995). Dissociation is less well characterized and is engaged when there is a perception that fighting is futile or fleeing impossible; the dissociative response is more internalizing and is hypothesized to help the individual prepare to survive injury. Peripheral blood flow decreases and heart rate goes down; the release of endogenous opioids and dissociation at the cognitive and emotional level occurs. In many cases, both of these adaptive responses will be activated during the same complex traumatic experience. Both response patterns can become sensitized, such that future stressors or challenges will activate the most common adaptive pattern used in a similar situation in the individual's past—for example, an infant physically abused in the context of a caregiving relationship who utilized a dissociative response to survive that inescapable painful event may, ten years later, "tune out" when the teacher raises his voice in frustration (see table 5.1).

As a child moves along the arousal–dissociative continuum in the face of novelty or threat, the internal state shifts. Different networks in the brain will activate while others deactivate. Although clearly oversimplifying the process, the more threatened the individual feels, the more functioning shifts from higher more complex and mature cortical networks to

TABLE 5.1  State-Dependent Functioning

| SENSE OF TIME | EXTENDED FUTURE | DAYS HOURS | HOURS MINUTES | MINUTES SECONDS | NO SENSE OF TIME |
|---|---|---|---|---|---|
| **Arousal Continuum** | REST | VIGILANCE | RESISTANCE<br>*Crying* | DEFIANCE<br>*Tantrums* | AGGRESSION |
| **Dissociative Continuum** | REST | AVOIDANCE | COMPLIANCE<br>*Robotic* | DISSOCIATION<br>*Fetal Rocking* | FAINTING |
| **Regulating Brain Region** | NEOCORTEX<br>Cortex | CORTEX<br>Limbic | LIMBIC<br>Diencephalon | DIENCEPHALON<br>Brainstem | BRAINSTEM<br>Autonomic |
| **Cognitive Style** | ABSTRACT | CONCRETE | EMOTIONAL | REACTIVE | REFLEXIVE |
| **Internal State** | CALM | ALERT | ALARM | FEAR | TERROR |

Different individuals may have different styles of adaptation to threat depending upon a wide range of factors, including age, nature of threat, history of previous exposure to trauma, and gender (Perry 2008; Perry et al., 1995). Some use a primary hyperarousal response; others use a primary dissociative response. Most use some combination of these two adaptive styles in any typical traumatic experience. If a child develops in an unpredictable, chaotic or threatening environment, her stress response systems become sensitized (see figure 5.1).

lower and more reactive systems. In the fearful child, this may manifest as a defiant stance. This typically is interpreted as a willful and controlling child. Rather than understanding the behavior as related to fear, adults often respond to the oppositional behavior by becoming angry and more demanding. The child, overreading the nonverbal cues of the frustrated and angry adult, feels more threatened and moves from alarm to fear to terror. These children may end up in a primitive minipsychotic regression or in a combative state. The behavior of the child reflects their attempts to adapt and respond to a perceived (or misperceived) threat.

Regression, a retreat to a less mature style of functioning and behavior, commonly is observed when we are physically ill, sleep deprived, hungry, fatigued, or threatened. During the regressive response to the real or perceived threat, less-complex brain areas mediate our behaviors. If a child has been raised in an environment of persisting threat, the child will have an altered baseline, such that the internal state of calm is rarely obtained. In addition, the traumatized child will have a sensitized alarm response, overreading verbal and nonverbal cues as threatening. This increased reactivity will result in dramatic changes in behavior in the face of seemingly minor provocative cues. All too often, this overreading of threat will lead to a fight or flight reaction and will increase the probability of impulsive aggression. This hyperreactivity to perceived threat can become a major problem in the home and classroom, impairing both social and cognitive development.

### State-Dependent Disruption of Healthy Developmental Experiences

The whole process of development involves the sequential and iterative process of being exposed to new experience, leaving a comfort zone, and ultimately making the once unfamiliar familiar. This process requires activation of the stress-response systems; all novel stimuli will cause the stress-response systems to activate until the new stimulus is categorized. Simply stated—all development and all learning requires doses of stress activation. In typical, healthy developmental circumstances, these tiny doses of stress activation play a role in helping build resilience. Unfortunately, in children with previous developmental adversity, chaos, or trauma, their stress-response systems have become so sensitized that even minor challenges will result in major activation—the transition from play to lunch will elicit a response that would be appropriate for a serious threat, the whisper becomes a shout, and "not now" becomes "never." The result is a confusing emotional and behavioral overreactivity that often confuses adults, peers, and the child (figure 5.1).

The major neural networks involved in the heterogeneous stress responses (see previous discussion) can become sensitized with patterns of activation that are unpredictable, extreme, and prolonged. This pattern of stress activation is common in maltreated and traumatized children—such as many children from international adoptions. When this occurs, the major adaptive style used by the infant, toddler, or child—either the hyperarousal (activate) or dissociation (shutdown) or, in some cases, both styles—becomes overactive and overly reactive. The results are profoundly disruptive for subsequent development as these overreactions to novelty and stress will inhibit and distort the accurate processing of new experiences even if these are predictable, consistent, nurturing, and enriching. A major consequence of this sensitization is that it shifts the state-dependence curve and narrows the developmental window (also known as the learning or therapeutic window; see figure 5.1). Simply stated, to acquire new capacities (i.e., make new associations in neural networks), the individual has to be exposed to novel experiences that, in turn, create novel patterns of neural activity. For optimal development (or learning or therapeutic change) this novelty has to have a "Goldilocks" effect—that is, enough novelty to challenge and expand the existing comfort zone (the set of previously acquired and mastered capabilities) but not so much novelty (or demand) that the capacity of the individual to process and assimilate is overwhelmed. When someone has a sensitized stress-response system, exposure to any novelty or unpredictability can rapidly move the person from active alert to a state of fear, thereby interfering with the process of learning. The more sensitized the stress response, the narrower this therapeutic–learning window is (see shaded areas in figure 5.1) and the less likely it will be that the child can benefit from typical or even optimal developmental experiences. The result is a profound frustration from the seemingly endless number of repetitions required for a child to master a concept or learn a behavior. The key to addressing this problem is to ensure that the child is regulated before expecting her to internalize any new social or cognitive content. A sense of safety is the key to beginning to overcome the sensitized stress

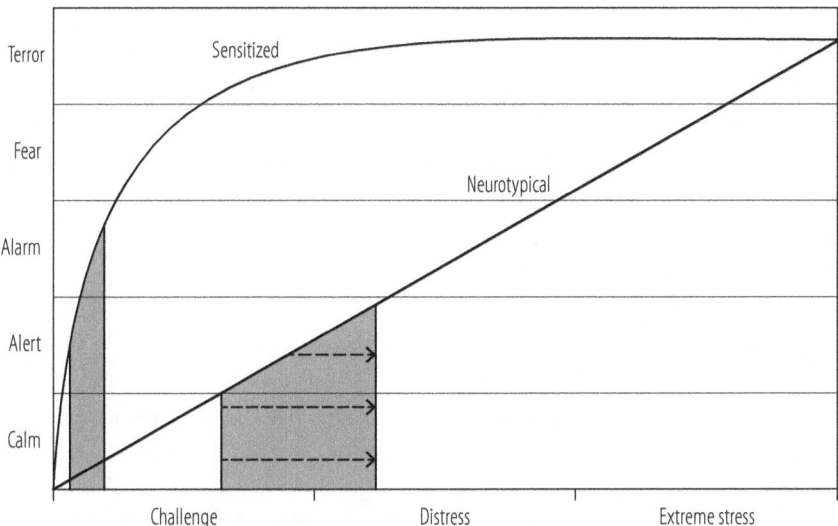

FIGURE 5.1 **The Developmental Window: State Dependence.** This figure illustrates two stress-reactivity curves; the straight black line indicates a neurotypical relationship between the level of external challenge, stress or threat and the appropriate proportional shift in internal state required to adapt, adjust, and cope with the degree of stress; with minor stressors, there are minor shifts in the internal state and with major stressors a larger shift in internal state is required. The top non-linear curve illustrates the distorted, sensitized stress-reactivity curve that results from patterns of extreme, unpredictable or prolonged stress activation such as is seen in many children from intercountry adoptions. In this case, there is a significant over-activity at baseline and an over-reaction even in the face of relatively minor challenges. Individuals with this level of sensitization require smaller "doses" of challenge. All learning—social, emotional, behavioral, or cognitive—requires exposure to novelty; a novel set of experiences that will, with repetition, ultimately become familiar and then 'internalized' or learned. The gray bars indicate the Developmental Window where enough—but not too much—stress activation (an appropriate "dose" of challenge) occurs to promote optimal learning. Too little novelty would lead to little stress activation and minimal learning, while too much activation leads to distress and inefficient internalization of information. With sensitized stress-response systems, the tolerable "dose" of challenge that can move the child into this optimal Developmental Window is very small (see thin gray bar); at the same time a neurotypical child can tolerate a larger "dose" of novelty (thick gray bar). In settings where the adult expectations for what a child or youth "should" be able to tolerate are not informed by an awareness of trauma-related alterations in these stress-reactivity curves, there are frequent misunderstandings that lead to escalation and significant behavioral problems.

responses that can disrupt development; in turn, the most powerful sense of safety comes from the sense of belonging—being part of a relationship, family, community, and culture. Unfortunately, this is one area of significant challenge for many intercountry and transracial adoptees; a core sense of belonging is linked to the fundamental capacity to form and maintain relationships.

### CLINICAL EXAMPLE

Edith is a 7-year-old Native American girl who was fostered from age 4 by a Caucasian mother and an African American father and then adopted by them at age 6. Key developmental adversities included prenatal exposure to alcohol, marijuana, and nicotine. She was removed from her biological mother following severe neglect in the first three months of life and lived in a dozen kinship and temporary shelter care and foster care settings during this time. The biological father was never involved in her life. Episodic efforts to establish and support the biological mother failed, and kin (all of them with significant challenges themselves) were unable to cope with the severity of her behavioral problems. During these many placements, Edith experienced additional chaos and trauma, including sexual abuse by an older foster child in one foster home. At the time of entering her ultimate adoptive home (age 4), she was nonverbal, unsocialized, and still in diapers. She had severe sleep problems and hypervigilance, with a profound behavioral reactivity to any challenge, frustration, or transition. Edith demonstrated a set of primitive self-soothing behaviors including rocking herself, biting and sucking her thumb, rhythmic humming, and hoarding of food. Despite her chronological age, she was developmentally below the 18-24 month level in most domains (i.e., cognitive, social, motor, and emotional) as determined by a set of standard developmental metrics and the Neurosequential Model of Therapeutics Metrics (NMT; see Perry, 2013).

During the first year in her adoptive home (age 4 to 5), a series of early intervention services were initiated; this included an occupational therapy evaluation with sensory "diet" recommendations, a specialized therapeutic day program (trained in the NMT). She required significant somatosensory soothing from caregivers and her foster/adoptive parents; this typically involved rocking, swinging, therapeutic massage (multiple times during the day for 8-10 minutes). She required a very structured nighttime ritual that involved the use of bathing, brushing teeth, having her hair dried and combed, reading stories, and a 10-12 minute backrub. Despite this she continued to wake during the night several times a week, requiring significant soothing. She was easily upset (especially when she did not have "control" or when there was an unpredictable change in her routine. These episodes occurred multiple times a day on most days in the beginning but decreased to a rate of several times a week by age 6. The duration of these episodes ranged from twenty minutes to three hours. The carers could not identify specific "triggers" on most occasions-aside from the word "no"-or "not getting her way." Edith entered public school and left the NMT-trained preschool setting at age 6. As she got older, the density of the somatosensory interventions was significantly decreased and her parents and school expected her to start to be more responsive to verbal direction, school and household rules, and age-typical social activities. She seemed to get worse; the rate of severe episodes increased. Consultation with mental health professionals resulted in diagnoses of ADHD and Oppositional Defiant Disorder and she was placed on a series of medications with no apparent positive impact (as is often the case, these clinicians did not view any of these symptoms through a "trauma-informed" lens). After a year of continuing severe symptoms and expulsion from her new school, the family consulted The ChildTrauma Academy.

On initial consultation with her family and clinical team (at age 6.5), we viewed this profound overactivity and over-reactivity in regulation as a predictable result of her chaotic, traumatic earlier life (see table 5.1 and figure 5.1) and related developmental adversities. Her resting heart rate at this time was 120 (significantly elevated and consistent with a child in a persisting high-alarm state (see table 5.1). In addition, Edith's reactivity (see figure 5.1) was such that minor frustrations (such as "no") were able to precipitate major behavioral outbursts; transitions were very challenging. Her ability to benefit optimally from the positive cognitive and social experiences provided in the home and school was compromised by her high arousal and high reactivity. As she matured cognitively and developed improved communication skills she asked if she "belonged" to mom or to dad and raised other questions suggesting she was beginning to notice that she "looked" different from both mom and dad.

With this reframing of her problems, school and family resumed a more somatosensory rich, relationally mediated schedule of activities including a schedule of

**CLINICAL EXAMPLE** (CONTINUED)

> 10-15 minute hand and neck massages, frequent sensory breaks in school, elements of collaborative problem solving and pairing academic lessons (and therapeutic interactions) with rhythm such as music and motor movement (e.g., walking, rocking desk, jump rope). The medications were discontinued with no observed negative effects. Over the ensuing six months the rate and intensity of "meltdowns" decreased; she resumed her earlier positive process of catching up in social and cognitive domains. She was capable of talking about her biological family, her multiple transitions, and her new family. Key recommendations included reconnecting her with Elders and others in her tribe of origin. The whole family was encouraged to participate in any tribal activities with the intent of creating meaningful cultural connections that could help her (and her family) negotiate and celebrate the complex and diverse cultural history that will be part of her life.

### The Intimacy Barrier

Humankind is a social species. We have survived and thrived on earth because we can form and maintain relationships to create larger, more functional, and flexible biological systems than the individual—we create families, communities, and cultures. Three of the most essential capabilities required for the survival of our species depend on "relational" neurobiology: the ability to (1) survive, (2) procreate, and (3) protect and support the vulnerable. First and foremost, to survive, a human needs other humans. We are born dependent and rely on the attention and supports (emotional and physical) of the adults in our life to survive. The relational nature of our very survival is obvious for infants and children but even into adult life, success depends on the capacity to connect, collaborate, coordinate, communicate, and be part of our "clan." A single human can never be truly independent; we are once and always interdependent. Complex neurobiological systems mediate this healthy interdependence. Second, procreation, in turn, is obviously a relational activity that is required for our species to continue. And, finally, there must be some "pull" for us to protect and nurture those in our family and clan who are more vulnerable and less capable of caring for themselves. Some complex neurobiological pull motivates and sustains the exhausted mother as she once again wakes in the night to feed and comfort the crying, needy infant; tens of thousands of times in our lifetime dozens of adults have given us time, energy, attention, and resources that have allowed us to survive and thrive.

These three core essential functional capabilities involve the very same relational neurobiology involved in the core feature of adoption—the creation of a relational connection or bond. Our early experiences with others—especially carers—can shape our relational neurobiology in powerful ways—both good and bad. When these bonds are characterized by mutual affection and love, the process of adoption is easier; yet many adoptions are complicated by challenges in the creation and maintenance of these loving bonds. For many adopted children, their earliest developmental experiences with parents, caregivers, and other human adults were characterized by inconsistency; unpredictability; and, sadly, confusion, threat, pain, and overtly traumatizing experiences. These experiences can influence the development of the core neurobiology required to form and maintain relationships, thereby making future positive relational interactions more difficult to establish and maintain.

A complex set of associations between the stress response, reward, and relational neural networks creates a three-part core of healthy human functioning. This triad of health and resilience is created through thousands of synchronous, mutual relational interactions in the first year of life (Szalavitz & Perry, 2010; Tronick & Perry, 2015). Through the patterned, repetitive bonding interactions of the attentive, attuned, and responsive caregivers with the infant, sensory integration, self-regulation, relational, and cognitive capacities emerge. Early bonding interactions create core "attachment" capabilities and related relational associations. The fundamental neurobiological capacity to create these bonds is a product of our genetic gifts and how these gifts are expressed as a function of the nature, timing, and pattern of relational experiences—especially when we are young.

One of the most interesting manifestations of these primary associations created by your earliest relational experiences is that we will interpret emotions, particularly expressions of fear, in context of our culture of origin (Chiao et al., 2008). The sensory attributes (e.g., skin tone, vocalizations, expressions, facial features) of our family and clan during our early life provide us with the relational templates through which we interpret all subsequent relational experiences. Thus, the sociocultural context changes a child's expectations for how to interpret his or her world—particularly signals of fear—and how to know when to come to the aid of a group member. Other research has shown that children have ingroup–outgroup biases and that children will consider other children who look similar to them to be nicer and smarter than children who do not (Dunham, Chen, & Banaji, 2013; for more discussion of this, see Szalavitz & Perry, 2010). This tendency to demonstrate bias is likely related to the long history of humankind's tribalism—throughout history the major threat to humans was other humans. There was, and still remains, a need for ingroup collaboration to help survive outgroup aggression. The implications for transracial adoption are significant; the adopted individual—even when adoption occurs early in life—may not feel safe or accurately interpret emotional cues in the new group. Basically, they may not feel as if they belong. This sense will be exacerbated if there is a history of adversity that involves security and attachment issues and impaired ability to interpret social cues.

A useful clinical concept, similar to the concept of personal space in proxemics (Hall, 1966) is the intimacy barrier (see figure 5.2). As described earlier, the set of early developmental experiences with caregiving adults creates an internal catalog of "associations" with human relational cues (e.g., tone of voice, eye contact, touch) and helps organize key areas of the brain involved in social affiliation and relational functioning, including the amygdala. The size of the amygdala in adult life, for example, a brain area very involved in interpreting and acting on threat related cues, correlates (positively) with the size and complexity of social networks (Bickart et al., 2011).

If the primary carers were present, attentive, attuned, and responsive, the child creates positive associations with human relational cues intended to convey interest, warmth, and comfort. Future positive social interactions with peers, teachers, and carers will be regulating and rewarding as long as they do not cross an invisible "intimacy" barrier. All humans have protective "boundaries" around specific emotional content (e.g., unsolicited conversation about your weight or sexual behaviors) and physical interactions (e.g., personal space, sexualized touch; Hall, 1966).

When this intimacy barrier is crossed without our permission, it is threatening. The stress-response systems (including the amygdala; Kennedy, Gläscher, Tyszka, & Adolphs, 2009) activate, and the individual

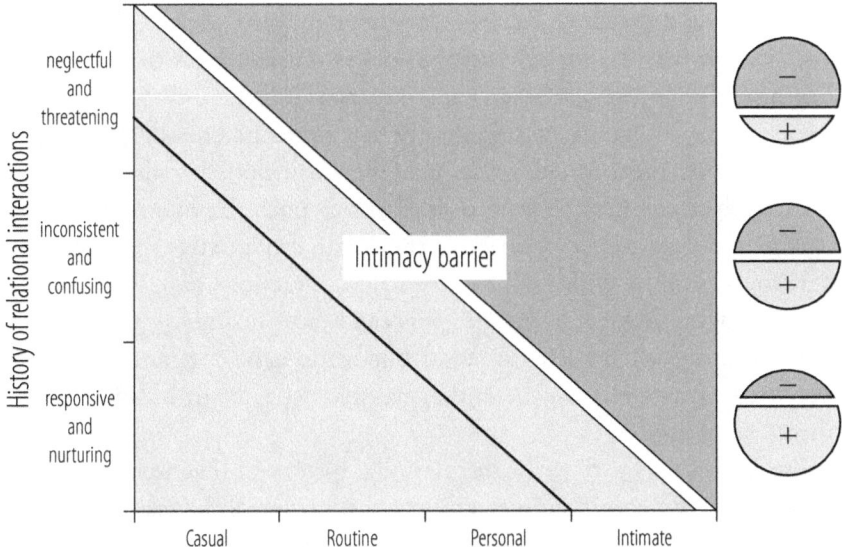

FIGURE 5.2 **The Intimacy Barrier.** As social interactions shift from casual to routinized (e.g., a structured social setting such as a classroom) to more personal and then finally intimate, the individual will interpret the social interaction in context of the 'sensitivity' of their Intimacy Barrier (the tangential white bar separating the dark gray from the light gray portions of the figure). If the individual had generally positive early life relational interactions (bottom "responsive and nurturing" row with larger light-gray "+"), his Intimacy Barrier will be "further out," making him capable of tolerating casual, routine and personal interactions without feeling threatened and activating a defensive set of responses (see table 5.1). If, however, either the personal or 'emotional' space boundary is crossed without permission and a sense of control, even neurotypical individuals feel threatened (see Kennedy et al., 2009). Like all brain-mediated functions, the "Intimacy Barrier" is state-dependent. When an individual feels threatened their sense of personal physical and emotional boundaries (i.e., the Intimacy Barrier) shifts (thin black tangential line). For many children and youth from intercountry adoptions, the combination of relational sensitivity following early life attachment disruptions and a sensitized stress response reactivity lead to very confusing and complex challenges with interpersonal interactions.

will engage in protective behaviors; a variety of stress-response strategies may be used depending on the sensitivity of your stress-response system (see figures 5.1 and 5.2) and the adaptive preferences the individual may have developed (see table 5.1; Perry, 1995). If the individual utilizes a flock–freeze–flight–fight response, when someone crosses this barrier, verbalizations (e.g., raised voice, profanity, threats) or behaviors (e.g., pushing, hitting) may be used to attempt to push the offending person back across the intimacy barrier. If the predominant style of adaptation is dissociation, the child will avoid social interactions and, if this is not possible, will passively disengage. This can be confusing for peers, carers, and educators when their intended nurturing behaviors and words are met with either overt hostile and aggressive behavior or indifferent and dismissive attitudes.

For individuals with early life relational history of inconsistent or abusive care (all too common in intercountry adoptions), the set of relational associations created will push the intimacy barrier out further than with typical individuals (see the top "neglectful and threatening" row in figure 5.2). A person with a high degree of relational sensitivity often will misinterpret neutral or positive social interactions from peers as threatening and respond by either avoiding or disengaging (which leads to problems with social learning and peer interactions) or, worse, by using aggressive, hostile, or hurtful words or even behaviors to push peers, teachers, and parents away. In extreme cases, as the child grows up, this relational sensitivity can result in significant antisocial or even assaultive behaviors. Individuals in prison (90 percent of whom have histories of interpersonal trauma in childhood) have a much larger sense of personal space than the average person (Wormith, 1984), and often will respond to personal space violations with aggressive and violent behaviors.

The tragic reality is that the maltreated child desperately wants to belong, wants to be loved and connected, but personal and intimate interactions elicit fear not comfort; unless the child initiates and controls the interactions, he or she will feel threatened. And if the child also has a sensitized stress-response system, even small violations of the emotional or personal space can result in extreme behaviors, including threats to kill or injure the parent.

The irony is that the more nurturing and loving the behaviors, the more overwhelming the child feels. These children rarely threaten to go kill a stranger—they threaten to kill the people or person who has been most caring and nurturing. Furthermore, when the threatened adult leaves or attempts to disengage from the disturbing interaction, the child (even as they say they hate you) will follow the adult and get even more dysregulated. This is likely due to the fact that they are not just sensitized to relational intimacy; they are sensitized to unpredictable abandonment. They want you present, but they don't want you too close; and, if physical or emotional intimacy is to be introduced, they want to be in control. They want to play the game their way; they want to get a hug when they want it; they want to talk about something overwhelming when they bring it up. The primary clinical strategy is to be present, parallel, patient, and persistent—a much easier thing to say than to do day in and day out with a challenging child. The consequences of this complex and somewhat-distorted set of relational associations can be destructive for the creation of the mutual loving bonds required for successful adoption.

These complex interpersonal dynamics are complicated by the additional challenges posed by being "different" (by virtue of ethnicity, race, culture, or country) than the adoptive family. Adopted "children will likely simultaneously occupy multiple positions within the socio-cultural-political and structural fabric of society" (Ortega & Faller, 2011, p. 31). These intersecting group memberships likely will affect quality of life given that the child may struggle more than other children to form an identity, particularly during adolescence, and that the child may feel conflicted between identifying with a culture that feels "right" or "natural" and the culture in which they actually are raised. Bicultural children have been shown to arrive at self-judgments by using different parts of their brain when primed by stimuli associated with one culture versus stimuli associated with the other culture (Chiao et al., 2009). This may indicate that transracial children are often balancing multiple views of themselves and trying out which self-representations are most adaptive in which environments. Despite the fact that this balancing and fluctuating ultimately may be adaptive, it is likely stressful and adds complexity to the social experience. Teasing and bullying by peers may be increased and further confirm that the world in which the child lives is not safe or that the child may not express certain parts of themselves in certain environments. Children may even feel reluctant to share these experiences with their adoptive parents given the perceived stress it might cause the family (Docan-Morgan, 2011).

**CLINICAL EXAMPLE: RELATIONAL SENSITIZATION**

Thomas is a 14-year-old boy adopted from an Eastern European orphanage at age 4 by a family in the United States who had two older biological children (9 and 12 at that time). In the first year in the U.S. he was noted to be in good physical health and seemed shy and somewhat overwhelmed by his new home but there were no major behavioral problems. He was somewhat touch defensive (although he would occasionally spontaneously seek physical affection from his mother). From age 4 to 6, his family provided much developmental enrichment with the intention of helping Thomas transition to a new country, new language, and new home. He had a language tutor, many "developmental" toys and video programs that he seemed to enjoy (possibly too much). He continued to be aloof to social engagement, had poor eye contact, and frequently rocked and quietly hummed when he was in social situations. The family viewed him as quiet and shy. His preference was to watch his "developmental" enrichment videos or play educational games on the computer. He was indifferent to peers in free-play situations and actively resisted their attempts (or adult encouragement) to socialize. His only major behavioral problems occurred when he was forced to stop his video games or when another person (adult, sibling, or peer) attempted to redirect his self-absorbed play. He was able to simply tune out verbal direction or interactions when he was engaged in an activity.

When in social interactions such as playing a game with a sibling, his behavior and mood were appropriate as long as he was in control (the game was of his choosing); he could change the rules to suit him; and he could order his partner around (and the partner would comply). Initially the siblings and parents tolerated this style of play. As he grew older, however, their efforts to teach him to share or follow the rules of the game precipitated odd and disruptive behavior (e.g., screaming, holding his hands over his ears, and rocking). When adults attempted to stop this, he would become very aggressive-biting, kicking, crying, and hitting. If left alone, these odd behaviors would last between 10 and 15 minutes, after which he would seem "fine" and act as if nothing had happened. When an aggressive episode was precipitated it would take over an hour to get back to baseline.

Thomas entered school at age 6. A long-lasting and serious deterioration ensued and his developmental progress plateaued. The episodes grew in frequency and intensity (as the social environment and relationally mediated demands of the teachers, aides, and carers increased). If left to his own devices his behaviors were odd but acceptable; he would make academic progress but in a pace and direction of his own choosing. He responded to imposed structure, redirection, and any physical proximity with a profound meltdown; when the teacher or staff attempted to physically withdraw him from the class (or physically comfort him) he would get aggressive, both verbally threatening and physically attacking them. He was expelled from school after school. Behavior at home deteriorated as well; he began to threaten his mother, especially when she attempted to be comforting or nurturing. Over time the family felt as if they were "walking on eggshells"—never knowing what would trigger Thomas and when he might have an aggressive meltdown.

A long history of failed placement at specialized schools, multiple mental health assessments, a parade of diagnoses (over twelve DSM diagnoses were assigned to him by various clinicians by the age of 13; more than twenty medications were used during this time, many simultaneously administered), and ultimately admissions to psychiatric hospitalizations and placements at residential treatment centers ensued. Along the way, any observed progress was short-lived. He was maintained in a series of out-of-home placements from age 8 to 14. At age 14 his treatment team consulted The ChildTrauma Academy.

Review of his history resulted in a reformulation of the traditional mental health perspective to a developmentally sensitive and trauma aware view. Among other core issues (he did demonstrate sensitized dissociative and hyperarousal behaviors; see table 5.1) was a profound relational sensitization. Physical and socioemotional interactions that might be considered "typical" and tolerable to most people were essentially evocative cues to him (see figure 5.2 and text on the Intimacy Barrier). These well-intended social and physical interactions provoked very reactive responses (see table 5.1 and figure 5.1). When the staff and family learned more about these processes and created parallel, predictable, patient, and regulated interactions where Thomas was given control over the frequency and intensity of intimate social and physical interactions, the number of aggressive episodes decreased and ultimately stopped. With a combination of regulating and relationally mediated educational, therapeutic, and enrichment experiences, Thomas made significant progress over the next six months and was able to return home with special in-home services supported by a developmentally informed school.

Children may be better at detecting emotional cues of people with similar backgrounds (Chiao et al., 2009), suggesting that children primed to be hypersensitive to threat may misread signals from unfamiliar cultural groups and potentially perceive threat when it does not exist. Just as institutionalized children have been described as having to learn English as their "second first language" (McCarthy, 2005, p. 9) given that they have language deficits in their native language and then are asked to learn a new language once arriving in the United States, children who have been transracially adopted may have similar struggles when "reading" emotional cues. Their ability to naturally interpret both threat and relational cues may be impaired because of a history of trauma, neglect, or institutionalization, and this impairment is exacerbated by difficulties interpreting facial expressions of unfamiliar racial or ethnic groups. The challenges for these children and their families under these circumstances can be considerable; the question remains what can we do to help?

### KEY POLICY AND PROGRAM IMPLICATIONS OF A NEURODEVELOPMENTAL PERSPECTIVE ON ADOPTION

1. Agencies involved in the care of orphaned children and the administration of adoptions should strive to become more developmentally and trauma informed. Administration, staff, and consulting professionals should be exposed to the fundamental principles of neurodevelopment, attachment, and traumatology that influence the children and adoptive families they serve.
2. Adopting families should be given educational and psychoeducational materials that help outline the basic principles of neurodevelopment, attachment, and the stress response. Supportive consultation services should be provided to ensure a more positive transition and the opportunity to identify the child's strengths and vulnerabilities to allow for proactive, rather than reactive, planning for educational, emotional, behavioral, and social needs.
3. Physicians and other professionals often involved in the care of intercountry and transracial adoptions must familiarize themselves with the various and complex challenges these children and youth face. Among the key areas of focus should be awareness and, ideally a mastery, of the emerging concepts related to trauma- and attachment-related problems often seen in this population.

## CONCLUSION: WHAT CAN CAREGIVERS AND PROFESSIONALS DO TO HELP?

One of the most important things we can do is give families hope; ultimately, 90 percent of adoptive parents of institutionalized children are pleased with their decision to adopt and would consider adopting again (Pearlmutter, Ryan, & Johnson, 2008). The vast majority of these children will make significant developmental progress when provided with attention, enrichment, nurturing, and developmentally informed early intervention services. Improvement in cognitive capabilities is seen in foster care and following adoption (Nelson et al., 2011). Many intercountry adoptees receive early intervention services; this may account for the observation that internationally adopted children may not be at greater risk of developmental adversity than domestically adopted children (Juffer & van Ijzendoorn, 2005). The Bucharest Early Intervention Project was designed to understand how effectively early cognitive deficits can be remediated (Zeanah et al., 2003) and followed 200 children from birth. Some remained in institutions and others were placed into a foster care system that was created by intervention developers. The average age of placement in foster care was 21 months. The study also employed a control group of children raised with biological parents. Results indicated that foster care led to increased intelligence and scores on developmental screeners compared with the children who remained institutionalized. Both groups, however, performed more poorly than children raised with biological parents. Results also showed that results were best for children who were removed at earlier ages. Similarly promising outcomes have been found in other studies (Bakermans-Kranenburg et al., 2008; Vanderwert et al., 2010).

Adoption has also led to improvements in cognitive functioning (van IJzendoorn, Juffer, & Poelhuis, 2005) compared with nonadopted biological siblings. Findings have suggested that adopted children's cognitive abilities may "catch up" to environmentally matched peers following adoption. Yet, regardless of increases in intelligence and performance superior to nonadopted siblings, institutionalized children consistently performed less well in school than environmentally matched peers and had an increased prevalence of learning disorders. In short, special education services remain indicated for institutionalized children many years postadoption, despite postadoptive gains in cognitive functioning. Additionally, gains in intelligence can occur irrespective of gains in social, emotional, and behavioral domains—and difficulties in these domains can mask cognitive gains. What is perhaps most difficult for caregivers is to understand why their child functions well in one domain and poorly in another, or well in one context in a certain domain and not in another. This patchwork of developmental strengths and weaknesses can be confusing and frustrating, especially when emotional age does not match the child's cognitive or developmental age (Perry, 2009).

Finally, a fundamental ingredient of all successful development is a sense of safety. For the child from a transracial or intercountry adoption, this sense of safety can be elusive. The potential trauma-related factors discussed earlier certainly can make this difficult; however, even without significant trauma-related issues, a sense of being different—in some ways, an outsider—often remains.

This sense of difference can be powerful and painful for the child. Children growing up in transracial households may feel constant pressure to acculturate and adopt cultural norms that are not their own. Helping the child learn about their country and culture of origin is important, as is allowing and encouraging peer and mentor relationships with other children who share similar racial, cultural, or ethnic backgrounds as the adopted child (e.g., Ortega & Faller, 2011). Simply being in a parenting or in the caregiving position confers power, and self-reflection and cultural humility is important to create a climate of acceptance and respect that can help a child feel fully embraced (Tervalon & Murray-Garcia, 1998). Family members who are equally interested in learning about, respecting, and, in some cases, adopting their child's cultural norms and traditions—even if the child is still learning those norms and traditions—could decrease stress on the entire family system. This can occur if family members are motivated to "instill the practice of adopting the client's values as their norms" (Fong, 2001, p. 5) in an effort to create a safe and inclusive environment that promotes the child's healthy development.

### DISCUSSION QUESTIONS

1. Discuss the role that early life relational disruptions may play in shaping the nature and severity of emotional and behavioral problems in the postadoption period. How is it that even brief periods of disruption in early life can continue to have such powerful impact later in life?

2. Describe the concept of "state dependence" and give examples of how a sensitized stress-response system can interfere with development even in safe, stable, and nurturing environment.
3. Describe the concept of the "intimacy barrier." Elaborate on why this is an important concept when trying to understand and work with many intercountry and transracial adoptees.

**REFERENCES**

Anda, R. F., Felitti, R. F., Walker, J., Whitfield, C., Bremner, D. J., Perry, B. D., Dube, S. R., Giles, W. G. (2006). The enduring effects of childhood abuse and related experiences: a convergence of evidence from neurobiology and epidemiology, *European Archives of Psychiatric and Clinical Neuroscience, 256*(3), 174–186.

Bakermans-Kranenburg, M. J., van IJzendoorn, M. H., & Juffer, F. (2008). Earlier is better: A meta-analysis of 70 years of intervention improving cognitive development in institutionalized children. *Monographs of the Society for Research in Child Development, 73*(3), 279–293.

Bickart, K. C., Wright, C. I., Dautoff, R. J., Dickerson, B. C., & Barrett, L. F. (2011). Amygdala volume and social network size in humans. *Nature Neuroscience, 14*, 163–164.

Bruce, J., Fisher, P. A., Pears, K. C., & Levine, S. (2009). Morning cortisol levels in preschool-aged foster children: Differential effects of maltreatment type. *Developmental Psychobiology, 51*, 14–23.

Chiao, J. Y., Harada, T., Komeda, H., Li, Z., Mano, Y., Saito, D. N., Parrish, T. B., Sadato, N., Iidaka, T. (2010). Dynamic cultural influences on neural representations of the self. *Journal of Cognitive Neuroscience, 22*(1), 1–11.

Chiao, J. Y., Iidaka, T., Gordon, H. L., Nogawa, J., Bar, M., Aminoff, E., Sadato, N., & Ambady, N. (2008). Cultural specificity in amygdala response to fear faces. *Journal of Cognitive Neuroscience, 20*(12), 2167–2174.

Chugani, H. T., Behen, M. E., Muzik, O., Juhasz, C., Nagy, F., & Chugani, D. C. (2001). Local brain functional activity following early deprivation: A study of post institutionalized Romanian orphans. *Neuroimage, 14*, 1290–1301.

De Bellis, M. (2005). The psychobiology of neglect. *Child Maltreatment, 10*(2), 150–172. doi:10.1177/1077559505275116

Dennis, W. (1973). *Children of the creche.* New York: Appleton-Century-Crofts.

Docan-Morgan, S. (2011). "They don't know what it's like to be in my shoes": Topic avoidance about race in transracially adoptive families. *Journal of Social and Personal Relationships, 58,* 336–355. doi:10.1177/0265407510382177

Dunham, Y., Chen, E., & Banaji, M. (2013). Two signatures of implicit intergroup attitudes: developmental invariance and early enculturation. *Psychological Science, 24*(6), 860–868 doi:10.1177/0956797612463081

Eluvanthingal, T. J., Chugani, H. T., Behen, M. E., Juhász, C., Muzik, O., Maqbool, M., & Makki, M. (2006). Abnormal brain connectivity in children after early severe socioemotional deprivation: A diffusion tensor imaging study. *Pediatrics, 117,* 2093–2100.

Fong, R. (2001). Culturally competent social work practice: Past and present. In Fong, R. & Furuto, S. (Eds.), *Culturally competent practice: Skills, interventions, and evaluations* (pp. 1–9). Boston: Allyn and Bacon.

Groark, C. J., McCall, R. B., & Fish, L. (2011). Characteristics of environments, caregivers, and children in three Central American orphanages. *Infant Mental Health Journal, 32*(2), 232–250.

Hall, E. T. (1966). *The hidden dimension.* New York: Doubleday.

Holland, J. (2011). *Unlikely friendships: 47 remarkable stories from the animal kingdom.* New York: Workman Publishing.

Johnson, D. E. (2002). Adoption and the effect on children's development. *Early Human Development, 68,* 39–54.

Johnson, D. E., & Gunnar, M. (2011). Growth Failure in Institutionalized Children, *Monographs of the Society for Reserach in Child Development, 76 (4),* 92–126.

Johnson, D. (n.d.). *Adopting an institutionalized child: What are the risks?* Retrieved from http://www.adoption-research.org/risks.html

Juffer, F., & van IJzendoorn, M. H. (2005). Behavior problems and mental health referrals of international adoptees. *JAMA, 293,* 2501–2515.

Kennedy, D. P., Gläscher, J., Tyszka, J. M., & Adolphs, R. (2009). Personal space regulation by the human amygdala. *Natural Neuroscience, 12,* 1226–1227. doi:10.1038/nn.2381

Lee, R. M. (2003). The transracial adoption paradox: History, research, and counseling implications of cultural socialization. *Counseling Psychology, 31*(6), 711–744. doi:10.1177/0011000003258087

Loman, M. M., Wilk, K. L., Frenn, K. A., Pollak, S. D., & Gunnar, M. R. (2009). Post institutionalized children's development: Growth, cognitive, and language outcomes. *Journal of Developmental Behavioral Pediatrics, 30*(5), 426–434. doi:10.1097/DBP.0b013e3181b1fd08

MacLean, K. (2003). The impact of institutionalization on child development. *Development and Psychopathology, 15,* 853–884.

Mason, P., & Narad, C. (2005). International adoption: A health and developmental perspective. *Seminars in Speech and Language, 26*(1), 1–9.

McCarthy, H. (2005). *Survey of children adopted from Eastern Europe.* Retrieved from http://www.eeadopt.org/index.php?option=com_content&task=view&id=48&Itemid=57

Mehta, M. A., Golembo, N. I., Nosarti, C., Colvert, E., Mota, A., Williams, S. C. R., & Sonuga-Barke, E. J. (2009). Amygdala, hippocampal and corpus callosum size following severe early institutional deprivation: The English and Romanian Adoptees Study Pilot. *Journal of Child Psychology & Psychiatry, 50,* 943–951.

Moffitt, T. E., Arseneault, L., Belsky, D., Dickson, N., Hancox, R. J., Harrington, H., Houts, R., Poulton, R., Roberts, B. W., Ross, S., Sears, M. R., Thomson, W. M., & Caspi, A. (2010). A gradient of childhood self-control predicts health, wealth and public safety. *PNAS Early Edition.* Retrieved from www.pnas.org/cgi/doi/10.1073/pnas.1010076108

Money, J. (1994). *The Kaspar Hauser syndrome of "psychosocial dwarfism": Deficient statural, intellectual, and social growth induced by child abuse.* Buffalo, NY: Prometheus Books.

Nelson, C. A., Bos, K., Gunnar, M. R., & Sonuga-Barke, E. J. S. (2011). The neurobiological toll of early human deprivation. *Monographs of the Society for Research in Child Development, 76*(4), 127–146.

O'Connor, C., Rutter, M., & English and Romanian Adoptees Study Team. (2000). Attachment disorder behavior following early severe deprivation: extension and longitudinal follow-up. *Journal of the American Academy of Child and Adolescent Psychiatry, 39,* 703–712.

Ortega, R. M., & Faller, K. C. (2011). Training child welfare workers from an intersectional cultural humility perspective: A paradigm shift. *Child Welfare, 90*(5), 27–49.

Pearlmutter, S., Ryan, S. D., Johnson, L. B., & Groza, V. (2008). Romanian adoptees and pre-adoptive care: A strengths perspective. *Child and Adolescent Social Work Journal, 25,* 139–156.

Perry, B. D. (2002). Childhood experience and the expression of genetic potential: What childhood neglect tells us about nature and nurture. *Brain and Mind, 3,* 79–100.

Perry, B. D. (2008). Child maltreatment: the role of abuse and neglect in developmental psychopathology. In T. P. Beauchaine and S. P. Hinshaw (Eds.), *Textbook of Child and Adolescent Psychopathology* (pp. 93–128). New York: Wiley.

Perry, B. D. (2009). Examining child maltreatment through a neurodevelopmental lens: Clinical application of the neurosequential model of therapeutics. *Journal of Loss and Trauma, 14,* 240–255.

Perry, B. D., Pollard, R. A., Blakley, T. L., Baker, W. L., & Vigilante, D. (1995). Childhood trauma, the neurobiology of adaptation, and "use-dependent" development of the brain: How "states" become "traits." *Infant Mental Health Journal, 16,* 271–291.

Piquero, A. R., Jennings, W. G., & Farrington, D. P. (2010). On the malleability of self-control: Theoretical and policy implications regarding a general theory of crime. *Justice Quarterly, 27*(6), 803–834.

Rutter, M., Andersen-Wood, L., Beckett, C., Bredenkamp, D., Castle, J., Grootheus, C., Keppner, J., Keaveny, L., Lord, C., O'Connor, T. G., & English and Romanian Adoptees Study Team. (1999). Quasi-autistic patterns following severe early global privation. *Journal of Child Psychology and Psychiatry, 40,* 537–549.

Rutter, M., & English and Romanian Adoptees Study Team. (1998). Developmental catch-up, and deficit, following adoption after severe global early privation. *Journal of Child Psychology and Psychiatry, 39,* 465–476.

Spitz, R. A. (1945). Hospitalism: An inquiry into the genesis of psychiatric conditions in early childhood. *Psychoanalytic Study of the Child, 1,* 53–74.

Spitz, R. A. (1946). Hospitalism: A follow-up report on investigation described in Volume I, 1945. *Psychoanalytic Study of the Child, 2,* 113–117.

Szalavitz, M., & Perry, B. D. (2010). *Born for love: Why empathy is essential and endangered.* New York: HarperCollins.

Tervalon, M., & Murray-Garcia, J. (1998). Cultural humility versus cultural competence: A critical distinction in defining physician training outcomes in multicultural education. *Journal of Heath Care for the Poor and Underserved, 9*(2), 117–125.

Tronick, E., & Perry, B. D. (2015). The multiple levels of meaning making and the first principles of changing meanings in development and therapy. In Marlock, G. & Weiss, H., with Young, C. & Soth, M. (Eds.), *Handbook of somatic psychotherapy.* Berkeley, CA: North Atlantic Books, 345–355.

U.S. Department of State. (n.d.). *Intercountry adoption.* Retrieved from http://adoption.state.gov/about_us/statistics.php

van IJzendoorn, M. H., Juffer, F., & Poelhuis, C. W. (2005). Adoption and cognitive development: A meta-analytic comparison of adopted and nonadopted children's IQ and school performance. *Psychological Bulletin, 131*(2), 301–316.

Vanderwert, R. E., Marshall, P. J., Nelson, C. A., Zeanah, C. H., & Fox, N. A. (2010). Timing of intervention affects brain electrical activity in children exposed to severe psychosocial neglect. *PloS ONE, 5*(7), 1–5.

Wormith, J. S. (1984). Personal space of incarcerated offenders. *Journal of Clinical Psychology, 40,* 815–827.

Zeanah, C. H., Nelson, C. A., Fox, N. A., Smyke, A. T., Marshall, P., Parker, S. W., & Koga, S. (2003). Designing research to study the effects of institutionalization on brain and behavioral development: The Bucharest early intervention project. *Development and Psychopathology, 15,* 885–907.

# 6

# Ethnic Identity Formation

ELLEN E. PINDERHUGHES, JESSICA A. K. MATTHEWS, AND XIAN ZHANG

"'Chinglish'... I'm part Chinese and I'm part English, so you would put the two words together and make that..."
7-year-old girl (Ponte et al., 2007)

"I didn't think [not being exposed to the black community impacted her], but now reading her answers... I thought maybe it was, to a degree."
Adoptive parent (Simon & Roorda, 2007, p. 93)

"I can't make her Chinese. I don't know how. I am not Chinese. I don't want people to think that Chinese language and dance is it. I don't want people to feel like I was trivializing the culture... we want to be respectful of the depth and richness of that culture."
Adoptive parent (Fong & Wang, 2000, p. 24)

"I've seen a lot of kids who have been transracially adopted and they are very confused."
Adult adoptee (Simon & Roorda, 2000, p. 38)

AS THESE REFLECTIONS INDICATE, the experiences of transracial adoptees (TRAs) are varied and reveal the complexities of growing up as an adopted person of color in the United States, as well as the challenges transracial adoptive parents face preparing their children to become successful adults. The communities and society in which we all live and work further complicate these families' lives.

Throughout our lives, identity development is central to the formation of a healthy sense of self. In today's world, we hear about "intersecting identities," a term that typically refers to the reality that each of us has multiple characteristics, given our race or ethnicity, gender, sexual or romantic orientation, religious background, socioeconomic status, and nationality (e.g., Rosenblum & Travis, 2012). For each of these characteristics, we have an identity—a view of ourselves and others sharing the respective characteristic (Tajfel, 1981). The different characteristics and identities combine in unique ways to form intersecting identities (Rosenblum & Travis, 2012). For those in the adoption triad, one's status (first or birth parent, adoptive parent, and adoptee) also is an important identity. Throughout the life span, adoptees face the task of incorporating an evolving adoptive identity with other developing identities.

Importantly, society confers different statuses (and privileges) for individuals with certain characteristics. For example, within the United States, European Americans, males, heterosexuals, Christians, individuals who are middle to upper income, and U.S. citizens have higher statuses and receive more societal resources and privileges than do their counterparts (e.g., African Americans, Latinos, Asian Americans, and Native Americans; females; homosexuals; people of Jewish, Islamic, and other or no faith; people who are low income; and immigrants; Feagin & Feagin, 2011). Many of us have intersecting identities that incorporate different status levels. For example, the three authors share the benefits associated with being well educated and also share the less privileged status of being female. The second author benefits from the status of being European American, whereas as an African American and an Asian immigrant, respectively, the first author and third authors have statuses conferring less privilege. As we incorporate these intersecting identities with different statuses, we must manage not only how we view these identities but also our interactions with others who may view our identities differently.

As we consider the issues of ethnic identity development for TRAs, it is essential to understand that they must integrate multiple identities that typically have lower status: being adopted; being a person of color; and, for intercountry adoptees, being an immigrant. Adoptees receive the benefits conferred upon their adoptive family, given the characteristics of their parents (Lee, 2003), but they also contend with experiences associated with lower status. Thus, adoptive parents must recognize that their transracially adopted children face challenges and stressors that parents themselves may not face.

This chapter addresses the ethnic identity development of people who are adopted transracially. Because ethnic identity is one of multiple identities that TRAs must integrate while growing up in the context of their family, community, and society, we briefly discuss contextual influences and then address several aspects of identity development—adoptive, cultural, and ethnic or racial—as well as challenges to healthy identity development and tasks parents face in promoting racial and ethnic identity development. We conclude the chapter with recommendations for how parents and professionals can support TRAs in this area. We draw from various sources about adoption, including research on children and families, adopted adults' retrospective accounts of their experiences in their families and communities, as well as more recent literature, including lessons learned from earlier waves of transracial adoption. In addition, we draw from certain writings from the literature on identity development of immigrant children, given the reality that internationally adopted TRAs are immigrants. But first, we turn inward.

### WHAT WE BRING TO THE TABLE

We are all cultural beings. Each of us, as a cultural being, has learned important lessons from our elders and ancestors, about relationships, interacting with strangers, work, how to get along with others, how to deal with our frustrations, how to resolve disagreements with others, and how to be happy in life. These essential lessons are the "stuff" of culture—the practices, beliefs, and rituals that ensure the physical, social, and economic survival of a group of people (Pinderhughes, 1989). As we all know, cultures and societies differ—sometimes subtly, other times dramatically—in the values, beliefs, and behaviors that underlie our interactions and who we are. In a country as diverse as the United States and with its historical tensions regarding differences, especially racial and ethnic differences, individuals who are noticeably physically different often find themselves as targets of comments and questions—whether intentional or unintentional—that call attention to their difference and that can leave them feeling invalidated or even threatened. Sue, Capodilupo, Torino, Bucceri, and Holder (2007) refer to these experiences as microaggressions, or "brief and commonplace daily verbal, behavioral, or environmental indignities, whether intentional or unintentional, that communicate hostile, derogatory, or negative racial slights and insults" (p. 271). In some cases, individuals also have direct experiences of bias, discrimination, or stigma. For example, two adolescent African American males were walking down the street in a summer resort town known for its historically amicable relations between African Americans and whites and heard a white man yell from a passing car, "COONS!" (Hereafter, we refer to all these experiences, intentional or not, as bias.) All individuals need to have ways of interacting with others in the context of or despite these experiences, and having a clear understanding of oneself as a cultural being can provide an important foundation.

Parents raising children in diverse countries such as the United States face the task of helping their children become successful adults as cultural beings, drawing from their own socialization experiences. When parents raise a child from a different cultural, racial or ethnic background, they face the added task of figuring out how to help their child develop a healthy identity, given his or her backgrounds and the potential lack of expertise possessed by the parents.

To help children develop a healthy sense of self as a cultural being, and develop skills in interacting with others across differences, parents face the task of facilitating conversations about differences. Children need to be able to come to their parents with questions and concerns. To facilitate these discussions, we must understand ourselves as cultural beings, including the attitudes, beliefs, and values we hold about ourselves and about others that can influence how we treat others, whether or not we are aware of the influence. In countless moments, we find ourselves giving children lessons without realizing it—through our actions and inactions and with words spoken and not spoken. Consider the following example: Waiting with her three-year old daughter to check out in a store, an African American parent, Paula, noticed a young white boy apparently with his mother and grandmother. While feeling sorry for the boy because his teeth were rotted, and assuming the family was quite poor, Paula was startled to realize that she and her child were objects of pity. The young boy innocently asked why the daughter's skin was brown and his mother and grandmother reacted with horror and embarrassment. Realizing the power of this teachable moment, yet humbled by the dual assumptions, Paula knelt alongside the boy and explained why her and her daughter's skin was brown and his and his family's skin was white.

Thus, we each must come to better understand who we are and what views or attitudes we bring to the table as we interact with others across difference and as we raise our children to do so. Myriad resources are available to support those who take on this task. Perhaps most immediately available, the Internet provides a vast array of resources that we can use to engage in self-reflection about our views and beliefs. To get readers started, we provide a brief description of a few we have found particularly helpful in our ongoing growth as cultural beings.

**RESOURCES**

TED Talks (www.ted.com) address a wide range of issues with thought- and emotion-provoking presentations. "The Danger of a Single Story" (2009) by writer Chimamanda Adichie calls on each of us to consider the ways that we make assumptions about others, given just a little information about their background (single story). In turn, she helps us connect to the experience of being the target of single story when someone else engages with us using assumptions about who we are. Actor Thandie Newton powerfully draws us into considering what it is like to be "othered" in her talk, "Embracing Otherness, Embracing Myself" (2011). Through her words as a biracial person facing messages from others about her background, we have a glimpse into the challenges experienced by those of us who are physically different. With this glimpse, parents and professionals can consider our own reactions to the pain inflicted and suffered and what it would mean for us to help our child manage such experiences.

Another useful tool for self-reflection is the Implicit Association Test (access the IAT at implicit.harvard.edu), which measures attitudes and associations that we might not be aware we hold (Greenwald et al., 2002). The IAT provides an opportunity to learn about our implicit tendencies to pair certain associations (e.g., race, gender, skin color) with certain evaluations (e.g., good, bad). Nosek, Greenwald, and Banaji (2007) have developed a range of IATs for varied characteristics. After taking the web-based test, you receive feedback that suggests the degree of preference you might have for people with a certain characteristic rather than others (e.g., degree to which you prefer white people to black people). You then have some information to consider in terms of how consistent it is with your explicit beliefs about difference and whether your implicit associations might affect your responses to others.

We encourage readers to access these and similar tools to stimulate ongoing self-reflection about oneself as a cultural being. This reflection provides an opportunity to read this chapter with a new (or for some, renewed) look at one's beliefs and values about cultural differences. As we have, we hope that readers find these tools useful to revisit periodically to maintain an ongoing self-reflection process, which is so critical to being prepared to support others who are working on themselves as cultural beings. Even the most progressive, reflective person has work to do in this area; an important lifelong process, this type of work is never finished. We now turn to contextual influences on identity development.

## CONTEXTUAL INFLUENCES

The modern adoptive family sits within a larger ecological context that is constantly changing over time. Any understanding of the adopted child must occur in context. Bronfenbrenner (1979) proposed what has become a commonly used framework for examining the levels of context for children and families: ecological systems theory, which includes the microsystem, mesosystem and exosystem, and macrosystem as contextual levels and processes, personal characteristics, contexts and time as a model of comprehensive constructs. Palacios (2009) used this framework to explore the extant research on adoption and identify gaps in the literature. For thoughtful discussion of these contextual concepts, we refer readers to the original sources; here we briefly address the concepts as they relate to TRAs and their families.

### Microsystem

The first level of ecology relevant for adoption is the microsystem. Consideration of the adoptive family microsystem, for example, involves attention to the child's characteristics, interaction processes with parents and siblings, and specifics of the family's home environment, and rearing practices all studied over time (Palacios, 2009). Few studies offer a comprehensive view of the entire microsystem that is the adoptive family (e.g., Palacios, Sánchez-Sandoval, & León, 2005; Quinton, Rushton, Dance, & Mayes, 1998; Rushton & Dance, 2006; Rushton, Mayes, Dance, & Quinton, 2003), and other microsystems that affect adopted children, school in particular, are underresearched (Palacios, 2009). Regarding the developmental process of identity formation in transracial adoption, examples of microsystem considerations might include the adoptee's understanding of adoption, the adoptive parents' race, ethnicity, and feelings of ethnic or racial affiliation or pride, as well as the amount, quality, and nature of communication between parent and child about adoption, race, and ethnicity. In schools, another microsystem, racial and ethnic diversity of the adoptee's school or communication about race and ethnicity by schoolteachers could be of particular importance. For example, professionals often advise parents to share information about intercountry adoption, and the particular country of origin, with their adopted child's class as an additional strategy for supporting their child's self-esteem given his or her cultural, racial, and ethnic background (Huh & Reid, 2000). Adoptees in school also might benefit from teachers' increased sensitivity to their needs, such as enabling discussion or study of their culture of origin, diversity education, or even native language instruction (Huh & Reid, 2000).

Adoptive family dynamics are similar to those of any other family, with the added layer of adoption. Previously, research focused on identifying differences between adoptive and nonadoptive families and how adoptive families dealt with those differences (e.g., Kirk, 1964). Although inconsistent (e.g., Lansford, Ceballo, Abbey, & Stewart, 2001; Lanz, Iafrate, Rosnati, & Scabini, 1999), findings generally demonstrated that adoptive and nonadoptive families have more similarities than differences in their interactions (Reuter, Keyes, Iacono, & McGue, 2009).

Although many developmental tasks are not affected by adoption, the adoptive family faces some additional unique tasks. For example, within identity development, the adoptive family must assist in scaffolding the child's emerging sense of self as an adopted person (Grotevant, Dunbar, Kohler, & Esau, 2000). Thus, identity development may include the adoptee's individual cognitive and affective processes, communication about adoption between adoptee and parents, and the salience and meaning attributed to adoption for each family member and the family as a whole (Brodzinsky & Pinderhughes, 2002).

#### FAMILY COMMUNICATION

Within adoptive families, communication is a critical ingredient for positive adoptee adjustment (Brodzinsky, 2006). At least three elements of communication are critical: family communication patterns (Rueter & Koerner, 2008), communication about adoption (e.g., Brodzinsky, 2011), and, for transracial adoptive families, communication about race and ethnicity (e.g., Suter, Reyes, & Ballard, 2011). Here, we discuss family communication patterns and communication about adoption; communication about race and ethnicity will be discussed later in this chapter.

High levels of family communication along with listening and warmth are linked to better emotional and behavioral adjustment among adoptees (i.e., less delinquency, hostility to parents, fewer externalizing behavior problems and fewer classroom problems; Rueter & Koerner, 2008). By contrast, having at least one adoptive parent who is controlling and engages in little communication, or having low levels of family communication, warmth, and listening, place adoptees at risk for adjustment problems. Positive and affirming communication is only one consideration. Adoptive families face the task of talking about adoption, including the adoption story and birth parents; for many, this is an ongoing process (Wrobel, Kohler, Grotevant, & McRoy, 2004). Openness in communication about adoption is linked to a more coherent and flexible adoptive identity in families with birth family contact (Von Korff & Grotevant, 2011) and to higher self-esteem and positive adjustment in children whose families varied in the degree of contact with birth parents (Brodzinsky, 2006).

Developmental considerations in adoption communication require our attention, as well. Brodzinsky (2011) reminds us of the importance of remaining aware of children's developmental level when parents discuss adoption with their children. (For a careful description of key developmental tasks regarding adoption for children from preschool through adolescence, see Brodzinsky, 2011.) Wrobel et al. (2004) have suggested three developmental stages to adoption communication: adoptive parents take the lead in sharing unsolicited information; next, adoptive parents respond to adoptees' curiosity and questions; and, finally, adoptees take the lead with pursuit of answers to their questions. This developmental sequence reflects the changing cognitive capacities of children as they develop and suggests that parents need to be prepared to support their child when she or he moves to the third stage and may pursue information within the context of the family or outside the family.

### ADOPTION VISIBILITY

Visibility is particularly important in understanding contexts for transracial adoptive families. *Adoption visibility* represents the relative ease with which it can be determined that a family was formed through adoption—that is, how "visible" the adoption is. This term was adapted from studies of adoptees in the context of feelings of difference. Brodzinsky (2011) noted that adopted children recognize their physical dissimilarities to their adoptive family members, but also notice both real and perceived differences in interests, personality, temperament, talents, and skills. Furthermore, this concept of adoption visibility extends outside the family context and must be applied within the larger societal context.

Lee (2003) describes transracial adoption as the most visible type of adoption because the differences between parent and child are more "apparent and immutable" (p. 712). Although many intercountry adoptions are transracial or transethnic, visibility falls on a spectrum. Some multiracial adoptive families share physical characteristics such that it is relatively difficult for the average person to determine the family was formed through adoption. Similarly, some inracial adoptive families look quite dissimilar, making their adoption more visible. One must also consider that the visibility of the adoption outside the family context does not necessarily correlate with how visible the child feels—as this may be due to within-family factors like personality or temperament differences. Thus, the perception of visibility and difference felt by the adoptee within the family should be considered.

### Mesosystem and Exosystem

The mesosystem involves the connections between settings (Palacios, 2009). Mesosystem considerations in a transracial adoption include issues such as whether adoptive parents educate teachers or classmates about adoption, and how adoptive families and teachers address potential bias in school because of the visibility of the adoption, as well as adoptive and birth parent contact.

The exosystem consists of elements that have an indirect impact on the adoptee. Within transracial adoption, exosystem facets like the influence and impact of the values of the extended family might be particularly important, as adoptees experience bias within their own families (e.g., http://youshouldbegrateful.tumblr.com). Additionally, adoption professionals are often the first people responsible for providing resources to transracial adoptive families, and their competency in so doing may have a distinct impact on the adoptive family. Other exosystem contextual considerations for transracial adoptive families would include issues such as neighborhood diversity, geographic location, or availability of cultural resources.

**Macrosystem**

Finally, when discussing the macrosystem, Palacios (2009) notes the long global history (chronosystem), the anthropology, and the sociology of adoption. This is especially important for international transracial adoptees (ITRAs) and transracial adoptive families, as there is a long history of debate about the value and ethics of transracial placements (Herman, 2012). Additionally, for international transracial adoptive families, macrosystem values about race, gender, ethnicity, culture, and adoption are communicated to the adoptee and the adoptive family. For example, the meaning of "adoption" in certain countries varies from the Western notion of adoption as severing the ties to one family and replacing them permanently with ties to another, which may have differential impacts on children adopted from countries that have a different cultural understanding of the word. Mezmur (2013) has discussed the impact on Ethiopian mothers who had placed their children for adoption understanding the arrangement more as "boarding" than a permanent severing of family ties, and adoptive families have reported the impact of these misunderstandings on the whole family (Pinderhughes, Matthews, Deoudes & Pertman, 2013).

One important macrosystem impact on ITRAs and citizenship lies in the intersection between immigration and intercountry adoption policies. In the past, children adopted into the United States did not automatically become naturalized citizens. The naturalization process requires the filing of paperwork on behalf of the adoptee by the adoptive parents. In some instances, children adopted from abroad have come to discover as adults that they are not U.S. citizens, and they have been deported to a country of origin with which they may have no familiarity, affiliation, or understanding of (e.g., Pertman, 2012). Many of these adult adoptees have discovered their illegal status when they apply for passports or have some sort of engagement with the U.S. legal system, thus making them subject to the 1996 Illegal Immigration Reform and Immigrant Responsibility Act that mandates deportation of noncitizens for criminal records for which a sentence to a year or more of prison time applies.

The Child Citizenship Act of 2000 made the process easier for people adopting internationally into the United States to guarantee citizenship for their children. If the adoption is finalized before reaching the United States, or the moment that families touch down on U.S. soil, their children will be U.S. citizens without the need to file extra paperwork. Those children adopted on different visas (i.e., IH-4 or IR-4), however, with adoptions originating in countries that are not signatories to the Hague Convention for Intercountry Adoption (HCIA) will require additional paperwork (Form N-600) once the adoption is officially finalized. If that paperwork has not been filed, those children may have difficulty getting college scholarships, working legally, voting, and enjoying other privileges offered to citizens.

Although no research suggests that TRAs are disproportionately affected by their adoptive parents' failure to complete the appropriate paperwork, significant evidence suggests that there is disproportionate minority contact within the juvenile and adult justice systems. Thus, it is of tremendous importance that parents adopting from non-HCIA countries file all necessary paperwork.

### IDENTITY DEVELOPMENT

The process of identity formation likely is more complicated for TRAs, who may face additional challenges in identity development, such as a lack of knowledge about their pasts, an inability to access or acquire information, and social attitudes that stigmatize adoption. Recent research recognizes the need to look at multiple layers of identity when describing the processes of identity formation in adoption (Grotevant, 1997; McGinnis, Smith, Ryan, & Howard, 2009).

### Adoptive Identity

Adoptive identity is defined as the sense of who one is as an adopted person (Grotevant et al., 2000). The adoptee's cognitive processes, family environment, and greater context are all important contexts for adoptive identity development (Grotevant et al., 2000). The nature of adoption for the adopted child involves complicated concepts like abandonment, rejection, grief, loss, and gratitude. Some of these concepts have the potential to be painful or even alienating for people who have been adopted. Challenges to adoptive identity development are evidenced by the many adopted individuals who have expressed concerns about "fitting in" or "belonging." Adopted individuals may feel that they belong neither to their adoptive families, nor to their biological families or birth countries (McGinnis et al., 2009).

Conversely, adoptees may find a way to incorporate and integrate aspects of both birth and adoptive families into their emerging identities. Children who are able to integrate these aspects into a positive sense of self tend to have parents who are more supportive, open, and empathic in their discussions with their children (Brodzinsky, Schechter, & Henig, 1992). Access to information about adoption and preplacement histories facilitates adoptive identity development (Brodzinsky et al., 1992; Grotevant, 1997). Families with more open styles of communication about adoption issues have fewer adolescent identity problems (Stein & Hoopes, 1985). Adoptive identity also remains important over the life span (McGinnis et al., 2009).

For ITRAs, cultural identity development may be a distinct process from adoptive identity. Adoptive families may have a cultural identity that may not align with the birth culture of the adoptee. Thus, the ITRA may face trying to navigate and incorporate additional cultures into his or her identity. This process may involve understanding a link to one's heritage and feeling connected to the country of origin; adoptive parents' support of this process will have an impact. Adoptees may incorporate the culture of their country of origin by learning about the cultural history, the language, the food, and the cultural celebrations, which may be distinct from those represented by the adoptive parents.

Cultural identity development may be particularly difficult for adoptees who are in cultural-resource-poor areas. For example, ITRAs living in rural or homogenous geographic areas may have a much more difficult time finding and accessing representations of their culture of origin; consequently, they face significant challenges formulating their cultural identity.

### Racial and Ethnic Identity

Racial and ethnic identity development was first studied with respect to minority race and ethnicity among nonadopted individuals. Debated as having either a biological or social definition, a modern understanding suggests that racial identity "refers to a sense of group or collective identity based on one's perception that s/he shares a common heritage with a particular racial group" (Helms, 1993, p. 3).

Early theories of racial identity development posited a process of initial identification with whites and internalization of racial stereotypes, disrupted by an encounter (often in adolescence or adulthood) that causes the individual to question white culture and values, seek information about and connection to one's own racial group and culture, and over time come to a balanced view of one's own racial group and culture and that of white culture (e.g., Cross, Parham, & Helms, 1991). More recently, scholars have articulated theoretical models of racial identity development for different racial groups (for African Americans, see Cross, Strauss, & Fhagen-Smith; 1999; for Asian Americans, see Kim, 2001), which suggest that children are socialized from infancy through adolescence with exposure to conversations with their same-race parents that may vary in the messages about the importance of their culture.

Ethnic identity refers to one's knowledge of self as a member of a group that shares a national or cultural origin, along with the emotional significance linked to that group membership (Feagin & Feagin, 2011; Tajfel, 1981). Ethnic identity has been shown to be important across diverse ethnic groups, including various white ethnic groups (e.g., Driedger, 1976). In an important study among nonadopted youth, Phinney (1992) showed that ethnic identity was significantly correlated with self-esteem among minority students and among white students who were a small minority in their school setting. Researchers have further explored the nature of ethnic identity by focusing on the components of ethnic identity, including self-identification, language, social networks, religious affiliation, positive attitudes, and varied cultural traditions and practices (Phinney, 1992). Ethnic identity is manifested normatively in the following ways: exploration of ethnicity through involvement in social activities or cultural traditions with other group members; positive or negative attitudes toward one's group demonstrated by ethnic pride or feelings about one's background and group membership; and, finally, commitment to one's ethnicity through expression of interest and awareness of ethnic identity (Phinney, 1992). Most of these aspects of ethnic identity are dimensional—for example, from high to low group esteem or from more to less confusion or ambivalence about ethnic identity.

Building on the literature on racial or ethnic identity development among nonadopted individuals, adoption researchers have begun to investigate racial and ethnic identity among TRAs. Some researchers have differentiated between racial and ethnic identity (e.g., Baden, 2002), but most have examined racial and ethnic identity together. In the following section, we refer to the terms used by the respective researchers.

### Within Transracial Adoptive Families

Adoptive parents are predominantly white (73 percent); thus, many intercountry adoptions are also transracial. The most common transracial placements have been the adoption of Asian children to white parents (Lee, 2003; U.S. Department of Health and Human Services, 2007). Given the high rates of adoption from countries like China, Ethiopia, and Guatemala, 40 percent of adoptive families in the United States find themselves part of bi- or multiracial families (U.S. Department of Health and Human Services, 2007).

Baden (2002) suggests that in transracial adoptive families, one must consider both the adoptee's and parents' cultural groups and racial groups as one is examining cultural identity and racial identity. In her cultural-racial identity model, the adoptee's racial identity is likely to reflect some impact of the values and beliefs from not only his or her racial group, but also his or her parent's racial group. Possible outcomes might include a pro-parent racial identity, in which adoptees endorse their parents' racial views and values; a pro-self racial identity, in which adoptees develop views and values consistent with their racial group; a biracial identity, in which adoptees have high endorsement of values and beliefs from both their parents' and their own racial groups; or an undifferentiated racial identity, in which adoptees might feel marginalized and uncertain of who they are.

Baden also suggests four similar outcomes for adoptees' cultural identities and notes that when both cultural and racial identities are jointly considered, the possible outcomes become even more complicated.

Lee (2003) suggests that although TRAs are ethnic minorities, they are perceived as members of the majority culture because they were adopted into white families—a phenomenon he calls the "transracial adoption paradox." McGinnis et al. (2009) found that many Korean ITRAs felt white and did not identify with their race until later adolescence and emerging adulthood (high school and college). Indeed, the authors described reports from adult Korean adoptees indicating they did not know they were Asian until they were informed by classmates.

Studies on ethnic identity among adoptees generally examine the extent to which adoptees use ethnic self-descriptors or express pride or comfort with their ethnicity (Lee, 2003). A meta-analysis of studies of domestic TRAs and non-white, inracial adoptees showed that TRAs had significantly lower racial/ethnic identities (Hollingsworth, 1997). Given the increase in ITRAs, however, and the increasingly popular opinion that adoptive parents should support the adoptee's access to and involvement with their birth-country culture (i.e., cultural socialization [CS]), this finding may be outdated. TRAs with the support of and access to racially and culturally appropriate role models and life experiences are better able to negotiate adoptive and ethnic identity development (Brodzinsky et al., 1992; McGinnis et al., 2009). Some adoptees in adolescence, however, resist their parents' attempts at CS because they seek to belong with their peers (Freundlich & Lieberthal, 2000).

Additional factors may influence identity, such as age at adoption, community diversity, and even developmental level of the adoptee. ITRAs placed at an older age identified more strongly with their ethnicities and races than those placed at a younger age (Wickes & Slate, 1996). Reflecting the influence of community diversity, studies in more ethnically homogenous settings like Sweden (e.g., Cederblad, Hook, Irhammar & Mercke, 1999) found weaker ethnic identity among TRAs. In the United States, some transracial adoptees' sense of race and ethnicity diminished by adolescence; importantly, this study found that parents' efforts to encourage birth-country ethnic identification also decreased (DeBerry, Scarr, & Weinberg, 1996). Other studies, however, found an increase in the birth-country ethnic identification of ITRAs from childhood into adulthood

(Freundlich & Lieberthal, 2000; McGinnis et al., 2009). We know little about whether gender is related to racial or ethnic identity development.

### IMPACT OF PARENTING

Parents of TRAs fall along a spectrum of parenting strategies concerning race and ethnicity. Some parents may seek ethnic or racial assimilation of their adopted child, such that they reject or downplay the unique racial and ethnic experiences of their children. Early studies suggested this was the case for many adoptive parents (e.g., Andujo, 1988; McRoy & Zurcher, 1983). More recent studies, however, have found that adoptive parents acknowledge differences within the family and promote the birth-country cultures and ethnic and racial heritages of their children (Carstens & Julia, 2000). This finding in part may be due to changes in intercountry adoption policies with the ratification of the HCIA, which includes, as a regulation for agency accreditation, that potential adoptive parents receive 10 hours of preadoptive training, including racial and cultural education (Hague Conference on Private International Law, 1993).

### WHEN ADOPTEES ARE IMMIGRANTS

Because 25 percent of adoptees are internationally placed (Vandivere, Malm, & Radel, 2009), and thus are immigrants, we look selectively to the literature on identity development among immigrant children. Of course, a critical distinction is that in stark contrast to other immigrant children, ITRAs experience the host culture alone within their families.

Among immigrants, Padilla (2006) found that although ethnic loyalty persisted across generations, knowledge about one's home culture decreased as years of residence in the United States increased. ITRAs are likely to have less cultural knowledge than are children raised by parents of the same racial or ethnic background, but their identification with an ethnic group can be strong. For example, although Korean adoptees were less likely to have a strong sense of belonging to their ethnic group, they identified more strongly with it (McGinnis et al., 2009). Separating cultural knowledge from ethnic loyalty might be useful in understanding identity development in ITRAs.

TRAs face the task of integrating multiple cultural identities. In this regard, the bicultural identity integration model, which focuses on bicultural individuals' perceptions of how compatible their cultural identities are (Benet-Martínez & Haritatos, 2005), might be helpful. Among Latin American adoptees in Italy, ethnic and national identification was related to more compatible cultural identities, which, in turn, were related to positive well-being (Manzi, Ferrari, Rosnati, & Benet-Martinez, 2014). Mistry and Wu (2010) point out the dynamic nature in which one navigates between multiple identities. Thus, in addition to considering whether a TRA's multiple identities are compatible, parents, researchers, and practitioners may focus on helping TRAs navigate between multiple identities to achieve a coherent sense of self.

## ETHNIC-RACIAL SOCIALIZATION

Ethnic–racial socialization (E-RS) encompasses several facets. Researchers used different terms such as ethnic socialization, racial socialization, and cultural socialization (CS) among others to capture various facets of racial and ethnic socialization. Hughes et al. (2006) hence clarified the usage of terminologies and proposed four themes describing racial and ethnic socialization. CS refers to activities that promote cultural pride and skills that enable a person to function as a member of a culture group, "preparation for bias" (PfB) refers to parents' efforts to make children aware of racism and to teach children how to cope with it. "Promotion of racial mistrust" emphasizes interracial mistrust; with "colorblind attitudes," parents with an "egalitarian" approach encourage children to look beyond race and promote an attitude that is silent about race. In this chapter, we focus on CS and PfB.

### Cultural Socialization

Many TRAs experience identity struggles (e.g., McGinnis et al., 2009). A positive ethnic identity, however, is predictive of better psychological adjustment in TRAs (DeBerry et al.; 1996; Tan & Jordan-Arthur, 2012; Yoon, 2000), and CS facilitates building a positive ethnic identity (Huh & Reid, 2000; Yoon, 2000).

Among African American TRAs and their parents, a family's degree of verbal and behavioral endorsement of E-RS predicted Afrocentric reference group orientation, which contributed to later adjustment (DeBerry et al., 1996). Participation in Korean cultural activities was associated with the extent of adoptees' identification with Korean culture (Huh & Reid, 2000). In international transracial adoptive families in which parents supported and participated in Korean ethnic socialization experiences, Korean adoptees showed better psychological adjustment (Yoon, 2000). In short, for TRAs, ethnic identity is related to well-being and adjustment, and CS is an important source of a positive ethnic identity.

For young adoptees, parents play an important role in CS. Some parents are more proactive and they initiate participation in cultural activities, whereas others choose to wait for their children to ask for such participation. Adoptees' interest in cultural activities was related to parents' proactivity (Bebiroglu & Pinderhughes, 2012). Quiroz (2012) argued that parents who waited for children to initiate CS relinquish their responsibilities for socialization, and this is an implicit form of cultural avoidance.

Often families must support TRAs and ITRAs who have special needs that may require substantial family resources, including time, energy, and finances. Some children with developmental delays may not understand concepts of racial or ethnic difference. In these family situations, parents must weigh what is best for the adoptee and family in terms of providing any exposure to CS. For example, the Windom family adopted Anthony at age 2 from India, knowing he had language delays. However, other special needs emerged after placement, notably reactive attachment disorder and severe tantrums, which disrupted many family activities in and out of the home. In combination, Anthony's disabilities were sufficiently serious to require intensive supports by his parents. Although Anthony's parents and older siblings initially had planned to incorporate Indian culture into their home to support him, it soon became clear that addressing his special needs had to take priority. His mother left work to be with him full-time, working to provide corrective emotional experiences, as well as to take him to his various therapies. Given the priorities to address Anthony's special needs, the Windoms decided that the best they could do was to incorporate Indian artwork and food.

Parents' racial and cultural attitudes also are important to CS. For example, parents endorsing colorblind attitudes were less likely to believe in the importance of CS, and in turn, provided less CS (Lee et al., 2006). The authors concluded that awareness of racial differences was insufficient to ensure CS practices; parents need to value the importance of providing cultural experiences to engage in CS behaviors. Little research has examined parents' or family ethnic identity and CS. Although parents' ethnic identity was not related to CS (Berbery & O'Brien, 2011), parent-reported family ethnic identity was related to parents' provision of CS and to their Chinese-born adopted children's ethnic labels (Pinderhughes et al., in press).

With limited knowledge and resources about a child's culture, transracial adoptive parents' provision of CS might not be sufficient for a child to develop a positive ethnic identity. Quiroz (2012) differentiated "cultural tourism," which features a consumer approach (e.g., purchase of ethnic meals, books, celebrations; sending child only to CS activities without family participation), from "culture keeping," which features deeper engagement in activities (e.g., language lessons, culture camp; regular contact with cultural experts). Quiroz (2012) noted that culture keeping provides more authentic exposure and is more likely to promote a positive ethnic identity. Korean adoptees, however, reported TRA-specific activities such as culture camps and ethnic festivals were insufficient to fully develop a positive ethnic identity (McGinnis et al., 2009). What helped, according to these adoptees, were "lived" experiences such as traveling to the birth country, attending racially diverse schools, and having role models of their own race and ethnicity. In another study, although African American adoptees were exposed to their ethnic culture to various degrees as a child, they had to "relearn" the culture when older (Samuels, 2010). This "relearning" experience was coined "reculturation" (Baden, Treweeke, & Ahluwalia, 2012) and refers to the individual's need to make sense of their culture as active adult participants.

Research supports beneficial effects of "lived experiences," such as heritage trips. For immigrants and their children who may experience alienation in their daily lives, heritage trips to ancestral lands satisfy longings for belonging (Cohen, 1979). Heritage trips, in the same way, provided ITRAs a potential sense of belonging and home (McGinnis et al., 2009; Wilson & Summerhill-Coleman, 2013) and were related positively to adult adoptees' ethnic identity (Song & Lee, 2009). More specifically, ITRAs reflected on their group-based heritage trips as providing opportunities to connect with other adoptees, create a coherent adoption narrative, relate to birth parents and share grief, and explore ethnic and racial background (Wilson & Summerhill-Coleman, 2013). Heritage trips, however, are not universally positive. Adoptees experience mixed feelings during their trips. Children who visited China felt positive emotions regarding the trip, but they found visiting the orphanage and the finding sites emotionally challenging (Ponte, Wang, & Fan, 2010). In some cases, adolescent adoptees have been so unsettled by their experience that they have needed therapeutic intervention upon return home (B. J. Lifton, personal communication, 2007). Thus, parents need to carefully consider if and when during their child's development to plan a heritage trip (Pinderhughes & Pinderhughes, 2010). An excellent resource for parents and professionals is *From Home to Homeland* (Jacobs, Ponte, & Wang, 2010), which features a collection of personal accounts and writings by professionals and researchers on the experience.

In sum, CS is indeed complex. Considerations include how much and how frequently CS should be provided, who should participate, and the extent to which a cultural expert engages with adoptees and their families. Parents who believe in the value of CS are more likely to provide CS, and their children are more likely to benefit from CS. As parents consider how they will incorporate CS into their family life, it might help to contemplate whether the family is multiracial or multiethnic or is American with a TRA.

### Preparation for Bias

Being visibly adopted and a member of an ethnic minority group make TRAs vulnerable to unsolicited public comments, whether with their parents (Wegar, 2000) or alone (Vashchenko, D'Aleo, & Pinderhughes, 2012). Across numerous retrospective accounts, whether research-based or personal accounts, almost all TRAs report being the target of bias (e.g., McGinnis et al., 2009; Oparah, Shin, & Trenka, 2006; Trenka, 2003). Despite this near-universal experience for adoptees, there is great variation in whether parents communicate with and provide support to help adoptees deal with their experiences. Family communication processes about adoption, notably visible adoption, are complex, complicated, and involve flexibility by adoptive parents (e.g., Harrigan 2009; Suter, Reyes, & Ballard 2011). Some adoptees' accounts of communication about bias suggest that they do not tell their families about their experiences because of prior parental unresponsiveness (Docan-Morgan, 2011). Other adoptees perceive that their parents will be unresponsive because "they don't know what it's like to be in my shoes" (Docan-Morgan, 2011, p. 345). Some adoptees feel the pull to blend into their white family's identity and not disrupt the family's life by talking about bias (Docan-Morgan, 2011). Parents' failure to model discussions about race can contribute to this pull: "So I think some of it was that my parents didn't bring [race] up" (Docan-Morgan, 2011, p. 346). Yet other adoptees seek to protect their family members from the reality of their experiences (Oparah et al., 2006). When TRAs do not feel that they can discuss issues of bias with their parents, they often hold their vulnerability quietly and alone, without guidance for how to deal with these painful experiences.

By contrast, some accounts indicate that some adoptees feel supported by their adoptive parents. Docan-Morgan (2011) reported that although most adoptees in her sample avoided telling their parents about bias, those who chose to talk with their parents had received prior validation and empathy from their parents. Docan-Morgan (2011) observed that these parents were comfortable enough to talk openly about race issues. She also noted that these adoptees' validating experiences were consistent with general family communication styles marked by the warmth, openness, and emotional or instrumental support that facilitated victims of bullying to tell their parents in nonadoptive families (Matsunaga, 2008). Our previous discussion about openness in adoption communication is directly relevant here: not only does adoption communication facilitate a positive experience of adoption but also likely enables parents and children to talk more openly about bias.

For transracial adoptive families, PfB is complicated in at least two ways. First, parents may not have experience navigating stigma related to their child's characteristics. Some adoptive parents understand the limitation that "the privilege of being White puts us at a disadvantage for helping our children cope in the world" (Harrigan, 2009, p. 643). Second, unlike most inracial adoptive families, transracial adoptive families face unsolicited comments and questions that often invalidate the adoptee, compromise the adoptive parent, or challenge their identity as a family (Wegar, 2000). Often comments intended for the parent are communicated in front of the adoptee because parents only become visible adoptive parents when their child is with them. As parents receive, consider possible actions, and respond to queries and comments, they also must remember that in that instant, they model for their children choices about dealing with bias. These processes are consolidated into brief teachable moments—so having practice with self-reflection about cultural differences can facilitate more effective choices during these experiences.

We know less about PfB in transracial adoptive families than we do about CS. The extant literature has focused on relations between PfB and children's functioning, with less attention given to associations between parents' role, provision of PfB activities, and children's functioning. PfB was associated with higher self-esteem (e.g., Mohanty, 2013) and lower levels of marginality (feeling like one belongs nowhere; Mohanty, 2013). In a study of discrimination frequency and stress among transracially adopted adolescents, youth receiving higher levels of PfB reported lower levels of stress than did youth receiving lower levels of PfB (Leslie, Smith, & Hrapczynski, 2013). Regarding parents' role, parents who believed in the value of PfB were more likely to provide it (Berbery & O'Brien, 2011). Parents with colorblind attitudes were less likely to provide PfB and, in turn, had fewer discussions with their children about racism (Lee et al., 2006).

Consider the following case: Jason was born in the United States to his Haitian mother and Ghanaian father, each an immigrant to the United States. Shortly after birth, he entered the foster care system, remaining there until he was adopted at age 4 years of age by the Bostrips, a white family. His family embraced his Haitian and Ghanaian backgrounds, posting artwork and seeking out students from these backgrounds from the local university. Over the years, the Bostrips were thrilled when different Haitian students would teach Jason words in Creole and Ghanaian students taught him some of their customs. The Bostrips, however, were horrified when they heard the students talking with Jason, now 12 years old, about racism, sharing lessons they learned about being black in the United States. The Bostrips adamantly instructed the students not to talk about race, citing their expectation that Jason not see himself as African American but rather as Ghanaian and Haitian. Confused and feeling invalidated, the students began an ongoing conversation with the Bostrips to help them understand what Jason already was experiencing but had not disclosed to his parents. Although they did not want issues of race and racism to enter family discussions, over time, the Bostrips came to understand it was a critical process to support Jason in dealing with bias.

In sum, from the limited research on PfB, we see that although PfB can benefit TRAs, parents' attitudes and beliefs about racial differences or the benefit of addressing these differences appear to be linked to their choices about providing PfB. More TRAs might be better supported in dealing with experiences of discrimination if parents acknowledged racial differences and could see the benefits associated with this activity. Personal accounts as well as research on TRAs' experiences with bias and family communication point to several important aspects of communication regarding bias experiences. Communication about bias *ideally* includes encouraging children to talk about their experiences, listening to adoptees' experiences, validating their vulnerability and hurt as a member of a targeted group, discussing ways to deal with future incidents, and advocating with others on the adoptee's behalf.

## CONCLUSION AND RECOMMENDATIONS

### Self-Reflection

As a foundation for our recommendations for professionals and families to promote children's ethnic identity, we first return to our call for ongoing self-reflection. This should be viewed as a critical foundational task and process in which adults engage. Responsible for providing the most formative context in which children grow up, parents set the tone for how children will view and experience transracial adoption through direct parent–child discussions, interactions with those outside the family, and degree of CS. Professionals fundamentally affect adoptees' lives by how they prepare families, with whom they place children, and the quality of postplacement services designed to support transracial placements. Whatever one's role, even the most enlightened people have ongoing work to do to remain aware of their multiple identities and the way in which their privileged statuses influence their attitudes, beliefs, and values and to consider ways to improve interactions with others. Moreover, the work professionals do in adoption, both with adoptees and with adoptive families, can always benefit from a deeper understanding of privilege and status as well as structural and institutionalized inequality (Fong, 2001). Our work on ourselves is never done. Whether in person, in chatrooms, or on listserves, this process should involve discussions with others who are engaging in similar journeys.

We place this suggestion first because unless one learns to be comfortable with and talking about one's views about race, culture, and stigma, parents may not be prepared to participate effectively in these typically difficult discussions with children or with others on behalf of children. Moreover, professionals who lack such practice are likely to experience difficulty facilitating these discussions with parents and risk intimidating parents from learning to have these discussions. For example, consider the first author's experience consulting with a predominantly white elementary school with some black students to provide support for teachers in their work with students. After two successful workshops on cultural diversity that facilitated teachers' initial work on self-reflection, the school leadership encouraged teachers to explore with black parents during parent-teacher conferences whether their children had faced difficult race-based experiences. Unfortunately, although interested in having these discussions, some teachers had not had sufficient practice and discussions went poorly.

With ongoing self-reflection as the foundational recommendation, we turn first to parents, and then to professionals because a key part of professionals' responsibilities is to understand and support parents' tasks. Our recommendations for parents address what parents should do to be as effective as possible in proactively and reactively supporting children. Proactive support involves planned activities and discussions designed to provide CS or PfB. Reactive support entails responses to situations that present as "teachable moments."

### SUGGESTIONS FOR PARENTS

- Your child needs you to share this journey of cultural exploration so she or he can have a healthy sense of self.
- You need to become comfortable with cultural and racial differences and with talking about differences to best support your child's journey.
- Your support should include planned (proactive) activities and discussions; but support also means being prepared for those teachable moments that happen unexpectedly (reactive).
- Your support should extend to teachers and other professionals working with your child. (You may be the only person who can help others hear your child's voice.)

**PARENTS**

### Communication About Adoption

TRAs are always visible, but they may not be heard. Their experiences and their voices need to be heard by their parents and other important adults in their world (see Brodzinsky, 2011, who provides twelve guidelines for how parents should communicate with children regarding adoption). As discussed, Brodzinsky (2011) notes that discussions should be dialogues between parent and child, start early, and evolve throughout their child's development; parents should be emotionally available and listen to and validate their child's experiences and questions, respect the birth family in discussing the adoption story, and be aware of their own feelings about the birth family, adoption, and their child's history. These guidelines directly apply to CS and PfB processes within transracial adoptions.

### Children Grow and Change

Parents must keep development in mind. As children develop, how, what, and how much parents talk with them about adoption, race and ethnicity and culture will shift. As parents of young children balance how much to share and how to deal with unknowns in the child's history, they must keep in mind that what they share likely will need revisiting, clarification, and elaboration as children grow older. Parents should remember that adoption communication has a developmental sequence that reflects children's changing cognitive capacities. How open parents are to discussions of adoption and race and cultural differences throughout childhood may shape the child's willingness to seek parental help (Wrobel et al., 2004). If parents find themselves feeling challenged by the adolescent adoptee's or young adult adoptee's interest in learning about his or her birth family or culture of origin, it is critical to remember that such curiosity and interest is normative. Parents also should be prepared to support their teen or young adult should she or he pursue adoption information within the context of the family or outside the family. A final developmental note is that one's child may resist CS at a number of points in time: "I don't want to go to Korean camp; I want to go to soccer camp with the rest of my friends." Just because one's child is not interested at that moment, does not mean she or he will never have renewed interest. It is important not to give up even if it seems that one's child has. If she or he does not want to participate, it may be up to parents to take the lead and pursue the information for their own benefit. At a point later in development, children also can benefit from what their parents have learned.

### Balance Multiple Identities

Parents should consider the importance of balancing family identity with supporting the development of children's multiple identities. How the family views itself racially, ethnically, and culturally may serve to provide a sense of connection or disconnection for a TRA. In line with ongoing self-reflection, parents should consider what choices they make for family-based activities, parent- and adoptee-based activities, and adoptee-only activities. As in all families, promoting a family identity that embraces all members should be balanced with supporting activities that enable individual family members to develop and integrate their multiple identities, including nonculturally based identities (e.g., athlete, artist).

### About CS

CS tends to involve more proactive and planned rather than reactive activities. CS is never a one-shot deal. No one activity, one idea, or one experience is sufficient to teach a child about their country of origin, race, ethnicity, or culture. Thus, parents should consider which activities to initiate or whether they should wait for the child to express interest, who should participate in which activities, and whether to engage cultural experts in the activities (e.g., language teacher, mentor from same cultural background).

### About PfB

PfB discussions should entail both proactive planned processes as well as—and especially—reactive discussions. Children need tools to deal with bias, and parents should be prepared to help children develop strategies or identify someone who can provide this support. Public settings present minefields for TRAs and families: How should they respond to insensitive comments or seemingly naïve questions? Parents should remain mindful that the story is their child's to tell. Because parents are always modeling for their children, self-reflective work on one's motivations for responding to different questions and comments might start with consideration of how comfortable one would be if the story being told was one's own story.

### Work on Behalf of Your Child

School, the neighborhood, and even extended family are settings in which children may need parental advocacy. As children develop, the opportunities presented by schools for parent engagement and advocacy on the adoptee's behalf change. Educating teachers and peers about the adoptee's culture of origin, including customs, practices, and rituals, would be appropriate in elementary years, but not likely an option in middle to high school. Addressing bias situations, however, will be advocacy that parents may find necessary at any point in the adoptee's elementary and middle and high school experiences. Parent advocacy may be less welcome by school administrators in the middle and high school years, but it may still be a necessary support for the adoptee. Thus, adoptive parents need to be prepared for such advocacy, as do other parents raising a child of color. As parents of color know, figuring out when to support one's child through home-based discussions about addressing bias or through direct advocacy at school is challenging. Transracial adoptive parents would directly benefit from being able to consult with other parents or adults of color or who have experience advocating with schools regarding bias. In short, having a community that can support parents in this area is important.

As one adoptive parent said, "You have to, yourself make some connections so that this child won't see his color/ethnicity as unnatural" (Simon & Roorda, 2007, p. 49). Parents raising TRAs need to consider not only the family identity they foster but also the broader community of support they provide for their adopted child and family. These considerations include where to live; a diverse community is likely to present fewer situations in which adoptees feel isolated, alone, and too visible. When parents cannot change their residence, it is important to actively cultivate friendships with adults and families from the child's cultural background or diverse cultural backgrounds as supports for themselves and for the adoptee. Possible settings include churches, local recreation centers, or universities. Family friends can provide direct support, whether through CS or PfB discussions, not only for parents as they work on their parenting challenges but also for adoptees.

## SUGGESTIONS FOR PROFESSIONALS

- We learn best through relationships. Parents need your help to see the difference that relationships make. You may be the family's first and last authority on raising a child of color.
- Given that you are the "expert" helping the family, you need to do the work to develop the expertise and become comfortable providing this support.
- This work includes developing relationships within and across cultural differences through which you learn about yourself and others.
- Your support of the family should not end when the adoption is finalized. Parents will need to access ongoing support as they raise children of color.

### PROFESSIONALS

In addition to ongoing self-reflection and related professional training, professionals should incorporate into preplacement preparation and postplacement content that would support parents to carry out the previous recommendations.

### Before Placement

Preplacement preparation should include training that includes self-reflection processes about parents' attitudes and beliefs about cultural and racial differences. Such training—provided before placement—would focus parents' attention on critical issues and questions they will face should they choose to raise an adopted child who does not share their racial or ethnic background. Training should include assigned readings or viewings from resources that subsequently are discussed in preadoptive parent groups. In addition to professionals facilitating these discussions, adult TRAs and seasoned transracial adoptive parents could serve as (compensated) consultants. As these supports are developed, it will be important for professionals to carefully evaluate their effectiveness.

### After Placement

Postplacement support for transracial adoptive families could include group-based experiences that are supplemented with individual or individual family sessions. Group-based services could include, as suggested for preplacement services, adult TRAs and seasoned transracial adoptive parents as consultants. The development of theoretically grounded and evidence-based postplacement supports will serve a critical advancement in the field.

Over the past two decades, camps have emerged to address TRAs' needs (and in some cases, families' needs). These camps typically focus either on adoption or providing culturally based experiences. A simple online search will point to a variety of camps across the United States. Given the diversity of camps available, one critical support adoption professionals could provide is assisting parents in assessing the quality of camp experiences and the potential fit of certain camps for specific child and family needs. A unique camp experience that directly addresses the needs of TRAs and families is offered by Pact, An Adoption Alliance, a California-based agency focusing on transracial placements (http://www.pactadopt.org/app/servlet/HomePage). The Pact Family Camp staff also provides consultation to other groups across the United States who seek to offer an integrated family-based camp experience by addressing issues faced by transracial adoptive families.

### Consultation with Other Professionals

Another important resource adoption professionals could provide to families is consultation to teachers and health professionals who regularly interact with TRAs and their families. Consultation that normalizes the challenges that TRAs and families face and that places relevant challenges in the context of school or community experiences might be especially helpful.

It is clear that parents raising transracially adopted or internationally transracially adopted children face multiple challenges. The task of scaffolding the identity of a child is indeed complex and ever changing, as our local and national contexts change. On behalf of children in need of loving, supportive, and affirming homes, it is important to support parents trying to navigate all the advice, recommendations, prescriptions, and demands of transracial adoptive parenting. Parents who have put in the work to seek information are taking critical steps to learn and understand how best to support their adopted children. Similarly, in the face of limited requirements for professional development in this area, adoption professionals who put in the additional time and effort to learn how best to support families position themselves to provide more effective services.

The task of TRAs' identity development is extremely important, especially because of its difficulty. This chapter has addressed the most important facets of identity development, including communicating about adoption, bias, race, and ethnicity; understanding the greater contexts the adoptee and adoptive family will face; understanding the different layers of identity related to adoption, culture, ethnicity, and race; and developing a process of exposing an adopted child to their culture of origin and helping them navigate bias—all in balance with the rest of the family, their agency, preferences, thoughts, feelings, values, and characteristics. As we conclude this chapter, we refer readers to the following two sets of resources: key questions for parents to consider regarding CS and PfB, and sample web- and print-based resources to support self-reflection about cultural differences in general and transracial adoption in particular.

**DISCUSSION QUESTIONS**

**Cultural Socialization Activities**

1. Why do I want my child to do this activity?
2. Why would my child want to do this activity?
3. What are short-term rewards for participating in this activity?
4. What are potential long-term rewards for participating in this activity?
5. How well does my child engage in the activity?
6. Why am I participating in this activity? Why aren't I participating in this activity with my child? What would it take to get me to participate in this activity?
7. What messages might I be giving to my child about this activity?
8. Who is responsible for imparting this cultural knowledge to my child and our family? Is it a cultural expert?
9. At what age does my child get a say in what kind of cultural activities we engage in as a family?
10. What if my child doesn't like this activity?

**Preparation for Bias**

11. Whom am I raising?
12. How would I describe my child? (ethnically, racially, culturally) How does my child describe himself or herself?

13. How comfortable am I raising a child who is seen by others as [stereotype: Black, Asian, Latino]?
14. When is my child old enough to describe herself?
15. When is my child old enough to tell his or her own story? And to decide who tells his or her story? Who gets to hear it?
16. What is my model for how I see our family? Did I simply adopt a child into my family? Did I incorporate a new culture into my family? How does the whole family practice this new culture? Is one member of my family no longer being exposed to aspects of the culture? Are all family members getting exposed to all aspects of everybody's culture?

### Context

17. Where do we live? How racially or ethnically diverse it our neighborhood? Is my child the only person from his or her racial or ethnic background in the neighborhood? Or is my child the only person of color? If yes, am I able or willing to move to a more diverse neighborhood? If not, am I willing to look to cultivate relationships or friendships with folks from my child's ethnic or racial background? Or with others from different backgrounds? Where can I look?
18. What about the racial diversity of my child's school? If the school is predominantly white, how does my child feel "being the diversity" in their school? How would I feel if I were the only member of my race at my school? What am I prepared to do to support my child?

### SAMPLE RESOURCES
#### Web- and Print-Based

Implicit Assumptions Test. Retrieved from implicit.harvard.edu

#### Videos, Movies, and Films

Chimamanda Ngozi Adichie. (2009). "TED Talk: Danger of a single story." Retrieved from http://www.ted.com/talks/chimamanda_adichie_the_danger_of_a_single_story

Thandie Newton. (2001). "TED Talk: Embracing otherness, embracing myself." Retrieved from http://www.ted.com/talks/thandie_newton_embracing_otherness_embracing_myself

Linda Goldstein Knowlton. (n.d.). *Somewhere between*. Retrieved from http://www.amazon.com/Somewhere-Between-Linda-Goldstein-Knowlton/dp/B009MBSWQW

People and Their Annoying Comments. Retrieved from https://www.youtube.com/watch?v=xFp61HAj-nk&index=3&list=PLN2q9hvme89ZtFRAW6Ns5xGhR5Cup4E3n

Adoption Inquisition. Retrieved from http://www.youtube.com/watch?v=GCjkJgn6VrQ&list=PLN2q9hvme89ZtFRAW6Ns5xGhR5Cup4E3n&index=1

A Perfect Answer to Annoying Question. Retrieved from http://www.upworthy.com/a-perfect-answer-to-a-super-duper-annoying-question-2?g=3

Mom's Photo-Series Spotlights Racist Comments Directed at Daughters. Retrieved from https://shine.yahoo.com/parenting/kim-kelly-wagner-photo-series-girls-adopted-china-191940669.html

### Blogs and Online Magazines

Sh*tty Things Adoptive Families Say to Adoptees. Retrieved from http://youshouldbegrateful.tumblr.com

Red Thread Broken: Exposing the Red Thread Myth in Relation to Adoption. Retrieved from http://redthreadbroken.wordpress.com/

Gazillion Voices (from Land of a Gazillion Adoptees). Retrieved from http://gazillionvoices.com

### Books

#### MEMOIRS AND TRIAD VOICES

Trenka, J. J. (2003). *The language of blood: A memoir*. Minneapolis: Minnesota Historical Society Press.

Fifield, A. (2001). *A blessing over ashes: The remarkable odyssey of my unlikely brother*. New York: HarperCollins.

#### RESEARCH/ACADEMIC (ALSO SEE REFERENCE LIST)

Simon, R. J., & Roorda, R. M. (2009). *In their siblings' voices: White non-adopted siblings talk about their experiences being raised with black and biracial brothers and sisters*. New York: Columbia University Press.

## REFERENCES

Adichie, C. N. (2009, July). "Chimamanda Ngozi Adichie: The danger of a single story" [Video file]. Retrieved from http://www.ted.com/talks/chimamanda_adichie_the_danger_of_a_single_story

Andujo, E. (1988). Ethnic identity of transethnically adopted Hispanic adolescents. *Social Work, 33*(6), 531–535.

Baden, A. L. (2002). The psychological adjustment of transracial adoptees: An application of the cultural–racial identity model. *Journal of Social Distress and the Homeless, 11*(2), 167–191.

Baden, A. L., Treweeke, L. M., & Ahluwalia, M. K. (2012). Reclaiming culture: Reculturation of transracial and international adoptees. *Journal of Counseling & Development, 90*, 387–399.

Bebiroglu, N., & Pinderhughes, E. E. (2012). Mothers raising daughters: New complexities in cultural socialization for children adopted from China. *Adoption Quarterly, 15*, 116–139.

Benet-Martínez, V., & Haritatos, J. (2005). Bicultural identity integration (BII): Components and psychosocial antecedents. *Journal of Personality, 73*, 1015–1050.

Berbery, M., & O'Brien, K. (2011). Predictors of white adoptive parents' cultural and racial socialization behaviors with their Asian adopted children. *Adoption Quarterly, 14*, 284–304.

Brodzinsky, D. M. (2006). Family structural openness and communication openness as predictors in the adjustment of adopted children. *Adoption Quarterly, 9*(4), 1–18.

Brodzinsky, D. M. (2011). Children's understanding of adoption: Developmental and clinical implications. *Professional Psychology: Research and Practice, 42*(2), 200–207.

Brodzinsky, D. M., & Pinderhughes, E. E. (2002). Parenting and child development in adoptive families. In M. Bornstein (Ed.), *Handbook of parenting: Vol. I. Status and social conditions of parenting* (2nd ed.). Hillsdale, NJ: Lawrence Erlbaum.

Brodzinsky, D. M., Schechter, M. D., & Henig, R. M. (1992). *Being adopted: The lifelong search for self.* New York: Doubleday.

Bronfenbrenner, U. (1979). Contexts of child rearing: Problems and prospects. *American Psychologist, 34*(10), 844–850.

Carstens, C., & Julia, M. (2000). Ethnoracial awareness in intercountry adoption: U.S. experiences. *International Social Work, 43*, 61–73.

Cederblad, M., Hook, B., Irhammar, M., & Mercke, A. (1999). Mental health in international adoptees as teenagers and young adults. An epidemiological study. *Journal of Child Psychology and Psychiatry, 40*(8), 1239–1248.

Cohen, E. (1979). A phenomenology of tourist experience. *Journal of the British Sociological Association, 13,* 179–201.

Cross, W. E., Parham, T. A., & Helms, J. E. (1991). The stages of Black identity development: Nigrescence models. In R. L. Jones (Ed.), *Black psychology* (3rd ed., pp. 319–338). Berkeley, CA: Cobb & Henry Publishers.

Cross, W. E., Strauss, L., & Fhagen-Smith, P. (1999). African American identity development across the life span: Educational implications. In R. H. Sheets & E. R. Hollins (Eds.), *Racial and ethnic identity in school practices: Aspects of human development* (pp. 29–47). Mahwah, NJ: Lawrence Erlbaum.

DeBerry, K. M., Scarr, S., & Weinberg, R. (1996). Family racial socialization and ecological competence: Longitudinal assessment of African-American transracial adoptees. *Child Development, 65,* 2375–2399.

Docan-Morgan, S. (2011). "They don't know what it's like to be in my shoes": Topic avoidance about race in transracially adoptive families. *Journal of Social and Personal Relationships, 28*(3), 336–355.

Driedger, L. (1976). Ethnic self-identity: A comparison of ingroup evaluations. *Sociometry, 39,* 131–141.

Feagin, J. R., & Feagin, C. B. (2011). *Racial and ethnic relations* (9th ed.). Boston: Prentice Hall.

Fong, R. (2001). Culturally competent social work practice: Past and present. In R. Fong, & S. Furuto (Eds.), *Culturally competent practice: Skills, interventions and evaluations.* Boston: Allyn and Bacon.

Fong, R., & Wang, A. (2000). Adoptive parents and identity development for Chinese children. *Journal of Human Behavior in the Social Environment, 3,* 19–33.

Freundlich, M., & Lieberthal, J. K. (2000). *The gathering of the first generation of adult Korean adoptees: Adoptees' perceptions of international adoption* (pp. 1–24). New York: Evan B. Donaldson Adoption Institute.

Greenwald, A. G., Banaji, M. R., Rudman, L. A., Farnham, S. D., Nosek, B. A., & Mellot, D. S. (2002). A unified theory of implicit attitudes, beliefs, self-esteem and self-concept. *Psychological Review, 109*(1), 3–25.

Grotevant, H. D. (1997). Coming to terms with adoption: The construction of identity from adolescence into adulthood. *Adoption Quarterly, 1,* 3–27.

Grotevant, H. D., Dunbar, N., Kohler, J. K., & Esau, A.M. L. (2000). Adoptive identity: How contexts within and beyond the family shape developmental pathways. *Family Relations, 49*(4), 379–387.

Hague Conference on Private International Law. (1993). *33: Convention of 29 May 1993 on Protection of Children and Co-operation in Respect of Intercountry Adoption, Contracting States.* Retrieved from http://www.hcch.net/index_en.php?act=conventions.status&cid=69

Harrigan, M. M. (2009). The contradictions of identity-work for parents of visibly adopted children. *Journal of Social and Personal Relationships, 26*(5), 634–658.

Helms, J. E. (1993). Introduction: Review of racial identity terminology. In J. E. Helms (ed.), *Black and white racial identity: Theory, research and practice.* Westport, CT: Praeger.

Herman, E. (2012). *The adoption history project.* Eugene, OR: Department of History, University of Oregon. Retrieved from http://pages.uoregon.edu/adoption/topics/specialneeds.html

Hollingsworth, L. D. (1997). Effect of transracial/transethnic adoption on children's racial and ethnic identity and self-esteem. *Marriage & Family Review, 25*(1–2), 99–130.

Hughes, D. Rodriguez, J., Smith, E. P., Johnson, D. J., Stevenson, H. C., & Spicer, P. (2006). Parents' ethnic-racial socialization practices: A review of research and directions for future study. *Developmental Psychology, 42,* 747–770.

Huh, N. S., & Reid, W. J. (2000). Intercountry, transracial adoption and ethnic identity. *International Social Work, 43,* 75–87.

Jacobs, D., Ponte, I. C., & Wang, L. K. (2010). *From home to homeland: What adoptive families need to know before making a return trip to China.* St. Paul, MN: Yeong & Yeong.

Kim, J. (2001). Asian American racial identity development theory. In Wijeyesinghe, C. L., & Jackson, B. W. III (Eds.), *New perspectives on racial identity development: Integrating emerging frameworks* (pp. 138–160). New York: New York University Press.

Kirk, H. D. (1964). *Shared fate: A theory of adoption and mental health.* New York: Free Press of Glencoe.

Lansford, J. E., Ceballo, R., Abbey, A., & Stewart, A. J. (2001). Does family structure matter? A comparison of adoptive, two-parent biological, single-mother, stepfather, and stepmother households. *Journal of Marriage and Family, 63,* 840–851.

Lanz, M., Iafrate, R., Rosnati, R., & Scabini, E. (1999). Parent-child communication and adolescent self-esteem in separated, intercountry adopted, and intact non-adoptive families. *Journal of Adolescence, 22*, 785–794.

Lee, R. M. (2003). The transracial adoption paradox: History, research, and counseling implications of cultural socialization. *Counseling Psychology, 31*(6), 711–744.

Lee, R. M., Grotevant, H. D., Hellerstedt, W. L., Gunnar, M. R., & The Minnesota International Adoption Project Team. (2006). Cultural socialization in families with internationally adopted children. *Journal of Family Psychology, 20*, 571–580.

Leslie, L., Smith, J., & Hrapczynski, K. (2013). Racial socialization in transracial adoptive families: Does it help adolescents deal with discrimination stress? *Family Relations, 62*, 72–81.

Manzi, C., Ferrari, L., Rosnati, R., & Benet-Martínez, V. (2014). Bicultural identity integration of transracial adolescent adoptees: Antecedents and outcomes. *Journal of Cross-Cultural Psychology*, 1–17.

Matsunaga, M. (2008). Parents don't (always) know their children have been bullied: Child-parent discrepancy on bulling and family-level profile of communication standards. *Human Communication Research, 35*, 221–247.

McGinnis, H., Smith, S. L., Ryan, S., & Howard, J. A. (2009). *Beyond culture camp: Promoting healthy identity formation in adoption*. New York: Evan B. Donaldson Adoption Institute.

McRoy, R. G., & Zurcher, L. A. (1983). *Transracial and inracial adoptees*. Springfield, IL: Charles Thomas.

Mezmur, B. D. (2013, February). *Adoption in Africa*. Lecture given at the Herbert and Elinor Nootbaar Institute on Law, Religion and Ethics Annual Conference, Intercountry Adoption: Orphan Rescue of Child Trafficking? February 8–9, 2013, Malibu, California.

Mistry, J., & Wu, J. (2010). Navigating cultural worlds and negotiating identities: A conceptual model. *Human Development, 53*, 5–25.

Mohanty, J. (2013). Ethnic and racial socialization and self-esteem of Asian adoptees: The mediating role of multiple identities. *Journal of Adolescence, 36*(1), 161–170.

Newton, T. (2011, July). "Thandie Newton: Embracing otherness, embracing myself" [Video file]. Retrieved from http://www.ted.com/talks/thandie_newton_embracing_otherness_embracing_myself

Nosek, B. A., Greenwald, A. G., & Banaji, M. R. (2007). The Implicit Association Test at age 7: A methodological and conceptual review. In J. A. Bargh (Ed.),

Social psychology and the unconscious: The automaticity of higher mental processes (pp. 265–292). New York: Psychology Press.

Oparah, J. C., Shin, S. Y., & Trenka, J. J. (2006). Introduction. In J. J. Trenka, J. C. Oparah, & S. Y. Shin (Eds.), *Outsiders within: Writing on transracial adoption* (pp. 1–15). Cambridge, MA: South End Press.

Padilla, A. M. (2006). Bicultural social development. *Hispanic Journal of Behavioral Sciences, 28*(4), 467–497.

Palacios, J. (2009). The ecology of adoption. In G. M. Wrobel & E. Neil (Eds.), *International advances in adoption research for practice* (pp. 71–94). West Sussex, UK: Wiley & Sons.

Palacios, J., Sánchez-Sandoval, Y., & León, E. (2005). Intercountry adoption disruptions in Spain. *Adoption Quarterly, 9,* 35–55.

Pertman, A. (2012). An unnerving reality: We're deporting adoptees. *Huffington Post Blog.* Retrieved from http://www.huffingtonpost.com/adam-pertman/an-unnerving-reality-were_b_1550747.html

Phinney, J. S. (1992). The multigroup ethnic identity measure: A new scale for use with diverse groups. *Journal of Adolescent Research, 7*(2), 156–176.

Pinderhughes, E. B. (1989). *Understanding race, culture and power: The key to efficacy in clinical practice.* New York: Free Press.

Pinderhughes, E., E., Matthews. J., Deoudes, G., & Pertman, A. (2013). *A changing world: Shaping best practices through understanding of the new realities of intercountry adoption.* New York: Evan B. Donaldson Adoption Institute.

Pinderhughes, E. E., & Pinderhughes, R. B. (2010). Before you pack: Developmental considerations in planning a heritage trip. In Jacobs, D., Ponte, I. C., & Wang, L.K., (Eds.), *From Home to Homeland.* St Paul, MN: Yeong and Yeong Press.

Ponte, I. C., Bebirolgu, N., Golden, K., Abo-Zena, M., Compitello, A., Shahab, M. Beneke, M., Sloane, J., Theodore, M., Dempsey, J., Fan, S., Vashchenko, M. & Pinderhughes, E. E. (2007). *Children adopted from China: Understandings of ethnicity and self.* Presented at Society for Research Biennial Meeting, Boston, MA.

Ponte, I. C., Wang, L. K., & Fan, S. P. S. (2010). Returning to China: The experience of adopted Chinese children and their parents. *Adoption Quarterly, 13*(2), 100–124.

Quinton, D., Rushton, A., Dance, C., & Mayes, D. (1998). *Joining new families: A study of adoption and fostering in middle childhood.* Chichester, NH: Wiley & Sons.

Quiroz, P. A. (2012). Cultural tourism in transnational adoption: "Staged authenticity" and its implications for adopted children. *Journal of Family Issues, 33*, 527–555.

Rosenblum, K., & Travis, T. (2012). *The meaning of difference: American constructions of race, sex and gender, social class, sexual orientation and disability.* New York: McGraw Hill.

Rueter, M. A., Keyes, M. A., Iacono, W. G., & McGue, M. (2009). Family interactions in adoptive compared to nonadoptive families. *Journal of Family Psychology 23*(1), 58–66.

Rueter, M. A., & Koerner, A. F. (2008). The effects of family communication patterns on adopted adolescent adjustment. *Journal of Marriage and Family, 70*, 715–727.

Rushton, A., & Dance, C. (2006). The adoption of children from public-care: A prospective study of outcome in adolescence. *Journal of the American Academy of. Child and Adolescent Psychiatry, 45*, 877–883.

Rushton, A., Mayes, D., Dance, C., & Quinton, D. (2003). Parenting late placed children: The development of new relationships and the challenge of behavioural problems. *Clinical Child Psychology and Psychiatry, 8*, 389–400.

Samuels, G. M. (2010). Building kinship and community: Relational processes of bicultural identity among adult multiracial adoptees. *Family Process, 49*, 26–62.

Simon, R. J., & Roorda, R. M. (2000). *In their own voices: Transracial adoptees tell their stories.* New York: Columbia University Press.

Simon, R. J., & Roorda, R. M. (2007). *In their parents' voices: Reflections on raising transracial adoptees.* New York: Columbia University Press.

Song, S. L., & Lee, R. M. (2009). The past and present cultural experiences of adopted Korean American adults. *Adoption Quarterly, 12*, 19–36.

Stein, L. M., & Hoopes, J. L. (1985). *Identity formation in the adopted adolescent.* New York: Child Welfare League of America.

Sue, D. W., Capodilupo, C. M., Torino, G. C., Bucceri, J. M., & Holder, A. M. (2007). Racial microaggressions in everyday life: Implications for clinical practice. *American Psychologist, 62*(4), 271–286.

Suter, E. A., Reyes, K. L., & Ballard, R. L. (2011). Parental management of adoptive identities during challenging encounters: Adoptive parents as 'protectors and educators' *Journal of Social and Personal Relationships, 28*(2), 242–261.

Tajfel, H. (1981). *Human groups and social categories.* New York: Cambridge University Press.

Tan, T. X., & Jordan-Arthur, B. (2012). Adopted Chinese girls come of age: Feelings about adoption, ethnic identity, academic functioning, and global self-esteem. *Children and Youth Services Review, 34,* 1500–1508.

Trenka, J. J. (2003). *The language of blood: A memoir.* Minneapolis: Minnesota Historical Society Press.

U.S. Department of Health and Human Services. (2007). The national survey of adoptive parents. Retrieved from http://aspe.hhs.gov/hsp/09/NSAP/

Vandivere, S., Malm, K., & Radel, L. (2009). *Adoption USA: A chartbook based on the 2007 National Survey of Adoptive Parents.* Washington, DC: U.S. Department of Health and Human Services, Office of the Assistant Secretary for Planning and Evaluation.

Vashchenko, M., D'Aleo, M., & Pinderhughes, E. E. (2012). "Just beyond my front door": Public discourse experiences of children adopted from China. *American Journal of Community Psychology, 49*(1–2), 246–257.

Von Korff, L., & Grotevant, H. D. (2011). Contact in adoption and adoptive identity formation: The mediating role of family conversation. *Journal of Family Psychology, 25*(3), 393–401.

Wegar, K. (2000). Adoption, family ideology, and social stigma: Bias in community attitudes, adoption research and practice. *Family Relations, 49*(4), 363–370.

Wickes, K. L., & Slate, J. R. (1996). Transracial adoption of Koreans: A preliminary study of adjustment. *International Journal for the Advancement of Counseling, 19,* 187–195.

Wilson, S. L., & Summerhill-Coleman, L. (2013). Exploring birth countries: The mental health implications of heritage travel for children/adolescents adopted internationally. *Adoption Quarterly, 16,* 262–278.

Wrobel, G. M., Kohler, J. K., Grotevant, H. D., & McRoy, R. G. (2004). The family adoption communication (FAC) model: Identifying pathways of adoption-related communication. *Adoption Quarterly, 7*(2), 53–84.

Yoon, D. P. (2000). Causal modeling predicting psychological adjustment of Korean-born adolescent adoptees. *Journal of Human Behavior in the Social Environment, 3,* 65–82.

# 7

# Mental Health Issues

▸ AMANDA L. BADEN, JONATHAN R. MAZZA,
ANDREW KITCHEN, ELLIOTTE HARRINGTON,
AND EBONY WHITE

THE HISTORY OF TRANSRACIAL AND international or intercountry adoptions has traversed many drastic changes over the past 60 years. As domestic transracial placements went from innovative family formations to ill-advised practice and then finally to popular practice once again, scholars and practitioners have learned a great deal about various aspects of the impact of transracial adoptive placements. Similarly, international adoption has had periods in which few sending countries have been active as well as times of high rates of international placements. Policies and laws like the Hague Convention on the Rights of the Child and the Multi-Ethnic Placement Act of 1994 continue to impact the prevalence and practice of transracial and intercountry adoption. Scholars and statisticians estimate that approximately 40 percent of all adoptions are transracial and 80–85 percent of international adoptions are transracial (Vandivere, Malm, & Radel, 2009).

The purpose of this chapter is to better understand the issues affecting adoption stakeholders by taking a critical lens to the literature and exploring the multiple influences on the mental health needs of individuals involved in transracial and intercountry adoption. Within the *adoption kinship network*, which is composed of birth or first parents, adoptees, adoptive parents, foster parents, siblings, grandparents, and other kin, the primary adoption stakeholders (also known as the adoption triad) are adoptees, birth parents, and adoptive parents. In particular, following a cultural humility perspective, we are interested in describing the mental health needs of the adoption triad given higher rates of mental health referrals (Miller et al., 2000) for adopted individuals.

Cultural humility is based on a commitment to lifelong self-reflection and self-critique of the power imbalances, social justice, and equity both within and outside cultural experiences (Tervalon & Murray-Garcia, 1998). Cultural competence is targeted at gaining cultural knowledge, whereas cultural humility is focused on understanding cultures of both self and others (Reynoso-Vallejo, 2009). As numerous scholars have noted, empirical attention rarely has been paid to the actual clinical treatment of adoptees as a whole, and the unique needs of transracial and international adoption stakeholders have been all but overlooked. As our colleagues throughout this book have done, we will use a perspective based on cultural humility to inform our work.

For decades, the primary questions asked in adoption-related research focused on the outcomes for adopted persons following adoption placement with transracial or same race adoptive families, identity concerns for adopted persons, and various psychological issues (e.g., attachment problems, depression, anxiety, externalizing behaviors, substance abuse). Ultimately, scholars were investigating the mental health outcomes associated with transracially and internationally adopted children and adolescents. More contemporary research questions have addressed the other arms of the adoption triad, namely the birth or first parents and adoptive parents. The research on adoptive parents has addressed the issues of parenting, attachment, adjustment to parenthood, parenting challenges, and cultural and racial socialization issues and practices for raising transracial and intercountry adoptees, whereas the scholarship on first parents has focused primarily on the effects of relinquishment on white birth parents within Western countries. Virtually absent from the literature has been examinations of the deeper mental health needs of the adoptive parents and birth parents who are stakeholders in international and transracial adoptions.

This chapter will explore the mental health issues experienced by adopted people, adoptive parents, and birth parents by reviewing the relevant literature, both empirical and theoretical, and applying the concepts of cultural humility. In particular, we will highlight the issues of racial and cultural differences and issues of social class, power, and privilege as they affect the adoption triad.

### ADOPTEES

A sizable body of literature has explored the prevalence of adoptees within clinical settings. Domestic, international, transracial, and special needs adoptees are all represented within adoption literature. A strong body of evidence suggests that adopted children generally present in clinical settings more than nonadoptees (Keyes, Sharma, Elkins, Iacono, & McGue, 2008; Miller et al., 2000; Slap, Goodman, & Huang, 2001). Although reports show that adopted children are at least twice as likely to be represented in a mental health setting (Keyes et al., 2008; Miller et al., 2008; Slap, Goodman, & Huang, 2001), explaining this phenomenon is a point of contentious debate. Some argue that this overrepresentation reflects a greater degree of clinical issues among adopted children (Keyes et al., 2008). By contrast, others explain this phenomenon by contending that adoptive parents have a greater tendency to seek out mental health services for their adopted children and have a lower threshold of referral to mental health services (Peters, Atkins, & McCay, 1999). Additionally, the utilization of mental health services varies among different types of adoptees. Half of all domestic foster care adoptees utilize mental health services, whereas roughly 40 percent of domestic private and international adoptees utilize these services (Tan & Marn, 2013). Several factors increase adoptees' probability of receiving mental health services, such as older age at placement (Harwood, Feng, & Yu, 2013; Tan & Marn, 2013), older age at assessment (Tan & Marn, 2013), special health care needs (Tan & Marn, 2013), and being male (Tan & Marn, 2013). These factors must be understood within the context in which transracial and intercountry adoption are practiced.

### Preadoptive History: Prerelinquishment Maltreatment and Poor Institutional Care

Prerelinquishment maltreatment and poor institutional care can greatly affect adoptees' development. Reports have found that the length of institutionalization among intercountry adoptees was related to the following issues: developmental delays (van Londen, Juffer, & van IJzendoorn, 2007; Weitzman, 2003); cognitive ability (O'Connor, Rutter, Beckett, Keaveney, & Kreppner, 2000; van Londen, Juffer, & van IJzendoorn, 2007); mental health issues (Weitzman, 2003); lags in physical growth; sensory processing difficulties; internalizing, externalizing, and attention problems; delays in social skills; and speech, language, and learning deficits (van Londen, Juffer, & van IJzendoorn, 2007). Some contest these finding by asserting that the conditions of the institution, not the time spent there, best determine the adopted child's outcome (Fisher, Ames, Chisholm, & Savoie, 1997). Either way, these findings highlight the potential impact that institutionalization can have on a child's development.

In addition to institutional care, prerelinquishment maltreatment also greatly affects the development of adoptees. Among a nationally representative sample of all adopted children living in the United States (including transracial and intercountry adoptees), those who experienced prenatal substance exposure and prior maltreatment were more prone to be identified with special health care needs, which then is associated with higher risk for receipt of mental health services, attachment disorders, and school performance issues (Harwood, Feng, & Yu, 2013). Preadoptive history along with the context in which relinquishment (voluntary and involuntary) occurred must be considered when considering potential risk factors, etiology of behaviors, and developmental outcomes.

**Mental Health Issues**

Numerous studies show that adoptees generally display higher rates of mental health challenges when compared with nonadoptees (Brodzinsky, Radice, Huffman, & Merkler, 1987; Hjern, Lindblad, & Vinnerljung, 2002; Keyes et al., 2008; Tieman, van der Ende, & Verhulst, 2005; Vandivere et al., 2009). More specifically, young adult intercountry adoptees are one and a half to nearly four times as likely to show serious mental health problems, according to Tieman et al. (2005). Research also suggests that Swedish intercountry adoptees, who are predominantly transracially adopted, display a high risk for severe mental health problems and social maladjustment in adolescence and young adulthood (Hjern, Lindblad, & Vinnerljung, 2002). By contrast, other studies postulate that adoptees and nonadoptees do not differ in rates of mental health (Cederblad, Höök, Irhammar, & Mercke, 1999; Slap, Goodman, & Huang, 2001). On the basis of a study of self-report data and parental interviews, international adoptees displayed similar rates of mental health when compared with nonadoptees

(Cederblad et al., 1999). More precisely, adoptees did not differ in various issues such as depression, aggression, low-self esteem, and substance abuse (Slap, Goodman, & Huang, 2001). It is unknown whether an attribution error or pathologization bias is targeting adoptees, thus potentially skewing rates of mental health issues observed among adoptees. The public perception of adoptees, frequently reinforced by the media, is often negative and achieved through popularizing "failed adoption stories" and painting a picture that all adoptees are defective (e.g., have attachment issues, fetal alcohol syndrome, or behavioral issues). Learning more about how this public perception influences the rates of *perceived* mental health issues among adoptees will be paramount in validating these findings.

Research has attempted to capture the specific differences present between adoptees and nonadoptees in various dimensions of mental health (Feigelman, 2005; Harwood, Feng, & Yu, 2013; Keyes et al., 2008; Slap et al., 2001; von Borczyskowski et al., 2006). Some of the more salient dimensions are as follows: (1) attention deficit hyperactivity disorder (ADHD); (2) depression; (3) substance use and abuse; (4) posttraumatic stress disorders (PTSD), attachment disorders, and trauma; and (5) suicide.

### ADHD

Evidence suggests that international adoptees are medicated for ADHD at a higher rate (Keyes et al., 2008) and general adoptees are twice as likely to be diagnosed with ADHD when compared with nonadoptees (Lindblad, Weitoft, & Hjern, 2010). Specifically, internationally adopted children are medicated for ADHD at a rate of 3.8 to 4.6 times higher than nonadoptees, according to Lindblad et al. (2010). The probability of being medicated for ADHD among international adoptees increased with higher age at adoption and rates were particularly high in the following areas: Eastern Europe, Middle East, Africa, and Latin America (Lindblad et al., 2010). These findings do not necessarily mean that adoptees have higher rates of ADHD. Because of a low threshold of referral and higher tendency to seek out mental health services among adoptive parents (Peters, Atkins, & McCay, 1999), adoptees may be disproportionately represented under this diagnosis. This means that adoptees may be treated and diagnosed for ADHD at a higher rate, but actually exhibit comparable rates of ADHD behavior when compared to nonadoptees.

## DEPRESSION

Most research suggests that adoptees do not present with higher rates of depression when compared to nonadoptees (Cederblad et al., 1999; Feigelman, 2001, 2005; Keyes et al., 2008; Passmore, Feeney, Peterson, & Shimmaki, 2006; Slap et al., 2001). Among rates of depression for adoptees as a whole, minimal differences have been observed in adolescents (Feigelman, 2005), young adults (Feigelman, 2005), and adults (Passmore et al., 2006) when compared to nonadoptees. Interestingly, rates of depression and emotional arousability did not differ among searching and nonsearching adoptees (Passmore et al., 2006), thus further disproving the myth that searching adoptees experience great affective turmoil. In slight contrast to the previous findings, a different report showed that young adult intercountry adopted men are almost four times as likely to have a mood disorder when compared with nonadoptees, although no significant difference was found for women (Tieman et al., 2005). Mood disorders, however, are a general diagnostic category that includes both depression and bipolar disorders. Our literature review revealed an absence of research specifically examining the presence of bipolar disorder in adoptees. Further exploring the prevalence of each diagnostic category is needed to better understand how this finding fits into the current literature.

## SUBSTANCE ABUSE

Although one report found no difference in substance abuse between adoptees and nonadoptees (Slap, Goodman, & Huang, 2001), other findings regarding international adoptees showed great disparities (Hjern, Lindblad, & Vinnerljung, 2002; Tieman et al., 2005). Young adult Dutch intercountry adoptees were twice as likely to meet the criteria for substance abuse or dependence compared with nonadoptees (Tieman et al., 2005). In a sample that included more than 11,000 Swedish international adoptees (77 percent born in Asia and 23 percent born in Latin America), international adoptees were five times more likely to be addicted to drugs and three times more likely to commit crimes and abuse alcohol when compared with nonadoptees (Hjern, Lindblad, & Vinnerljung, 2002). These findings show that international adoptees may be at great risk for substance abuse and dependence.

## PTSD, SELF-ESTEEM, AND TRAUMA

The findings regarding PTSD, attachment disorders, and trauma among adoptees are varied. As expected, a report found that prior maltreatment among adoptees increased the rate of being diagnosed with PTSD or an attachment disorder (Harwood, Feng, & Yu, 2013). A concerning finding from the National Longitudinal Survey of Adolescent Health was that adopted females from all types of adoptions (e.g., transracial, intercountry, stepparent) were nearly three times as likely to report being victims of rape when compared with nonadoptees (Feigelman, 2001). A study conducted on Romanian adoptees found that one out of every five children exhibited PTSD (Hoksbergen et al., 2003). In this same study, the children that exhibited PTSD stood out from others because of their high rates of externalizing behavior and excessive attention seeking (Hoksbergen et al., 2003). These traits, however, can be seen as adaptive survival behaviors within an institutional setting (Hoksbergen et al., 2003). Given that some adoptees, regardless of type of adoption, are relinquished or enter child welfare settings because of maltreatment, adoptees are likely to present with higher rates of PTSD and trauma than nonadoptees. Depending on where a child is relinquished may determine higher or lower rates of PTSD and trauma. For instance, in a country like China where the family planning "one-child" policy is enforced, most children may be relinquished because of adherence to this government-imposed sanction rather than because of maltreatment. Thus, one might suspect that rates of PTSD may be relatively low among Chinese adoptees when compared with other international adoptees. Other factors, however, that frequently play into the circumstances of international adoptees may have a significant role in the onset of PTSD, but they have not yet been empirically explored.

## SUICIDE

Some studies reported a higher incidence of suicide among adoptees when compared with nonadoptees (Hjern et al., 2002; Slap, Goodman, & Huang, 2001; von Borczyskowski, Hjern, Lindblad, & Vinnerljung, 2006). Among adolescents, adoptees are twice as likely to have attempted suicide when compared with nonadoptees, according to Slap, Goodman, & Huang (2001). More specifically, international adoptees have displayed higher rates of suicide and suicide attempts than domestic adoptees (von Borczyskowski et al., 2006). Although both domestic and international adoptees were found to present with increased risk of suicide when compared with their siblings and the general population (von Borczyskowski et al., 2006), evidence also suggests that Swedish international adoptees born in Asia and Latin America were three to four times more likely to have significant mental health issues, such as suicide, suicide attempts, and psychiatric admissions (Hjern, Lindblad, & Vinnerljung, 2002). On the contrary, a different study found no difference in suicide, suicidal ideation, and suicide attempts between adoptees and nonadoptees (Feigelman, 2005). Even though several studies reported higher rates of suicide among adoptees, some authors contend that the great majority of adopted children do not attempt suicide (Slap, Goodman, & Huang, 2001).

A variety of risk factors predicted the presence of mental health diagnoses among a mixed race sample of domestic adoptees, such as older age at adoptive placement, white race, male gender, having more than one placement, and a history of sexual abuse (Hussey, Falletta, & Eng, 2012). Despite these risk factors and all of the research that has mixed and often dire predictions for the outcomes for transracial and international adoptees, a meta-analysis of eighty-eight studies on self-esteem found the following: (1) no difference between adoptees and nonadoptees; (2) no difference between international, domestic, and transracial adoptees; and (3) no difference between transracial and same-race adoptees (Juffer & van IJzendoorn, 2007).

**Attachment**

One of the most widespread themes surrounding adoption is attachment. A central question to the discussion of attachment essentially queries whether adoptees form healthy attachments. The short answer to this question is yes. Some contend that children who are exposed to extreme institutional conditions are able to form attachment relationships (Chisholm, 1998). Among a sample of only thirty adopted Chinese girls, no difference in attachment security was noted 2 years postadoption when compared to nonadoptees (Cohen & Farnia, 2011). In this same sample, adoptees' ability to form new attachments with their adoptive mothers was not hindered by the moderate degree of emotional deprivation experienced (Cohen &

Farnia, 2011), thus supporting the idea that periods of emotional deprivation (i.e., poor institutional care or preadoption maltreatment) may have little impact on adoptees' ability to form new attachments. This contention is corroborated in a meta-analysis study of attachment, stating that adopted children are equally as capable as nonadopted children at overcoming early adversity and risks and forming secure attachments (van den Dries, Juffer, van IJzendoorn, & Bakermans-Kranenburg, 2009). By contrast, this same meta-analysis also found that adoptees showed more disorganized attachments, strictly based on observational assessments. When including self-report data in conjunction with observational assessments, no differences were found between adoptees and nonadoptees. These conflicting findings may represent a confirmation bias among observers. A popular belief in the public consciousness is that all adoptees have attachment issues. Therefore, observers may be assessing attachment issues in the behavior of adoptees based on a misinformed core belief or bias. Looking further into this issue will be crucial before making confident deductions regarding these particular findings.

Several variables predict attachment difficulties in adoptees. One of the most salient predictors of attachment difficulties is age at adoption. Various reports agree that later age at adoption results in more attachment difficulties (Chisholm, 1998; Irhammar & Bengtsson, 2004; Levy-Shiff, 2001; Niemann & Weiss, 2012; van den Dries et al., 2009). There is consensus in the literature that children adopted after 12 months are at increased risk for adoption difficulties (Levy-Shiff, 2001; van den Dries et al., 2009). Children adopted between 6 and 12 months demonstrated equally secure attachments when compared to nonadoptees (Levy-Shiff, 2001; van den Dries et al., 2009). The majority of international adoptees were able to form secure attachments, according to van Londen, Juffer, & van IJzendoorn (2007). Consistent with the aforementioned findings regarding attachment difficulties for general adoptees, additional findings concur that age at adoption may increase an international adoptee's probability of developing an insecure attachment (Irhammar & Bengtsson, 2004; Niemann & Weiss, 2012). Age at adoption appears to be the biggest predictor for later attachment difficulties, both for international and general adoptees. Some additional noted risk factors for unresolved or disorganized attachments are as follows: memories from the time before the adoption, divorce, lack of contact in the adoptive family with the child's origin, and a tendency in adoptees not to think about their biological background (Irhammar & Bengtsson, 2004).

> **CASE ILLUSTRATION**
>
> Anja was abandoned in a busy street market in Mumbai, India, when she was approximately 2 years of age. She was malnourished and had severe eczema. She was in an institution for 2 more years until she was adopted by a white single mother from Washington State. When Anja was in first grade, she was diagnosed with ADHD and a moderate learning disability. By the time she reached middle school, Anja struggled with friendships and social skills. She was experiencing bullying and had numerous instances in which she was targeted and teased for her dark complexion. She was uncomfortable with her Indian heritage and avoided the few other South Asian students in her school. She became depressed and refused to attend school. When her mother was at work, she began hanging out with older teens and she began using alcohol and marijuana. Her mother's attempts to discipline her were ineffective and outpatient therapy was unsuccessful. The therapists had little experience with adoption; the impact of institutionalization; and the racial, ethnic, and adoption identity challenges that Anja was facing. Her last therapist facilitated Anja's admission to a residential treatment center. As part of Anja's therapy, she was required to journal and she began writing poems to her birth mother.
>
> Case Discussion
>
> In the case study of Anja, several common mental health issues were identified that have implications for the impact of both adoption and Anja's cultural context. Using a cultural humility perspective to analyze this case, therapists can reflect on the social and power imbalances that existed in Anja's birth origins and that continue to exist in her lived experience. Having been abandoned in a street market near many impoverished neighborhoods, Anja's origins were likely lacking social class privilege, and her birth family also may have experienced multiple oppressions resulting from poverty and other identities in which they lacked privilege. Once adopted, Anja was raised in a racially and culturally different environment than her birth heritage. The oppressions she experienced as a result of her status as a person of color in a largely white environment, as an adopted

person, and as a child and adolescent with educational and mental health challenges likely have been significant in her current presentation. Her therapists must understand the impact of these multiple oppressions and appreciate that analysis of her history from an adoption-competent perspective explains her current mental health and social issues in ways that depathologize her and provide pathways to understanding and treating her more effectively.

### Adult Adjustment

The research seems to be split regarding the adjustment of adult adoptees. Some evidence indicates that adult adoptees do adjust well (Levy-Shiff, 2001; Tieman, van der Ende, & Verhulst, 2006), whereas other evidence indicates that adult adoptees do not adjust well when compared with nonadoptees (Cubito & Brandon, 2001). In a study conducted among people of the Netherlands, young adult intercountry adoptees were found to exhibit similar psychosocial functioning and reach similar educational and professional attainment when compared with nonadoptees (Tieman et al., 2006). By contrast, this same sample was less likely than nonadoptees to maintain intimate relationships, to live with a partner, and to be married (Tieman et al., 2006). In a sample of predominately white-Caucasian adult adoptees (91 percent), reports showed that adoptees scored higher on levels of distress when compared with the norms (Cubito & Brandon, 2001). Additional research suggests that Israeli adult adoptees display more pathological symptomatology and have a less positive self-concept when compared with nonadoptees (Levy-Shiff, 2001). Ultimately, it appears that young adult intercountry adoptees generally may adjust well but struggle in the area of intimacy. Adoptees also may struggle with self-concept more than nonadoptees because of the identity issues present in the adoption process (i.e., genealogical bewilderment, psychic homelessness, and transracial adoption).

To contextualize the findings on adjustment in transracial and international adoption, scholars have explored some of the cultural factors in adjustment. Feigelman (2000) noted that residing in predominantly white communities affected adjustment negatively, resulting in discomfort of adoptees. Levy-Shiff (2001) found a correlation between developing mental health issues and residing in predominantly white communities. When these issues occurred, they affected male adoptees more than female adoptees (Levy-Shiff, 2001). In domestic adoption, adoptive parents relied heavily on mental health professionals, with Latino adoptees having the highest treatment rates for emotional problems and Asian adoptees having the lowest rates of seeking help from counselors and doctors (Basow, Lilley, Bookwala, McGillicuddy-DeLisi, 2008; Feigelman, 2000). Evidence also suggested that denying adoptees information about their birth stories and cultures could negatively affect well-being (Basow et al., 2008).

### Identity Formation

Identity formation is a crucial component of a person's development and a lifelong process. The process of identity formation can be difficult to navigate and is further complicated when considering adoptees. Erikson placed a large amount of focus on identity in his psychosocial model of human development (Sokol, 2009). He believed that the achievement of identity formation yielded positive outcomes but failure at this process led to confusion and mistrust (Sokol, 2009). Although identity generally has been defined as an understanding and sense of self, people cannot be understood outside of their social context (Bronfenbrenner, 1994; Sokol, 2009). Thus, when conceptualizing identity, it is important to consider race, ethnicity, and culture and the intersectionality of each (Baden, Treweeke, & Ahluwahlia, 2012). In addition, when working with adoptees, birth culture, adoptive culture, and their interplay must be examined. Although race is a social construction, it is especially relevant in adoption because race classifies groups of people by visible differences (Baden, Treweeke, & Ahluwahlia, 2012). As such, an understanding of the impact of race, the shared experiences of ethnic groups, and the shared beliefs and customs within a culture is necessary for identity formation.

Because the importance of race, ethnicity, and culture in identity development has been established, the complexity of identity formation becomes more apparent when considering transracial adoptees, whose birth culture and lived adopted culture differ. Limited exposure to birth culture leads to multiple unknowns, which can cause difficulties in identity development (Baden, Treweeke, & Ahluwahlia, 2012). Curtis and Pearson (2010) researched adjustment of adoptees in domestic adoption and their participants reported myriad of difficulties, including struggles with self-identification and identity formation. The complicated identity path of an adopted person could result in a lower level of self-acceptance, higher incidences of maladjustment, and challenges in developing a healthy sense of racial identity (Basow et al., 2008; Butler-Sweet, 2011; Levy-Shiff, 2001; Westhues & Cohen, 1998). Also, given that society may view adoptees' birth cultures as inferior to the majority culture, adoptees may develop a sense of shame and negative self-image (Basow et al., 2008).

In many cases of transracial adoption, authentic exposure to birth culture may be minimal, leading many adoptees to identify with the culture of their adopted families. Identification with the lived culture of their adoptive parents (often white, middle-class culture) can result in dissonance when trying to reconcile treatment by others based on misperceptions regarding cultural identities (Baden, Treweeke, & Ahluwahlia, 2012). Although transracial adoptees may be given an honorary white status within their families and neighborhoods, parents may fail to consider their children's experiences beyond these boundaries, where that status no longer exists (Baden, Treweeke, & Ahluwahlia, 2012; Davies, 2011). Because transracial adoptees are forever associated with their birth culture by the larger society due to visible features, they may feel a need to resolve their dissonance by connecting with their own racial and ethnic background and seeking out people with physical similarities (Basow et al., 2008).

Humans have a strong desire to receive affection from others and feel a sense of belonging in their group, and will work hard to achieve this goal (Maslow, 1943). Thus, the desire to connect with one's birth culture and develop relationships with people who share that culture is not only a natural instinct, but it can lead to the development of a strong ethnic identity, thereby shielding adoptees from negative stereotypes, contributing to decreased feelings of marginality and enhancing psychological well-being (Basow et al., 2008; Butler-Sweet, 2011; Mohanty & Newhill, 2011). Although the benefits of exposure to and immersion in birth culture are apparent, many transracial adoptive parents struggle to teach their children about their birth culture or fail to expose them to individuals from their ethnic groups (Westhues & Cohen, 1998). In a study of thirty-two young black adults, nine of whom were transracially adopted, Butler-Sweet (2011) found that adoptive parents minimized racial differences and inadequately assisted them in understanding their ethnicities. These challenges in racial and cultural socialization and confusion about ethnic identity have been linked to behavioral problems and psychological distress (Butler-Sweet, 2011).

The transracial adoption of black children by white families has a long history of empirical and social attention, but the discourse regarding the advisability of transracial placements remains mixed. Butler-Sweet (2011) postulated that white families may not be equipped to help black children navigate a racist society and develop a healthy identity, echoing the concerns expressed by the National Association of Black Social Workers in 1972. Westhues and Cohen (1998), however, found that some white families were able to facilitate their children's understanding of their birth culture through the use of books, music, television, and movies and that they were able to foster a healthy sense of identity by attending diverse churches, celebrating holidays, and choosing godparents of color.

### Summary

Various studies support the finding that adoptees present in clinical settings at a higher rate than nonadoptees (Keyes et al., 2008; Miller et al., 2000; Slap, Goodman, & Huang, 2001). This disproportionate representation has partially led to an investigation of the psychological well-being of various types of adoptees (i.e., international, domestic, foster, transracial). There is some disparity among the different states of psychological well-being present among these varied groups. Each type of adoption carries a unique experience that leads to assorted states of psychological well-being for the adoptee. This chapter offers a mere overview of these distinctions and the implications that follow. Much of the literature presented in this section focuses on the experience of international adoptees; however, 80–85 percent of international adoptions are transracial (Vandivere et al., 2009). Therefore, the findings regarding international adoptees may be generalized to transracial adoptees as well, although with some caution.

CASE ILLUSTRATION

Tracy is a 42-year-old woman who was adopted when she was 3 years of age. She identifies as biracial and she reports having a black birth mother and a white birth father. Tracy was adopted by a white heterosexual couple who had one son by birth. They lived on a working farm in a rural town in Pennsylvania where Tracy was the only child of color in her elementary school classes. Tracy reported feelings of depression and anxiety for the past 15 years. Upon assessment, Tracy revealed that she drinks wine with dinner each night and when she was in college, she drank heavily. She denies having a drinking problem but estimates that she drinks approximately two to four glasses of wine each night. Tracy has a master's degree in literature and works as a receptionist in a public relations firm at which she reports a high level of stress on the job. She admitted to taking sleeping pills daily. Tracy searched for her birth mother and found relatives but her birth mother had died before Tracy's contact. She continues to grieve the inability to meet her birth family. She sought therapy at this time to deal with multiple issues: (1) her divorce that was finalized 8 months ago, (2) her struggles with her career and underemployment, (3) her adoption, (4) challenges with race and culture, and (5) her desire to have a child as a single parent. Tracy had been in therapy several times in the past but felt that the therapists "never really understood her adoption issues." She was frustrated with "just talking about her attachment issues" even though she knew that her dating history had always been "rocky" and "too intense."

### Case Discussion

The problems exhibited by Tracy reflect the complexity that can present in adult adoptees. Her educational achievements and the absence of any chronic, debilitating mental illness show strengths and coping resources, whereas her history of depression, anxiety, and substance abuse of alcohol and sleeping pills along with relationship instability indicate ongoing mental health issues. Tracy's comments about the lack of adoption-competent therapists and her own challenges with the impact of having been relinquished and transracially adopted reflect the need for the development of a comprehensive theoretical and practical understanding of the combined effects of relinquishment, adoption, race, culture, ethnicity, and identity. Tracy's experiences as a biracial adoptee who struggles to connect with other people of color also suggest the need for more attention to her process of reclaiming aspects of her birth culture and heritage (Baden, Treweeke, & Ahluwahlia, 2012).

### ADOPTIVE PARENTS

Adoption literature predominately has been dedicated to the psychological, intellectual, and physical outcomes and vulnerabilities of adopted children (Wegar, 1995). Although there are many similarities that exist between adoptive parents and biological parents, adoptive parents may face some unique challenges and experiences, such as infertility issues; financial stress related to adopting a child; evaluation of parental fitness; social stigma; and difficulties associated with developmental, medical, or psychological issues in their adopted children (Baden, Gibbons, Wilson, & McGinnis, 2013). Stressors associated with adopting transracially and internationally may come in multiple forms, ranging from expressions of racism and oppression to internal struggles with having visible or conspicuous adoptive families. The stressors take many forms yet little research specifically explores the impact of transracial and intercountry adoptions on adoptive parents. In exploring mental health issues of adoptive parents, the contextual factors of racial status and privilege as well as social class likely play a qualitatively different role in the experiences of adoptive parents than those same factors play in the experiences of adoptees or even birth parents, given that many adoptive parents come from privileged statuses (e.g., white, middle class, and highly educated).

The literature that does exist on adoptive parents primarily has focused on adoptive parents' postadoption outcomes and mental health. Although adoptive parents and the mental health community have benefited from the attention that postadoption issues have received, there is a continuing need to address any preexisting mental health needs of adoptive parents that were in existence before the adoption of their children (Baden et al., 2013; McKay, Ross, & Goldberg, 2010). This section on the possible mental health issues that adoptive parents may experience will be separated into preadoption and postadoption issues.

#### Preadoption Mental Health Concerns of Adoptive Parents

The preadoptive functioning of adoptive parents is affected by multiple factors, including their own social relationships that encompass their early relationships and attachments, mental health history, adjustment, and identity issues (Baden et al., 2013).

MENTAL HEALTH ISSUES

### RESOLVING INFERTILITY ISSUES OF ADOPTIVE PARENTS

The ability of adoptive parents to resolve conflict surrounding their own infertility is believed to contribute to a negative view of adoptive parents' self-images, especially surrounding their sense of masculinity and femininity (Menning, 1980). Early literature on adoptive parents first suggested that if adoptive parents are unable to resolve their infertility issues, then they may manifest symptoms of anxiety, mood disturbances, impaired self-esteem, marital problems, sexual dysfunction, and social isolation (Edelmann & Connolly, 1986; Mathews & Mathews, 1986; Seibel & Taymor, 1982). More recent research has suggested that adoptive parents may experience shame or have feelings of inferiority because of their actual or perceived infertility that can have significant impact on the adoptive parents (Baden et al., 2013; Miall, 1994). Although infertility is just one reason families adopt, the stigma that links infertility to adoption is one often experienced by adoptive parents (Krusiewicz & Wood, 2001). The failure to resolve any unsettled feelings or thoughts surrounding infertility can lead to various internalizing and externalizing problems that mental health professionals will need to address.

#### CASE ILLUSTRATION

A white heterosexual couple—Jim, 35 years old, and Mary-Anne, 33 years old—have been trying to conceive their first child for the past year. After a year of being unsuccessful in their attempts to conceive a child, they decided to obtain medical consultation. After completing a physical exam and gathering sexual histories of both partners, Mary-Anne was asked by her OB/GYN to undergo several blood tests, an ultrasound of her ovaries, and a hysterosalpingography (an X-ray of the uterus and fallopian tubes). Mary-Anne's doctor did not find any abnormalities in Mary-Anne's reproductive system to explain their infertility issues.

Jim, who consulted his primary care physician, underwent a physical examination and his doctor found a noticeable bulge under the skin above Jim's left testicle. After further testing, Jim's doctor diagnosed him with varicocele, a condition that causes abnormally shaped sperm and can lead to infertility in men. Jim elected to undergo corrective surgery, but the procedure was not able to help Jim's infertility issue.

**CASE ILLUSTRATION** (CONTINUED)

The couple continued to try to conceive a child after Jim's surgery, but continued to be unable to do so. After another year of being unsuccessful, the couple stopped trying to conceive a child. Afterward, Jim became increasingly irritable and withdrawn from social events, such as family celebrations. Jim and Mary-Anne's relationship slowly began to deteriorate because of an increase in unresolved arguments between the couple. Jim would quickly become angry and Mary-Anne began avoiding talking to Jim. Mary-Anne became increasingly depressed as time continued and consulted her primary care physician for medication for depression. A family friend urged Mary-Anne and Jim to seek counseling to help them with their marital problems. They are considering adoption, but Jim is not sure he wants to adopt. They both agree, however, that if they do adopt, they will take "any child who needs a home" because for them, "race doesn't matter."

### Case Discussion

Individuals who learn they are infertile often experience emotional distress similar to that felt by those who are grieving a loss. Anxiety, depression, social withdrawal, anger, frustration, and marital problems are all common manifestations of infertility in adoptive couples. Mental health professionals must be prepared to address loss issues that may manifest regarding fantasized biological children that arise because of unresolved infertility issues. Before couples consider adoption, both members of the couple must be fully prepared to parent a child through adoption. They must work to develop realistic expectations of adoption, race, and cultural issues. Using a cultural humility perspective, therapists can help couples develop awareness and understanding of their own racial identities, racial privilege, and their ability to address the various forms of oppression that affect transracial adoptive families.

## Adoptive Parents' Transition to Parenthood

Even before being able to take their children home for the first time, most adoptive parents experience a unique transition to parenthood that occurs after a long and intense period of paperwork, evaluations, home visits, waiting periods, possible false starts, and preparation of home, family, and friends to this alternative path for forming a family (Baden et al., 2013).

In a study with fifty-two preadoptive couples (Levy-Shiff, Bar, & Har-Even, 1990), the expectation that adoptive parents may experience more psychological stress and struggle with adjustment to parenthood because of unique adverse effects associated with adoption during the expectancy period was not supported. Levy-Shiff et al. (1990) proposed that adoptive couples may be better able to transition to parenthood because of their infertility struggles and painful failures to bear children. They suggested that adoptive couples were likely to feel (1) a strong sense of impending fulfillment with the approaching arrival of their baby resulting from their basic deprivation of the right of parenthood; (2) a sense of fulfillment that may overshadow the unique stresses associated with adoptive parenthood and overall parenthood; (3) a sense that adoptive parents' older ages may prepare them to handle parenting stress; and (4) more financially secure and established.

Although many protective factors and strengths may help adoptive parents handle the stress of adopting a child and transitioning to the role of parenthood, adopting transracially and internationally may include additional stressors and challenges. Smit (2010) reported that after surveying 107 adoptive parents (104 mothers and 3 fathers) of internationally adopted children, some parents self-disclosed that they were uncertain about their parenting skills and wanted more support and information that would help them in their family's transition. Smit (2010) noted that parents, particularly those with limited child care experience, had many questions about what to expect and do with their child after placement in the home.

### Postadoption Mental Health Concerns of Parents

Just as biological parents need to adapt to the postpartum period of parenthood, adoptive parents experience a series of challenging transitions and unique obstacles as they themselves adjust to the postadoption period (Fontenot, 2007). During this postadoption period, transracial adoptees and their families must choose how they plan to address the differences in race and ethnicity of each of its family members. White adoptive parents who belong to the dominant group most likely have not experienced racial discrimination or prejudice and may not know how to handle or react to racial bias. McGinnis, Smith, Ryan, and Howard (2009) recommended that postplacement support for adoptive parents with transracial children should be expanded to help adoptive parents prepare their children to cope with racial bias. Adoptive parents of transracial and international adoptees must decide how they can help their children relate to and identify with their birth cultures and countries of origins (Baden, Treweeke, & Ahluwahlia, 2012). Adoptive parents help dictate to what extent the family system incorporates children's birth cultures and heritage into the family system. Brabender and Fallon (2009) acknowledged that adoptive parents often are encouraged to live and school their children in communities in which their children will encounter individuals from their birth countries and racial groups.

### UNDERSTANDING SOURCES OF STRESS IN ADOPTIVE PARENTHOOD

Adoptive parents, like all parents, must deal with the daily tasks of parenthood that can induce stress (Crnic & Low, 2002). However, adoptive parents must also be able to resolve "adoptive strains" or stress that is directly linked to the role of adoptive parenthood (Bird, Peterson, & Miller, 2002). Using the Parenting Stress Index (PSI) to assess 109 adoptive mother–father pairs who had adopted children internationally from Eastern Europe, Judge (2003) found that 10 mothers (8.3 percent) and 4 fathers (3.7 percent) who completed the PSI obtained a score that indicated a clinically significant level of stress. Similarly, in one study, 13 percent of adoptive parents of children with prenatal substance exposure had clinically significant PSI scores (McCarty, Waterman, Burge, & Edelstein, 1999) and in another study, 34.3 percent of adoptive parents' PSI scores fell into the clinically significant range (McGlone, Santos, Kazama, Fong, & Mueller, 2002). Although the majority of adoptive parents cope adequately with the stress of adoptive parenthood, some may need additional support.

When working with adoptive parents, mental health professionals should understand and be able to identify risk factors that may lead to stress in adoptive parenthood. Some risk factors contributing to adoptive parent stress include the following: (1) the simultaneous adoption of siblings (Sanchez-Sandoval & Palacios, 2012); (2) child behavior problems in a sample of Romanian adoptees (Judge, 2003; Mainemer, Gilman, & Ames, 1998); (3) adoptive parents' perceptions of similarities and differences within their families in comparison with nonadoptive families (Sanchez-Sandoval & Palacios, 2012); and (4) overemphasis on differences in discussions about adoption coupled with extreme communication patterns that overpathologize adoption as causing family dysfunction (Sanchez-Sandoval & Palacios, 2012). Recommendations include the acceptance of differences, facilitation of open communication, and validation of any feelings of loss or search for adoptees' birth parents, and discussion of similarities between family members (Sanchez-Sandoval & Palacios, 2012).

## ASSESSING DEPRESSION IN ADOPTIVE PARENTS

Postadoption depression appears to be relatively common in adoptive mothers (McKay, Ross, & Goldberg, 2010). In a recent study, international adoptive mothers experience increased stress and life changes that can put them at risk for developing depression similar to what biological mothers experience during the postpartum period (Mott, Schiller, Richards, O'Hara, & Stuart, 2011). Postpartum depression (PPD) was assessed in 13 percent of women following childbirth (Gavin et al., 2005) and 15.4 percent of international adoptive mothers were assessed with depression during the postadoption period (Senecky et al., 2009). This finding is complicated by the assessment of depression in adoptive mothers during preadoption as well.

In another study, Gair (1999) found that among nineteen mothers who adopted children age 5 years old and younger, six mothers (32 percent of participants) scored above the clinical cutoff on the Edinburgh Postnatal Depression Scale (EPDS), indicating probable major depression. Of those six mothers above the clinical cutoff, five reported caring for babies with colic and experienced severe sleep deprivation. Gair (1999) suggested that both sleep deprivation and colic are important factors that could account for distress and depression in mothers during the postadoption period, just as they would for many nonadoptive mothers as well. Several other risk factors for postadoption depression among mothers who adopted internationally were identified in the literature, including increased difficulty with and time spent in the adoption process, history of infertility, self-reported history of psychological disorders, and marital dissatisfaction (Mott et al., 2011). Women who experienced these factors had more depressive symptoms during the first year following adoption than women who did not report these factors (Mott et al., 2011).

Assessment of depression by mental health professionals during the postadoption period for adoptive mothers should be conducted because of the increased stress and significant life changes that adoptive mothers experience (Mott et al., 2011). This is especially important because maternal depression is associated with internalizing and externalizing symptoms (Campbell, Morgan-Lopez, Cox, & McLoyd, 2009), cognitive difficulties (Hay, Pawlby, Waters, & Sharp, 2008), and later depressive symptoms (Bureau, Easterbrooks, & Lyons-Ruth, 2009) in children. Common depressive symptoms among adoptive mothers include physical complaints, social difficulties, medical problems, child behavioral and emotional problems, and parenting stress. Similar depressive symptoms are experienced by biological mothers with PPD (O'Hara & Swain, 1996).

### ASSESSING ANXIETY IN ADOPTIVE MOTHERS

According to Mott et al. (2011), women who adopted internationally experienced significantly fewer symptoms of anxiety, including social anxiety, panic, and traumatic intrusions and they experienced greater well-being than postpartum nonadoptive mothers. The authors noted that this diminished well-being may be related to the biological changes associated with childbirth or pregnancy and delivery complications that nonadoptive mothers may experience, which have been shown to increase the risk for anxiety disorders during the postpartum period (Wenzel, 2011), that adoptive mothers do not experience. Gjerdingen and Froberg (1991) reported that they surveyed 108 married first-time adoptive mothers, who were found to have significantly better mental health outcomes when compared with first-time nonadoptive mothers and married women without children. Adoptive mothers scored significantly lower on the anxiety subscale of the Mental Health Inventory (MHI) when compared with other groups. Screening practices and selection criteria used by adoption agencies to choose prospective mothers also may contribute to the lower levels of anxiety symptoms present in adoptive mothers (Mott et al., 2011). Mental health professionals, however, should still be aware that adoptive parents may be at risk for increased anxiety during the postadoption period because of the increased stress that parenthood may bring (Mott et al., 2011).

### INTIMATE PARTNER RELATIONSHIP SATISFACTION

South, Foli, and Lim (2012) suggested that because adoptive parents face unique challenges, such as a higher likelihood of a period of infertility (Cudmore, 2005); are more likely to parent a child with behavioral or emotional problems (Glidden, 2000); and often have a child from a different racial or ethnic group (Lazarus, Evans, Glidden, & Flaherty, 2002), they are likely to encounter additional sources of stress that might lead to a decrease in marital satisfaction if they do not have adequate coping strategies and support networks in place. Although few studies explored the relationship satisfaction of adoptive parents, findings are mixed, with one study reporting high levels of happiness and satisfaction (Leve, Scaramella, & Fagot, 2001) and another reporting decreases in love and increases in ambivalence and conflict across the transition to adoption in all types of couples who adopted across the first year of parenthood (Goldberg, Smith, & Kashy, 2010).

The research depicts adoptive parents' mental health with a mixed snapshot. Very little of the research on adoptive parents, however, specifically addresses issues related to transracial and international adoption. As adoptive parents, they are best positioned in terms of power, privilege, and often social class to navigate the challenges of adoption parenthood, yet there is much we still must understand about the role of race, culture, and differences to better understand their impact.

### CASE ILLUSTRATION

Amanda, 35 years old, and John, 40 years old, recently brought home their adopted daughter Christina from Colombia. The couple had decided to adopt because they were advised by their physician that Amanda was at a high-risk for having health complications during a potential pregnancy and delivery. The couple still wanted to have children and sought to adopt a child to start a family. Christina was adopted at 11 months of age and did not have any reported medical condition; however, her preadoption history was incomplete.

Christina was the couple's first child, and this was the couple's first experience parenting. John was able to take several days off from work to spend the first couple of days with Amanda and Christina at home, but had to return to work soon after. Christina took over most of the caretaking responsibilities during the day while her husband John was at work. The first few weeks during the postadoption period were the toughest for Amanda. As soon as John left for work, Christina would uncontrollably cry and protest her separation from John by sitting by the door refusing to move. Amanda would try to console Christina and play with her, but Christina would continue to cry for extended periods of time without

## CASE ILLUSTRATION (CONTINUED)

resolution. Amanda felt saddened, shameful, and worthless that she was unable to help Christina stop crying when John left. She began to question her parenting skills and became increasingly anxious when John would leave the home. After returning from work, John would help Amanda with Christina until her bedtime. Christina, however, frequently woke up during the night and cried until Amanda or John came to her side. Christina did not sleep soundly throughout the night and required constant reassurance from Amanda and John. John and Amanda frequently did not get adequate amounts of sleep and felt constantly tired throughout the day. As a result, John became irritable and the couple frequently argued. The couple began reaching out to friends and family for support and parenting advice, because they both felt overwhelmed, tired, stressed, and frustrated.

When the family was out with Christina, they would be questioned about their adoption by strangers and friends, leading Amanda and John to feel overwhelmed with having to answer so many questions about her origins and their adoption process. They had promised their adoption agency that they would seek out Colombian cultural activities, but they have not had the energy or interest in doing so.

### Case Discussion

First-time parenthood can be a stressful time for adoptive and nonadoptive parents alike. Adoptive parents can become stressed and overtired, which can cause relationship problems, feelings of depression, anxiety, and cause lower self-esteem. Mental health professionals may need to address these issues in counseling and provide resources for adoptive parents to help them with parenting skills and coping skills. Furthermore, visible racial differences within families can lead to more intrusive questions about adoption and race from others and adoptive parents may struggle to cope with and deal appropriately with these responses. They also may need support in seeking racial and ethnic communities that will provide the diversity and lived cultural experiences that their children need.

## BIRTH PARENTS

Birth parents and their families are considered the least studied and possibly most misunderstood members of the adoption triad (Freundlich, 2007; Wiley & Baden, 2005). Despite the prevalence of international and transracial adoptions over the past 60-plus years, birth parents of color as well as birth parents from other countries rarely have been studied in any systematic way. With the exception of a couple of empirical studies of birth parents from other countries (e.g., Johnson, Banghan, & Liyao, 1998; Roby & Matsumura, 2002), little is known about the actual lived experiences and mental health of birth parents. Per the practice of cultural humility, the scarcity of literature on the mental health needs of this population demands reflection on the possible influence of issues of equity and social justice that create this gap. This review of mental health issues in transracial and international adoption for birth parents will utilize the extant literature to theorize about the mental health issues that birth parents of color and foreign birth parents experience.

Given the dearth of information, both empirical and even anecdotal, on birth parents of color and birth parents whose relinquished children are placed transracially, we will briefly note several areas unique to transracial adoption and intercountry adoption that may present challenges to the mental health and adjustment of first parents. The main areas of concern involve the impact of disparities in social class, race, power, privilege, social stigma, and community and social supports.

### Relinquishment and First Families' Mental Health

Without question, one of the most predominant mental health concerns for first parents is depression (Wiley & Baden, 2005). The ongoing grief and loss experienced by birth parents cuts across race, culture, and types of adoptions. Birth parents who relinquished voluntarily or involuntarily to same-race adoption, transracial adoption, or international adoption have reported long-term feelings of loss, which often is manifested by the relinquishment itself.

Multiple studies (Christian, McRoy, Grotevant, & Bryant, 1997; DeSimone, 1996; Jones, 2000; Wiley & Baden, 2005) confirm that, "women who place their children for adoption are at significant risk of long-term physical, emotional, and interpersonal difficulties" (Freundlich, 2007, p. 329). Logan (1996) states that it is clear that "loss of a child through adoption profoundly affects coping mechanisms and may contribute to longstanding distress" (p. 621). In her study of twenty-eight birth mothers, almost three-quarters considered themselves as having mental health problems;

most attributed this to the experience of relinquishment. Studies by Clifton (2012), Triseliotis, Feast, and Kyle (2005), and Cicchini (1993) reported similar findings with respect to birth fathers. Despite these findings, placement is often viewed as a simple solution and one-time event for birth parents, who are then freed to "move on" with their lives with minimal effect. Logan (1996) and Neil (2013) point out that in some cases there may have been a preexisting condition, social forces, or a predisposition to mental health challenges at play. They both caution the reader against pathologizing the depression and mental distress experienced by birth mothers who have relinquished.

The context in which relinquishment occurs is also likely to have a significant impact on mental health outcomes. Birth mothers having preexisting mental health issues, including substance abuse or dependence may experience even more significant issues. First families who relinquish internationally or transracially often face more complicated judgments and negative outcomes for relinquishment in contexts in which (1) legal relinquishment is impossible (e.g., China); (2) coercion coupled with misinformation is prominent (e.g., the Republic of the Marshall Islands; Roby & Matsumura 2002); (3) cultural norms may discourage voluntary relinquishment; and (4) power, oppression, and social class may result in higher rates of terminations of parental rights. These contextual factors likely further complicate the impact of relinquishment on first families, but to date, little is known empirically about birth families of color and who placed internationally (Baden et al., 2013; Wiley & Baden, 2005).

### Context of Relinquishment

Relinquishment abroad. In one of the few studies that focused on birth mothers in international adoption, Roby and Matsumura (2002) explored the experiences of seventy-three birthmothers in the small Western Pacific island nation of the Marshall Islands. The study underscored the importance of cultural understanding in international adoption. The Western view of modern adoption is that a formal proceeding takes place during which a child becomes a permanent member of the adoptive family. Adoption in the Micronesian region is considered to be of a more informal nature that results in only a partial transfer of the child into the adoptive family. In a remarkable example of cultural difference, more than 82 percent of the birth mothers in the study by Roby and Matsumura (2002) believed that their adoption arrangement was open when it was not. These same women also were under the misapprehension that their children would return to them when they turned 18 years old to take care of their family of origin, after having become wealthy and educated in the United States. Disturbingly, most of the birth mothers had been told these falsehoods by adoption agency personnel and adoptive parents.

The disconcerting findings of the work of Roby and Matsumura (2002) afford professionals the opportunity to reflect on the role of cultural humility in their work. More than 41 percent of those in the study felt pressure from adoption agency personnel to place their child for international adoption. As is the case in many international adoptions, poverty was a primary reason for placement in the large majority of the relinquishments; the adoptions were made more attractive by the promise of financial security for all members of the birth family (Roby & Matsumura, 2002). As reported by the Evan B. Donaldson Institute (2007), "research findings consistently show that women who feel pressured into placing their children suffer from poorer grief resolution and greater negative feelings" (p. 5). The application of the self-reflection and self-critique required for the practice of cultural humility may have created markedly different results in the decisions and lives of these birth parents.

### CHILD ABANDONMENT AS RELINQUISHMENT

Child abandonment has been an especially notable practice in China. Information is difficult to obtain about the health and well-being of those who abandon their children in the hopes of adoption. Johnson et al.'s 1998 study of 237 birth families who abandoned their children found that the "birthmothers frequently expressed emotional pain and remorse for the act" of abandonment (p. 474). First parents in China who abandon their children may be required to pay a penalty; they often are subjected to ridicule and disapproval by those in their towns and workplaces. The results of such shunning may be detrimental to the well-being of the birthparents.

First parents or birth parents may first place their children in foster care before their adoption placements. Interestingly, although the majority of scholarship on the experiences of birth parents focuses on white birth parents who relinquished to same-race adoption placements, foster care is an area in which some research begins to address the experiences of birth parents of color. Parents of color, particularly those of African descent, were more likely (44 percent) to have their children enter foster care than their white counterparts (Knott & Donovon, 2010).

### FOSTER CARE AND TERMINATION OF PARENTAL RIGHTS

First parents or birth parents may first place their children in foster care before their adoption placements. Parents of color, particularly those of African descent, were more likely (44 percent) to have their children enter foster care than their white counterparts (Knott & Donovon, 2010). Particularly notable stressors for parents whose children are in state or foster care include stigma, disenfranchised grief, and struggles with parental identity (because of a quasi-parental status; Schofield et al., 2011).

Racism and sexism in the diagnosis of mental illness has been long documented in the United States (Fernando, 2012; Garb, 1997; Greer, 2011; Kim, 2014; Oyserman, Mowbray, Meares, & Firminger, 2000). The repercussions of this systemic form of prejudice are evident not only on the larger societal level but also extend to individual families. With respect to mental health, overdiagnosis and misdiagnosis of mental health conditions have been shown to disproportionately affect people of color (Eack & Newhill, 2012). As a result, biological parents of color may suffer higher rates of parental rights terminations. Mental health issues, including substance abuse, may be common reasons given for terminating parental rights, but scholars and practitioners must begin to examine the context in which these issues occur and account for the issues of privilege, oppression, social class, and race on relinquishments, both voluntary and involuntary.

### Open Adoption Versus Closed Adoption

Although considerable evidence documents the effects of relinquishment, research on open adoption has demonstrated the benefits to mental health and well-being for birth parents in open adoptions (Cushman, Kalmuss, & Namerow, 1997; Ge et al., 2008; Grotevant & McRoy, 1998), including decreased stress because of voluntary open adoption (Ge et al., 2008; Grotevant & McRoy, 1998) and greater postplacement adjustment for first mothers related to greater openness and satisfaction (Ge et al., 2008). Birth mothers who had at least some openness with adoptive families reported better psychological outcomes with "lower levels of grief, regret, and worry, and higher levels of relief and peace with the adoption decision, than do other birth mothers" (Cushman et al., 1997, p. 17). Additionally, positive effects on the well-being of first mothers was associated with being able to participate in selecting adoptive parents for their children (Cushman et al., 1997; Henney, Ayers-Lopez, McRoy, & Grotevant, 2007), a practice rarely possible in international adoption and involuntary placements (termination of parental rights). Although some samples represented transracial adoptions (e.g., Ge et al., 2008) in brief, the results that were reported did not address racial or cultural issues just as most studies on birth parents' outcomes and adjustment do not use samples of birth parents of color or birth parents from abroad. In cases of involuntary placement (in which parental rights have been terminated), ongoing contact between first families and their children after placement in foster care or adoptive families is virtually absent in practice and from the literature. Although multiple studies have been performed with respect to the benefits and potential complications of open adoption, almost none have focused on racial composition of the birth parent sample and the role of race in placement planning.

Along with openness, reunion has been shown to have positive effects on the well-being of first parents. According to a study by Field (1992), those who had not yet achieved reunion show markedly more negative affect and poorer levels of psychological well-being. Few birth parents that have placed internationally have had the option or ability to attempt reunification, and therefore have not been afforded the positive benefits of the experience (Roby & Matsumura, 2002).

**CASE ILLUSTRATION**

Elena is a 23-year old woman who lives in an urban area in the Eastern United States. Her parents are from Mexico; she is the oldest child of four, and first-generation born in the United States. Elena was diagnosed with moderate depression at 20 years old, for which she was placed on antidepressants; she also has a history of panic attacks. Three weeks ago, Elena placed her newborn daughter, Katie, in an open adoption with a white, heterosexual, upper-middle-class couple who resides in a different state. Elena's boyfriend is living several hours

**CASE ILLUSTRATION** (CONTINUED)

away from where she currently is living with her parents. Elena was employed in a small, family-owned business at the beginning of her pregnancy, but she was let go when she missed too many days of work because of her extreme morning sickness. Although she now lives with her parents, neither her mother nor her father are emotionally supportive of her. Her father rejected her early in her pregnancy based on his conservative religious views. Her mother disagrees with Elena's decision to place the baby for adoption. Elena's panic attacks have returned, and her mood seems to have plummeted since Katie's birth. In fact, Elena lacks the energy and interest in seeing a doctor for help.

### Case Discussion

One of the greatest helps to Elena would be follow-up contact by her placing agency. She should be screened for PPD and given an appropriate referral to a medical doctor. A medical exam would be especially important because Elena was instructed to stop taking her antidepressants as soon as she found out that she was pregnant, and she may need assistance with resuming her medication. She could be concerned about whether Katie inherited a predisposition to depression. Many other factors may be negatively affecting Elena. Although her mental health issues predated her pregnancy, her current state might be a result of her preexisting conditions combined with some postrelinquishment reactions that are common to birth parents. She may be experiencing the feelings of guilt, shame, failure, and rejection that many birth parents encounter; these feelings often are compounded by general society's negative attitude toward relinquishment. These emotions may be magnified by a sense of betrayal of her own racial identity and heritage because the placement of Katie with a non-Hispanic couple. She may be concerned over how matters of race and cultural identity will be handled by the adoptive parents. Her placing agency should help her to assert her wishes about maintaining a connection with Katie's birth heritage through letters and other contact with the adoptive parents. Elena's panic attacks may have returned as a result of feelings of a loss of control during a crucial period of her life. It is important that she express any unaddressed feelings of coercion or disempowerment that she experienced during her pregnancy, and the birth, adoption planning, and relinquishment of Katie, as well as in her relationship with the adoptive parents.

## PRACTICE AND POLICY HIGHLIGHTS

- Clinicians must seek education and training to adequately understand the impact of multiple oppressions experienced by transracial and international adoptees, including adoption stigma as well as racial and ethnic discrimination.
- The gains and losses inherent in adoption must be acknowledged and addressed in therapy to appropriately treat adoptees, adoptive parents, and birth parents.
- Clinicians must carefully navigate the boundary between adequately acknowledging adoption and dismissing adoption impact.
- Mental health professionals must be able to identify risk factors that may lead to stress in adoptive parents.
- Clinicians must be prepared to address racial, ethnic, and cultural issues that will affect transracial adoptive families.
- Effective clinical treatment opportunities for foreign birth parents and birth parents of color must be developed and made widely available both domestically and internationally.
- Clinicians must be trained to work effectively with parents considering relinquishment or coping with termination of parental rights.
- The overrepresentation of adoptees in mental health settings must be addressed through improved adoption competence among all clinicians.

## CONCLUSION

We hope that mental health professionals will be able to use the information in this chapter to better inform and familiarize themselves with the mental health issues that may directly affect adoption stakeholders to better provide services and counseling to this important and often-overlooked group of individuals. Problems arise when mental health professionals are not adoption knowledgeable but still provide services to adoptees, adoptive parents, and birth parents (Brabender & Fallon, 2013). This may occur because adoption is often minimized or ignored in mental health settings or is overemphasized and associated with pathology (Bonovitz, 2006). As a result, adoption triad members often struggle to find an adoption-competent mental health professional. Riley (2009) reported that some adoptive parents sought help from up to ten different therapists before finding a counselor who understood adoption-related issues and the needs of an adoptive family. It is essential that more mental health professionals become knowledgeable and competent in adoption-related issues to ensure that they are providing the best possible treatment and services to adoptive parents and their families.

When working with the adoption kinship network, mental health professionals will need to be aware of their own preexisting biases and beliefs about adoptive parents, other members of the adoption triad, and adoption itself. If mental health professionals are not cognizant of their own internal schemas surrounding adoption, they may continue to perpetuate a long history of stigma that members of the adoption triad may have encountered throughout their life, making treatment ineffective and potentially harmful. The messages that mental health professionals send to all members of the adoption triad are extremely powerful and have significant long-lasting effects on the client.

A few of the most salient themes present in the literature regarding the adoption triad were examined in this chapter, including identity, mental health, attachment, preadoptive and preplacement history, relinquishment, and adjustment. The literature has shown that international and transracial adoptees generally do well in these various areas but that adoptive parents and birth parents of color (including birth parents from abroad) must receive more empirical attention to better understand the impact of culture, race, power, privilege, and other disparities on their mental health. Exploring the implications behind these findings and excavating confounding variables will help to arrive at a more accurate understanding of the scholarship that exists and the issues for which additional attention can be paid. Many areas of the literature yielded inconclusive or conflicting results. Future research will be needed to reach a more valid consensus regarding the impact of intercountry and transracial adoption on adoptees, first parents, and adoptive parents.

As this review of the literature on mental health issues for transracial and intercountry adoptees reflects, much more research is needed to address several areas. We recommend that scholars, practitioners, and training programs work to address several areas needing more attention.

1. Develop clinical applications based on theory that are specifically designed to effectively treat adoption-related mental health issues for all adoption stakeholders, including those affected by transracial or international adoption.
2. Conduct rigorous research to develop evidence-based best practices in the treatment of mental health issues that have been developed and specifically validated with transracial and international adoptees, birth parents, and adoptive parents.
3. Develop and implement comprehensive adoption-competency training programs for clinical practitioners-in-training and all clinical practitioners, including education and awareness training regarding attitudes and judgments about adoption that contribute to the stigma that accompanies adoption.
4. Design and implement empirical research that more effectively and fully accounts for and identifies the racial, cultural, and other disparities that are hallmarks of transracial and international adoption.
5. Conduct research with birth families of color and international birth families whose children were adopted transracially or internationally to best understand the mental health issues that affect them.

**DISCUSSION QUESTIONS**

1. How might you utilize a cultural humility approach when working with transracially adopted adolescents who are depressed because they don't feel like they fit in with their adoptive families or their fellow peers?
2. What sort of biases or countertransference might you have when working with adoptees? How would this affect the relationship with your clients?
3. As a mental health professional, what might you discuss with adoptive parents who do not see the benefit of exposing their internationally adopted children to the children's birth cultures?
4. How would you help adoptive parents incorporate their children's birth culture into the family system's values and traditions?
5. How might you help an adoptive mother who is experiencing common postadoption symptoms of depression, including physical complaints, social difficulties, and increased stress from parenting?

6. What are some cultural considerations when working on mental health issues with birth parents involved in domestic transracial adoption?
7. What system changes might be put into place to more effectively support the mental health of birth parents involved in international adoption?
8. In what ways might the mental health concerns of birth parents involved in international adoption differ from those involved in transracial domestic adoption? How might they be similar?

**RESOURCES**

Child Welfare Information Gateway. This is the direct link to a list of organizations/coalitions by state for both adoptees and adopters. https://www.childwelfare.gov/pubs/reslist/rl_dsp.cfm?rs_id=32&rate_chno=W-00113

Donaldson Adoption Institute. Great resource with free adoption publications for adoptive families covering a wide range of topics, including adoption from foster care, international adoption, adoption best practices, support for gays and lesbians who adopt, etc. Sign-up for their free newsletter on adoption, as well as check out the events page for adoption events. http://adoptioninstitute.org/

Light of Day Stories. This website provides stories of transracial adoptees and their experiences. Adoptees are able to communicate with one another through a discussion format. http://lightofdaystories.com/tag/transracial-adoptees/

National Resource Center for Permanency and Family Connections. This service of the Children's Bureau provides training, technical assistance, and information services regarding a variety of permanency issues, including the topic of birth family support and education. http://www.hunter.cuny.edu/socwork/nrcfcpp/info_services/birth-family-issues.html

NCFA Adoption Counseling Program—Pregnancy Counseling Training. Online pregnancy options counseling training. https://www.adoptioncouncil.org/adoption-professionals/training

On Your Feet Foundation. Dedicated to empowering birth mothers of adopted children. With physical locations in Northern California and Illinois. www.oyf.org

Pact, An Adoption Alliance. This organization has information and resources for everyone in the adoption triad. They also host events and have a forum where people can communicate with one another. http://www.pactadopt.org/adoptees/resources.html

U.S. Department of Health & Human Services: Administration for Children & Families: Child Welfare Information Gateway—National Foster Care & Adoption Directory Search. Find adoption resources by state, including public and private adoption agencies, adoption and foster care support groups, birth family and adoptee search support groups, and information on how to access adoption records. https://www.childwelfare.gov/nfcad/

U.S. Department of Health & Human Services: Administration for Children & Families: Child Welfare Information Gateway—National Foster Care & Adoption Directory Search. Resource list for transracial adoptive families compiled by U.S. Department of Health & Human Services. https://www.childwelfare.gov/adoption/types/families/trans_info.cfm

U.S. Department of Health & Human Services: Administration for Children & Families: Child Welfare Information Gateway—National Foster Care & Adoption Directory Search. Training opportunities for adoptive parents on topics such as helping deal with loss and brief, how to talk about adoption, and transracial parenting. https://www.childwelfare.gov/adoption/adopt_parenting/training.cfm

### REFERENCES

Baden, A. L., Gibbons, J. L., Wilson, S. L., & McGinnis, H. (2013). International adoption: Counseling and the adoption triad. *Adoption Quarterly, 16*(3/4), 218–237. doi:10.1080/10926755.2013.794440

Baden, A. L., Treweeke, L. M., & Ahluwahlia, M. K. (2012). Reclaiming culture: Reculturation of transracial and international adoptees. *Journal of Counseling & Development, 90*(4), 387–399.

Basow, S.A., Lilley, E., Bookwala, J., & McGillicuddy–DeLisi, A. (2008). Identity development and psychological well-being in Korean-born adoptees in the U.S. *American Journal of Orthopsychiatry, 78*(4), 473–480.

Bird, G. W., Peterson, R., & Miller, S. H. (2002). Factors associated with distress among support-seeking adoptive parents. *Family Relations, 51*(3), 215–220. Retrieved from http://search.proquest.com/docview/213934082?accountid=12536

Bonovitz, C. (2006). Unconscious communication and the transmission of loss. In K. Hushion, S. Sherman, & D. Siskind (Eds.), *Understanding adoption:*

*Clinical work with adults, children, and parents* (pp. 11–34). Lanham, MD: Jason Aronson.

Brabender, V. M., & Fallon, A. E. (Eds.). (2009). *Working with adoptive parents: Research, theory, and therapeutic interventions.* Hoboken, NJ: Wiley & Sons.

Brodzinsky, D. M., Radice, C., Huffman, L., & Merkler, K. (1987). Prevalence of clinically significant symptomatology in a nonclinical sample of adopted and nonadopted children. *Journal of Clinical Child Psychology, 16*(4), 350–356. doi:10.1207/s15374424jccp1604_9

Bronfenbrenner, U. (1994). Ecological models of human development. In *International Encyclopedia of Education, 3*(2), 37–43.

Bureau, J. F., Easterbrooks, M. A., & Lyons-Ruth, K. (2009). Maternal depressive symptoms in infancy: Unique contribution to children's depressive symptoms in childhood and adolescence? *Developmental & Psychopathology, 21,* 519–537.

Butler-Sweet, C. (2011). "A healthy black identity" transracial adoption, middle-class families, and racial socialization. *Journal of Comparative Family Studies, 42*(2), 193–212.

Campbell, S. B., Morgan-Lopez, A. A., Cox, M. J., & McLoyd, V. C. (2009). A latent class analysis of maternal depressive symptoms over 12 years and offspring adjustment in adolescence. *Journal of Abnormal Psychology, 118,* 479–493.

Cederblad, M., Höök, B., Irhammar, M., & Mercke, A. (1999). Mental health in international adoptees as teenagers and young adults. An epidemiological study. *Journal of Child Psychology and Psychiatry, 40*(8), 1239–1248. doi:10.1111/1469-7610.00540

Chisholm, K. (1998). A three year follow-up of attachment and indiscriminate friendliness in children adopted from Romanian orphanages. *Child Development, 69*(4), 1092–1106. doi:10.2307/1132364

Christian, C. L., McRoy, R. G., Grotevant, H. D., & Bryant, C. M. (1997). Grief resolution of birthmothers in confidential, time-limited mediated, ongoing mediated, and fully disclosed adoptions. *Adoption Quarterly, 1*(2), 35–58.

Cicchini, M. (1993). *The development of responsibility: The experience of birth fathers in adoption.* Sydney, New South Wales, Australia: Adoption Research and Counseling Services.

Clifton, J. (2012). Birth fathers and their adopted children. *Adoption & Fostering, 36*(2), 43–56.

Cohen, N. J., & Farnia, F. (2011). Children adopted from China: Attachment security two years later. *Children and Youth Services Review, 33*(11), 2342–2346. doi:10.1016/j.childyouth.2011.08.006

Crnic, K., & Low, C. (2002). Everyday stresses and parenting. In M Bornstein (Ed.), *Handbook of parenting: Vol. 5 Practical issues in parenting* (2nd ed., pp. 243–267). Hillsdale, NJ: Erlbaum.

Cubito, D. S., & Brandon, K. O. (2000). Psychological adjustment in adult adoptees: Assessment of distress, depression, and anger. *American Journal of Orthopsychiatry, 70*(3), 408–413. doi:10.1037/h0087856

Cudmore, L. (2005). Becoming parents in the context of loss. *Sexual and Relationship Therapy, 20,* 299–308.

Curtis, R., & Pearson, F. (2010). Contact with birth parents: Differential psychological adjustment for adults adopted as infants. *Journal of Social Work, 10*(4), 347–367.

Cushman, L. F., Kalmuss, D. D., & Namerow, P. B. (1997). Openness in adoption: Experiences and social psychological outcomes among birth mothers. *Marriage & Family Review, 25*(1/2), 7–18.

Davies, M. (2011). Intercountry adoption, children's rights and the politics of rescue. *Adoption and Fostering, 35*(4), 50–62.

DeSimone, M. (1996). Birth mother loss: Contributing factors to unresolved grief. *Clinical Social Work Journal, 24*(1), 65–76.

Eack, S. M., & Newill, C. E. (2012). Racial disparities in mental health outcomes after psychiatric hospital discharge among individuals with severe mental illness. *Social Work Research, 36*(1), 41–52. doi:10.1093/swr/svs014

Edelmann, R. J., & Connolly, K. J. (1986). Psychological aspects of infertility. *British Journal of Medical Psychology, 59,* 209–219.

Evan B. Donaldson Institute. (2007). *Safeguarding the rights and well-being of birthparents in the adoption process* (Monograph). New York: Author.

Feigelman, W. (2000). Adjustments of transracially and inracially adopted young adults. *Child and Adolescent Social Work Journal, 17*(3), 165–183.

Feigelman, W. (2001). Comparing adolescents in diverging family structures: Investigating whether adoptees are more prone to problems than their non-adopted peers. *Adoption Quarterly, 5*(2), 5–36. doi:10.1300/J145v05n02_02

Feigelman, W. (2005). Are adoptees at increased risk for attempting suicide? *Suicide and Life-Threatening Behavior, 35*(2), 206–216. doi:10.1521/suli.35.2.206.62873

Fernando, S. (2012). Race and culture issues in mental health and some thoughts on ethnic identity. *Counselling Psychology Quarterly, 25*(2), 113–123. doi:10.1080/09515070.2012.674299

Field, J. (1992). Psychological adjustment of relinquishing mothers before and after reunion with their children. *Australian and New Zealand Journal of Psychiatry, 26*(2), 232–241.

Fisher, L., Ames, E. W., Chisholm, K., & Savoie, L. (1997). Problems reported by parents of Romanian orphans adopted to British Columbia. *International Journal of Behavioral Development, 20*(1), 67–82. doi:10.1080/016502597385441

Fontenot, H. B. (2007). Transition and adaptation to adoptive motherhood. *Journal of Obstetric, Gynecologic, and Neonatal Nursing, 36,* 175–182.

Freundlich, M. (2007). Research contributions: Strengthening services for members of the adoption triad. In R. A. Javier, A. L. Baden, F. A. Biafora, A. Camacho-Gingerich (Eds.), *Handbook of adoption: Implications for researchers, practitioners, and families* (pp. 327–347). Thousand Oaks, CA: Sage.

Gair, S. (1999). Distress and depression in new motherhood: Research with adoptive mothers highlights important contributing factors. *Child and Family Social Work, 4,* 55–66.

Garb, H. (1997). Race bias, social class bias, and gender bias in clinical judgment. *Clinical Psychology-Science and Practice, 4*(2), 99–120.

Gavin, N. I., Gaynes, B. N., Lohr, K. N., Meltzer-Brody, S., Gartlehner, G., & Swinson, T. (2005). *Obstetrics & Gynecology, 106,* 1071–1083.

Ge, X., Natsuaki, M., Martin, D., Leve, L., Neiderhiser, J., Shaw, D., Villareal, G., Scaramella, L., Reid, J. B., & Reiss, D. (2008). Bridging the divide: Openness in adoption and postadoption psychosocial adjustment among birth and adoptive parents. *Journal of Family Psychology, 22*(4), 529–540.

Gjerdingen, D. K., & Froberg, D. (1991). The fourth stage of labor: The health of birth mothers and adoptive mothers at 6 weeks postpartum. *Family Medicine, 23,* 29–35.

Glidden, L. M. (2000). Adopting children with developmental disabilities: A long-term perspective. *Family Relations, 49,* 397–405.

Goldberg, A. E., Smith J. Z., & Kashy, D. A. (2010). Preadoptive factors predicting lesbian, gay, and heterosexual couples' relationship quality across the transition to adoptive parenthood. *Journal of Family Psychology, 24,* 221–232.

Greer, T. M. (2011). Coping strategies as moderators of the relationship between race- and gender-based discrimination and psychological symptoms for African American women. *Journal of Black Psychology, 37*(1), 42–54. doi:10.1177/0095798410380202

Grotevant, H. D., & McRoy, R. G. (1998). *Openness in adoption: Exploring family connections.* Thousand Oaks, CA: Sage.

Harwood, R., Feng, X., & Yu, S. (2013). Preadoption adversities and postadoption mediators of mental health and school outcomes among international, foster, and private adoptees in the United States. *Journal of Family Psychology, 27*(3), 409–420. doi:10.1037/a0032908

Hay, D. F., Pawlby, S., Waters, C. S., & Sharp, D. (2008). Antepartum and postpartum exposure to maternal depression: Different effects on different adolescent outcomes. *Journal of Child Psychology & Psychiatry, 49*, 1079–1088.

Henney, S., Ayers-Lopez, S., McRoy, R., & Grotevant, H. (2007). Evolution and resolution: Birthmother's experience of grief and loss at different levels of adoption openness. *Journal of Social & Personal Relationships, 24*(6), 875–889.

Hjern, A., Lindblad, F., & Vinnerljung, B. (2002). Suicide, psychiatric illness, and social maladjustment in intercountry adoptees in Sweden: A cohort study. *The Lancet, 360*(9331), 443–448. doi:10.1016/S0140-6736(02)09674-5

Hoksbergen, R. C., ter Laak, J. J., van Dijkum, C. C., Rijk, S. S., Rijk, K. K., & Stoutjesdijk, F. F. (2003). Posttraumatic stress disorder in adopted children from Romania. *American Journal of Orthopsychiatry, 73*(3), 255–265. doi:10.1037/0002-9432.73.3.255

Hussey, D. L., Falletta, L., & Eng, A. (2012). Risk factors for mental health diagnoses among children adopted from the public child welfare system. *Children and Youth Services Review, 34*(10), 2072–2080. doi:10.1016/j.childyouth.2012.06.015

Irhammar, M., & Bengtsson, H. (2004). Attachment in a group of adult international adoptees. *Adoption Quarterly, 8*(2), 1–25. doi:10.1300/J145v08n02_01

Johnson, K., Banghan, H., & Liyao, W. (1998). Infant abandonment and adoption in China. *Population and Development Review, 24*(3), 469–510. doi:10.2307/2808152

Jones, M. B. (2000). *Birthmothers: Women who have relinquished babies for adoption tell their stories.* Lincoln, NE: iUniverse.com, Inc.

Judge, S. (2003). Determinants of parental stress in families adopting children from Eastern Europe. *Family Relations, 52*, 241–248.

Juffer, F., & van IJzendoorn, M. H. (2007). Adoptees do not lack self-esteem: A meta-analysis of studies on self-esteem of transracial, international, and domestic adoptees. *Psychological Bulletin, 133*(6), 1067–1083. doi:10.1037/0033-2909.133.6.1067

Keyes, M. A., Sharma, A., Elkins, I. J., Iacono, W. G., & McGue, M. (2008). The mental health of US adolescents adopted in infancy. *Archives of Pediatric and Adolescent Medicine, 162*(5), 419–425.

Kim, M. (2014). Racial/ethnic disparities in depression and its theoretical perspectives. *Psychiatric Quarterly, 85*(1), 1–8. doi:10.1007/s11126-013-9265-3

Knott, T., & Donovan, K. (2010). Disproportionate representation of African-American children in foster care: Secondary analysis of the National Child Abuse and Neglect Data System, 2005. *Children and Youth Services Review, 32*(5), 679–684.

Krusiewicz, E. S., & Wood, T. J. (2001). "He was our child from the moment we walked in that room": Entrance stories of adoptive parents. *Journal of Social and Personal Relationships, 18,* 785–803.

Lazarus, C., Evans, J. N., Glidden, L. M., & Flaherty, E. M. (2002). Transracial adoption of children with development disabilities: A focus on parental and family adjustment. *Adoption Quarterly, 6,* 7–24.

Leve, L. D., Scaramella, L. F., & Fagot, B. L. (2001). Infant temperament, pleasure in parenting, and marital happiness in adoptive families. *Infant Mental Health Journal, 22,* 545–558.

Levy-Shiff, R. (2001). Psychological adjustment of adoptees in adulthood: Family environment and adoption-related correlates. *International Journal of Behavioral Development, 25*(2), 97–104. doi:10.1080/01650250042000131

Levy-Shiff, R., Bar, O., & Har-Even, D. (1990). Psychological adjustment of adoptive parents-to-be. *American Journal of Orthopsychiatry, 60,* 258–267.

Lindblad, F., Weitoft, G., & Hjern, A. (2010). ADHD in international adoptees: A national cohort study. *European Child & Adolescent Psychiatry, 19*(1), 37–44. doi:10.1007/s00787-009-0038-3

Logan, J. (1996). Birth mothers and their mental health: Uncharted territory. *British Journal of Social Work, 26*(5), 609–625.

Mainemer, H., Gilman, L. C., & Ames, E. W. (1998). Parenting stress in families adopting children from Romanian orphanages. *Journal of Family Issues, 19,* 164–180.

Maslow, A. H. (1943). A theory of human motivation. *Psychological Review, 50*(4), 370–396.

Mathews, A. M., & Mathews, R. (1986). Perspective on the social psychology of infertility and involuntary childlessness. *Family Relations, 35,* 479–487.

McCarty, C., Waterman, J., Burge, D., & Edelstein, S. B. (1999). Experiences, concerns, and service needs of families adopting children with prenatal substance exposure: Summary and recommendations. *Child Welfare, 78,* 561–577.

McGinnis, H., Smith, S. L., Ryan, S., & Howard, J. A. (2009). *Beyond culture camp: Promoting healthy identity formation in adoption.* New York: Evan B. Donaldson Adoption Institute.

McGlone, K., Santos, L., Kazama, L., Fong, R., & Mueller, C. (2002). Psychological stress in adoptive parents of special-needs children. *Child Welfare, 81,* 151–171.

McKay, K., Ross, L. E., & Goldberg, A. E. (2010). Adaptation to parenthood during the post-adoption period: A review of the literature, *Adoption Quarterly, 13,* 125–144.

Menning, B. E. (1980). The emotional needs of infertile couples. *Fertility and Sterility, 34,* 313–319.

Miall, C. E. (1994). Community constructs of involuntary childlessness: Sympathy, stigma, and social support. *Canadian Review of Sociology & Anthropology, 31,* 392–421.

Miller, B. C., Fan, X., Grotevant, H. D., Christensen, M., Coyl, D., & van Dulmen, M. (2000). Adopted adolescents' overrepresentation in mental health counseling: Adoptees' problems or parents' lower threshold for referral? *Journal of the American Academy of Child & Adolescent Psychiatry, 39*(12), 1504–1511. doi:10.1097/00004583-2

Mohanty, J., & Newhill, C.E. (2011). Asian adolescent and young adult adoptees' psychological well-being: Examining the mediating role of marginality. *Children and Youth Services Review, 33,* 1189–1195.

Mott, S. L., Schiller, C. E., Richards, J. G., O'Hara, M. W., & Stuart, S. (2011). Depression and anxiety among postpartum and adoptive mothers. *Archives of Women's Mental Health, 14,* 335–343.

Neil, E. (2013). The mental distress of the birth relatives of adopted children: "Disease" or "unease"? Findings from a UK study. *Health & Social Care in the Community, 21*(2), 191–199. doi:10.1111/hsc.12003

Niemann, S., & Weiss, S. (2012). Factors affecting attachment in international adoptees at 6 months post adoption. *Children and Youth Services Review, 34*(1), 205–212. doi:10.1016/j.childyouth.2011.10.001

O'Connor, T. G., Rutter, M., Beckett, C., Keaveney, L., & Kreppner, J. M. (2000). The effects of global severe privation on cognitive competence: Extension and longitudinal follow-up. *Child Development, 71*(2), 376–390. doi:10.1111/1467-8624.00151

O'Hara, M. W., & Swain, A.M. (1996). Rates and risk of postpartum depression—a meta-analysis. *International Review of Psychiatry, 8,* 37–54.

Oyserman, D., Mowbray, C. T., Meares, P., & Firminger, K. B. (2000). Parenting among mothers with a serious mental illness. *American Journal of Orthopsychiatry, 70*(3), 296–315. doi:10.1037/h0087733

Passmore, N. L., Feeney, J. A., Peterson, C. C., & Shimmaki, K. (2006). Depression, emotional arousability, and perceptions of parenting in adult adoptees and non-adoptees. *Adoption Quarterly, 9*(2–3), 23–35. doi:10.1300/J145v09n02_02

Peters, B. R., Atkins, M. S., & McKay, M. (1999). Adopted children's behavior problems: A review of five explanatory models. *Clinical Psychology Review, 19*(3), 297–328. doi:10.1016/S0272-7358(98)00028-2

Reynoso-Vallejo, H. (2009). Support group for Latino caregivers of dementia elders: Cultural humility and cultural competence. *Ageing International, 34* (1–2), 67–78. doi:http://dx.doi.org/10.1007/s12126-009-9031-x

Riley, D. (2009). Training mental health professionals to be adoption competent. *Policy & Practice, 67,* 33–44.

Roby, J., & Matsumura, S. (2002). If I give you my child, aren't we family? A study of birthmothers participating in Marshall Islands-U.S. adoptions. *Adoption Quarterly, 5*(4), 7–31.

Sanchez-Sandoval, Y., & Palacios, J. (2012). Stress in adoptive parents of adolescents. *Children and Youth Services Review, 34,* 1283–1289.

Schofield, G., Moldestad, B., Höjer, I., Ward, E., Skilbred, D., Young, J., & Havik, T. (2011). Managing loss and a threatened identity: Experiences of parents of children growing up in foster care, the perspectives of their social workers and implications for practice. *British Journal of Social Work, 41*(1), 74–92.

Seibel, M. M., & Taymor, M. L. (1982). Emotional aspects of infertility. *Fertility and Sterility, 37,* 137–145.

Senecky, Y., Agassi, H., Inbar, D., Hoersh, N., Diamond, G., Bergman, Y. S., et al. (2009). Post-adoption depression among adoptive mothers. *Journal of Affective Disorders, 115,* 62–68.

Slap, G., Goodman, E., & Huang, B. (2001). Adoption as a risk factor for attempted suicide during adolescence. *Pediatrics, 108*(2), 1–8.

Smit, E. M. (2010). International adoption families: A unique health care journey. *Pediatric Nursing, 36,* 253–258.

Sokol, J. T. (2009). Identity development throughout the lifetime: An examination of Eriksonian theory. *Graduate Journal of Counseling Psychology, 1*(2), 1–11.

South, S. C., Foli, K. J., & Lim, E. (2012). Predictors of relationship satisfaction in adoptive mothers. *Journal of Social and Personal Relationships, 30*, 545–563.

Tan, T., & Marn, T. (2013). Mental health service utilization in children adopted from US foster care, US private agencies and foreign countries: Data from the 2007 National Survey of Adoption Parents (NSAP). *Children and Youth Services Review, 35*(7), 1050–1054. doi:10.1016/j.childyouth.2013.04.02000012000-00011.

Tervalon, M., & Murray-Garcia, J. (1998). Cultural humility versus cultural competence: A critical distinction in defining physician training outcomes in multicultural education. *Journal of Health Care for the Poor and Underserved, 9*(2), 117–125. Retrieved from http://search.proquest.com/docview/220583378?accountid=12536

Tieman, W., van der Ende, J., & Verhulst, F. C. (2005). Psychiatric disorders in young adult intercountry adoptees: An epidemiological study. *American Journal of Psychiatry, 162*(3), 592–598. doi:10.1176/appi.ajp.162.3.592

Tieman, W., van der Ende, J., & Verhulst, F. C. (2006). Social functioning of young adult intercountry adoptees compared to nonadoptees. *Social Psychiatry and Psychiatric Epidemiology, 41*(1), 68–74. doi:10.1007/s00127-005-0995-x

Triseliotis, J., Feast, J., and Kyle, F. (2005). *The adoption triangle revisited*. London: BAAF.

van den Dries, L., Juffer, F., van IJzendoorn, M. H., & Bakermans-Kranenburg, M. J. (2009). Fostering security? A meta-analysis of attachment in adopted children. *Children and Youth Services Review, 31*(3), 410–421. doi:10.1016/j.childyouth.2008.09.008

van Londen, W., Juffer, F., & van IJzendoorn, M. H. (2007). Attachment, cognitive, and motor development in adopted children: Short-term outcomes after international adoption. *Journal of Pediatric Psychology, 32*(10), 1249–1258. doi:10.1093/jpepsy/jsm062

Vandivere, S., Malm, K., and Radel, L. (2009). Adoption USA: A chartbook based on the 2007 National Survey of Adoptive Parents. Washington, DC: U.S. Department of Health and Human Services, Office of the Assistant Secretary for Planning and Evaluation.

von Borczyskowski, A., Hjern, A., Lindblad, F., & Vinnerljung, B. (2006). Suicidal behaviour in national and international adult adoptees: A Swedish cohort study. *Social Psychiatry and Psychiatric Epidemiology, 41*(2), 95–102. doi:10.1007/s00127-005-0974-2

Wegar, K. (1995). Adoption and mental health: A theoretical critique of the psychopathological model. *American Journal of Orthopsychiatry, 65,* 540–548.

Weitzman, C. (2003). Developmental assessment of the internationally adopted child: Challenges and rewards. *Clinical Child Psychology and Psychiatry, 8*(3), 303–313. doi:10.1177/1359104503008003002

Wenzel, A. (2011). *Anxiety in childbearing women: Diagnosis and treatment.* Washington, DC: APA Press.

Westhues, A., & Cohen, J. S. (1998). Ethnic and racial identity of internationally adopted adolescents and young adults. *Adoption Quarterly, 1*(4), 33–55.

Wiley, M., & Baden, A. (2005). Birth parents in adoption: Research, practice, and counseling psychology. *Counseling Psychologist, 33*(1), 13–50.

# 8

# Medical Issues

▸ DANA E. JOHNSON AND JUDITH K. ECKERLE

THROUGHOUT HUMAN HISTORY, loss of parental nurture and protection through death or abandonment placed a child's survival at immediate risk. Standing in stark contrast to other options, the elevation of an abandoned or orphaned child to a position indistinguishable from a birth child within a family through formal or informal adoption was the superior mode of ensuring survival and well-being in a harsh world. Adoption, however, sometimes came with a price: the loss of the child's cultural, ethnic, and racial ties.

In the twenty-first century, adoption is broadly accepted and an important part of our shared cultural experience in the United States. The U.S. National Foster Care Adoption Attitudes Survey revealed that almost three-fourths of respondents were at least somewhat familiar with adoption and that two-thirds or more had a favorable to extremely favorable opinion of intercountry, private, or foster care adoption. About 40 percent of respondents reported that a family member or close friend had been adopted (Dave Thomas Foundation, 2013). Numerically, adoption is an important way in which families are built in the United States. More than 1.5 million adopted children, about one of every forty children less than 18 years of age, were living in families in 2010. If one includes stepchildren, one in fifteen children have a relationship with an adoptive parent (Kreider & Lofquist, 2014).

## EVOLUTION OF TRANSRACIAL DOMESTIC AND INTERCOUNTRY ADOPTION IN THE UNITED STATES

Diversity is a central characteristic of contemporary adoption in the United States. On the basis of the 2007 National Survey of Adoptive Parents, 40 percent of adopted children were involved in a transracial, transethnic, or transcultural adoption (Vandivere, Malm, & Radel, 2009). In 2009–2011, almost 438,000 transracially adopted children, 28 percent of all adopted children under 18 years of age, lived within homes in the United States (Kreider & Lofquist, 2014). Although informal adoption has a centuries-long tradition in the United States and a legal foundation for adoption has existed since 1851 (Herman, 2012f), because of the historical stringent racial boundaries in the United States, transracial domestic and intercountry adoption entered the mainstream only after the humanitarian tragedies of the mid-twentieth century and changes in attitudes toward race following World War II.

### Transracial Domestic Adoption

The first recorded transracial adoption of an African American child by a Caucasian family in Minnesota, took place in 1948 (Herman, 2012h). However, organized activity in North America to promote transracial adoption dates to 1960 when the Open Door Society in Montreal, Quebec, attempted to place black children in same-race homes but recruited white families if these efforts failed. A similar organization, Parents to Adopt Minority Youngsters, was founded in Minnesota in 1961. Because children of color always have been disproportionately represented in foster care, additional agencies began transracial placement in situations in which same-race homes were unavailable (Simon, 2006). Further breakdown of racial barriers during the sixties increased interest in transracial adoption and during 1971, 2,574 black children were adopted by white families in the United States (Simon, 2006). In 1972, concerned about a child's loss of racial and cultural identity, the National Association of Black Social Workers issued a strongly worded response against this growing trend of transracial adoption, affirming "the inviolable position of black children in black families where they belong physically, psychologically and culturally in order that they receive the total sense of themselves and develop a sound projection of their future" (Herman, 2012g, p. 1).

This organized opposition immediately decreased the number of transracial adoption of black children by white families to about 1,000 in 1973, down 71 percent from 1971 (Simon, 2006). Although the number of domestic transracial adoptions slowly increased from the 1973 nadir, the trajectory was to change again in the nineties when Congress enacted the Multiethnic Placement Act of 1994 as amended by the Interethnic Provisions of 1996, a federal civil rights law enacted to speed placement of children in foster care into permanent homes (Hollinger & The ABA Center on Children and the Law, 1998). This legislation prohibits using race, color, or national origin for decisions either delaying or denying a child in foster care of adoptive placement or for denying individuals the opportunity to become a foster or adoptive parent. States must be diligent in recruiting foster and adoptive parents who reflect the racial and ethnic diversity of the children who need homes. Following passage of that legislation, transracial adoptions from the public foster care system increased from 11 percent in 1995 to 15 percent in 2004 (Eschelbach Hansen & Simon, 2004).

### Intercountry Adoption

Children adopted internationally constitute 37 percent of transracially adopted children in the United States (Kreider & Lofquist, 2014). Following World War II, thousands of children who were orphaned, abandoned by their soldier-fathers, or separated from parents needed homes. Military personnel in the occupying forces were the first to step forward to bring these children into their families. Between 1948 and 1962, U.S. families adopted 1,845 German, 744 Austrian, and 2,987 Japanese children. Additional waves of adopted children arrived in the United States following subsequent conflicts, including the Greek Civil War (3,116 from 1948 to 1962), the Korean War (4,162 from 1953 to 1962) the Vietnam War (3,267 between 1963 and 1973), and the war in El Salvador (2,083 between 1980 and 1990; Alstein & Simon, 1991; Herman, 2012e).

Because of the growing shortfall of adoptable infants in the United States secondary to increasing availability of support for single parents as well as legal abortion, beginning in 1968, the number of children placed from abroad rose consistently (Alstein & Simon, 1991). Children from Central and South America, India, and the Philippines, as well as an increasing number of children from Korea, boosted the total number of intercountry adopted people to nearly 10,000 year by the mid-eighties. A sharp increase in intercountry adoptions during 1990–1995 accompanied the fall of Communism in Eastern Europe and the dissolution of the United Soviet Socialist Republic. Augmenting this rise was the liberalization of Chinese adoption policy in response to the rise in abandonment of infant girls secondary to strict population control measures. Although rates of adoption from Romania flared briefly in 1991 (2,594), the number of children adopted from Russia and China rose steadily during the ensuing decade. By 1995 Korea had been supplanted as the top-placing country, and in fiscal year (FY) 2003, China and Russia accounted for 56 percent of intercountry adoption placements in the United States. In 2004, a record number of 22,884 orphan visas were issued in the United States (U.S. Department of State, 2014c).

Since that peak, the total number of intercountry adoptions has decreased progressively (7,092 in FY 2013) back to levels comparable to the eighties. The reasons for this decline are complex and include implementation of the Hague Convention on Intercountry Adoption and the Intercountry Adoption Act, the recent recession, political tensions (e.g., Russia), more restrictive requirements for adoption (e.g., China), internal political turmoil (e.g., Ukraine), and emerging domestic adoption programs in many countries that once placed children abroad, as well as perceived or documented fraud and abuse within the system. For these and no doubt other reasons, the most recent U.S. National Foster Care Adoption Attitudes Survey showed that international adoption was not viewed as favorably as it had been in the past (Dave Thomas Foundation, 2013). Nevertheless, internationally adopted people account for a significant component of transracially adopted people in the United States. The U.S. Census Community Survey in 2009–2011 identified 244,869 children who were internationally adopted, a total of 16 percent of adopted children less than 18 years of age (Kreider & Lofquist, 2014).

The most recent data on the breakdown of transracial adoption in the United States comes from the 2007 National Survey of Adoptive Parents, which found that 27 percent of adoptions from foster care, 21 percent of private domestic adoptions, and 84 percent of intercountry adoptions were transracial. The growing number of transracial adoption over the past half-century appears to parallel the increase in approval of interracial marriages. In 2011, a Gallup poll reported that 86 percent of American (96 percent blacks, 84 percent whites) approved of black–white marriages, an increase from an overall approval rate of 4 percent in 1958. Although only 66 percent of surveyed individuals 65 years old or older sanctioned marriage between blacks and whites, 97 percent of 18- to 29-year-olds approved. If comparisons between approval of interracial marriage and adoption are valid, transracial adoptions likely will increase in the future.

### Medical Issues in Adoption

Despite the leadership role of prominent pediatricians at the turn of the twentieth century, such as Dwight Chapin, in supporting adoption as a means to decrease the extraordinarily high rates of infant mortality and morbidity within orphanages (Sherman, Aldrich, Bonar, Carr, & McCulloch, 1938), the discipline of pediatrics, until recently, has failed to appreciate the full range of issues faced by adoptive families and the special medical and development needs of children residing in or adopted from orphanage or foster care. As late as 2000, most standard textbooks on general pediatrics failed to even to mention the topic (Johnson, 2005). In the late eighties, investigators identified a high prevalence of medical problems in children adopted internationally that jeopardized not only the health of the child but also of the adoptive family and greater community (Hostetter, Iverson, Dole, & Johnson, 1989; Hostetter et al., 1991; Jenista, 1993; Jenista & Chapman, 1987; Lange, Kreider, & Warnock-Eckhart, 1987; Lange & Warnock-Eckhart, 1987; Lange, Warnock-Eckhart, & Bean, 1989). Following these reports, the American Academy of Pediatrics (AAP) published specific guidelines for postadoption screening for children from abroad (Committee on Infectious Diseases, 1994).

Over the ensuing 25 years, investigators focused considerable attention on adopted children spurred on not only by the surge in intercountry adoptions and the burgeoning population in foster care but also by rapidly increasing knowledge on the short- and long-term effects of early deprivation on child health and development.

## MEDICAL PROBLEMS AND RISK FACTORS IDENTIFIED IN POSTINSTITUTIONALIZED CHILDREN

- Growth impairment (Albers, Johnson, Hostetter, Iverson, & Miller, 1997; Johnson et al., 1992; Mason & Narad, 2005; Miller & Hendrie, 2000; Miller, Kiernan, Mathers, & Klein-Gitelman, 1995)
- High risk of prenatal alcohol exposure (Gronlund, Aring, Hellstrom, Landgren, & Stromland, 2004; Landgren, Svensson, Stromland, & Andersson Gronlund, 2010; Miller et al., 2009; Miller et al., 2006; Robert et al., 2009)
- Hearing and vision problems (Eckerle et al., 2014)
- Nutrient deficiencies (Fuglestad et al., 2013; Fuglestad et al., 2008; Gustafson, Eckerle, Howard, Andrews, & Polgreen, 2013)
- Developmental delays (Albers et al., 1997; Groze & Ileana, 1996; Johnson et al., 1992; Miller et al., 1995; Rutter, 1998)
- Sensory processing problems (Cermak & Daunhauer, 1997; Wilbarger, Gunnar, Schneider, & Pollak, 2010)
- Emotional and behavioral issues (Ames, 1997; Gunnar & van Dulmen, 2007; O'Connor & Rutter, 2000; O'Connor, Rutter, Beckett, Keaveney, & Kreppner, 2000; Rutter, 1999; Rutter, Kreppner, & O'Connor, 2001; Zeanah et al., 2009)

During the past decade, the AAP has taken a leadership role in educating child care practitioners in this area. *Fostering Health: Healthcare for Children and Adolescence in Foster Care* was published in 2005 (Task Force on Health Care for Children in Foster Care, 2005). The AAP Council on Foster Care, Adoption, and Kinship Care (COFCAKC) was formed in 2011 by merging the Section on Adoption and Foster Care (founded in 2000); relevant parts of the Committee on Early Childhood, Adoption, and Dependent Care; and the Task Force on Foster Care. This council generates policy, creates educational programming and resources, develops and promotes advocacy initiatives, and supports translation of policy and education into practice. In 2014, the AAP and COFCAKC published the first comprehensive overview of adoption for child health professionals *Adoption Medicine: Caring for Children and Families* (Mason, Johnson, & Albers Prock, 2014).

Adoption professionals also experienced a steep learning curve about the specific health needs of adopted children. In the mid-eighties, we queried long-standing and highly respected adoption agencies in our community about the wisdom of establishing an adoption medical clinic. One response was particularly illustrative of the prevailing view, "You won't get much business because all the kids we place from abroad are healthy." Although this viewpoint was no doubt heavily influenced by the high percentage of truly healthy Korean infants being placed at that time, once the long-term sequelae of severe deprivation were recognized in postinstitutionalized Romanian, Russian, and Chinese children in the early nineties, the notion that love and good food were sufficient for child well-being was discredited. Currently, education on medical and developmental issues is a mandatory component of preadoption education for most parents adopting internationally (U.S. Department of State, 2014b) and is incorporated into most training programs for parents adopting from foster care.

### Preadoption Contact with Adoptive Parents: The Preadoption Medical Review

Because health issues and health service utilization are of paramount concern for adoptive parents (Ames, 1997; Le Mare, Audet, & Kurytnik, 2007), families often consult with health care professionals before adoption about general health issues in children adopted from foster care or from abroad or may seek to understand the medical needs of a specific child referred to them for adoption. Discussions at this point in the adoption process prepare parents to more knowledgably ascertain whether their financial and emotional resources, social network, marriage, and family structure are in line with the likely needs of a particular child. The preadoption visit is also an opportunity for a health care provider to establish a relationship with the adoptive family that will ensure appropriate health care and guidance throughout childhood.

This is the time when a professional trained in adoption medicine plays a unique role. Once limited to guidance regarding common malformations, such as cleft lip and palate, or infectious diseases, such as hepatitis B, areas of knowledge have expanded dramatically over the past two decades to include interpreting medical terminology from various countries, ascertaining the short- and long-term effects of institutional rearing, and highlighting changing regional differences in medical risk. For example, heavy prenatal alcohol use historically has been high in Eastern Europe but is rising in other nations (e.g., South Korea) that are experiencing rapid Westernization (Lee, Shin, Won, Kim, & Oh, 2010).

The accuracy of medical and social information for children in the process of adoption varies widely depending on the quality of the medical system in the country of origin as well as the training, experience, and personal biases of the professionals responsible for collecting and reporting referral information. The experience of a medical professional trained in adoption medicine can help families accurately interpret the often-confusing referral information and realistically gauge whether additional information should or even could be obtained. For example, Korea has a medical system that is similar to the United States with medical information that is typically comprehensive, reliable, and up to date. Follow-up information as well as additional diagnostic testing is readily available. China has the potential for sophisticated medical care but significant regional variations exist in diagnostic capabilities. While procuring follow-up information or additional diagnostic testing is possible, the cost in time and money for the child's institution is often the limiting factor. Referrals from Eastern Europe frequently list a number of diagnostic terms that are used inaccurately and indiscriminately. In these cases, a provider's experience in discerning actual conditions from the multiple diagnoses that carry no weight in Western medicine is often critical in setting appropriate expectations for adoptive families.

A health care professional can play an important role in the preadoption process through nonjudgmental discussions regarding the families' motivations to adopt and by helping them understand whether their resources are sufficient to enable a child to navigate medically and culturally through their life course. It is important during the preadoption process for the family to develop an extended view of possible outcomes of their decision. Most families will research what it means to have a child with HIV before adoption but some might not realize the implications of the child's culture and race. Considering what it will mean to parent a transracial child, not only as a cute little infant, but also as a young student, a surly adolescent, and an independent young adult, is a parental exercise that health care professionals should support. Faced with sometimes-candid statements by adoptive parents about their comfort level in adopting children of certain racial backgrounds, we may not agree with their view but we need to help them engage in more self-reflection and assist them in knowing how their beliefs will intersect with the reality of raising a child who is transracially and transculturally adopted.

### Cultural Sensitivity and Awareness During Preadoption Counseling

Addressing the overall issue of cultural sensitivity and awareness in the delivery of health care, the American College of Obstetrics and Gynecology stated the following:

> Culture is defined as the dynamic and multidimensional context of many aspects of the life of an individual (Wells, 2000). It includes gender, faith, sexual orientation, profession, tastes, age, socioeconomic status, disability, ethnicity, and race. Cultural competency, or cultural awareness and sensitivity, is defined as, "the knowledge and interpersonal skills that allow providers to understand, appreciate, and work with individuals from cultures other than their own." It involves an awareness and acceptance of cultural differences, self awareness, knowledge of a patient's culture, and adaptation of skills. (ACOG Committee on Health Care for Underserved Women 2011, p. 1)

The cultural sensitivity and awareness checklist, designed to facilitate understanding and communication within health care settings, helps to operationalize the process of determining which cultural aspects surrounding adoption require awareness and sensitivity from health care professionals (Seibert, Stridh-Igo, & Zimmerman, 2002). Several items on this checklist are particularly relevant for providers as they begin relationships with parents choosing to build their family through adoption, including communication method and language barriers, cultural identification, beliefs, and health care provider bias.

## CULTURAL SENSITIVITY AND AWARENESS CHECKLIST

1. Communication method: Identify the patient's preferred method of communication.
2. Language barriers: Identify potential language barriers (verbal and nonverbal).
3. Cultural identification: Identify the patient's culture.
4. Comprehension: Double-check: Does the patient or family comprehend the situation at hand?
5. Beliefs: Identify religious and spiritual beliefs. Make appropriate support contacts.
6. Trust: Double-check: Does the patient or family appear to trust the caregivers? Remember to watch for both verbal and nonverbal cues.
7. Recovery: Does the patient or family have misconceptions or unrealistic views about the caregiver, treatment, or recovery process? Make necessary adjustments.
8. Diet: Address culture-specific dietary considerations.
9. Assessments: Conduct assessments with cultural sensitivity in mind. Watch for inaccuracies
10. Health care provider bias: We all have biases and prejudices. Examine and recognize yours.

### COMMUNICATION METHOD AND LANGUAGE BARRIER

Establishing our clinic in 1986, we chose the name Foreign-Born Adoption Clinic and then distributed promotional literature to adoption agencies in our community. Shortly after opening our doors, the clinic received a call from Marietta Spencer, a social worker at Children's Home Society of St. Paul, who had authored "The Terminology of Adoption" for The Child Welfare League of America (Herman, 2012b). She patiently explained that "foreign-born" carried negative connotations, whereas the term "international" was neutral. Her Positive Adoption Language, which later evolved into Respectful Adoption Language, included vocabulary that "acknowledges those involved in adoption as thoughtful and responsible people, reassigns them authority and responsibility for their actions, and, by eliminating the emotionally charged words which sometimes lead to a

## GUIDELINES FOR POSITIVE ADOPTION LANGUAGE

- Do you or others use the word with a silent, but intended, "only" in front of it?
- Does your language honor the connections that exist?
- Does your language reflect the reality of the situation, both legally and practically?
- Do you ask others involved how they would like to be addressed or referred to?
- Do you continue to use language that others find offensive?

subconscious feeling of competition or conflict, helps to promote understanding among members of the adoption circle" (Johnson, 2001, p. 1).

Spencer's visit not only prompted a name change to the "International Adoption Clinic" but also a change in the language that we used with our families. Although terms such as illegitimate and legitimate already had been stricken from our lexicon, terms such as "real" or "natural" parent became birth parent and terminology that labeled a child were dropped (e.g., Korean child became simply a child). Rather than memorizing a table of appropriate terms, the following guidelines are helpful (Romanchik, 2013).

### Cultural Identification

Clearly, a child adopted transracially or internationally is from a different culture, but an important question is whether the context of adoptive and birth families differ. Is there a culture of adoption that is relevant for medical providers? In the case of birth parents, assuming a pregnancy was planned, the most likely reason a baby is conceived is to expand their family. This is a common reason why parents adopt as well, but other factors enter into the decision-making process, such as wanting to provide a permanent home for a child and infertility (Vandivere et al., 2009).

One common question posed by professionals unacquainted with adoption is why adopt a child from abroad when thousands of children are waiting in domestic foster care for a permanent home? Most individuals who pursue intercountry adoption desire the entire spectrum of parenting experience and therefore seek as young a child as possible. At the end of FY 2012, only 22 percent of children awaiting adoption from foster care through public agencies were less than 3 years old (U.S. Department of Health and Human Services, 2013). During the same interval, 53 percent of children adopted internationally were less than 3 years of age (U.S. Department of State, 2014c). Adoptive parents also choose intercountry adoption because of concerns about the child's relationship with her or his birthparents and about potential health issues in fostered children. In the 2002 National Adoption Attitudes Survey, a majority of respondents stated that if they were thinking about adopting, a major concern would be making sure that the birthparents would not later decide to reclaim their parental rights (Dave Thomas Foundation for Adoption, 2002). Other families are concerned about open adoption and wish to avoid ongoing interactions with their child's birthparent(s). In addition, medical problems and mental health issues were identified as major worries when adopting from foster care. Intercountry adoption does provide some degree of security that birthparents will not contact or reclaim their adopted child. However, excluding domestic adoption in hopes of avoiding medical or behavioral problems is flawed reasoning as the children currently available for adoption from abroad share many of the same risk factors and medical and behavioral problems as children in domestic foster care (Chernoff, Combs-Orme, Risley-Curtiss, & Heisler, 1994; Garwood & Close, 2001; Halfon, Mendonca, & Berkowitz, 1995; Simms, Dubowitz, & Szilagyi, 2000; Takayama, Wolfe, & Coulter, 1998).

Humanitarian disaster triggers a resolve to adopt in many people, as was evident following the depiction of the plight of children in Romanian orphanages in 1990–1991 (Hunt, 1991), selective abandonment of infant girls in China (Evans, 2000), the Southeast Asian (Brown, 2005) and Japanese tsunamis (Doukopil, n.d.), and the Haitian earthquake (Seabrook, 2010). Family origins or an affinity with the child's country of origin also may weigh heavily in this choice. Finally, some families seek special needs children with correctible handicaps who otherwise would not be treated, or parents may wish to share skills they acquired dealing with long-term disabilities in children with similar problems (e.g., blindness or deafness). In these situations, health care professionals should help families focus on the primary goal of identifying and parenting a child whose needs they can meet rather than "saving" a child or expecting gratitude for a child's so-called rescue.

Finally, for optimal communication, professionals must be aware that while taxing events lead up to the arrival of a child in both birth and adoptive families, the stresses experienced are often quite different. Adoptive parents have little to no control and often no knowledge of the gestational milieu in which their child develops or the caregiving environment that surrounds their child after birth. Adoptive parents endure intense scrutiny during their home study and approval process, a waiting period often far longer than 9 months, extensive out-of-pocket fees not covered by health insurance, travel to unfamiliar countries, and the ever-frustrating necessity of dealing with government bureaucracy and legal systems both at home and abroad. These events shape an identity with similarities as well as clear differences from the experiences of a birth parent.

**Beliefs**

Religious beliefs play a powerful, central role in many adoption decisions. Judeo-Christian tradition holds individuals who adopt in high esteem, and in Islam, taking custody of a foundling is deemed an act of piety (Pollack, Bleich, Reid, & Fadel, 2004). Two pioneering families in transracial and intercountry adoption were motivated in large part by their religious beliefs. The "One-Family United Nations" of Helen Doss and her Methodist-minister husband Carl that graced the pages of *Reader's Digest* and the cover of *Life* in the mid-twentieth century was the first intercountry adoption "poster family" (Doss, 1949, 1954; Herman, 2012d). Because the couple was infertile but desiring children, the Doss family ultimately adopted twelve children, some with special needs, who were considered unadoptable because of their mixed-race parentage. The children represented Korea, Japan, Philippines, Spain, France, Malaysia, Burma, Mexico, Hawaii, and three Native American Chippewa, Blackfoot, and Cheyenne tribes. Two of the most prominent figures in the early history of intercountry adoption in the United States, Bertha and Harry Holt, shared the same roots and motivations (Herman, 2012a). Already birthparents of six, the Holt's eventually made the decision to adopt eight Korean orphans after hearing a presentation from the director of World Vision at a Sunday evening service at their church. They would later go on to help shape the adoption landscape on a global level.

Although the evangelical community has a long-standing commitment to orphan care (Joyce, 2013), increasing involvement is being catalyzed through the Christian Alliance for Orphans (2014). One of the core principles of this organization follows: "To act upon God's call to care for orphans is not merely a matter of duty or reaction to need. It is first a response to Gospel: the loving Father who sought us, adopted us, and invites us to live as His sons and daughters" (Christian Alliance for Orphans, 2014, p. 1). Thus, it is not uncommon for individuals with a strong faith-based approach to adoption to view a child's referral as divinely ordained and therefore unquestionable. Rather than directly challenging parents to consider whether this child is a correct fit for the family, it is appropriate for a health care professional to approach the consultation process as an opportunity to inform the family about the likely spectrum of services the child will require, explore what options might be available in their community, and discuss what the long-term care of the child might entail.

### Health Care Professional Bias

Our closely held beliefs emerge not only through decades of our own experiences but attitudes also are transmitted vertically to us through our parents and extended family. Consequently, we all have biases, some of which are inconsequential in our professional lives, but others that interfere with our ability to optimally relate to our patients. Socrates stated that an unexamined life is not worth living, which should remind professionals that biases have the most destructive power when unacknowledged. In terms of adoption, child health providers have strong feelings that may extend beyond the transracial or transcultural aspects of adoption. Adoption is a common method for lesbian, gay, bisexual, and transgender people to form families (Mallon, 2008). When the American Academy of Pediatrics promulgated a policy that supported adoption by same-sex parents (Committee on Psychosocial Aspects of Child and Family Health, 2002), a group of pediatricians broke away to form the American College of Pediatricians (n.d.) as they felt that any child-rearing situation aside from a heterosexual, two-parent family was not in the best interest of children. Others have challenged the wisdom of allowing children with special needs from abroad to be adopted by families in the United States through the feeling that it adds to our shared economic burden. Whether such views are right or wrong, some providers will feel conflicted with elements of the culture surrounding transracial or intercountry adoption. Acknowledging our biases and exploring their roots is the most important step in providing competent and sensitive care to individuals who differ physically, culturally, or socially.

### ASSESSING THE CULTURE OF AN ADOPTED CHILD

Irrespective of whether an adoption is transracial, it would outwardly appear that that each adopted person is born into a rich and diverse culture. The intrauterine environment provides even the youngest infant the sounds of language and music, the tastes of food through the surrounding amniotic fluid as well as the daily rhythms of her mother. These earliest experiences are reinforced throughout the first years of life during the most critical period of brain development. In the situation of the developing child, the definition of culture by Hoebel as an "integrated system of learned behavior patterns which are characteristic of the members of a society and which are not a result of biological inheritance" is particularly helpful (Hoebel, 1966, p. 52). The critical question in terms of adopted children is whether they developed within an environment in which they were able to integrate these experiences into developmental gains, behaviors, and memories that would be typical in their birth culture.

Until the late-eighties, most children adopted internationally were from Korea. Relinquished by healthy women stigmatized by single parenthood, these children were raised in foster families, provided a high level of medical care, and adopted as infants. In contrast, in the twenty-first century, many internationally adopted children are far more likely to be abandoned by poorly nourished, destitute mothers many of whom have abused alcohol or intravenous drugs, be cared for within grossly inadequate institutional care settings, receive inadequate medical care and nutrition, and join their adoptive families as toddlers or older children (Johnson, 2000, 2002). Normal enculturation of children within the foster care system is likewise compromised by neglect and abuse before placement and multiple placement changes in families and schools after entering the foster care system (Casey Family Programs, 2011). In other words, the developmental contexts of children adopted from domestic foster care and from abroad are qualitatively indistinguishable. As a group, it is difficult to argue that these children are ever fully able to benefit from the culture in which they appear to reside without the benefit of permanency.

We contend that the most pervasive influence for most people adopted transracially or internationally is a developmental environment (culture) characterized by prenatal risk and postnatal social, nutritional, and medical deprivation. Within this environment, children experience unbuffered periods of stress, generally referred to as "toxic stress," which exacts an extreme and often lifelong toll in most developmental areas (Danese & McEwen, 2012; Shonkoff et al., 2012). In institutionalized children who were randomized to foster care, sensitive periods can be identified during early childhood beyond which recovery is less optimal even if children enter a more nurturing environment. For example, children raised in institutions since birth have fewer mental health problems if placed in foster care before 6 months of age and grow best if placed before 12 months of age. Language outcomes are best if placed before 18 month, social skills before 20 months, and cognition and attachment before 24 months (Nelson, Fox, & Zeanah, 2014). This information reveals not only the prompt, pervasive, and profound effects of adversity on early development but also provides guidance about the developmental status of adopted children at the time they enter their families and the areas in which intervention might be necessary.

### Medical Assessment After Arrival

One of the benefits of specialty care in a clinic focused on adopted children is the comprehensive team approach to a neglected child coming from a "culture" of deprivation. In determining the effects of neglect and assuring a successful transition into the adoptive family, providers must consider all realms of socioemotional, nutritional, and medical deprivation experienced by the child. An initial examination is recommended 2–3 weeks after a child arrives in his or her adoptive home. Assuming the child is not acutely ill, this brief hiatus between arrival and first visit allows the family to recover from jetlag, improves child cooperation during the initial assessment, and permits the family to formulate specific questions.

An optimal first visit includes testing for major infectious diseases, vaccination status, growth delays, and nutritional deficiencies. Arrangements should be made for vision and hearing testing by specialized pediatric providers. A mental health professional should be available to explore attachment and family adjustment and a pediatric occupational therapist should assess developmental and sensory integration skills to plan for a home program and initiate referrals when appropriate, to early intervention programs. Finally, specific referrals are made to address known or discovered medical problems.

We recommend that all children are rescreened 6 months postplacement. At this time, the growth trajectory is assessed and necessary infectious disease and health screening tests are finalized. Catch-up growth is usually so robust that most children are now within the normal range in height, weight, and head circumference. If not, further diagnostic work-up is warranted, including screening for Helicobacter pylori or other sources of inflammation (Miller, Kelly, Tannemaat, & Grand, 2003). Calorie intake is an important factor in catch-up growth and feeding problems are common in children with sensory-motor problems or a history of adverse early feeding experiences (Rowell, 2012). Referral to a dietician or feeding specialist may be helpful in these cases. Referral to a pediatric endocrinologist also may be appropriate as growth hormone therapy may be indicated (Miller et al., 2010). This is a good time to evaluate family adjustment as the "honeymoon period" may be waning and issues with sleep, eating, attachment, tantrums, and rocking or other self-stimulating behaviors may be emerging. Parents know much more about their child at this time point and are better able to integrate discussions on further medical referrals, developmental and behavioral interventions, and other parenting practices.

### INFECTIOUS DISEASE AND GENERAL HEALTH LABORATORY SCREENING

The following tests are performed at the University of Minnesota International Adoption Clinic for all newly arrived international adoptees:

- Viral
    - Hepatitis A total Ig (with reflex testing for IgM if total Ig positive)
    - Hepatitis B (SAg, SAb, Core Ab)**
    - Hepatitis C Ab*
    - HIV 1 and 2 Ab*
- Bacterial
    - Syphilis screening (antitreponemal Ab, RPR or VDRL)
    - Tuberculin skin test (TST) if less than 5 years old*
    - TST or QuantiFERON blood test if 5 years old or older*

## INFECTIOUS DISEASE AND GENERAL HEALTH LABORATORY SCREENING (CONTINUED)

- Parasitic
  - Stool examination for ova and parasites (x 3)
  - Giardia Stool antigen
- Vaccine Preventable Infection Titers (if documentation of prior immunization)
  - Measles, Mumps, and Rubella Ab
  - Diphtheria and Tetanus Ab
  - Haemophilus influenza type b Ab
  - Polio Types 1 and 2 neutralizing Ab
  - Varicella Ab
  - Alternative approach is revaccination according to current guidelines
- General Health Screening
  - Complete blood count with differential, including a peripheral eosinophil count and red blood cell indices*
  - Vitamin D total*
  - Iron panel including C-reactive protein*
  - Thyroid stimulating hormone (TSH) and free thyroxine (free T4)
  - Lead
  - Haiti specific: G6PD, hemoglobin electrophoresis, malaria thick/thin smear if coming from a malaria-endemic area

*Note:* Ig, immunoglobulin; IgM, immunoglobulin M, Ab, antibody; SAg, surface antigen, SAb, surface antibody; RPR, Rapid Plasma Reagin test.

\* Retest at 6 months.

\*\* Retest at 6 months if test results are negative on initial testing.

Source: Adapted from Jones et al. (2012).

### ONGOING ASSESSMENTS

Although preadoption counseling and the initial homecoming health assessment are important, additional time points for further evaluation are worth consideration. Entry into kindergarten is a time when expectations for academics, attention, and behavior increase for any child, and children who exhibit difficulties in these areas may benefit from further medical evaluation.

Neuropsychological testing is especially important at this time as it identifies areas of strength and weakness, which can assist the school system in focusing on a child's actual needs. Further screening should be done at several time points for signs of fetal alcohol spectrum disorder (FASD) as children in the adoption system are at higher risk (Astley, Stachowiak, Clarren, & Clausen, 2002; Landgren et al., 2010).

Medical providers also can encourage families to access appropriate mental health professionals when the experience of early adversity is likely interfering in attachment or family dynamics. Other problems that frequently require intervention include sensory processing problems, speech and language issues (table 8.1) (Glennen & Masters, 2002), and developmental delays. Early referral to appropriate specialists is critical for optimal outcome.

Another important time point is late childhood when we encounter premature or accelerated puberty. A national survey on central precocious puberty (onset in girls less than 8 years and in boys less than 9 years) from thirty-four pediatric endocrinology clinics in Spain found that the risk of this condition in internationally and domestically adopted children was more than 27-fold greater than birth children. The risk of early puberty was particularly high in girls (Soriano-Guillen et al., 2010). Data from Denmark confirmed the increased risk in internationally adopted girls and showed that the average age of both breast development (9.5 years) and menarche (12.1 years) were approximately 1.3 years earlier than girls born in Denmark. Overall, 16 percent of girls adopted internationally entered puberty before 8 years of age (Teilmann, Main, & Skakkebaek, 2005; Teilmann, Pedersen, Jensen, Skakkebaek, & Juul, 2005; Teilmann et al., 2009). This is an issue in which health care providers should not take a "wait and see" approach for children who have experienced early adversity. Effects on

TABLE 8.1  Suggestions for Referral to a Speech and Language Pathologist

| AGE AT ADOPTION | SUGGESTED REFERRAL CRITERIA |
|---|---|
| 0–12 months | Refer as if primary English speaker |
| 13–18 months | Refer if not producing fifty words or two-word phrases at 24 months |
| 19–24 months | Refer if not using English by 24 months, fifty words at 28 months, or two-word phrases at 28–30 months |
| 25–30 months | Refer if not using English within several weeks at home or not speaking fifty English words or two-word phrases by 31 months |

emotional development and final adult stature can be significant and referral to a pediatric endocrinologist familiar with this problem is prudent.

Mid- to late adolescence is a time when health care visits are infrequent. Providers, however, should maintain contact with the adoptive family and child as questions regarding identity and relationships often arise. It is also a time to address issues of independence and future educational and vocational prospects if the child has struggled with learning. Screening for chronic adult diseases should also begin at this time (see the following discussion).

### U.S. Adoption and Citizenship

The administrative process of intercountry adoption may seem beyond the scope of health care professionals, but providers can play an important role in ensuring maximum legal protection for newly adopted children. Although most U.S. state courts do recognize the legitimacy of a foreign adoption decree, it is not a requirement, and one can only imagine the scenarios in contested divorces or in dissolutions of parental partnerships where unions lack formal recognition. Formal adoption of the child in the United States guarantees that the courts of all fifty states will recognize the adoption. Once a child is adopted or readopted in state court, parents can request that a state birth certificate be issued. Having this document on file guarantees that a child can always obtain a certified copy simply by contacting the appropriate state agency. Birth certificates from abroad, once lost or destroyed, are extremely difficult to replace.

The issue of U.S. citizenship is likewise important when registering to vote or applying for college financial aid, jobs, or a U.S. passport. More ominous is the specter of conviction for a crime and, as a noncitizen, facing deportation. Because of the Child Citizenship Act of 2000, many parents no longer need apply separately for a child's naturalization but for those who do, health care professionals should stress the importance of citizenship and encourage parents to complete the necessary paperwork to achieve this goal (U.S. Department of State, 2014a).

### Horizontal and Vertical Identity

In the first chapter of his superb book, *Far from the Tree,* about raising children who differ significantly from their parents, Andrew Solomon explores the concept of vertical and horizontal identity (Solomon, 2012).

Vertical identity such as ethnicity and skin color is transmissible from one generation to the next, and as such, the presence of these elements is an expectation in birth children. In the case of transracially or transculturally adopted children, these traits may not be shared with their adoptive parents, which forces children to acquire identity from a peer group who share these similarities. Health care professional can help parents promote this identification process and accept it as a normal and necessary part of establishing their child's identity particularly during the critical years of adolescence. As one adopted person stated, "Children adopted from China don't want to eat Chinese food with their parents. They want to eat it with their Chinese friends."

### Establishing Horizontal Identity

Observant individuals are continuously reminded that we live in a racist society with wide-ranging discrimination against individuals who do not share the same skin color, ethnicity, or language with the white majority. Such discrimination clearly affect all facets of life, including health. Given the undeniable fact that we do not live in a colorblind society, the following assertion in the 1972 Position Statement Against Transracial Adoption, by the National Association of Black Social Workers is truthful, at least in part, for all people adopted transracially (Herman, 2012g, p. 1):

> In our society, the developmental needs of black children are significantly different from those of white children. Black children are taught, from an early age, highly sophisticated coping techniques to deal with racist practices perpetrated by individuals and institutions. These coping techniques become successfully integrated into ego functions and can be incorporated only through the process of developing positive identification with significant black others. Only a black family can transmit the emotional and sensitive subtleties of perception and reaction essential for a black child's survival in a racist society.

Because a large percentage of adoptive parents are white and unfamiliar or totally ignorant of the strategies needed, can health care professionals provide such guidance? Although professionals from several disciplines provide competent care for children, at least in the case of children adopted internationally, 92 percent received care from a pediatrician or pediatric nurse practitioner (Eckerle et al., 2014). Are pediatricians or pediatric nurse practitioners likely to be familiar with the particular challenges of transracial adoption within a racist society? If racial demographics of pediatric health care providers are any indication of competency in this area, the answer is "not likely." A 2013 survey of fellows of the American Academy of Pediatrics revealed that 75 percent were white. Only 15 percent were Asian, 4.1 percent were black/African American, and 6 percent were Hispanic (American Academy of Pediatrics, 2013). White pediatricians were far less likely to have minority patients than their Asian, Hispanic, and black colleagues (Basco, Cull, O'Connor, & Shipman, 2010). The situation is likely even more extreme for pediatric nurse practitioners. In a 2007 survey of nurse practitioners and clinical nurse specialists from many disciplines, 94% of respondents were white (Kenward, 2007).

At the time, concerns expressed by the National Association of Black Social Workers were at least partially warranted as studies in the era following this statement showed that many white parents who adopted African American children at that time tended to exhibit colorblind racial attitudes and were ambivalent about enculturation and racialization (McRoy & Zurcher, 1983). A more recent study of parents who adopted internationally, however, found relatively low mean scores on colorblind racial attitudes and relatively high mean scores on enculturation and racialization parenting beliefs (Lee, Grotevant, Hellerstedt, Gunnar, & Minnesota International Adaption Project, 2006). Thus, health care professionals likely will encounter families who are aware of the issues that must be addressed as their child matures and who are interested in whatever guidance and reminders that can be provided by professionals who are willing to be educated about the subject. The Children's Bureau offers the following counsel for those considering transracial and transcultural adoption (U.S. Department of Health and Human Services, n.d.).

### VERTICAL IDENTITY FOR CHILDREN ADOPTED TRANSRACIALLY AND TRANSCULTURALLY

Despite the fact that it may appear inaccessible, all adopted children have a vertical or personal identity tied to their birth family that should be explored. In terms of domestic adoption, U.S. adoption records were open to adopted persons, birth parents, and adoptive parents before

# REFLECTION ON TRANSRACIAL/TRANSCULTURAL ADOPTION BY A COLORBLIND PARENT

The first time I held my infant son in my arms he smiled. Only weeks earlier he lay critically ill in his Calcutta orphanage near death from the monsoon-related enterovirus epidemic that was ravaging the nursery. Rather than mourning, however, I stood at the arrival gate transfixed by joy at his first smile ever—the word had indeed become flesh. At that time, the fact that I was adopting a child of color was the last thought on my mind and therein laid the problem. Of course, our social worker had addressed this issue and encouraged us to explore own beliefs and attitudes about race and ethnicity, but I was blindly confident that our family was up to the challenge. As my 10-year-old daughter definitively stated when asked about having a brown brother, "I wouldn't care if he's green or purple. I'd love him anyway" I should have taken our social worker's advice more seriously.

The father returning Gabriel's smile was tall, blond, blue-eyed, highly educated, and professionally successful. Not only had I never been personally exposed to racial discrimination, I had lived an essentially insular life in white neighborhoods and schools and had no friends of color until college. Raised in an evangelical religious tradition, I planned on becoming a medical missionary and lived for a year during medical school in the Democratic Republic of Congo. Spending time as a member of a distinct racial minority, however, imparted few lessons as missionaries were accorded an elevated status as medical providers. Not only were my personal experiences woefully inadequate to teach my son to live in a racist society, but the choices we made in terms of neighborhood, schooling, and family friends during my son's childhood minimized rather than celebrated diversity.

I was a member of a generation of adoptive parents who grew up enthusiastically singing:

> "Jesus loves the little children
> All the children of the world
> Red & yellow, black & white
> They are precious in his sight
> Jesus loves the little children of the world"
>
> Clare Herbert Woolston (1856–1927)

Emergence from this colorblind innocence began only when I witnessed or was told of racial microaggressions my son experienced, such as the distinct surprise on the faces the parents of his white prom date when they greeted him at the front door. Then came the overt racism. First, in high school while riding in the back seat of his friend's car with a group of white friends, he was singled out by police officers and questioned about drugs and guns. On another occasion, he was arrested for a trivial traffic violation by police officers in a predominately white suburb.

A further personal revelation came during my attempt to reconcile the song I sang in Sunday school with the unease I felt when boys or men of color approached me on an empty sidewalk—individuals who were the same color as my son. I was troubled to realize that while raised by an exceptionally loving and nurturing family, their attitudes, which reflected the pervasive racism and anti-Semitism of the fifties, had been instilled in me as well.

Although I can't universalize my own experience and acknowledged short comings in this area to other adoptive parents, I now understand the concern of the National Association of Black Social Workers regarding how ill-equipped most white parents are to "teach from an early age, highly sophisticated coping techniques to deal with racist practices perpetrated by individuals and institutions" (Herman, 2012g, p. 1). But how does this existential anxiety translate into health care advice for parents who adopt children from another race or culture? Certainly many issues, such as identity formation and the development of positive self-esteem, are important and have a major bearing on the future of a child, but my epiphany as both parent and pediatrician was a talk given by a black social worker from Los Angeles about risks faced by children adopted transracially. He related stories of young men of color raised by white parents in white neighborhoods who were unschooled in dealing with law enforcement officers. Stopped in their own communities and being unaware of either the raciest attitudes of the police or appropriate coping strategies, they refused to follow instructions or exhibited emotional outrage at being profiled on their own streets. Not only did this result in arrest but also raised the possibility of having such actions perceived as aggression and met with deadly force.

When I recently apologized to my son for failing to provide appropriate education in this area, he was gracious and stated that he "was a fast learner." Indeed, he is an intelligent man with good self-awareness, which no doubt helped in his adaptation to the harsh racial realities in our society. The fact, however, that my child or any child in his situation could be killed or seriously injured certainly emphasizes the importance of this area of education. Although the necessity for racialization goes far beyond this issue, this scenario provides health care professionals a powerful entrée to the subject material, particularly for parents, like me, who exhibit colorblind attitudes.

## PREPARING FOR A TRANSCULTURAL OR TRANSRACIAL ADOPTION

- Examine your beliefs and attitudes about race and adoption and ethnicity
- Think about your lifestyle
- Consider adopting siblings
- Become intensely invested in parenting
- Tolerate no racially or ethnically biased remarks
- Surround yourselves with supportive family and friends
- Celebrate all cultures
- Talk about race and culture
- Expose your child to a variety of experiences so that he or she develops physical and intellectual skills that build self-esteem
- Take your child to places where most of the people present are from his or her race and ethnic group

World War II. During the next three decades, however, state laws were enacted to deny easy access to birth records by birth parents and then by adopted adults (Carp, 2006a; Herman, 2012c; Norris 2006). The reasons behind this change centered on the perceived benefits of confidentiality for members of the triad. The effect of this change, however, permitted perpetuation of attitudes and myths about adoption that were prevalent at time: that birth outside of marriage was shameful and should be hidden, that parents need not confront the fact that adoptive families are inherently different, and that contact with other members of the adoption triad inevitably would lead to emotional trauma. In response to this change, adopted individuals banded together and attempted to influence policy on sealed records through such organizations as the Life History and Study Center (1953), Orphan Voyage (1962) and the American Adoption Congress (1978) all founded by Jean Paton and Adopted Persons' Liberty Movement Association founded by Florence Fisher in 1971. Although these groups had little success overturning confidentiality laws in state and federal courts, their arguments did persuade social work professionals, agencies, and state legislatures to pass statutes and alter policy to enable searches that maintained privacy of triad members through such instruments as mutual-consent voluntary adoption registries or confidential intermediaries (Carp, 2006a).

For many adopted individuals, however, access to information on parentage and culture is considered a fundamental human right. For these individuals, any strategy short of complete access to information was unacceptable. Bastard Nation, an outspoken adoption activist organization founded in 1996, has achieved some success in restoring the rights of adopted individuals to receive their original birth certificate. Although a small number of states permit unconditional access, court orders are still required in most states (Carp, 2006a, 2006b). To further complicate this field, the issue of open records has entered the turmoil of the abortion debate as some feel that removing the option of privacy would lead to more abortions.

Concurrent with the growing desire to identify and contact birth parents, a cadre of amateur and professional identity investigators, adoptee support groups, and access to the Internet permit many individuals adopted both domestically or internationally access to their birth histories (Pertman, 2000). Concerns about this loss of personal identity are being addressed proactively through open adoptions in which birth parents, adoptive parents, and the child remain in contact. Contemporary studies indicate improved outcomes for children when avenues of communication remain open among adoption triad members (Barth & Berry, 1988; Berry, 1991; Grotevant, 1997; Grotevant & McRoy, 1998; Grotevant, McRoy, Wrobel, & Ayers-Lopez, 2013; Grotevant et al., 2008; Von Korff, Grotevant, & McRoy, 2006).

The exponential growth of DNA analysis and commercial DNA databases over the past decade now permits low-cost, conclusive parent, sibling, half-sibling, and first cousin matches. As advancing technology permits cost-effective analysis of even more genomic variations, the identification of ever-more-distant relatives will be possible. A shared interest in one's forbearers undoubtedly will expand the use of these genomic databases in other countries continuing to revolutionize this search process. Now one need only submit a simple saliva sample through the mail and then await notification of possible family matches through services that integrate extensive crowd-sourced family pedigrees with DNA analysis (e.g., Ancestry.com). These developments may soon render moot the debate about birth record confidentiality and permit contact or closure in situations such as international adoption for which resolution was once thought impossible. Health care professionals counseling adopted individuals exploring these mechanisms to establish family ties should strongly encourage consideration of the benefits and burdens of sharing genetic information as well as the ability of different DNA analytic techniques to provide the answers desired (Lucassen, Hill, & Wheeler, 2010; Research-China.Org, 2011).

## TRANSITION TO ADULTHOOD

Most children adopted from foster care or internationally have experienced significant periods of deprivation; thus, an important question is whether these adverse experiences will have an effect on their future health. The Adverse Childhood Experiences (ACE) study is based on more than 17,000 Kaiser Permanente Health Maintenance Organization members who, when undergoing a comprehensive physical examination in 1995–1997, chose to answer ten questions about their childhood experience of abuse (emotional, physical and sexual), neglect (emotional, physical), and family dysfunction (mother treated violently, household substance abuse, household mental illness, parental separation or divorce). The ACE score was determined by adding up the affirmative answers (0–10). The outcome of the study was that the risk for many major health problems (e.g., ischemic heart disease, diabetes, stroke, chronic obstructive pulmonary disease, depression, alcoholism, liver disease) increases in a strong and graded fashion as the ACE score increases (Centers for Disease Control and Prevention, 2014).

Another indicator of the adverse effects of early deprivation is shortening of the specialized nucleoprotein complexes on chromosomes (telomeres) that promote chromosomal stability. Telomere length shortens with each successive cellular division and when length reaches a critical point, cell division ceases and the cell dies. Without regenerative abilities, tissues and organs deteriorate and malfunction. Accelerated telomere length shortening has been associated with normal aging as well as cigarette smoking, radiation exposure, oxidative stress, and psychological stress, including a history of early maltreatment. The Bucharest Early Intervention Project, the first randomized controlled study of foster versus institutional care, recently studied telomere length in their subjects at 8 years of age finding it inversely related to the length of time children were institutionalized (Drury et al., 2012). Thus, early deprivation makes children old before their time.

## CONCLUSION

Adoption is a lifelong journey and medical professionals should orient their practice with adopted individuals in this fashion. First, preadoption counseling and advice is key to address challenges that should be anticipated so families are prepared to meet a child's likely needs. Second, health care professionals should comprehensively assess a child's status after arrival. This involves attention not only to medical issues but also the psychological processes involved in incorporating a child successfully into the family. Third, parents must be informed of the necessity to enculturate and racialize their children. Finally, ongoing vigilance will help identify problems that may appear at key developmental horizons or advancing age. As key contacts to children and families throughout their lifetimes, health care providers have the opportunity and obligation to inform individuals with a history of adversity that they are at increased risk of developing a variety of chronic adult diseases, which could affect their quality of life and longevity if unrecognized and untreated. Screening should start during childhood and adolescence and continue throughout adulthood. A healthy lifestyle and regular health check-up will substantially improve prospects for good health.

Although challenges are faced by all transracially and internationally adopted individuals, this chapter ends with an optimistic note. Data accumulated over the past half-century leave no doubt regarding the positive effects of adoption on children's development. Out of calamity and loss, adoption is by far the most effective means to help children recover and become functionally and emotionally competent adults within the environment of a permanent family (Johnson, 2002).

### DISCUSSION QUESTIONS

1. What is the makeup (racial, international versus domestic) of adopted persons in the United States?
2. What are the initial major medical concerns in internationally adopted children especially those coming from institutional care environments?
3. Besides the initial postarrival evaluation, at what ages and time points should medical or developmental reevaluation be considered and what issues should be addressed?

## REFERENCES

ACOG Committee on Health Care for Underserved Women. (2011). *Cultural sensitivity and awareness in the delivery of health care*. Retrieved from http://www.acog.org/Resources_And_Publications/Committee_Opinions/Committee_on_Health_Care_for_Underserved_Women/Cultural_Sensitivity_and_Awareness_in_the_Delivery_of_Health_Care

Albers, L. H., Johnson, D. E., Hostetter, M. K., Iverson, S., & Miller, L. C. (1997). Health of children adopted from the former Soviet Union and Eastern Europe. Comparison with preadoptive medical records. *Journal of the American Medical Association, 278*(11), 922–924.

Alstein, H., & Simon, R. J. (1991). Introduction. In H. Alstein & R. J. Simon (Eds.), *Intercountry Adoption: A Multinational Perspective* (pp. 1–20). New York: Praeger.

American Academy of Pediatrics. (2013). *Percent of pediatricians by ethnicity*. Retrieved from http://www.aap.org/en-us/professional-resources/Research/pediatrician-surveys/PublishingImages/slide7_2013.jpg

American College of Pediatricians. (n.d.). Retrieved from http://www.acpeds.org

Ames, E. W. (1997). *The Development of Romanian Orphanage Children Adopted to Canada*. Burnaby, BC, Canada: Simon Fraser University.

Astley, S. J., Stachowiak, J., Clarren, S. K., & Clausen, C. (2002). Application of the fetal alcohol syndrome facial photographic screening tool in a foster care population. *Journal of Pediatrics, 141*(5), 712–717.

Barth, R. P., & Berry, M. (1988). *Adoption and Disruption*. Hawthorne, NY: Aldine de Gruyter.

Basco, W. T., Jr., Cull, W. L., O'Connor, K. G., & Shipman, S. A. (2010). Assessing trends in practice demographics of underrepresented minority pediatricians, 1993–2007. *Pediatrics, 125*(3), 460–467.

Berry, M. (1991). The practice of open adoption. *Children and Youth Services Review, 13*, 379–395.

Brown, S. (2005). *Rush to adopt tsunami orphans may end in tears*. Retrieved from http://reliefweb.int/report/indonesia/rush-adopt-tsunami-orphans-may-end-tears

Carp, E. W. (2006a). Adoption search movement. In K. Shepperd Stolley & V. L. Bullough (Eds.), *The Praeger Handbook of Adoption* (pp. 41–43). Westport, CT: Praeger.

Carp, E. W. (2006b). Bastard Nation. In K. S. Stolley & V. L. Bullough (Eds.), *The Praeger Handbook of Adoption* (98–139). Westport, CT: Praeger.

Casey Family Programs. (2010). *Foster care by the numbers.* Retrieved from http://www.fostercareandeducation.org/portals/0/dmx/2013%5C07%5Cfile_20130719_111354_0StS_0.pdf

Centers for Disease Control and Prevention. (2014). *Adverse childhood experiences (ACE) study.* Retrieved from http://www.cdc.gov/violenceprevention/acestudy/index.html

Cermak, S. A., & Daunhauer, L. A. (1997). Sensory processing in the postinstitutionalized child. *American Journal of Occupational Therapy, 51*(7), 500–507.

Chernoff, R., Combs-Orme, T., Risley-Curtiss, C., & Heisler, A. (1994). Assessing the health status of children entering foster care. *Pediatrics, 93*(4), 594–601.

Christian Alliance for Orphans. (2014). *Core principles.* Retrieved from http://www.christianalliancefororphans.org/about/core-principles

Committee on Infectious Diseases. (1994). *1994 Red Book: Report of the committee on infectious diseases* (23 ed.). Elk Grove Village, IL: American Academy of Pediatrics.

Committee on Psychosocial Aspects of Child and Family Health. (2002). Coparent or second-parent adoption by same-sex parents. *Pediatrics, 109*(2), 339–340.

Danese, A., & McEwen, B. S. (2012). Adverse childhood experiences, allostasis, allostatic load, and age-related disease. *Physiology and Behavior, 106*(1), 29–39.

Dave Thomas Foundation for Adoption. (2013). *National foster care adoption attitudes survey.* Retrieved from https://davethomasfoundation.org/wp-content/uploads/2013/07/DTFA-HarrisPoll-REPORT-USA-FINAL1.pdf

Dave Thomas Foundation for Adoption. (2002). *National adoption attitudes survey.* Retrieved from http://adoptioninstitute.org/publications/2002-national-adoption-attitudes-survey/

Doss, H. (1949). Our international family. *Readers Digest* (August), 58–59.

Doss, H. (1954). *The family nobody wanted.* Boston: Little, Brown.

Doukopil, T. (n.d.) *Where will the tsunami orphans go?* Retrieved from http://www.thedailybeast.com/articles/2011/03/26/japans-tsunami-where-will-the-orphans-go.html

Drury, S. S., Theall, K., Gleason, M. M., Smyke, A. T., De Vivo, I., Wong, J. Y., et al. (2012). Telomere length and early severe social deprivation: linking early adversity and cellular aging. *Molecular Psychiatry, 17*(7), 719–727.

Eckerle, J. K., Hill, L. K., Iverson, S., Hellerstedt, W., Gunnar, M., & Johnson, D. E. (2014). Vision and hearing deficits and associations with parent-reported behavioral and developmental problems in international adoptees. *Maternal Child Health Journal, 18*(3), 575–583.

Eschelbach Hansen, M., & Simon, R. J. (2004). Transracial placement in adoption with public agency involvement: What can we learn from the AFCARS data? *Adoption Quarterly, 8*(2), 14–55.

Evans, K. (2000). *The lost daughters of China*. New York: Penguin.

Fuglestad, A. J., Georgieff, M. K., Iverson, S. L., Miller, B. S., Petryk, A., Johnson, D. E., & Kroupina, M. G. (2013). Iron deficiency after arrival is associated with general cognitive and behavioral impairment in post-institutionalized children adopted from Eastern Europe. *Maternal Child Health Journal, 17*(6), 1080–1087.

Fuglestad, A. J., Lehmann, A. E., Kroupina, M. G., Petryk, A., Miller, B. S., Iverson, S. L., Johnson, D. E., et al. (2008). Iron deficiency in international adoptees from Eastern Europe. *Journal of Pediatrics, 153*(2), 272–277.

Garwood, M. M., & Close, W. (2001). Identifying the psychological needs of foster children. *Child Psychiatry and Human Development, 32*(2), 125–135.

Glennen, S., & Masters, M. G. (2002). Typical and atypical language development in infants and toddlers adopted from Eastern Europe. *American Journal of Speech and Language Pathology, 11*, 417–433.

Gronlund, M. A., Aring, E., Hellstrom, A., Landgren, M., & Stromland, K. (2004). Visual and ocular findings in children adopted from Eastern Europe. *British Journal of Ophthalmology, 88*(11), 1362–1367.

Grotevant, H. D. (1997). Coming to terms with adoption: The construction of identity from adolescence to adulthood. *Adoption Quarterly, 1*(1), 1–27.

Grotevant, H. D., & McRoy, R. G. (1998). *Openness in adoption*. Thousand Oaks, CA: Sage.

Grotevant, H. D., McRoy, R. G., Wrobel, G. M., & Ayers-Lopez, S. (2013). Contact between adoptive and birth families: Perspectives from the Minnesota Texas Adoption Research Project. *Child Development Perspectives, 7*(3), 193–198.

Grotevant, H. D., Wrobel, G. M., Von Korff, L., Skinner, B., Newell, J., Friese, S., et al. (2008). Many faces of openness in adoption: Perspectives of adopted adolescents and their parents. *Adoption Quarterly, 10*(3–4), 79–101.

Groze, V., & Ileana, D. (1996). A follow-up study of adopted children from Romania. *Child and Adolescent Social Work Journal, 13*(6), 541–565.

Gunnar, M. R., & van Dulmen, M. H. (2007). Behavior problems in postinstitutionalized internationally adopted children. *Developmental Psychopathology, 19*(1), 129–148.

Gustafson, K. L., Eckerle, J. K., Howard, C. R., Andrews, B., & Polgreen, L. E. (2013). Prevalence of vitamin D deficiency in international adoptees within the first 6 months after adoption. *Clinical Pediatrics, 52*(12), 1149–1153.

Halfon, N., Mendonca, A., & Berkowitz, G. (1995). Health status of children in foster care. The experience of the Center for the Vulnerable Child. *Archives of Pediatrics and Adolescent Medicine, 149*(4), 386–392.

Herman, E. (2012a). Bertha and Harry Holt. *Adoption History Project.* Retrieved from http://www.uoregon.edu/~adoption/people/holt.htm

Herman, E. (2012b). Child Welfare League of America, "Adoption terminology," 1980s. *Adoption History Project.* Retrieved from http://darkwing.uoregon.edu/~adoption/archive/CwlaAT.htm

Herman, E. (2012c). Confidentiality and sealed records. *The Adoption History Project.* Retrieved from http://www.uoregon.edu/~adoption/topics/confidentiality.htm

Herman, E. (2012d). The family nobody wanted—1954. *The Adoption History Project.* Retrieved from http://www.uoregon.edu/~adoption/topics/familynobodywanted.htm

Herman, E. (2012e). International adoptions. *The Adoption History Project.* Retrieved from http://www.uoregon.edu/~adoption/topics/internationaladoption.htm

Herman, E. (2012f). Massachusetts Adoption Act, 1851. *Adoption History Project.* Retrieved from http://www.uoregon.edu/~adoption/archive/MassACA.htm

Herman, E. (2012g). National Association of Black Social Workers, "Position statement on tans-racial adoption," September 1972. *The Adoption History Project.* Retrieved from http://www.uoregon.edu/~adoption/archive/NabswTRA.htm

Herman, E. (2012h). Transracial adoptions. *The Adoption History Project.* Retrieved from http://www.uoregon.edu/~adoption/topics/transracialadoption.htm

Hoebel, A. (1966). *The study of man.* New York: McGraw-Hill.

Hollinger, J. H., & The ABA Center on Children and the Law. (1998). *A guide to the Multiethnic Placement Act of 1994 as amended by the Interethnic Adoption Provisions of 1996.* Retrieved from http://www.americanbar.org/content/dam/aba/administrative/child_law/GuidetoMultiethnicPlacementAct.authcheckdam.pdf

Hostetter, M. K., Iverson, S., Dole, K., & Johnson, D. (1989). Unsuspected infectious diseases and other medical diagnoses in the evaluation of internationally adopted children. *Pediatrics, 83*(4), 559–564.

Hostetter, M. K., Iverson, S., Thomas, W., McKenzie, D., Dole, K., & Johnson, D. E. (1991). Medical evaluation of internationally adopted children. *New England Journal of Medicine, 325*(7), 479–485.

Hunt, K. (1991). The Romanian baby bazaar. *New York Times Magazine, 140* (March 24), 24–53.

Jenista, J. A. (1993). Infectious disease and the internationally adopted child. *Current Opinions in Infectious Disease, 6*, 576–584.

Jenista, J. A., & Chapman, D. (1987). Medical problems of foreign-born adopted children. *American Journal of Diseases of Children, 141*(3), 298–302.

Johnson, D. E. (2000). Medical and developmental sequlae of early childhood institutionalization in international adoptees from Romania and the Russian Federation. In C. Nelson (Ed.), *The effects of early adversity on neurobehavioral development* (pp. 113–162). Mahwah, NJ: Lawrence Erlbaum.

Johnson, D. E. (2002). Adoption and the effect on children's development. *Early Human Development, 68*(1), 39–54.

Johnson, D. E. (2005). International adoption: What is fact, what is fiction, and what is the future? *Pediatric Clinics of North America, 52*(5), 1221–1246.

Johnson, D. E., Miller, L. C., Iverson, S., Thomas, W., Franchino, B., Dole, K., et al. (1992). The health of children adopted from Romania. *Journal of the American Medical Association, 268*(24), 3446–3451.

Johnson, P. (2001). *Adoption language.* Retrieved from http://www.comeunity.com/adoption/adopt/adopt-language.html

Jones, V. F., High, P. C., Donoghue, E., Fussell, J. J., Gleason, M. M., Jaudes, P. K., et al. (2012). Comprehensive health evaluation of the newly adopted child. *Pediatrics, 129*(1), e214–223.

Joyce, K. (2013). *The child catchers: Rescue, trafficking, and the gospel of adoption.* New York: PublicAffairs.

Kenward, K. (2007). Role delineation study of nurse practitioners and clinical nurse specialists. Retrieved from https://http://www.ncsbn.org/06_LPN_RoleDelStudy_NCLEX_30_Web.pdf

Kreider, R. M., & Lofquist, D. A. (2014). *Adopted children and stepchildren: 2010.* Retrieved from http://www.census.gov/prod/2014pubs/p20-572.pdf

Landgren, M., Svensson, L., Stromland, K., & Andersson Gronlund, M. (2010). Prenatal alcohol exposure and neurodevelopmental disorders in children adopted from Eastern Europe. *Pediatrics, 125*(5), e1178–1185.

Lange, W. R., Kreider, S. D., & Warnock-Eckhart, E. (1987). Hepatitis B surveillance in Korean adoptees. *Maryland Medical Journal, 36*(2), 163–166.

Lange, W. R., & Warnock-Eckhart, E. (1987). Selected infectious disease risks in international adoptees. *Pediatric Infectious Disease Journal, 6*(5), 447–450.

Lange, W. R., Warnock-Eckhart, E., & Bean, M. E. (1989). Mycobacterium tuberculosis infection in foreign born adoptees. *Pediatric Infectious Disease Journal, 8*(9), 625–629.

Le Mare, L., Audet, K., & Kurytnik, K. (2007). A longitudinal study of service use in families of children adopted from Romanian orphanages *International Journal of Behavioral Development, 31*(3), 242–251.

Lee, R. M., Grotevant, H. D., Hellerstedt, W. L., Gunnar, M. R., & Minnesota International Adaption Project, T. (2006). Cultural socialization in families with internationally adopted children. *Journal Family Psychology, 20*(4), 571–580.

Lee, S. H., Shin, S. J., Won, S. D., Kim, E. J., & Oh, D. Y. (2010). Alcohol use during pregnancy and related risk factors in Korea. *Psychiatry Investigation, 7*, 86–92.

Lucassen, A. M., Hill, C. M., & Wheeler, R. (2010). "Ethnicity testing" before adoption: A help or hindrance? *Archives of Disease in Childhood, 95*(6), 404–405.

Mallon, G. P. (Ed.). (2008). *Social work practice with lesbian, gay, bisexual and transgender people.* New York: Routledge.

Mason, P., & Narad, C. (2005). International adoption: a health and developmental prospective. *Seminars in Speech and Language, 26*(1), 1–9.

Mason, P. W., Johnson, D. E., & Albers Prock, L. (Eds.). (2014). *Adoption medicine: Caring for children and families.* Elk Grove Village: American Academy of Pediatrics.

McRoy, R. G., & Zurcher, L. A. (1983). *Transracial and inracial adoptees: The adolescent years.* Springfield, IL: Charles C Thomas.

Miller, B. S., Kroupina, M. G., Iverson, S. L., Masons, P., Narad, C., Himes, J. H., et al. (2009). Auxological evaluation and determinants of growth failure at the time of adoption in Eastern European adoptees. *Journal of Pediatric Endocrinology and Metabolism, 22*(1), 31–39.

Miller, B. S., Kroupina, M. G., Mason, P., Iverson, S. L., Narad, C., Himes, J. H., et al. (2010). Determinants of catch-up growth in international adoptees from Eastern Europe. *International Journal of Pediatric Endocrinology, 2010*, 1–8. doi:10.1155/2010/107252

Miller, L. C., Chan, W., Litvinova, A., Rubin, A., Comfort, K., Tirella, L., et al. (2006). Fetal alcohol spectrum disorders in children residing in Russian orphanages: A phenotypic survey. *Alcohol Clinical and Experimental Research, 30*(3), 531–538.

Miller, L. C., & Hendrie, N. W. (2000). Health of children adopted from China. *Pediatrics, 105*(6), E76.

Miller, L. C., Kelly, N., Tannemaat, M., & Grand, R. J. (2003). Serologic prevalence of antibodies to Helicobacter pylori in internationally adopted children. *Helicobacter, 8*(3), 173–178.

Miller, L. C., Kiernan, M. T., Mathers, M. I., & Klein-Gitelman, M. (1995). Developmental and nutritional status of internationally adopted children. *Archives of Pediatrics and Adolescent Medicine, 149*(1), 40–44.

Nelson, C. A., Fox, N. A., & Zeanah, C. H. (2014). *Romania's abandoned children: Deprivation, brain development and the struggle for recovery*. Cambridge: Harvard University Press.

Norris, B. L. (2006). Closed adoption. In K. S. Stolley & V. L. Bullough (Eds.), *The Praeger Handbook of Adoption* (pp. 161–165). Westport, CT: Praeger.

O'Connor, T. G., & Rutter, M. (2000). Attachment disorder behavior following early severe deprivation: extension and longitudinal follow-up. English and Romanian Adoptees Study Team. *Journal of the American Academy of Child and Adolescent Psychiatry, 39*(6), 703–712.

O'Connor, T. G., Rutter, M., Beckett, C., Keaveney, L., & Kreppner, J. M. (2000). The effects of global severe privation on cognitive competence: extension and longitudinal follow-up. English and Romanian Adoptees Study Team. *Child Development, 71*(2), 376–390.

Pertman, A. (2000). *Adoption nation*. New York: Basic Books.

Pollack, D., Bleich, M., Reid, C. J., & Fadel, M. H. (2004). Classical religious perspectives of adoption law. *Notre Dame Law Review, 79*(2), 693–753.

Research-China.Org. (2011). *DNA technology improving for sibling testing.* Retrieved from http://research-china.blogspot.hk/2011/09/dna-technology-improving-for-sibling.html

Robert, M., Carceller, A., Domken, V., Ramos, F., Dobrescu, O., Simard, M. N., et al. (2009). Physical and neurodevelopmental evaluation of children adopted from Eastern Europe. *Canadian Journal of Clinical Pharmacology, 16*(3), e432–440.

Romanchik, B. (2013). *A few words on words in adoption*. Retrieved from http://library.adoption.com/articles/a-few-words-on-words-in-adoption.html

Rowell, K. (2012). *Love me, feed me*. St. Paul: Feeding Dynamics.

Rutter, M. (1998). Developmental catch-up, and deficit, following adoption after severe global early privation. English and Romanian Adoptees (ERA) Study Team. *Journal of Child Psychology and Psychiatry, 39*(4), 465–476.

Rutter, M. L. (1999). Psychosocial adversity and child psychopathology. *British Journal of Psychiatry, 174*(6), 480–493.

Rutter, M. L., Kreppner, J. M., & O'Connor, T. G. (2001). Specificity and heterogeneity in children's responses to profound institutional privation. *British Journal of Psychiatry, 179*(2), 97–103.

Seabrook, J. (2010). *The last babylift.* Retrieved from http://www.newyorker.com/reporting/2010/05/10/100510fa_fact_seabrook

Seibert, P. S., Stridh-Igo, P., & Zimmerman, C. G. (2002). A checklist to facilitate cultural awareness and sensitivity. *Journal of Medical Ethics, 28*(3), 143–146.

Sherman, D. H., Aldrich, C. A., Bonar, B. E., Carr, W. L., & McCulloch, H. (1938). *Semi-centennial volume of the American Pediatric Society 1888–1938* (Vol. 64). Menasha, WI: George Banta.

Shonkoff, J. P., Garner, A. S., Siegel, B. S., Dobbins, M. I., Earls, M. F., McGuinn, L., et al. (2012). The lifelong effects of early childhood adversity and toxic stress. *Pediatrics, 129*(1), e232–e246.

Simms, M. D., Dubowitz, H., & Szilagyi, M. A. (2000). Health care needs of children in the foster care system. *Pediatrics, 106*(4 Suppl), 909–918.

Simon, R. J. (2006). Transracial Adoption. In K. S. Stolley & V. L. Bullough (Eds.), *The Praeger Handbook of Adoption* (pp. 632–640). Westport, CT: Praeger.

Solomon, A. (2012). *Far from the tree.* New York: Scribner.

Soriano-Guillen, L., Corripio, R., Labarta, J. I., Canete, R., Castro-Feijoo, L., Espino, R., et al. (2010). Central precocious puberty in children living in Spain: incidence, prevalence, and influence of adoption and immigration. *Journal of Clinical Endocrinology and Metabolism 95*(9), 4305–4313.

Takayama, J. I., Wolfe, E., & Coulter, K. P. (1998). Relationship between reason for placement and medical findings among children in foster care. *Pediatrics, 101*(2), 201–207.

Task Force on Health Care for Children in Foster Care. (2005). *Fostering health: Health care for children and adolescence in foster care.* Elk Grove Village: American Academy of Pediatrics.

Teilmann, G., Main, K., & Skakkebaek, N. (2005). High frequency of central precocious puberty in adoptee and immigrant children in Denmark. *Hormone Research, 64,* 41–47.

Teilmann, G., Pedersen, C. B., Jensen, T. K., Skakkebaek, N. E., & Juul, A. (2005). Prevalence and incidence of precocious pubertal development in Denmark: an epidemiologic study based on national registries. *Pediatrics, 116*(6), 1323–1328.

Teilmann, G., Petersen, J. H., Gormsen, M., Damgaard, K., Skakkebaek, N. E., & Jensen, T. K. (2009). Early puberty in internationally adopted girls: Hormonal and clinical markers of puberty in 276 girls examined biannually over two years. *Hormone Research, 72*(4), 236–246.

U.S. Department of Health and Human Services. (n.d.). *Transracial and transcultural adoption.* Retrieved from http://centerforchildwelfare2.fmhi.usf.edu/kb/cultcomp/Transracial%20and%20Transcult%20adoption.pdf

U.S. Department of Health and Human Services. (2013). *The AFCARS report.* Retrieved from http://www.acf.hhs.gov/programs/cb/resource/afcars-report-20

U.S. Department of State. (2014a). *Acquiring U.S. citizenship for your child.* Retrieved from http://adoption.state.gov/us_visa_for_your_child/citizenship.php

U.S. Department of State. (2014b). *Intercountry adoption.* Retrieved from http://adoption.state.gov

U.S. Department of State. (2014c). *Intercountry adoption: statistics.* Retrieved from http://adoption.state.gov/about_us/statistics.php

Vandivere, S., Malm, K., & Radel, L. (2009). *Adoption USA: a chartbook based on the 2007 national survey of adoptive parents.* Retrieved from http://aspe.hhs.gov/hsp/09/nsap/charournatbook/index.cfm

Von Korff, L., Grotevant, H. D., & McRoy, R. G. (2006). Openness arrangements and psychological adjustment in adolescent adoptees. *Journal of Family Psychology, 20*(3), 531–534.

Wells, M. I. (2000). Beyond cultural competence: a model for individual and institutional competence development. *Journal of Community Health Nursing, 17,* 189–199.

Wilbarger, J., Gunnar, M., Schneider, M., & Pollak, S. (2010). Sensory processing in internationally adopted, post-institutionalized children. *Journal of Child Psychology and Psychiatry, 51*(10), 1105–1114.

Zeanah, C. H., Egger, H. L., Smyke, A. T., Nelson, C. A., Fox, N. A., Marshall, P. J., et al. (2009). Institutional rearing and psychiatric disorders in Romanian preschool children. *American Journal of Psychiatry, 116,* 777–785.

# School Issues

JAERAN KIM AND BETH HALL

OUTSIDE OF HOME, CHILDREN SPEND more of their lives at school than anywhere else. (For this chapter, we are focusing on children in public and private educational settings, and therefore do not include children who are homeschooled.) For six or more hours a day, the average school-age child or adolescent spends their time in an environment that is not necessarily well-equipped to be responsive to transracially and internationally adopted children and their families. Teachers, school administrators, and staff, as well as other children and their families, may have only a cursory understanding of the transracial and international adoption experience. Curriculum generally is developed from the perspective of the dominant society; in the United States, the "norm" is often assumed to be white, intact families where children are living with their biological parents. The paucity of research on the educational outcomes for transracially and internationally adopted children means we do not know the extent to which educators understand or support the transracially adopted child's educational development (Raleigh & Kao, 2013). To fully support their transracially and internationally adopted children, parents must pay close attention to the children's educational experiences and act as educators, advocates, and even agitators to ensure that their children's needs are being met. In this chapter we will review what transracial and intercountry adoptees and their adoptive parents tell us about their experiences with schools; some of the ways racism and adoptism are expressed in schools; how developmental challenges faced by transracially and internationally adopted students can affect their learning experiences; how issues of race and adoption impact students with special needs; and, finally, practical interventions that individual educators can make (and parents can advocate for) in classroom assignments and school environments.

Children learn more than how to read and write in school; they learn *who they are* outside their immediate family systems, as citizens of the world. Transracially and internationally adopted (TRA/ICA) children entering formal school systems have more developmental and identity tasks to perform than their peers. Like other children, TRA/ICA children and youth undertake the tasks of physical, neurological, emotional, moral, and identity development; however, TRA/ICA children must integrate additional tasks related to their adoption (Brodzinsky, Schechter, & Henig, 1993). Similarly, although all children of color must navigate their racial, ethnic, and cultural identity in the context of white privilege, TRA children often address these identities without the benefit of adult role models of color in their home or extended family. In addition, some TRA/ICA children have one or more physical, intellectual, developmental, learning, or emotional and behavioral disability that affects learning (Kreider & Lofquist, 2014; Vandivere & McKlindon, 2010). Each of these identities mark a TRA/ICA child as "other" and may make him or her subject to differential or discriminatory treatment.

For ease, this chapter will refer to transracial adopted children as TRA and international (also referred to as intercountry) adopted children as ICA. As authors we apply a few conventions of terminology as well based on the following assumptions: (1) the large majority of transracial adoptions are of children of color by white parents, although any adoption of a child by parents of a different race is in fact a transracial adoption; (2) most (but not all) intercountry adoptions are also transracial adoptions and as such have more commonality than not in terms of children's experience of race and adoption; (3) there are significant differences in experiences between TRA and ICA children that are *not* transracially adopted (e.g., children adopted internationally by U.S. citizen parents that share the child's race, ethnicity, and culture), which are more similar in experience to in racial domestic placements than transracial international placements because the child's experience of adoption does not intersect directly with their experience of race; and (4) when we use the term TRA, we are applying it to both transracially adopted domestically born and internationally born children.

Despite listing these categories as discrete spheres, TRA/ICA children experience what Kimberlee Crenshaw (1989) defines as *intersectionality*—that is, they must navigate multiple, simultaneous, interconnected identities that the dominant group perceives as violations of spoken or unspoken norms. The TRA/ICA child, through no choice of her own, violates norms of kinship, race, and ability because she (1) is not genetically related to the family she lives with, in a society that privileges biological kinship connections; (2) crosses racial lines, in a society that privileges racial matching within families; and (3) may have a disability, in a society that privileges physical, cognitive, and mental ability. As concrete thinkers, children are confused by these intersections and cannot, without adult help, understand their experience in the context of the larger systems at play (Brodzinsky et al., 1993; Piaget & Inhelder, 1974). These intersections, then, become critical to understanding both the TRA/ICA child's experience and their successes or struggles within the school system.

Most research on TRA/ICA children in schools has focused on educational outcomes (Dalen, 2002; Raleigh & Kao, 2013; Tirella, Chan & Miller, 2006). For example, a study of 193 internationally adopted children in Norway found that compared with their nonadopted peers, the internationally adopted children had lower educational achievement outcomes (Dalen, 2002). Using longitudinal data, Raleigh and Kao (2013) examined whether differences exist between transracially adopted children and white, same-race adoptive placements. Tirella et al. (2006) found that 61 percent of the eighty-one Eastern European adopted children in their study had an Individualized Education Plan (IEP). Despite the amount of time that children in school spend interacting with teachers and peers, there have been no significant studies on the interaction between the teacher–child relationships or school environment on TRA/ICA racial, ethnic, and cultural identity. Research on the impact of racial and ethnic socialization in the school environment for TRA/ICA children has focused on the role of white adoptive parents, as opposed to teachers or classmates (Crolley-Simic & Vonk, 2008; Lee, 2003; Snyder, 2012; Vonk, 2001).

The authors approach this topic both as adoption professionals and as individuals with personal connections to adoption and real-life experiences of school-related issues faced by TRA/ICA children and youth. JaeRan Kim was adopted as a 3-year-old from South Korea into a white family living in a predominantly white town in Minnesota, attending nondiverse schools. She is now a child welfare professional and researcher who specializes in issues related to adoption and foster care. Beth Hall was raised in a white, same-race adoptive family, as a nonadopted sibling, and later became an adoptive parent to two TRA children. Beth was born and raised in the San Francisco Bay Area, where she also raised her children. She and her children attended both public and private schools, in the context of a racially diverse community where schools nevertheless often are segregated along racial and socioeconomic lines. Beth is a cofounder of Pact, An Adoption Alliance, where she has worked with adopted children of color and their families for more than 20 years. Pact is a nonprofit organization whose mission is to serve adopted children of color. To best serve children's needs, Pact provides not only adoptive placement but lifelong education, support, and community for adoptees and their families on issues of adoption and race with the goal that every child should feel wanted, honored, and loved—a cherished member of a strong family with proud connections to the rich cultural heritage that is his or her birthright. Pact offers educational workshops in California as well as online webinars for transracial adopters. The "jewel in the crown" of Pact's educational programs is Pact Family Camp, a weeklong summer retreat where adopted children of color and their families can share their experiences while learning from experts and each other.

Few organizations have a sole mission to serve children of color in adoption, although some individual support groups and adult adoptee groups are either web based or serve regional constituencies (e.g., Land of Gazillion Adoptees, Adoption Mosaic, International Korean Adoptee Association [IKAA]) and several international adoption–focused groups attract many transracial families, such as Families with Children from China (FCC) and Korean Adoptee and Adoptive Parent Network (KAAN). Some placement agencies focus is race centric (Institute for Black Parenting, Institute for Latino Parenting), although their postplacement programming often is focused more on same-race adoptive families than transracial families. Finally, there are several culture camps throughout the country, often with a focus on a particular country of birth for internationally born adoptees (Holt Camps, Colorado Heritage Camps) as well as programs that provide opportunities for birth country travel to both families and adopted youth, called homeland tours.

Both authors have experience educating school staff and administrators on ways that schools can become TRA/ICA sensitive. Each has a child who has been diagnosed with a learning disability and therefore has personally navigated the educational system for a child of color with special needs. This chapter seeks to combine professional and personal experience to provide a window into the firsthand experiences of TRA/ICA children and their parents in the school environment.

## WHAT TRANSRACIAL AND INTERCOUNTRY ADOPTEES TELL US ABOUT THEIR EXPERIENCES WITH SCHOOLS

It is important to acknowledge that adoptees themselves—not parents, teachers, or other professionals—are the foremost experts on what it *feels like* to be an adopted person in a school environment. TRA/ICA adults and children describe their school experiences as riddled with incidents in which they were forced to reveal or explain their adoption history to peers, to teachers, and in assignments.

> My son's teacher called today. He hasn't been turning in his assignments for 11th grade Humanities. He is an A student but is so far behind on this paper and presentation about how his family came to America, the teacher is worried he will fail the class. He has to interview two family members and then present their answers to his class. How can I get him back on track? I know these family-related topics are sensitive for him as an adopted kid, but he doesn't want to tell his teacher about his feelings so she just assumes he is being either lazy or defiant when really he just doesn't want to have to explain his personal history and struggle with identity to a stranger yet again.
>
> Pact client

"Narrative burden" (Ballard, 2013; Leinaweaver, 2008) is the presumption that one's personal narrative and history is public property, open to the curiosity and interest of strangers. For TRA/ICA adults and children, narrative burden can be focused on adoption, race, or a combination of both. Assignments and curriculum (such as family trees or family histories) that force them to put their personal experiences or feelings into the public sphere before they are ready, or that do not give the student an authentic choice about sharing this aspect of their life, is a form of narrative burden. A TRA/ICA child may "check out" of a classroom expectation or assignment as a way to disengage from confronting their personal history in the school setting. Teachers and parents may see such disengagement as a function of the child's cognitive, social, or emotional limitations rather than as an emotional response to being forced to explore their adoption in a public context.

> In my eighth-grade Geography class when we were learning about countries in Asia, my teacher wrote a bunch of scribbles on the chalkboard to "demonstrate" what Chinese writing looked like and imitated what he thought Chinese language sounded like by speaking some "ching-chong" type utterances. He then said, "Well, this isn't really Chinese, but you get the idea." Everyone in the class turned and looked at me, expecting a response, as I shrunk in my seat with embarrassment. Adoption-based "narrative burden" experiences I experienced as a child and adolescent included having to explain why I had an "American" name, why I was adopted and didn't look like my parents, and people wanting to know what it felt like to be abandoned and/or adopted.
>
> JaeRan Kim

TRA/ICA students experience bias and discrimination from their peers, teachers, and other school staff. In the Donaldson Adoption Institute study of adult adoptees, adult adoptees were surveyed about their racial, ethnic, and adoptive identity. Of the 179 adult Korean adoptees who responded, 75 percent reported experiencing racism from classmates and 39 percent reported racism from teachers (McGinnis, Smith, Ryan, & Howard, 2009). Parents and teachers often assume that TRA/ICA students will report bullying by peers around adoption, race, ethnicity, or cultural issues, but often they do not. TRA/ICA students perceive that both adoption and race should be minimized in an attempt to neutralize the differences between them and their nonadopted family members and community members (Samuels, 2009, 2010). Sara Docan-Morgan (2011) examined how adopted Koreans communicate with their white adoptive families around issues of race and adoption. More than three-fourths of the thirty-four participants in the study reported being raised in predominantly white communities. The participants' experiences with racism in school included three types of attacks by classmates or peers: attacks by classmates or peers based on their appearance (such as having children pull at the corners of their eyes to mimic the almond shaped eye), attacks on ethnicity (most often by using racial slurs), and physical attacks (often in conjunction with one or both of the other types of racially based actions). The determining factor in whether these adoptees shared these experiences at school with their parents was whether their parents validated and affirmed these experiences in the past, or minimized or discounted them.

Even in more racially diverse environments, students report being questioned by peers and adults regarding their membership in their family because of their visible difference from their parents. These questions can come both from people of color who may share the child's racial or ethnic group, as well as those who do not, is always the result of a lack of understanding of the child's transracial family context.

> As a transracial adoptive family, whenever we change schools or move into a new community, we are faced with the challenge of explaining who we are and how we are connected. I remember when my son was starting fourth grade at his new school. As usual, it went smoothly for the first several days, because people hadn't matched us up yet. Of course eventually everyone realized that neither of his parents looked like him, and so the questions began. It was my husband's day for pick-up. As he and our son James walked next to the chain-link fence that surrounded the school, Dexter, another little boy who was in James' class and black like James, worked to get James' attention.
>
> "Hey, James," Dexter called out, "James, is that your dad?"
>
> James tried to ignore him at first, but Dexter was persistent.
>
> "James, James, is that your dad?"
>
> Letting James respond to his friend, my husband took James' backpack and continued the trek to the other end of the block. James was walking with his head down, looking like he wanted to sink into the sidewalk itself. By the end of the block it was clear that Dexter was not going to give up. As if in front of a firing squad, James turned and spat out his response:
>
> "No, he isn't my dad!"
>
> Time stopped. The instant was transformed into something bigger and more potent than any of the three could have planned or imagined. It was one of those split seconds that parents and TRA children fear—a moment

of truth. As soon as they were safely alone in the car, my husband turned to James and said:

"James, I just want you to know that I know that you love me."

James collapsed in the arms of his father and sobbed, wracked with the pain of denying this man he loved and worshipped because of his desire to fit in with a boy he as yet hardly knew. It was about James trying to manage the walk between fitting in with his same-race peers and loyalty to his family—race vs. adoption vs. his own personal identity. Walking along that block, between his black friend and his white father—this is the journey of TRA children, caught between the parents they love and the people in the world with whom they want to feel a connection.

Beth Hall

## WHAT TRANSRACIAL AND INTERCOUNTRY ADOPTIVE PARENTS TELL US ABOUT THEIR EXPERIENCES WITH SCHOOLS

Adoptive parents are different; their children have entered their families in a different way than those who gave birth to create a family. Because of this, adoptive parents sometimes feel like a targeted group when others question whether their children are "theirs" or ask whether they are their children's "real" parents, which seems to imply that they are not as legitimate as parents who give birth to their children. Like any other group, however, adoptive parents are not a monolithic community. Each parent has a different approach to, and understanding of, adoption, so it is critical to ask parents how they handle adoption and racial issues within their family rather than assuming one knows because one has worked with other adoptive parents in the past.

Educators often have a limited understanding of the losses and challenges associated with adoption, particularly given the lack of training educators receive on the topic (Smith & Riley, 2006; Wood & Ng, 2001). Educators may believe that adopted children should be able to behave and perform similarly to their nonadopted counterparts because of an underlying assumption that placement solves all of the adopted child's experiences with loss, grief, and trauma. In one study, parents of adopted children gave lower ratings on their child's school adjustment compared with parents of children who were born to them and reported higher rates of complaints about children's behaviors when the child was adopted (Howard, Smith, & Ryan, 2004). Adoptive parents themselves may or may not understand how their child's experience of loss, grief, and trauma manifest as behaviors, including depression, rage, school failure, drug and alcohol involvement, sexual activity, and juvenile justice interactions. When these behaviors are displayed in school, parents report that they feel blamed by teachers and administrators for their children's struggles, rather than treated as partners in helping to unlock the impact of past experiences and the ongoing issues that their children are experiencing.

The most common school-related question we hear from adoptive parents is whether or not they should tell the school and their children's teachers that their child is adopted for fear that teachers and staff will assume that their children have "problems" based on preconceived stereotypes about adopted children (Smith & Riley, 2006). Educators may unwittingly engage in *adoptism*, defined as the bias that exists within society to privilege families that are connected genetically over those made through adoption. Adoption-sensitive teachers and educators recognize that the world often treats adoptive parents and adopted children as "second-best" families, and use their skills and knowledge to advocate for these families and their unique needs and partner with adoptive parents to create a TRA/ICA-sensitive learning environment.

### Race and Adoption in the Schools

> Last year, when he was a kindergartener at the local public school, my son took another child's show-and-tell toy and hid it in his cubby. He was sent to the principal's office with a formal disciplinary referral for stealing. It landed him an in-school detention and a call home from the principal. I never imagined I'd have to discuss with school personnel the absurdity of applying "zero tolerance" policies to five-year-olds.
>
> Pact client

Race, ethnicity, and culture matter in the classroom, whether the TRA/ICA child is in a diverse school and community or in a predominantly white community or school. Bias and discrimination by classmates, teachers, school staff, and administrators exists for all children of color (Tatum, 2003). Race and ethnicity also factor into educational outcomes

(Kao & Thompson, 2003). TRA children, who do not always feel authentically connected to their same-race peers or adults, may interpret the racism they experience as inherent to being transracially adopted. Even in environments in which supportive and well-developed racial sensitivity exists, TRA students may feel unable to seek assistance from staff. During one discussion session facilitated by JaeRan with a group of adolescents at Pact Family Camp (where adopted children of color and their families can explore feelings about race and adoption with others who share their experiences), parents were surprised and upset to hear their children describe racist incidents experienced in school and that teachers and administrators often minimized these incidents or allowed them to continue—or were themselves the perpetrators.

Bias and discrimination are not limited to blatant actions by racists or adoptists but also are evident in the everyday lived experiences known as microaggressions. (We define adoptists as those who treat adopted and fostered people as damaged, pathologizing their experience. Adoptists believe that all nonadopted people are inherently healthier, more competent, and therefore better than their adopted and fostered counterparts.) Coined by Chester Pierce (1974), the term "microaggressions" describes brief, everyday exchanges that send denigrating messages to people of color because they belong to a racial minority group. Micro-aggressions are delivered in the form of subtle snubs or dismissive looks, gestures, and tones whose impact is minimized as being unintended or innocuous (Sue et al., 2007). Baden and Pinderhughes (2014) found that microaggressions apply to adoption as well. Examples of microaggressions in school include white teachers rarely calling on students of color or schools placing adopted children in lower-level reading groups without evidence that this is appropriate to the particular child. Microaggressions may also masquerade as compliments, as when white teachers express surprise when a student of color is high-achieving. A meta-study by Tenebaum and Ruck (2007) found that teachers' expectations on their student's learning abilities varied depending on the child's race or ethnicity. Microaggressions impair performance by sapping the psychic and spiritual energy of their recipients. When a child must direct part of his energy each day to coping with these kinds of interactions, he has been forced to direct his energy and attention away from learning, participating in class, completing his work, and building healthy relationships with other children. Microaggressions have a significant, cumulative, and harmful impact on the developing adopted child of color.

When thinking about racism it can be easy to focus on interpersonal dynamics and ignore the larger context of institutional racism. Racism, sexism, heterosexism, ablism, and adoptism are all enforced and maintained by a society's institutions. Educational institutions are fundamentally influenced by the societal mores and assumptions of the dominant culture in which they exist. For parents and educators to serve the transracially adopted child, they must first understand the institutional power dynamics at play in their lives, so that they can begin to confront the multiple oppressions that these youth face and can advocate for systematic change. Widespread racial disparities exist in education, as demonstrated by the school-to-prison pipeline and racial achievement gaps documented nationally (Alexander, 2012; Gregory, Skiba, & Noguera, 2010; Morris, 2013). A recent report by the U.S. Department of Education (2014) found that children of color, particularly African American children, are three times more likely to be suspended or expelled from school compared with white children, starting as far back as preschool. Children of color are also more likely to be categorized as needing special education services (Rebora, 2011).

To eradicate racism, we must change institutional structures that reproduce and reinforce racism. To address institutional changes, we must confront two aspects of bias: *intent* and *impact*. Many "good-hearted" people and organizations do not set out to hurt anyone (intent), yet are sometimes unintentionally racist (impact) without realizing or recognizing why. White adults in particular can fall into the trap of focusing on *intent* when they respond to situations with dismissive comments, such as "I'm sure she didn't mean it like that" or "the school is trying to serve children of color better, but the problem is bigger than each of us." Despite the difficulty, individuals and institutions must hold themselves accountable for the *impact* of their actions and attitude even when the intent was well-meaning, by making reparations through personal growth as well as systemic advocacy for change.

## DEVELOPMENTAL CONSIDERATIONS FOR TRANSRACIAL AND INTERCOUNTRY ADOPTED STUDENTS

Creating an educational setting that is sensitive to the needs of TRA/ICA children is not a one-size-fits-all solution. At each age, the transracially or internationally adopted child will experience different challenges.

> Within a year after my adoption from South Korea at age 3, I was able to recognize other Asian people, pointing to them and saying "like me!" to my adoptive family in my newly acquired English language.
>
> JaeRan Kim

People are often surprised to learn that children begin to recognize racial differences in the toddler years (Mayer, 2012). It is often assumed that transracially or internationally adopted children must not notice or understand race if they haven't asked questions or talked about it aloud. Yet, as Van Ausdale and Feagin (2001) found in their study of preschool children, children not only notice race but also are actively exploring what racial difference means to them in their interactions with each other. To make things more complicated, when children do talk about racial difference, it often is expressed in ways that make white adoptive parents and teachers uncomfortable. The adults may worry that the child sounds racist and respond in ways that may shame the child, which in turn leads the child to understand that it is not okay to talk about race. Or the child may be concerned that if they "notice" race, they will no longer feel as connected to their parents and family. As Crumbley (1999) reminds us, it is common for TRA children to express a desire to be white like their parents in an effort to reinforce this connection.

Consciously or unconsciously, these attitudes and responses can work against the child's developmental need to explore physical and racial characteristics, inadvertently hindering the TRA/ICA child in terms of their immediate and long-term identity exploration. It is important to remember that children need to go through each developmental stage in chronological order no matter their pace; if well-meaning adults minimize or delay racialized exploration, the child will struggle to move to the next stage in their necessary development. Tatum (2003) reminds us that preschool-age children are developmentally on target when they notice differences in how people look physically. Children are naturally curious, pointing out skin color or hair color and texture differences; this is developmentally appropriate and reflects their growing observational skills. TRA/ICA preschoolers need supportive teachers and school staff to validate and acknowledge racial differences and also need to recognize and intervene if actions move into discriminatory or bullying behavior, such as refusing to let a child be part of an activity based on race or adoption status.

Along with the developmental tasks that all children undertake, adopted children have additional developmental tasks to work through (Brodzinsky, Schechter, & Henig, 1993). For children and youth of color, the significant losses that led to their placement are necessarily racialized. Factors such as the loss of the first family or first culture and heritage complicate the developmental progression of children of color, particularly as they move beyond the preschool years and through adolescence (Brodzinsky, Smith, & Brodzinsky, 1998; Crook, 2000; Feagin & Sikes, 2006). Educators often experience the TRA/ICA student's struggle with these developmental tasks through the child's behaviors, particularly if these behaviors are challenging and externalized to the point at which they are interfering with learning for other children in the classroom. Adoptive parents may not know the extent to which these behaviors are occurring in the classroom, and they may not always understand that these behaviors can be connected to their child's early preadoption experiences.

Many behaviors that present as problematic in the classroom and home stem from the survival skills that adopted children developed as a way to cope with their traumatic experiences. These behaviors might look like delays, regression, anxiety, oppositional attitudes, ADD, or ADHD. For example, an adoptive-sensitive educator working with a child who is acting clingy at age 8, in a way that doesn't seem age-inappropriate, will consider whether this behavior is tied to the child's multiple disruptions that interrupted or delayed the child's development of trust and individuating from his nonadopted peers.

Although attachment disorder gets a lot of media attention and often is associated with adoption, educators should know that an adopted child who appears disconnected and angry with her parents may be quite capable of attachment and is acting out of fear of losing or being rejected by yet another family or parent figure. From a developmental standpoint, it makes sense that adoption in and of itself interferes with or interrupts typical development. When educators do not understand the additional complexities that TRA/ICA children are trying to manage, and how these complexities affect learning and performance in the school setting, they are much more likely to misdiagnose or misunderstand these children and their needs.

At the same time, it is essential to understand these differences without pathologizing the experience of being adopted—as if adopted children or adults are somehow permanently damaged in a way that sets them up as less than their nonadopted counterparts. Adults should understand that adoption results in normative crises (Pavao, 1998) that, in turn, predict that certain issues and trigger points are likely to be salient for the population, rather than viewing them as inherently or permanently damaged.

We suggest that adoption does not prevent development but rather may disrupt development in such a way that the child's milestones may not match the child's chronological age. For example, given that an infant's task is to trust that his needs will be taken care of, imagine how the disruption of leaving his birth or first family for new caregivers affects the child's current and future developmental tasks of trust and attachment. (The phrase "first parents" is being used increasingly as a way to refer respectfully to the people who brought an adopted child into the world; it acknowledges that throughout their lives they will never cease to be the individuals who created that child. Among some adopted individuals and families of origin, "birth parents" has come to signify a devaluation of their status to one strictly defined by biology and the moment of childbirth.) When children are institutionalized, neglected, or traumatized, they can get stuck developmentally at that particular age, yet too often we continue to hold expectations and discipline them as if they were older children, as if their development and chronological ages were identical (Schooler, Keefer Smalley, & Callahan., 2010; van Gulden, 2010). When milestones are not met, adults become frustrated and too often label the child as having a "problem." Yet we would never expect a baby of 3 months to be able to crawl. Similarly, a child that did not learn to trust due to multiple disruptions of caregivers must continue to work on this task even as they reach the age when other children are working on individuating and autonomy.

Educators must understand that the adoption experience can be quite varied; how a child adopted as an infant at birth understands his or her experience will likely be very different than a child adopted at an older age. Children in open adoptions who are able to interact with their first or birth family may have a different perspective than those children who have no contact. Children adopted as toddlers and preschoolers will be adjusting to, at minimum, a transition between their birth or first family and their adoptive family, and many have experienced placement(s) in foster care or institutional care as well. These transitions mean becoming adjusted to everything that is new to them—new parents, new homes, new beds, new neighborhoods, new routines, new rules, new food, and often new schools and peers and friends. The magnitude of the stress associated with these transitions spills over into the classroom. Children are remarkably resilient, but a great deal of psychological energy must be devoted to the transition, so to expect them to be firmly attached or settled in the early stages of their transition is unrealistic. Even when children appear to be quickly acclimatized to a new family setting, it is useful to remember that their apparent connection to their new family is initially a survival reaction that requires time to develop into a firmly attached relationship.

Educators may see challenging behaviors at transition times such as arriving and settling into the classroom, saying goodbye to parents, preparing to leave at the end of the day, and transitioning between activities, classrooms, or teachers and staff. Remember that these children must focus on the tasks of connecting to their new family and environment during a time when they have experienced a lot of change and had little to no control over their situation, which may have included trauma, abuse, neglect, or institutionalization. As parents are likely to be managing these same behaviors at home, school staff and parents benefit from working together to find ways to manage transition-related behaviors.

> Every year my son has a major meltdown at the end of the school year. While all his classmates and teachers plan end-of-the-year celebrations and field trips, my son is the one refusing to go to school, disrupting the classroom, and acting out against his friends and beloved teachers. It took me a few years to understand that this transition was actually traumatic for him; it meant the end of a relationship with a teacher he cared about, friends, and even a routine that he depended on. Before we adopted him, my son had experienced both the loss of his birth family and had been in many foster homes. Given all the losses in his young life, it is no wonder he saw the end of a school year as another round of people disappearing from his life.
>
> Adoptive parent

Other developmental tasks that might be disrupted as a result of an adoption include issues around food or sleep during lunch, snack, or nap times. Children who have experienced food insecurity may hoard or steal food. Some children have had limited diets. Rigid attempts to control food or eating issues in school typically only reinforce the child's fears of food scarcity or exacerbate a child's unhealthy eating behaviors (Rowell, 2012). Being mindful that adopted children may have issues related to sleeping, and working with parents to develop strategies for managing them, is important in the context of younger children who still nap and also older children when asked to participate in sleep-away field trips or other overnight activities. Author and educator Jane Katch (2011) describes working with the parents of a child adopted from Russia to reduce problematic eating and napping issues in the classroom, including having two lunches from which the child could choose to eat, and setting the child's nap cot closer to her friends so that when she woke up she was surrounded by familiar faces.

Many ICA children are adopted during the late infant through early preschool years, a critical period of language development. Their language development is interrupted as a result of their adoption and the transition to learning English. As a result, these children may have additional difficulties communicating because they are losing their ability to communicate in a first language that may not be fully developed, and yet they may not be able to understand English. In addition to affecting reading and writing skills (Dalen, 2002), relationship skills necessary for communicating with teachers and classmates are likely to be affected.

**PRACTICE NOTES**

Adoption may interrupt developmental tasks, including the following:
- Ability to manage transition times in school including drop-off and pick up times, recess, lunch or snack, or change in classrooms or teachers
- Food issues during lunch or snack times, including stealing or hoarding food, refusing to eat, or developing unhealthy eating habits
- Sleep issues, such as sleeping in class, disrupted nap participation
- Language, writing, and communication skills
- Peer group relationship management
- Delayed behaviors that may be misinterpreted as oppositional or diagnosed as ADD/ADHD or anxiety rather than as residual coping mechanisms based on previous placements and early childhood experiences of trauma

Young children may have been told they were adopted, but that does not mean they have a full understanding of what adoption means. There are several critical developmental milestones in children's progressive understanding of adoption (Brodzinsky et al., 1993). Around age 6 or 7 years old, children begin to understand cognitively that to gain their new (adoptive) family they must have lost another family (Brodzinsky et al., 1993). This understanding enables them by age 9 years old or so to think about their first or birth parents and to wonder whether their first or birth parents are thinking about them as well. In the middle school years and later in the teen years, children focus even more on why adoption happened to them. They are coming to grips with who they are, relative both to the family with whom they live and their first or birth family, about whom they may have little or overwhelmingly negative information (Brodzinsky et al., 1993). These realities present additional developmental challenges for TRA/ICA children that they must integrate along with all the developmental tasks that other nonadopted children of color are facing.

As adopted children begin to realize that to get their adoptive family they had to first lose another family, they may begin to recognize far more complex and sometimes buried feelings about adoption. Adoption is an "ambiguous loss." Boss (2000) describes two different types of ambiguous loss: *physical absence coupled with psychological presence,* such as divorce, parent incarceration, soldiers missing in action, foster care, and adoption; and *physical presence coupled with psychological absence.* When the ambiguous loss is physical absence, the status of the "lost" person (such as a first or birth parent) is not known; yet the grieving person is thinking about and grieving for them on a regular basis. Boss points out that ambiguous loss is difficult to resolve because unlike when a death occurs, society does not have a familiar symbolic ritual for this type of loss; in addition the loss is not socially recognized or is kept hidden from others and the person suffering this loss is not acknowledged as grieving or is expected to "get over it."

Adopted persons, including children, are often told they should be grateful for having such a wonderful adoptive family. Expectations to be grateful for an experience that also makes one feel sad can lead to feeling invalidated (Boss, 2000). According to Boss, "The greater the ambiguity surrounding one's loss, the more difficult it is to master [the loss] and the greater one's depression, anxiety and conflict" (p. 7). Adoption, which we are taught to think of as positive and happy, can create a huge amount of ambiguity for the child, who might struggle with their sad or grieving feelings that go unvalidated by parents or other adults or peers.

The awareness that it is different to be adopted deepens in middle childhood. Children are concrete thinkers and imagine themselves at the center of everything (Piaget & Inhelder, 1974). If something good happens, it is because they have been good. If something bad happens, it is their fault. Children of color adopted by white parents may decide that their skin color is the reason or at least part of the reason that their birth family did not parent them. A child with medical problems or learning disabilities might similarly think that their first or birth parents couldn't take care of her because of her special needs. Even children who suffer the worst forms of abuse at the hands of their first or birth parents often believe that they were hurt because they were bad children. Managing their feelings about their first family and the (sometimes multiple) other placements they may have experienced before joining their adoptive family can interfere with engaging in school-related learning tasks. When a TRA/ICA child is struggling in school, in addition to an assessment for learning disabilities, parents and educators should consider these factors to ensure that they are not being misconstrued as inattention or lack of academic commitment.

Adolescence can be a tumultuous time for every child, but adopted youth of color must do a lot of extra psychological heavy lifting during their preteen and teen years. Normal adolescence involves a crisis in identity; adopted teenagers will face additional complications. "Tweens" and teens often express their reactions to loss by rebelling against parental standards. Knowing that they have a different origin may contribute to their need to define themselves autonomously. On the other hand, adopted adolescents may conform to others' behavior, beliefs, or expectations, to fit in or out of a sense of guilt or responsibility to their adoptive parents. Peer group membership becomes of ultimate importance during adolescence. Because membership is signified by "being the same as," TRA tweens and teens may have a more difficult time trying to figure out where they fit in.

According to Riley and Meeks (2005), despite being 2 percent of the overall teen population, adopted teenagers make up 5–17 percent of adolescents using mental health services in the United States. Adopted teens and their families require therapists and clinicians who are educated about their unique struggles. Riley and Meeks (2005) identified six common "stuck spots":

- *Reason for adoption*: Adopted tweens and teens often have myriad feelings of unresolved grief about why they were placed. When adopted adolescents are flooded by feelings of uncertainty and rejection, they need to know that not everyone will leave them.
- *Missing or difficult information*: Teens often look for detailed facts about themselves and their first on birth family that may not be available or known, bringing up feelings about loss of control. This loss needs to be acknowledged and processed.
- *Difference*: Feeling different from peers in adolescence is a profoundly difficult experience and can affect a child's sense of self-worth and security. This may play out in the context of racial and cultural differences when kids are adopted across racial lines and have grown up without a peer group of either other youth of color or other adoptees.
- *Permanence*: Tweens and teens who have already lost one set of parents may exhibit new anxiety reactions and behaviors relating to the possibility of losing their adoptive parents. This can manifest as misbehavior or testing behavior to see whether parents will let them go if their behavior is "bad" enough or result in kids who are afraid to leave the adoptive home. Others may struggle with retaining relationships because they consider themselves unworthy of long-term security.
- *Identity*: The questions of "who am I?" and "where did I come from?" are central to the adolescent adoptee. This often leads to increased interest in birth family search or connections, and for TRA/ICA youth, an increased focus on finding their place racially and culturally.
- *Loyalty*: Many adopted teens experience guilt about their interest in their birth parents, which they are afraid may hurt or upset their adoptive parents. Teens often need explicit permission from their adoptive parents to feel comfortable exploring feelings about and connections to their birth family; this can be complicated when the child is of a different race, ethnicity, or culture than their adoptive parents.

For adopted children of color, racial identity development can be especially intense and is made more complex by our society's confusion between race and class. For TRA/ICA children raised in nondiverse schools and communities, several challenges exist: they must manage relationships with classmates and teachers who have uninformed or preconceived beliefs, biases, or ideas about their racial, ethnic, or cultural group; teachers and administrators may not recognize or respond to subtle or overt teasing and bullying based on race, ethnicity or culture; and a racially or culturally inappropriate or insensitive school culture often remains unchallenged.

Children raised in diverse communities have different challenges. They may feel pressure to join (or conversely experience rejection by) their racial, ethnic, and cultural peers. Teens in closed adoptions or without racial or ethnic mentors in their lives may actively seek people of their own race in the school or community without guidance on how to evaluate appropriate relationships within that community. Conversely, they may shun same-race peers because of fear of rejection or learned stereotypes about people of their heritage community. These issues of authenticity or clashing values can result in a child feeling isolated, and this in turn will likely affect that child's academic performance.

We know that learning environments are far more successful when children see themselves reflected in their environment (Derman-Sparks & The A.B.C. Task Force, 1989) and that includes seeing and hearing reflections of their adoption and racial experience. Without these supports, children who still need to process their adoption experiences or racial identity will approach important school-age milestones in ways that teachers might attribute to lack of focus or learning disabilities. For this reason, it is essential that careful and professional assessments be conducted.

### Race, Disability, and Special Education Issues

Without an understanding of the challenges the adopted child, birth family, and adoptive family can face, schools and other community institutions often, unwittingly, work against the best interests of adoptees and adoptive families. . . . All of the children who are adopted, or who are foster children, or who are in other complex family situations and working hard to make sense of these complexities, have emotional obstacles to dealing with these challenges and divided loyalties. This extra emotional work—what I would call a normative crisis under challenging circumstances—influences the learning styles of these children.

Joyce Maguire Pavao (1998)

Performance and behavior in school are often the impetus for a child's referral for an assessment for a disability. In general, adopted children are more likely than nonadopted children to receive special education services (Brodzinsky & Steiger, 1991; Howard, Smith, & Ryan, 2004). Sometimes TRA/ICA children have preadoption experiences that include poor prenatal care, prematurity, low birth weight, prenatal exposure to alcohol or drugs, mentally ill birth parents, abuse, neglect, multiple placements, or institutionalization (Smith & Riley, 2006). McCarthy (2005) found that 40 percent of the 293 children adopted from Eastern European countries received special education services. In another study, 32 percent of ICA children and 40 percent of children adopted from foster care received special education services (Howard, Smith, & Ryan, 2004). These experiences may contribute to the child having a developmental delay or disability that requires additional educational support.

Children with disabilities experience discrimination and bias in the schools. The U.S. Department of Education (2014) found that children with disabilities were twice as likely to experience a suspension or expulsion compared with their nondisabled classmates. Students with disabilities are also subjected to the most severe forms of discipline, such as seclusion and physical and mechanical restraints, at much higher rates than their classmates without disabilities (U.S. Department of Education, 2014). The intersection of race and disability also matters, particularly for African American, American Indian, and multiracial children with disabilities, who are disproportionately suspended from school at rates higher than white children with disabilities (McFadden, Marsh, Price & Hwang, 1992; U.S. Department of Education, 2014).

The Individuals with Disabilities Education Act (IDEA) is the current law that ensures children with disabilities have access to quality, free, public education. IDEA specifies parents' rights related to special education, which include the right to request an assessment; to be informed in writing whether the school initiates an assessment; to give or withhold approval for an evaluation; to obtain an independent evaluation; to be provided with copies of their child's school records and to request corrections of incorrect information; and to file a complaint with the Office of Civil Rights if discrimination or misdiagnosis has occurred (National Learning Center for Disabilities, n.d.).

Unfortunately, educators can sometimes become defensive when parents feel the need to advocate for their children or raise questions about how a student is being treated related to his race, adoption status, or learning challenges. Children's needs will be best served when administrators and teachers see adoptive parents as *partners* in supporting the TRA/ICA child. In an ideal world, schools would be supportive of parents who are pursuing the following strategies:

- Parents need to insert themselves into the school's bureaucratic processes, which often are not set up to be inclusive to parents; it is essential to be educated about the rules and rights that govern the school system's responsibility to educate your child, which might mean continuing to ensure success and advocate even after receiving multiple "no's" from school staff or administrators.
- Parents should closely monitor their child's performance in school. Maintaining records and periodically checking in with the child's teachers beyond regularly scheduled conferences should be seen as a positive enhancement that will allow each to learn from the other as they sort out the multiple intersections likely to be influencing the TRA/ICA child's educational progress.
- Parents should ask questions and be invited to clarify their beliefs regarding whether teachers are either minimizing or overemphasizing areas of need or concern, particularly as it relates to adoption histories and racial needs if those are not areas of expertise or extensive experience of the school staff.
- If a school is not responsive, parents should search for organizations locally and nationally that can provide guidance and help them understand their rights. National organizations include the National Center for Learning Disabilities (n.d.), which has great advice for parents about how to recognize and advocate for their children with learning differences or other special needs, and Wrightslaw (n.d.), which has information about special education law and advocacy for special needs children.

Teachers and other important adults can make a huge difference in how children perceive themselves and process the experience of having learning disabilities, special needs, or ADD and ADHD. When teachers and school administrators see TRA/ICA children in terms of their *abilities* rather than their *disabilities*, they can help the children see their learning issues within the context of their other differences without making assumptions that their learning issue is determined by their race or caused by their adoption.

> My son never loved school but he sees himself as a learner. This is what my son wrote for one of his high school papers: "My personal challenge is that I have a learning difference called dyslexia. Dyslexia is a learning issue that affects how I learn but does NOT mean I am not as smart as anyone else. There are some big super-stars that have dyslexia like Thomas Edison and Danny Glover. I had to learn that I am as smart as anyone else in this world. Learning differently has made me patient because when you have a learning disorder you take longer to get some things than other kids, like multiplication facts. Frustration is one of the biggest things you'll run into if you are teaching a kid with learning disabilities. I remember when I was younger that homework would only take my other classmates ten minutes and it would take me MUCH longer. I wouldn't be able to go outside until my homework was all done. I would get so mad that they got to play and I didn't. Sometimes you have to learn to fight for yourself because the people who are trying to help you under-estimate you. Sometimes I have to speak out and say, "This is too easy, can I please have something harder?" Overall I feel that I am a better, stronger person with more understanding of others who are challenged because of my own learning differences.
>
> Beth Hall

### INDIVIDUAL EDUCATOR INTERVENTIONS IN THE CLASSROOM

Part of what a child learns about in school is how the world operates beyond her own home. If he is lucky he is taught to search for commonality and to appreciate difference, first among his classmates and then in the wider community. As mentioned earlier, children who don't see their lives reflected in their assignments and by their teachers may react in a number of ways: with anger, withdrawal, or noncompliance with the assignment. Ensuring that books and other learning materials represent a spectrum of human diversity, including positive portrayals of adoptive families, is critical. A diverse curriculum and classroom materials benefit TRA/ICA children by providing much-needed reflection and validation of their racial, ethnic, and cultural heritage and adoption identity, but it is equally important in normalizing diversity and difference for the white and nonadopted students, who otherwise are prone to assuming their own experience is "normal."

We focus here are two areas of concern that can have a huge impact on the experience of transracially adopted children in schools: classroom assignments and school ecology or environment.

### Classroom Assignments

One way that children are taught about the world and people around them is through assignments that focus on family and society. When these assignments are inclusive and respectful of many diverse family models, cultures, and racial groups, all children benefit. TRA/ICA students growing up in unique families especially benefit from seeing their families reflected as part of the spectrum of human experiences. Too often, however, these assignments are not sensitively designed and actually can undermine the well-being and sense of learning readiness for TRA/ICA children.

Most assignments can be modified to allow everyone to feel included while still reaping the benefits and meeting the learning goals. Usually, simply offering examples that give children options and choices will ensure that children and families from all kinds of backgrounds and histories can find at least one option that validates their own situation and gives them choices about what kind of personal information they wish to share.

#### FAMILY TREES

My daughter came home from her elementary school with a "family tree" assignment. It's a form with boxes and circles that the kids are supposed to fill in: mom and dad, brothers and sisters, grandparents. When we suggested that she could use either our family or her birth family, either was okay with us, she ripped the paper in half and screamed with tears streaming down her face, "I hate school." What are we doing wrong?

Pact client

Parents and educators are tasked with helping transracially adopted youth process and understand their feelings and also to be an ally in thinking about how to advocate for changes for children who don't fit the "standard" family tree configuration. Parents can help children process their feelings by offering some of their own. "I keep thinking about all the different kinds of families that don't fit into this kind of form. What about Jenny who lives with her mom and grandma, but doesn't know her dad? How about Jimmy, who has two moms, how is he supposed to fill it in? And what about you and other adopted kids: they have two sets of parents and they shouldn't feel like they have to choose. I like your teacher, but I don't think this assignment is good for a lot of different kinds of families. What do you think?"

Wood and Ng (2001) recommend some alternative assignments teachers can assign:

- Draw a picture of the people in your life who love you and you consider family.
- Draw a picture of who lives in your home and what their relationship to you is.
- Create your loving tree or caring tree and tell something about each person that does something important for you or teaches you something.
- Create a kinship tree or genogram that shows people who you are related to genetically as well as those who are part of your family because you live with them or because you care about or take care of each other.

### Personal Timelines and Birthdays

Our kindergarten daughter, who was born in China, joined our family when she was two years old. The first assignment of the school year turns out to be a ME board project in which the kids are supposed to tell the story of their birth and family through pictures and descriptions. What do we do?

Pact client

Many adoptees and foster children cannot complete an assignment that is based on their birthday, and that alone makes it inappropriate. Similar assignments include personal timelines or baby picture guessing games (particularly uncomfortable when a child's photo is all too easy to guess because she or he is the only student of color). Many ICA and some TRA children know little if anything about the circumstances of their birth and often find it embarrassing if they are the only one to bring in a picture of themselves at age 2 years old or with an orphanage identification number when all the other kids have newborn or hospital photos. Celebrations or rituals on children's birthdays can present challenges as well because some adopted children do not know the time, place, or date of their birth. Alternative assignments include:

- Ask kids to bring in pictures from "when they were younger"—ones they like or were taken on a day that was important to them. This gives them an opportunity to share what they choose. They can bring in something relatively recent without feeling like they can't do what the teacher asked.
- Invite kids to create a "significant events in my life" timeline showing or describing five or ten chosen events. This way they can choose events that may or may not have anything to do with when they entered their family. Give examples like: "I learned to walk" or "I got a bicycle" or "I started school."
- Celebrations are important so we urge teachers to work carefully with parents to understand whether there are any sensitivities about these issues among their students. Celebrations and rituals can be tailored to avoid pointing out difficulties or painful aspects. For a child who does not know his or her birth date, a teacher could find out whether the family knows what month the child was born in, and create celebration rituals for that class that focus on all the children's birth months.

### Mother's Day and Father's Day

For children who have more than one mother or father or are being raised by someone other than a parent, these celebrations can bring up circumstances (painful or simply private) they may not want to explore in the classroom setting. Alternative assignments could include having the child create something to give to a maternal or paternal figure or someone who is important to them or drawing a picture or writing something about someone in their life who has made a difference or taught them something.

### Names

Adopted and foster children often are given different names by their birth parents and adoptive parents or are named by someone who is no longer in their life, such as in the case of many ICA children who were named at their orphanage. Alternatively, we suggest asking children to share their name and tell each other one thing they like or don't like about their name or something about the meaning or history of their name in different cultures. It is fine to explore the meaning of names but that should not be confused with requiring children to reveal their personal naming history.

### Cultural Holidays

Educators often point to particular holidays or "ethnic" study units that happen once a year or for a special occasion as a reflection of incorporating diversity. Unfortunately, this approach creates a kind of tourist curriculum that minimizes or treats them as exotic. For example, if the only element of a school's curriculum that acknowledges a Latino tradition is a festival on Cinco de Mayo, the school's implicit message to its students is that there is no other meaningful history, literature, or cultural celebration in Latino culture. To create a curriculum that is truly diverse means that multicultural awareness is not pushed to the periphery but rather emphasized within literature choices, in historical texts, in year-round school displays, and in daily classroom discussions. Truly diversifying the curriculum benefits not only those who belong to nondominant races or cultures but every child who needs to be prepared to live in a diverse world.

## TEACHING RACIALLY CHARGED HISTORY OR CURRICULUM

Children understand that what is "important" is reflected in the books they are assigned to read and the history they are required to know and understand. Assess whether all of the "main characters" in a school's textbooks are European in background, Christian, and born to their families. Does the curriculum include at its center the views of all the people affected and involved, such as African American, Japanese American, and Native American people, or does it include only a white, Euro-American point of view on topics such as slavery, World War II, Japanese internment, or Indian reservations.

When TRA/ICA children are in predominantly white schools or community, it is common for teachers to ask a TRA/ICA child to become the "poster child" for teaching moments related to their heritage. Although younger children may embrace the opportunity to share some of their racial, ethnic, or cultural heritage, older TRA/ICA children are often uncomfortable being singled out in this way. Older TRA/ICA children and adolescents must manage their racial identity development at the same time the curriculum becomes less celebratory about race and culture. Although curriculum may include sessions on slavery, the Civil War, and the civil rights movement, other historical experiences of people of color are often excluded or are given minimal inclusion. This can be an embarrassing and shameful time for adopted students of color. In predominantely white classrooms, TRA/ICA children and youth may be expected to be content experts or held to a higher standard of knowledge in these lessons; in addition, they may be asked to comment more in classroom discussions or represent "their people." Confronted with curricula written from a predominantly white perspective and by white authors, the TRA/ICA student may come to believe that this partial or unbalanced information is the full story of her racial, ethnic, and cultural group; on the other hand, a TRA/ICA student who is well-educated on the topic may have critiques about the content or feel that the way it is being presented perpetuates racial, ethnic, or cultural stereotypes. In this situation, the student may feel unsafe expressing those concerns, given the power differential between a white teacher and a student of color.

> One family we worked with, whose son was unprepared to interview his African American adoptive parents because he knew that his birth family was Ethiopian, came up with the idea of writing a paper on international adoption in general. He interviewed several adult and teen adoptees regarding their thoughts and feelings on the subject so that he didn't have to reveal his own personal story. Another student wrote a very personal narrative that included interviews with her birth family, but was allowed to make a video of her presentation that was only viewed by her teacher instead of the whole class because of the student's desire to keep some of the information private.
>
> Beth Hall

Whatever the solution, parents and teachers must be children's allies in recognizing and acknowledging the child's frustration and anger about being asked to explore unresolved identity issues in front of their classmates. Helping them find a workaround that allows them to pass their classes is important, but even more important is creating classroom and school environments that anticipate such issues and offer assignments that do not precipitate these crises in the first place.

### SCHOOL ECOLOGY AND ENVIRONMENT

Early in first grade at my daughter's school, each child is given a special day when she gets to help the teacher in prominent ways and make important choices (like who gets to stand first in line). Classmates interview the child of the day, and the teacher records the answers on a big poster. My daughter was the first of two adopted children in her class to have a special day, and inevitably questions about adoption came up— although, the teacher reported, they were afterthoughts. The class had just finished interviewing my daughter, and the teacher was about to move on, when a classmate asked, "Weren't you adopted?"

I got a message from the teacher that afternoon saying that adoption had come up and that my daughter had handled the situation with confidence and pride. The teacher then read to the class a book called *Families Are Different*. In it a girl adopted transracially from Korea talks about her white parents, her Korean sister, and the occasional discomfort of being different from other families. But she looks around the neighborhood and notices that while in some families everyone looks alike (even the dog), in others there are many differences. All families, she concludes, are held together "by a special kind of glue called love."

I was glad the teacher had read the book, and I was gratified to hear that my daughter had enjoyed her special day. So I was surprised, when I picked up my daughter that afternoon, to see her looking sad. It turns out that the interview was fine. She had enjoyed talking about herself and didn't mind the questions about adoption. She loved the book and was pleased that her teacher had read it aloud. But there was still a problem.

One child had asked if the two adopted girls in *Families Are Different* were real sisters. And the teacher had answered, "They're kind of sisters." It's possible that no one except my daughter picked up on the subtext of that answer. But some kids catch all the nuances when grownups talk about adoption. Mine has her radar fine-tuned. She heard that the teacher wasn't sure just how "real" those sisters were. My daughter doesn't have a sibling, but she has adopted friends who do. Weren't Betty and Zoe real sisters, she asked?

I explained that sometimes grownups not in adoptive families aren't always good at answering questions about adoption. What's confusing, I explained, is that before Zoe was adopted, she and Betty weren't sisters, but that from the moment of adoption on, they were sisters forever. And by the way, would she like me to come talk to the class about adoption next week?

Amy Klatzkin, How I Explained Adoption to the First Grade,<br>Adoptive Families Magazine

Children perform better in school when they feel their families are supported in the ecology that is their school. Solomon (1976) argues that oppressive habitats in schools and neighborhoods carry negative valuations on the people and children who inhabit them, creating "an overriding sense of one's powerlessness to direct one's own life." Students who experience acceptance at school are more highly motivated, engaged in learning, and committed to school (Osterman, 2000). Students in schools that have a greater sense of community are more academically motivated and have higher educational aspirations (Bryk & Driscoll, 1998; Solomon et al., 2000) and are also more likely to develop social and emotional competencies and enjoy school more (Schaps, Battistich, & Solomon, 1997). More recently, educators have been looking at how schools must create welcoming environments to serve diverse populations:

> When asking students to explore issues of personal and social identity, teachers must provide safe spaces where students are seen, valued, cared for and respected. Teachers can show they value students' lives and identities in a variety of ways. Some are small, like taking the time to learn the proper pronunciation of every student's name or getting to know young people's families. Others require more time and investment, like building curriculum around personal narratives or incorporating identity-based responses into the study of texts. At the community level, it is important to understand neighborhood demographics, strengths, concerns, conflicts and challenges.
>
> Critical Practices for Anti-Bias Education

It is therefore critical to increase family involvement and teach respect for diversity both within the school and in the world beyond so all students and families feel safe and welcomed. To create a welcoming and inclusive school environment, staff and teachers can begin by understanding each child's unique family structure in the following ways:

- Asking what children call each parent and caregiver or guardian and using that language with the child and when referring to their family.
- Consulting parents or children to see whether they are open to sharing how they talk about their family, including how it was formed and who is part of their family.
- Being careful not to "out" a student as being adopted (or fostered) or a different race than their parents, unless they or their parents share this information themselves.
- Ensuring that assumptions or biases about people based on racial or ethnic group are explicitly challenged and talked about as wrong in the classroom and throughout the school by those with power (teachers and administrators).
- Making sure that institutional language and policies are inclusive. School forms should be inclusive of all kinds of caregivers and are not gender-specific, eliminating distinction between "kinds" of parents or guardians. Letters should be addressed to all family members or caregivers rather than specifying "mother and father."
- Developing a robust antibias, antibullying policy that includes plans and policy for addressing specific problems as they arise. Children and youth report being bullied about both family structure and race.
- Funding trainings for teachers and staff about how to support adopted and foster children and their families, as well as families of color, and then moving beyond those two categories as separate experiences to understand how they intersect in the lives of transracially adopted children.

Transracial adoptive families benefit when a school is welcoming to families of all races and economic backgrounds. An inclusive school works to diversify and empower its own staff; showcases all students' unique talents; holds events for parents and caregivers at times when those who work can attend; provides childcare so single parents can participate; uses multiple communication methods to stay in touch with families; invites and is responsive to parents' input; offers a wide variety of ways to get involved in the school community, and doesn't make fundraising the sole focus on parental involvement.

Triggering language becomes a barrier for children and parents in recognizing allies. As mentioned earlier, adoptive and foster parents respond to the use of the term "real parent" or "real brother or sister" negatively. Adopted and fostered people have at least two sets of parents, adoptive and first or birth—more if you include former foster parents, and they can all be "real" to the child and parents. Similarly triggering is "biological child" versus adopted child. All people—whether adopted or not—are born, which means they all are biological beings. For this reason we suggest avoiding the term "biological" to describe children who are not adopted.

Sometimes educators, particularly those who are white, state they "don't see color" or race. However well intentioned, this attitude minimizes the reality that significant racial disparities still exist in our society. As Samuels (2009) reminds us, colorblind models serve to deny the experience of people of color and the legacy of racism on which this country was founded. To "see color" is actually part of seeing people for who they are, just as we see gender or eye color. In the absence of a proactive approach regarding race and adoption, education will support the status quo. Unless schools provide children with the tools they need to talk about bias and difference, children will assume that their schools approve of the biases children perceive in the world. A school's failure to discuss differences will imply to students of color that their school, in some sense, "approves" of bias against them. For white children, the implication will be that bias and prejudice is okay and not something with which they need to concern themselves.

Multicultural education may sound straightforward, but it has multiple interpretations. It is challenging to establish priorities regarding learning about one another's history, lifestyles, contributions, traditions, attitudes, and how (or how much) schools should reflect the world's diversity. To become truly multicultural, schools must incorporate diversity and acceptance of difference into the core curriculum through books and materials being used as well as through the active pursuit of an antibias mind-set (Scharf, 2013). Schools can consider having affinity groups for diverse families, which can promote connections based on shared experiences.

Increasingly, the thought is to move institutions, including schools, beyond the goal of diversity to embrace the goals of equity and inclusion. Equity means fairness whereas diversity is variety. One can have diversity without achieving equity or inclusion. An equity approach to education recognizes that different people have different needs and therefore designs programs to fit different populations differently to address each individual or group's needs. To achieve equity, schools must build in equity assessments explicitly; otherwise, they are likely to be subject to implicit bias, whether recognized or not. Schools that already consider equity (not diversity) a high priority are likely to be able to apply the same standards to the situation of transracial and intercountry adoption. Race Forward (2014) has identified equity goals to create a successful school community: (1) build in decision-making guides that take equity for underserved or underrepresented constituencies into consideration; (2) foster active engagement and empowerment of stakeholders; (3) give distinct, specific, and sufficient attention to key disparities and inequities; (4) support and implement strategies to remove barriers; and (5) systematically analyze potential impacts of disadvantaged groups. Studies conducted on schools that have employed such strategies have documented that these principles are in fact effective, creating schoolwide change through individual teacher education and focus on equity goals (Deshmukh Towery, Oliveri, & Gidney, 2007).

Schools are a great place to start challenging institutional racism, because they are community based. The "racial achievement gap" (Gregory, Skiba, & Noguera, 2010) is often a reflection of a *resource* gap, where unequal inputs yield unequal outcomes. Parents, teachers, and administrators can intervene by asking questions, talking with students about their experiences, requesting public documents, organizing parents, talking to elected officials, notifying the media, and taking public action. White allies do not have to wait for people of color to complain before taking action. White allies can be change *agents* and *agitators,* by speaking out when something's wrong. As Hall and Steinberg (2013) advocate, all children need to know that the following:

- Heroes come from every race and ethnicity and include adopted people. Ensure your school and classroom includes literature, images, and real-life examples that embody this principle. Adopted children of color need heroic role models that reflect them.
- White middle-class America is not the measure against which all other lifestyles must be compared. Do not tolerate an environment in which mainstream or normal means "white." No child should ever be held out as the one "example" of their race, either in their classroom or community.

- Race matters. Adoption matters. We are a race-conscious, adoptist society and children deserve and need guidance to learn how to negotiate that reality. Children also deserve the opportunity to become who they want to be based on what is inside them, not on their physical appearance or origins. Freedom of opportunity can emerge only when we teach students to evaluate history from more than one point of view, holding multiple viewpoints without emphasizing one as better than another.

**CONCLUSION**

A review of the literature on adoption and education tells us that very little work has been done to establish evidence-based practice regarding the service and support of TRA/ICA and their families in the schools. This review suggests that topics of transracial and intercountry adoption are missing from teacher education programs and curriculum and highlights the lack of rigorous research on the impact of teacher knowledge or classroom ecology on the educational outcomes for TRA/ICA students.

Teachers are guides, leading students from the known to the unknown, from ignorance to wisdom, from the past to the future. To a child the teacher is the world, the embodiment of knowledge. Twenty-first-century teachers stand before classes far more complex than those of their counterparts a generation ago. Dramatic social changes call on teachers to be ever more sensitive to the needs of diverse populations, which must include transracially and internationally adopted youth. Clearly with the ever-growing numbers of these children in the school system, this research is essential to allow educators to have benchmarks and guidelines for how best to serve the TRA/ICA constituency.

We offer the following suggestions for what educators and schools can do to become TRA/ICA-competent as well as some pointers that agencies can offer to families to help them make decisions and assessments about the schools their children attend:

- *A diverse population of students, families, faculty, and administration.* We have seen that children with complex needs do best in schools that already are well versed in working with complex families. This means creating environments inclusive of many kinds of families, including multiracial and nontraditionally formed families. School communities that focus on serving monolithic communities often struggle to create a welcoming envi-

ronment for nontraditional families, increasing the likelihood TRA/ICA children might experience bullying or rejection by their peers or educators.
- *Successful students with various gifts and challenges.* Diversity is not the only or ultimate goal; schools need to be striving for equity for all their students, particularly for students who have differing needs and experiences. Pay attention to attrition rates for students of color or students with special education needs. It is not enough for schools to focus on the recruitment of students of color; there needs to be equal emphasis on the retention of students of color. If the graduating class consists of students of various races, family constellations, and special needs all graduating with honors and accolades, the school likely has directed resources toward supporting and strengthening students with different gifts and challenges.
- *Curriculum that includes specific as well as embedded TRA/ICA-sensitive lessons.* Faculty and administrations open to hearing from experts within the adoption community about the sensitivities of adopted children and their needs will create adoption-sensitive educators who incorporate adoption content and resources into the curriculum, highlight visibility of TRA/ICA families in the materials and books students use, and modify curriculum that is particularly sensitive to TRA/ICA issues in such a way that is inclusive of all kinds of families.
- *Teachers are trained to respond to students' questions and concerns using respectful language and educated explanations of transracial and international adoption.* Generally, school administrators determine the in-service education offered to teachers. TRA/ICA children should not have to hope they receive an individual teacher educated to their needs. An adoption-sensitive school includes administrators who recognize the importance of a staff well educated on transracial and intercountry adoption.
- *A school environment in which students with different capacities and challenges are valued equally.* Special needs children sometimes are seen as a drain on educational resources, and these kinds of schools are not likely to be supportive of the special needs that often are associated with adopted children whether they are expressed in terms of educational, emotional, or behavioral challenges.

Furthermore, we call on the research community to prioritize research on transracial and intercountry adoption, particularly for research that promotes evidence-based teaching strategies and interventions that inform and lead to adoption-competent practices in the school. To start, there is a need for data that would help build an adoption-competent education workforce, including: understanding how teacher or administrator attitudes toward transracial and intercountry adoption shape school and classroom ecology as well as TRA/ICA student outcomes; the impact of adoption-sensitive curriculum on TRA/ICA students; classroom instruction methods that educators implement for adopted children with histories of early deprivation, developmental delay, or trauma; and how teachers mediate and intervene in TRA/ICA-related bullying or discrimination of TRA/ICA students by peers. In particular, little is known about the extent to which educators receive TRA/ICA-specific information or teaching strategies in their undergraduate or graduate curricula or continuing education through trainings or conference sessions. Much more information on the depth and breadth of TRA/ICA content in teacher education is needed.

Educators and classroom environments play a crucial role in the development of a child, influencing and shaping all aspects of a child's trajectory in ways that go far beyond grades and performance outcomes. When a child knows and believes that the teachers and school staff understand his or her family, this adds to a feeling of safety at his or her school, which in turn leads to a more successful learning environment for that child. When teaches and staff model language and attitudes for other students, they are helping to create an environment that feels better for children in all kinds of different family structures because they see that differences are seen as "normal" and "okay." In

PRACTICE HIGHLIGHTS

Schools can increase their transracial and intercountry adoption competency in the following ways:
- Creating and sustaining an environment inclusive of diverse family types, including multiracial and nontraditionally formed families
- Ensuring that children with diverse strengths and needs have opportunities for successful educational outcomes
- Including TRA/ICA representation in curriculum, such as in assignments and reading materials
- Including in-service staff training on transracial and intercountry adoption
- Prioritizing an environment in which students of diverse capabilities and challenges are valued

a transracial-adoption-sensitive school, every adult—the principal, teachers, specialists, lunch staff, bus monitors, custodians, and paraprofessionals—play a critical role, sharing responsibility for all of the students by listening to their experience and creating sensitive and inclusive curriculum and environments that will support them as full members of their school community. When this happens, the children's learning and growth is optimized.

**DISCUSSION QUESTIONS**

1. This chapter presented a number of typical assignments that can be triggering or difficult for children with transracial and intercountry adoption histories. What additional classroom assignments might pose difficulties for transracial and intercountry adopted children and youth, and how could those be adapted to be more inclusive?
2. What are ways that school administrators and staff could create a welcoming and adoption-sensitive environment for transracial and intercountry adoptive students and families?
3. In this chapter, we presented the ways in which allies who do not share firsthand experience with adoption or as a person of color can act as allies to transracial and intercountry adopted children and their families in school environments. What are some ideas that this chapter has given you that might be implemented in your school?

**REFERENCES**

Alexander, M. (2012). *The New Jim Crow: Mass incarceration in the age of colorblindness.* New York: New Press.

Baden, A. L., & Pinderhughes, E. P. (2014, May). Identifying and addressing racial and adoption microaggressions. Paper presentation at the St. John's University 8th Biennial Adoption Initiative Conference, Queens, NY.

Ballard, R. L. (2013). Narrative burden: A qualitative investigation of transnational, transracial adoptee identity. *Qualitative Communication Research, 2*(3), 229–254.

Brodzinsky, D. M., Schechter, M. D., & Henig, R.M. (1993). *Being adopted: The lifelong search for self.* New York: Anchor Books.

Brodzinsky, D., Smith, D., & Brodzinsky, A. (1998). *Children's adjustment to adoption: Developmental and clinical issues. Developmental Clinical Psychology and Psychiatry Series.* Thousand Oaks, CA: Sage.

Brodzinsky, D. M. & Steiger, C. (1991). Prevalence of adoptees among special education population. *Journal of Learning Disabilities, 24,* 484–489.

Boss, P. (2000). *Ambiguous loss: Learning to live with unresolved grief.* Cambridge, MA: Harvard University Press.

Bryk, A., & Driscoll, M. (1998). *The high school as community: Contextual influences and consequences for students and teachers.* Madison, WI: National Center on Effective Secondary Schools.

Crenshaw, K. W. (1989). Demarginalizing the intersection of race and sex: A black feminist critique of antidiscrimination doctrine, feminist theory and antiracist politics. *University of Chicago Legal Forum, 140,* 139–167.

Crolley-Simic, J., & Vonk, M. E. (2008). Racial socialization practices of white mothers of international transracial adoptees. *Journal of Ethnic and Cultural Diversity in Social Work, 17*(3), 301–318.

Crook, M. (2000). *The face in the mirror: Teenagers and adoption.* Vancouver, BC: Arsenal Pulp Press.

Crumbley, J. (1999). *Transracial adoption and foster care: Practice issues for professionals.* Washington, DC: CWLA Press.

Dalen, M. (2002). School performances among internationally adopted children in Norway. *Adoption Quarterly, 5*(2), 39–58.

Derman-Sparks, L., & The A.B.C. Task Force. (1989). *Anti-bias curriculum: Tools for empowering young children.* Washington, DC: National Association for the Education of Young Children.

Deshmukh Towery, I., Oliveri, R., & Gidney, C.L. (2007). *Peer-led professional development for equity and diversity: A report for teachers and administrators based on findings from the SEED Project (Seeking Educational Equity and Diversity).* Cambridge, MA: Schott Foundation for Public Education. Retrieved from http://www.nationalseedproject.org/about-us/timeline

Docan-Morgan, S. (2011). "They don't know what it's like to be in my shoes": Topic avoidance about race in transracially adoptive families. *Journal of Social and Personal Relationships, 28*(3), 336–355.

Feagin, J., & Sikes, M. (2006). *Systemic Racism: A Theory of Oppression.* New York: Routledge.

Gregory, A., Skiba, R. J., & Noguera, P. A. (2010). The achievement gap and the discipline gap: Two sides of the same coin? *Educational Researcher, 39*(1), 59–68.

Hall, B., & Steinberg, G. (2013). *Inside transracial adoption.* London: Jessica Kingsley Publishers.

Howard, J. A., Smith, S. L., & Ryan, S. D. (2004). A comparative study of child welfare adoptions with other types of adopted children and birth children. *Adoption Quarterly, 7*(3), 1–30.

Kao, G., & Thompson, J. (2003). Race and ethnic stratification in educational achievement, *Annual Review of Sociology, 29*, 417–442.

Katch, J. (2011). *Far away from the tigers: A year in the classroom with internationally adopted children.* Chicago: University of Chicago Press.

Klatzkin, A. (2001). How I explained adoption to the first grade. *Adoptive Families Magazine* (June/July 2001). Retrieved from https://www.adoptivefamilies.com/talking-about-adoption/talking-with-first-graders/

Kreider, R. M., & Lofquist, D. A. (2014). *Adopted children and stepchildren: 2010.* U.S. Census Bureau. Retrieved from http://www.census.gov/hhes/socdemo/children/data/acs.html

Lee, R. M. (2003). The transracial adoption paradox: History, research and counseling implications of cultural socialization. *Counseling Psychologist, 31*(6), 711–744.

Leinaweaver, J. (2008). *The coordinated management of a culturally diffused identity: Internationally adopted people and the narrative burden of self* (doctoral dissertation). Retrieved from http://www.dissertation.com/book.php?method=ISBN&book=1612337619

Mayer, A. (2012, August). How babies see race. *Scientific American, 23*(4), 17.

McCarthy, H. (2005). *Survey of children adopted from Eastern Europe.* Retrieved http://www.eeadopt.org/index.php?option=com_content&task=view&id=48&Itemid=57

McFadden, A. C., Marsh, G. E., Price, B. J., & Wang, Y. (1992). A study of race and gender bias in the punishment of handicapped school children. *Urban Review, 24,* 239–251.

McGinnis, H., Smith, S. L., Ryan, S. D., & Howard, J. A. (2009). Beyond culture camp: Promoting healthy identity formation in adoption. Evan B. Donaldson Adoption Institute, New York.

Morris, M. (2013). *Black stats: African Americans by the numbers in the twenty-first century.* New York: New Press.

National Center for Learning Disabilities. (n.d.). *How parents can be advocates for their families.* National Center for Learning Disabilities. Retrieved from http://www.ncld.org/parents-child-disabilities/ld-rights/how-parents-can-be-advocates-for-their-children.

Osterman, K. F. (2000). Students' need for belonging in the school community. *Review of Educational Research, 70*(3), 323–367.

Pavao, J. M. (1998). *The family of adoption*. Boston: Beacon Press.

Piaget, J., & Inhelder, B. (1974). *The child's construction of quantities: Conservation and atomism*. New York: Basic Books.

Pierce, C. (1970). Offensive mechanisms. In F. Barbour (Ed.), *The Black seventies*. (pp. 265–282). Boston, MA : Porter Sargent.

Pierce, C. (1974). Psychiatric Problems of the Black Minority. In S. Ariete (Ed.), *American Handbook of Psychiatry* (pp 512–523). New York, New York.

Race Forward. (2014). *Moving the race conversation forward: Racial discourse change in practice*. Race Forward: Center for Racial Justice Innovation. Retrieved from https://www.raceforward.org/research/reports/moving-race-conversation-forward

Raleigh, E., & Kao, G. (2013). Is there a (transracial) adoption achievement gap? A national longitudinal analysis of adopted children's educational performance. *Children and Youth Services Review, 35*(1), 142–150.

Riley, D., & Meeks, J. (2005). *Beneath the mask: Understanding adopted teens*. Silver Springs, MD: CASE Publications.

Rebora, A. (2011). Keeping special ed in proportion. *Education Week*, October 13. Retrieved from http://www.edweek.org/tsb/articles/2011/10/13/01disproportion.h05.html?intc=fall11_tsbem

Rowell, K. (2012). *Love me, feed me: The adoptive parents guide to ending the worry about weight, picky eating, power struggles and more*. St. Paul, MN: Family Feeding Dynamics.

Samuels, G. M. (2009). "Being raised by white people": Navigating racial difference among adopted multiracial adults. *Journal of Marriage and Family, 71*, 80–94.

Samuels, G. M. (2010). Building kinship and community. *Family Process, 49*, 26–42.

Schaps, E., Battistich, V., & Solomon, D. (1997). School as a caring community: A key to character. In A. Molnar (Ed.), *The construction of children's character. 96th Yearbook of the national society for the study of education part 2*. (pp. 127–139). Chicago: National Society for the Study of Education.

Scharf, A. (2013). *Classroom culture. Critical practices for anti-bias education*. Teaching Tolerance: A Project of the Southern Poverty Law Center. Retrieved from http://www.tolerance.org/publication/classroom-culture

Schooler, J., Keefer Smalley, B., & Callahan, T. (2010). *Wounded children, healing homes: How traumatized children impact adoptive and foster families*. Colorado Springs, CO: NavPress.

Smith, S., & Riley, D. (2006). *Adoption in the schools: A lot to learn.* Donaldson Adoption Institute. Retrieved from http://adoptioninstitute.org/publications/adoption-in-the-schools-a-lot-to-learn/

Snyder, C. R. (2012). Racial socialization in cross-racial families. *Journal of Black Psychology, 38*(2), 228–253.

Solomon, B. (1976). *Black empowerment: Social work in oppressed communities.* New York: Columbia University Press.

Solomon, D., Battistich, V., Watson, M., Schaps, E., & Lewis, C. (2000). A six-district study of educational change: Direct and mediated effects of the Child Development Project. *Social Psychology of Education, 4,* 3–51.

Sue, D. W., Capodilupo, C. M., Torino, G. C., Bucceri, J. M., Holder, A. M. B., Nadal, K. L., & Esquilin, M. (2007). Racial microaggressions in everyday life: Implications for clinical practice. *American Psychologist, 62*(4), 271–286.

Tatum, B. D. (2003). *Why are all the black kids sitting together in the cafeteria? And other conversations about race.* New York: Basic Books.

Tenebaum, H. R., & Ruck, M. D. (2007). Are teachers' expectations different for racial minority than for European American students? A meta-analysis. *Journal of Educational Psychology, 99*(2), 253–273.

Tirella, L. G., Chan, W., & Miller, L. C. (2006). Educational outcomes of children adopted from Easter Europe, now ages 8–12. *Journal of Research in Childhood Education, 20*(4), 245–254.

U.S. Department of Education. (2014, March). *Civil rights data collection data snapshot: Discipline.* Issue brief no. 1. Retrieved from http://www2.ed.gov/about/offices/list/ocr/docs/crdc-discipline-snapshot.pdf

Van Ausdale, D., & Feagin, J. R. (2001). *The first R: How children learn race and racism.* Lanham, MD: Rowman & Littlefield.

van Gulden, H. (2010). *The dance of attachment: An adoptive and foster parents guide to nurturing healthy development.* Lulu.com: Author.

Vandivere, S., & McKlindon, A. (2010). The well-being of U.S. children adopted from –foster care, privately from the United States and internationally. *Adoption Quarterly, 13*(3–4), 157–184.

Vonk, M. E. (2001). Cultural competence for transracial adoptive parents. *Social Work, 46*(3), 246–255.

Wood, L., & Ng, N. (2001). *Adoption and the schools: Resources for parents and teachers.* Palo Alto, CA: FAIR.

Wrightslaw. (n.d.). Retrieved from www.wrightlslaw.com

# 10

# The Need for Adoption-Competent Mental Health Professionals

▸ DEBBIE B. RILEY AND ELLEN C. SINGER

MANY CHILDREN ADOPTED TRANSRACIALLY AND from other countries have experienced trauma from abuse, neglect, abandonment, and institutionalization, which result in emotional, cognitive, social, and behavioral challenges, leading adoptive parents to seek professional help. Adoptive families who seek help to address mental health issues within their families often find it difficult to find adoption-competent mental health professionals who can address their unique needs. This chapter will highlight the critical need for knowledgeable professionals and explain what makes a professional "adoption competent," with an emphasis on the effects of preadoptive traumatic experiences. Through case examples and presentation of effective therapies, we will explore how professionals can assist families in addressing children's adjustment in families who are of a different racial and ethnic background, adapt to new home and country environments different from their country of origin, promote attachment, help heal from trauma, and cope with feelings of loss and grief. Strategies for finding adoption-competent practitioners are provided.

The need for adoption-competent mental health services has been well documented (Brodzinsky, 2013; Freundlich, 2006; Lenerz, Gibbs, & Barth, 2006; Smith, 2014). Many children who have been adopted through intercountry adoptions come from compromised beginnings. Research shows that children with traumatic experiences of abuse, neglect, abandonment, and challenging behaviors are at high risk of presenting with adjustment problems during their development. As a result of these mitigating factors, adoptive families are three to four times more likely to engage their children in counseling and five to seven more times likely to send their child to a residential treatment facility (Howard, et al., 2004; Landers, Forsythe, & Nickman, 1996; Price & Coen, 2012; Vandivere, et al., 2009). All too frequently, adoptive parents identify the complexities of compromised beginnings in intercountry adoption as the primary contributors to family stressors. Issues related to ethnic and racial differences in adoptive families often are identified as well, although it is also true that parents may be unaware of how this factors into the challenges they are experiencing. Access to adoption-competent mental health services is a critical factor in promoting positive outcomes for adoptive families.

Adoptive parents consistently report that their greatest post adoption support need is mental health services provided by someone who understands adoption (Atkinson & Gonet, 2007; Brodzinsky, 2013; Smith, 2014). Some families reported seeking therapy from as many as ten different therapists before finding one who understood adoption issues, if they found such a therapist at all (Casey Center for Effective Child Welfare Practice, 2003). So it is not surprising that studies indicate that most mental health professionals lack the training to meet the diverse and complex clinical needs of adoptive families (McDaniel & Jennings, 1997; Sass & Henderson, 2002). In a study investigating the level of preparation psychologists have related to adoption and the need for further education, out of 210 participants, only 51 percent rated themselves as "Somewhat prepared" with the second largest group (23 percent) rating themselves as "not very prepared." Ninety percent reported they needed more education in adoption. Only sixty-seven participants reported taking courses that dealt with adoption as part of their formal education, and they averaged only 1.3 courses during their undergraduate education, and 1.5 during graduate school (Sass & Henderson, 2000).

Many intercountry adoptive families face mental health crises with their children that place the adoption itself at risk. Issues arise that in some cases can undermine the safety of the child or other members of the family. Factors such as prenatal complications, including poor prenatal care and prenatal exposure to toxic substances (Barth & Brooks, 2000), early childhood breaks in attachment, maltreatment and trauma related to emotional abuse, physical and sexual abuse, exposure to violent acts, unresolved grief and loss, nutritional and emotional deprivation, and the impact of institutionalization (including multiple caregivers), along with genetic vulnerabilities, contribute to the risk (Barth & Brooks, 2000; Briere, Kaltman, & Green, 2008). Studies of children adopted from orphanages in China, Russia, and Romania found that the most significant factor affecting future problems was the length of time in institutionalized care (Meese, 2005). It is the profound impact of these early life experiences as well as ethnic and racial differences that create challenges for the children and their families, creating the need for effective clinical intervention and other postadoption supports.

> "Every time I left my son's therapist's office I felt like a failure. He is so angry at me for being white."
>
> Coleen, adoptive mom, age 43

> "I was sitting in the hospital after trying to kill myself and the social worker lady told me I should be "happy" that I was adopted as my parents had gotten me out of that horrible orphanage."
>
> Andrew, adoptee, age 16

Many of the issues related to children's racial identity and socialization emerge most fully long after the adoption is finalized. As transracially adopted children enter adolescence, these issues are likely to have particular salience (Smith et al., 2008). Feigelman (2000) found that appearance discomfort was linked with higher levels of adjustment difficulties in transracially adopted young adults. Studies that include qualitative methods find that many transracial adoptees report a struggle to fit in with peers, the community in general, and, sometimes, their own families (Freundlich & Lieberthal, 2000; John, 2005; Simon & Alstein, 2002; Trenka, Oparah, & Shin, 2006).

Without access to adoption-competent mental health services, adoptions can and do fail. Children may enter state child welfare agencies through "forced relinquishments" or place their children in residential treatment facilities or wilderness programs, choices parents make when they lack access to the appropriate resources. Most alarming were the recent media reports regarding "rehoming" (Twohey, 2013). The report revealed desperate adoptive parents, feeling unable to parent their children connecting with strangers via the Internet, handing over "custody" to strangers, often placing their children in abusive, dangerous situations. In this horrific practice, the investigation found that there were more than 5,029 posts spanning a 5-year period advertising adopted children available for rehoming. According to the investigation, children ranged from 6 to 14 years of age and all were adopted abroad (Twohey, 2013).

In addition, one cannot forget the Tennessee mother, who in May 2012, sent her 7-year-old adopted son on a plane alone back to Russia, claiming she could not handle his severe behavioral problems. She sent the boy alone with a note that partially read; "I am sorry to say that for the safety of my family, friends, and myself, I no longer wish to parent this child" (CBS/Associated Press, 2012). As horrific and surprising as this is, it is reflective of the fact that too often, families are unprepared for the parental task of parenting children who come from compromised beginnings or of a different culture, ethnicity, or race. Sadly, the absence of adequate resources to assist them leaves families floating adrift with no lifeline.

## A RESPONSE TO THE NEED: SUPPORTING ADOPTIVE FAMILIES

Recognizing the need for a responsive system of care, the Center for Adoption Support and Education (C.A.S.E.) was created in 1998, to provide pre- and postadoption counseling and educational services to foster and adoptive families, as well as training for educators, child welfare staff, and mental health providers in Maryland, Northern Virginia, and Washington, DC. C.A.S.E. has become a national resource for foster and adoptive families and for professionals through its training programs, publications, and distance consultations. Cited in the Donaldson Institute October 2014 research publication, *Keeping the Promise: The Case for Adoption Support and Preservation*, C.A.S.E was identified as a promising practice providing leadership and innovative programming for postadoption services.

C.A.S.E. has more than 17 years of experience in service delivery to more than 5,500 foster and adopted children, adolescents, and their families; adult adoptees and their families; and expectant and birth parents and their families as well as to more than 20,000 professionals. Their clinical interventions have resulted in successful transitions from foster care or institutionalization to permanency; healing of early trauma, loss, and grief; stabilization of families in crisis; the promotion of secure attachments; an increase in self-regulatory behaviors in children; improvement in children's adjustment; higher functioning in school and community; and, most important, adoption preservation.

To achieve its mission, C.A.S.E integrates evidence-based best practices and promising practices along with innovation to provide premier resources and training that advance permanency for children and the healthy growth and development of families.

### Building the Framework

The C.A.S.E. promising practices model of comprehensive family-focused treatment addresses the complex needs of adopted children and their families. The conceptual framework was deeply embedded in the guiding principles of the work of the National Consortium for Post Legal Adoption Services: Adoption Support and Education (Arneaud et al., 1996). The model further predicates that families should have access to an array of services that range from advocacy to psychosocial services. This framework was further solidified by the integration of several theoretical models, including family systems theory, attachment, grief and mourning, and trauma-informed treatment.

*Family systems theory* embodies the view of families as dynamic, changing, interacting compilations of emotional and behavioral systems and subsystems. Family systems theory is key in the treatment of adoptive families. Many of the challenges facing international adoptive families are seen as connected to developmental processes or normative crises in the development of the adoptive family (Falicov, 1988; Pavao, 1992). Recognizing the complexities of relationships that bind the ties in adoption, early work by Reitz and Watson suggested that problems experienced by a client could be treated within the context of the extended family systems, birth and adoptive, created through adoption: "Although the family system for treatment remains the primary family system of the client, it is essential to the provision of effective service that a professional work within the conceptual context of the many systems involved" (1992, p. 12).

*Attachment* is the term for the social, psychological, and affective relationship between a child and one or more specific persons with whom the child interacts regularly; it is a mutual and reciprocal emotional connection between a child and a caregiver (Hirschi, 1969; Wilson & Hernstein, 1985). On the basis of early life experiences with their caregivers, children develop a cognitive model of themselves, their caregivers, and the world around them (Bowlby, 1969, 1973, 1988). This cognitive model is transferred to other relationships. To develop secure attachments and confidence about relationships, children must receive sensitive, nurturing care (Carlson, Cicchetti, Barnett, & Braunwald, 1989.) Attachment theory emphasizes the role of a child's birth parents in shaping the child's ability to form emotional bonds (Bowlby, 1988; Fahlberg, 1979). For adopted children, attachment theory suggests that the preplacement history of the adopted child can deeply influence the quality of later adoptive family relationships (McRoy et. al., 1988).

*Grief* is the reaction to loss and *mourning* is the expression of grief that is integral to the grieving process. Loss in adoption is explored later on in the chapter. Psychologists and researchers have outlined various models or phases of grief. In 1969, Elisabeth Kubler-Ross identified five linear stages of grief with which most people are now familiar: denial, anger, bargaining, depression, and acceptance (Kubler-Ross, 2014).

Kubler-Ross originally developed this model to illustrate the process of grief associated with death, but she eventually adapted the model to account for any type of grief. Kubler-Ross noted that everyone experiences at least two of the five stages of grief, and she acknowledged that some people may revisit certain stages over many years or throughout life (Kubler-Ross & Kessler, 2014). The theory of "ambiguous loss" developed by Pauline Boss has significant relevance to treatment of internationally placed children and will be discussed later on in the chapter (Boss, 2000).

*Trauma-informed treatment* refers to treatment that incorporates (1) an appreciation for the high prevalence of traumatic experiences in individuals who receive mental health services; (2) a thorough understanding of the profound neurological, biological, psychological, and social effects of trauma and violence on the individual; and (3) clinical skills and interventions that address the effects of trauma (Jennings, 2004). Models of trauma-informed treatment are discussed later in the chapter.

## DEFINING ADOPTION COMPETENCY

Research continues on the specific features of clinical practices that distinguish them as "adoption competent." These achievements are components of a multiyear initiative to which C.A.S.E. has provided leadership since 2007, the Training and National Certification for Adoption Competent

## DEFINITION: AN ADOPTION-COMPETENT MENTAL HEALTH PROFESSIONAL

This definition was developed by the Center for Adoption Support and Education in collaboration with a National Advisory Board, which is composed of leading adoption practitioners, researchers, advocates and policy makers, and, importantly, adoptive parents.

An adoption-competent mental health professional has the following skills:

- The requisite professional education and professional licensure;
- A family-based, strengths-based, and evidence-based approach to working with adoptive families and birth families;
- A developmental and systemic approach to understanding and working with adoptive and birth families;
- Knowledge, clinical skills, and experience in treating individuals with a history of abuse, neglect, or trauma; and
- Knowledge, skills, and experience in working with adoptive families and birth families.

An adoption-competent mental health professional understands the nature of adoption as a form of family formation and the different types of adoption; the clinical issues that are associated with separation and loss and attachment; the common developmental challenges in the experience of adoption; and the characteristics and skills that make adoptive families successful.

An adoption-competent mental health professional is culturally competent with respect to the racial and cultural heritage of children and families.

An adoption-competent mental health professional is skilled in using a range of therapies to effectively engage birth, kinship, and adoptive families toward the mutual goal of helping individuals to heal, empowering parents to assume parental entitlement and authority, and assisting adoptive families to strengthen or develop and practice parenting skills that support healthy family relationships.

An adoption-competent mental health professional is skilled in advocating with other service systems on behalf of birth and adoptive families (C.A.S.E., 2007).

Mental Health Practitioners. The long-term goals of the initiative are to expand the access of prospective adoptive parents, adopted individuals, birth families, adoptive families, and kinship families to adoption-competent mental health professionals.

Although the terms "adoption competent" and "adoption sensitive" frequently have been used, there was no standardized, well-accepted definitions for these terms. To address the need for a comprehensive definition, in 2007, C.A.S.E. convened a group of nationally recognized experts, including parents, who identified the specific knowledge, skills, and values competencies that mental health practitioners need and helped to develop a definition of an adoption-competent mental health professional using an expert-consensus process.

Findings reported in this chapter are from a survey of adoptive parents and other members of the adoption kinship network conducted in early 2011. The central purpose of the survey was to determine whether members of the adoption kinship network agree with the definition developed by experts and to examine more closely their views on the specific elements of the expert-developed definition. Additional questions were asked about their own experiences with mental health services and the availability of various types of assistance with accessing mental health services.

### Respondents

A total of 400 people from thirty-eight states and five countries outside the United States responded to the survey (Atkinson et al., 2013). Eighty-seven percent were adoptive parents, 7.6 percent were adopted persons, and 9.1 percent were members of an adoptive family.

More than 81 percent of respondents reported they had seen one or more mental health professionals or had been involved with the treatment of another family member. Eighty-two percent of adoptive parents and almost 66 percent of adopted persons reported having seen one or more mental health professionals.

### Experience with Mental Health Professionals

Of the 319 respondents who reported they had seen a mental health professional, 24.1 percent reported that the mental health professionals were adoption competent, 26.3 percent reported the mental health professionals were not adoption competent, and 49.5 percent reported that some were and some were not adoption competent.

Nearly one-quarter of respondents found that therapists had a lack of knowledge about attachment, trauma, loss, adoption language, or any real understanding of adoption. Several parents reported that therapists did not understand that the underlying issues were adoption related. Findings from this survey are consistent with those reported in the Evan B. Donaldson Adoption Institute's *Keeping the Promise* (2010).

### Importance of Adoption-Competency Training

When asked how important it is for a therapist to have specialized training or a certificate to provide services to adoptive families, almost 80 percent rated training as "very important" and about 17 percent rated it "moderately important." Only 2.5 percent rated the training "a little important" and less than 1 percent reported it not important.

## THE TAC MODEL AND OTHER POSTADOPTION TRAINING PROGRAMS

Over the past two decades, various levels of postgraduate adoption-competency training programs have been developed across the country. Some programs are geared toward child welfare staff, and others combine both mental health professionals and child welfare professionals. In *A Need to Know: Enhancing Adoption Competence Among Mental Health Professionals* (Brodzinsky, 2013), there were at least sixteen programs around the country providing training in the psychology of adoption and foster care. In Brodzinsky's analysis of the current program, he states "although there is a considerable overlap across programs in many of the core adoption issues covered in their curricula, differences in course content do exist and there is considerable variability in length—from 45 to 96 training hours. In addition, some programs have a strong clinical focus, whereas others do not" (Brodzinsky, 2013, p. 34). To view a complete listing of current adoption-competent training programs and their descriptions, please see the appendix in *A Need to Know* (Brodzinsky, 2013).

The following discussion will focus on the model created by C.A.S.E to deliver a manualized, rigorously evaluated protocol that can be replicated effectively with high fidelity to content delivery throughout the United States.

Creating a definition of an adoption-competent mental health professional was not only an invaluable contribution to the body of knowledge with regard to adoption competent mental health practice but also has served as the foundation for the development of C.A.S.E.'s TAC (Training in Adoption Competency). The TAC curriculum was developed and pilot-tested in 2009 at the University of Maryland School of Social Work. It currently is being implemented in fourteen sites across the United States (Connecticut, Georgia, Indiana, Iowa, Massachusetts, Minnesota, Missouri, Nebraska, North Carolina, Northern California, Ohio, and Virginia)(2). A rigorous evaluation has been conducted throughout the implementation of the TAC, beginning with the pilot-test. (To learn about other adoption-competency trainings program, please see *A Need to Know* [Brodzinsky, 2013].)

### The TAC Training

Working closely with a national advisory board, C.A.S.E. detailed eighteen areas of knowledge, values, and skills that mental health professionals must have to be considered "adoption competent." Using these competencies, C.A.S.E. developed a comprehensive training program for postmaster's mental health professionals.

**C.A.S.E. ADOPTION COMPETENCY TRAINING FOR MENTAL HEALTH PROFESSIONALS: TRAINING SESSIONS**

Introduction to Adoption Competent Mental Health Practice

- Adoption History, Law, and Process
- Clinical and Ethical Issues in Planning, Preparing for, and Supporting Adoption
- Clinical Issues in Providing Therapeutic Services: Separation, Grief, Loss, and Identity Formation
- Clinical Issues: Part 2: Attachment and Genetics and Past Experiences
- Trauma and Brain Neurobiology
- Family-Based Therapeutic Strategies: Coaching Adoptive and Foster Families
- Adoptive and Birth Families
- Adoptive Family Formation, Integration, and Developmental Stages
- Openness in Adoption and Birth Family Culture
- Race and Ethnicity
- Adjunct Therapies and Cross Systems and Community Practice
- Integrating Knowledge, Values, and Skills

### TAC: Evaluation Highlights

The pilot program and all replications have been subject to ongoing, rigorous evaluation designed to assess training delivery, outcomes, and effectiveness by Policy Works, LTD.

#### TRAINING EFFECTIVENESS

TAC participants scored an average 37.87 points higher on post-tests than control groups of comparably qualified professionals not enrolled in the training (see table 10.1).

#### TRAINING OUTCOME: CHANGES IN CLINICAL PRACTICE

TAC participants are asked at the midpoint and conclusion of training to identify and comment on the aspects of practice influenced by information or insights gained from the training. On the basis of 410 responses that contained 1,920 separate narrative responses describing ways practices were influenced by the training, the following information was reported:

- All TAC participants to date report change in at least two of the six defined aspects of practice
- 55.65 percent report change in all five aspects at the individual clinician level.
- 56.85 percent report change in programming and services at the organizational level.

There is a sound and growing body of evidence that the TAC is a high-quality, effectively delivered training program that increases knowledge and changes clinical practices in ways associated with adoption competency.

### Integrating Adoption Competency Into Practice

Meeting the diverse needs of adoptive families will require mental health providers to infuse knowledge gained through specialized adoption-competency training that influences one's assessment protocol, diagnoses, treatment planning, and interventions.

In many clinical practices, adoption issues are not addressed in the assessment. At best, the question of adoption status may be posed simply as "Are you adopted?" For the therapist, the first step in affirming adoption is

TABLE 10.1  TAC Evaluation Highlights

| | |
|---|---|
| Reasons surrounding the parents' decision to build their family through adoption. | Preadoptive experiences of adoptive parents play a large role in determining the later functioning of the adoptive family. Adoptive parents might have their own unresolved grief and loss issues, and special attention needs to be paid to the "fit" between parental expectations and the child. |
| The adoption story. | A thorough "adoption history" is obtained through questions such as when was the child placed, at what age, where the child lived before joining the family (if the child was not placed at birth), and other related questions. |
| Impact of trauma. | The neurodevelopment impact of neglect and traumatic stress in childhood is assessed. |
| Pre- and postnatal history. | Parents are asked about their knowledge of the pregnancy and delivery (complications), birth family medical and social history, as well as the child's developmental milestones. |
| Communication around adoption. | The family's comfort level with talking about adoption is assessed, including how the child's adoption story was presented to the child, as well as the child's age and reactions. |
| Attitudes and feelings toward birth family. | Therapists need to know whether the adoptive parents met the birth parents, agreements around postplacement contact, and comfort level in acknowledging the importance of the birth family to the child. |
| Extended family members and social support system. | Relationships with extended family members and social supports with regard to their acceptance of the adoption are assessed. |
| Entitlement and claiming. | Questions are aimed at determining the parents' sense of their right to parent the child as well as their efforts to "claim" their child. |
| The experience of being an adoptive family. | Each family member's feelings about being part of an adoptive family are explored, including their awareness of how their life has been affected by adoption. |
| Transracial and transcultural adoption. | Therapists assess the family's acceptance of themselves as a multicultural, multiracial family, including what the family has done to integrate the child's racial or ethnic difference into his or her identity, and how the child has been prepared to handle racism and diversity in the larger social context. |
| Six tasks inherent to adoption. | All family members must come to terms with the six fundamental dynamics of the adoption experience: reasons for adoption, missing or difficult information, difference, identity, permanence, and loyalty (Riley & Meeks, 2006). |

demonstrating their own comfort level in discussing the topic of adoption and the potential questions and feelings that may be raised in the assessment process (Riley & Meeks, 2006). The significance of adoption-related issues may be largely ignored or minimized by clinicians where the focus of treatment becomes the myriad of externalizing behaviors.

The assessment process is a thorough psychosocial evaluation integrating the complexities of adoption. The assessment may involve up to three sessions, including meetings with the parents, the child, and sometimes other family members and, if indicated, collateral and extended kinship family. Exploring the experience of adoption with both children and their parents must be an integral component of the assessment interviews. Assessments also include communication with the child's school and other treatment professionals and a review of previous child welfare reports as well as educational, psychological, and psychiatric evaluations.

The assessment interview involves exploration of the following: Mental health providers must understand that adoption is a significant emotional event that cannot be ignored within the framework of offering mental health services affecting the adoptee, his or her family of origin, and the adoptive family. Although parents may be well intentioned or may have had access to preadoption education, adoptive parents often do not comprehend the causative factors of their child's issues or behaviors and have an even less awareness as to the appropriate and effective interventions that would be helpful. Too often, healthy family systems are taxed so profoundly by children whose symptomatology is so severe that by the time they reach out for support they are perceived by the practitioner as the one who needs treatment, not the child. This is evident in families in which children have been exposed to prolonged periods of deprivation, maltreatment, and unpredictable stressors. In recent years, research has advanced our understanding as to the neurological implications of trauma and brain development and recommended treatment protocols influencing more positive outcomes for these children and familial stability.

It is the pervasive complexity of presenting problems, each child's unique adoption experience, and the "temperament of the family system" that will and does require specialized adoption-competent mental health services from highly skilled professionals who have the knowledge and skills to treat these confounding issues. The nature, complexity, and severity of issues are best served by clinicians who possess a diverse repertoire of clinical knowledge and skills that are embedded in attachment theory, family systems theory, and ecological theory. Grounded experiences with an emphasis in child and family development that are trauma informed and culturally competent are more likely to be effective in supporting intercountry and transracial adoptive families.

In the past few years, there has been a heavy focus on the utilization of a specific, evidence-based protocol, but experience leads us to conceptualize a broader "clinical toolkit." Research involving family surveys has stressed the need for services that are easily accessible and that allow families flexibility to access services that match their needs at different stages throughout the adoption life cycle (Atkinson & Gonet, 2007). The range of services will be the most effective when they are preventative, are supportive, and include an array of treatment interventions that are responsive to the family's needs. Furthermore, it is essential that adoption-competent mental health services are embodied in a fluid, flexible time frame that leaves the door open versus services that are rigid and time limited. Such a malleable system of care has been linked to more positive outcomes for the families being served (Atkinson & Gonet, 2007).

**Continuum of Needs**

In any discussion of adjustment in intercountry and transracially adopted children, it is important to recognize that the vast majority of adoptees are functioning normally and that their adoptive parents are highly satisfied with their adoptions. Even among groups of adopted children coming from higher risk situations, such as institutions or those in foster care who were removed from abusive or neglectful homes, most children are in the normal range on standardized measures of behavioral and emotional problems (Howard & Smith, 2003; Howard, Smith, & Ryan, 2004; Rosenthal & Groze, 1992, 1994; Simmel, 2007).

Understanding the challenges and how they are manifest is a prerequisite to addressing them and maximizing children's development to their fullest potential. Adoption scholars have identified critical developmental tasks confronting adoptive families as they work through core adoption issues at each stage of psychosocial development (Brodzinsky, Schechter, & Henig, 1992; Brodzinsky, Smith, & Brodzinsky, 1998; Hajal & Rosenberg, 1991; Schooler & Norris, 2002).

The needs of adopted children and their families after adoption fall along a continuum—some families face only a few challenges that they are able to handle successfully without professional help. A significant percentage, however, will struggle and seek counseling. Some families will seek help to weave the complexities of their children's adoption experience through an intricate developmental lenses, whereas others may seek support to ensure their child has access to other adopted children so as to "normalize" their experience as an adoptee and not feel so alone, and yet other families will be navigating the journey of search and reunion.

Some adopted children come to their families from higher risk situations that bring additional stresses to any family adopting them. By contrast, some adoptive parents have characteristics that pose challenges for adoption adjustment. Their own unresolved loss and grief issues and "attachment injuries" may complicate their ability to support their child's loss and grief issues and to help them successfully attach. Parents may come into placement with unrealistic expectations for themselves and the child. All of these challenges may lead to adoptive families seeking therapeutic counseling at various times throughout their lives.

Most parents express that adopting their child is a life-changing event. What often is not taken into account, however, is the need to adequately prepare parents for the ways in which adopted children manifest with a variety of psychological characteristics and behaviors that may differ significantly from other children. Many parents embark on the task of raising an adopted child ill prepared for understanding or coping with the behavioral manifestations of a child with a complex history.

According to a survey of adoptive parents' training programs, the following top ten behaviors were identified as a reason to seek help (Freundlich, M. C.A.S.E. 2009, TAC Module 9):

- Anger Outbursts
- Lying
- Stealing
- Eating Disorders and Food Issues
- Sexualized Behavior
- Fire-Setting
- Sleep Problems
- Self-Destructive Behavior

- Running Away
- Wetting and Soiling

Within the framework of adoption-competent practice, parents are educated to understand the underpinnings of their child's behavioral and emotional challenges as well as to understand that it is the parents, not the therapist, who plays the primary role in helping his or her child heal from past trauma. While engaging adoptive parents to be collaborative partners in treatment, it is imperative to remove viewing the family as pathological and to lift the blame from the parents: "We as adoptive parents are not to blame—we did not cause the problem, but we desperately desire to be an integral part of the solution" (K. D., parent of twelve adopted children). We must help adoptive parents understand how adoptive parenting is different from parenting by birth, particularly when the child has been exposed to the risks factors previously discussed. Engaging the family is essential to the child's recovery and family well-being.

## THERAPEUTIC APPROACHES AND CASE EXAMPLES

Armed with the understanding of all the potential factors and experiences that have affected clients when they walk through our doors, an adoption-competent therapist will be equipped to address the common themes that are most likely to present in almost all families they treat. In addition, they will have a repertoire of therapeutic approaches, strategies, and tools that have been found to be effective with intercountry and transracial adoptive families. Following a discussion of these themes and therapeutic approaches, we have provided several case examples to demonstrate how these themes and approaches are interwoven into the clinical treatment of these families.

### Four Major Themes of Adoption-Competent Clinical Practice

#### LOSS AND GRIEF ISSUES IN INTERCOUNTRY AND TRANSRACIAL ADOPTIONS

Loss and grief is recognized as *a* if not *the* key issue in understanding clinical issues in adoption. Internationally adopted children, no matter what their age, embark upon their new lives facing loss—of their birth parents, birth siblings, extended birth family members, former caregivers, and supports (e.g., foster parents, orphanage staff, teachers, therapists, friends), genealogical continuity; racial, ethnic, and cultural origins; self-identity; the sense of "fitting in" in terms of looking like other family members; and privacy with regard to the adoption being "public." These children have lost familiar smells, tastes, and sounds; the way they do things; material items; their language; and their daily routines.

In her book, *Ambiguous Loss*, Pauline Boss (2000) describes how grieving the losses in adoption are complicated because they are "ambiguous." A child's birth relatives may be physically absent but psychologically present (in their thoughts and feelings), as is often the case in intercountry adoption. Adoptive parents often need help in understanding how to identify their children's grief and assist them through their grief issues. They also may need assistance in acknowledging the lifelong processing of the losses, including any they may have experienced themselves before becoming adoptive parents (Grotevant & Brodzinsky, 2009, TAC Module 4).

### ATTACHMENT ISSUES IN INTERCOUNTRY AND TRANSRACIAL ADOPTIONS

Children adopted internationally have experienced the trauma of severed attachments. Many children have experienced multiple caregivers—birth family, foster family, and orphanage staff. The quality and the experience of the relationships with caregivers are as significant as the loss or separation from them. When a young child's needs are not met in a consistent, responsive manner, a child's ability to form healthy, loving attachments to adults can be severely compromised. Some children have never successfully attached to another adult; others have experienced insecure or ambivalent attachments. Combined with unresolved feelings of loss and grief, many children will go to great lengths to protect themselves from the very thing they need most to heal—attaching successfully to their adoptive parents.

Children who have learned to expect rejection, abandonment, and maltreatment at the hands of caregivers learn to depend on themselves and not trust adults. They usually experience serious fears of getting close to their adoptive parents, and many of their behaviors serve the purpose of maintaining emotional distance from them (Malchiodi & Crenshaw, 2014).

Older transracially adopted children may experience many challenges around feeling like they truly fit in or belong to their families when they look so different from them. Ethnic, racial and cultural differences between their adoptive families and previous experiences with caregivers—birth family, foster families, and orphanage staff can impede their ability to adapt and attach to their new families.

It is equally important when addressing attachment issues to assess the role of the parents' own attachment histories as it affects their ability to support healthy attachments for their child (Hughes, 2009) Adoptive parents often are surprised to find that racial differences are affecting their ability to attach to their new children, regardless of age. Parents with either birth children or same-race adopted children are often especially vulnerable to this unexpected challenge. In addition, transracial adoptive families are affected by societal reactions. Negative responses to their families can seriously undermine a family's sense of validity as a family, which can further impact attachment.

## TRAUMA ISSUES IN INTERCOUNTRY AND TRANSRACIAL ADOPTION

As we have discussed throughout the chapter, many of the children and adolescents we treat come from histories embedded in trauma. We have referred to "trauma histories," but many children have experienced what is termed "complex trauma." Complex trauma is defined by Courtois and Ford (2009, p. 1) as "including traumatic stressors that (1) are repetitive and prolonged; (2) involve direct harm and/or neglect and abandonment by caregivers or ostensibly responsible adults; (3) occur at developmental vulnerable times in the victim's life, such as early childhood; and (4) have great potential to severely compromise a child's development." Children adopted from abroad have likely experienced several traumatic breaks in attachment. Preadoption experiences, especially in orphanage care, suggest the possibility of having experienced emotional neglect (lack of nurturance and stimulation), physical neglect (lack of adequate nutrition and medical care), sexual and physical abuse, and witnessing violence and abuse.

Extensive research substantiates the physiological changes in brain structure and chemistry with profound and prolonged effects, compromising all aspects of development. Early trauma will affect problem-solving skills, social awareness, ability to learn, attachment, physical health, self-esteem, and emotional regulation. It can have an impact on the developmental milestones that every child must master for healthy emotional and intellectual growth.

### PARENTING A CHILD OF A DIFFERENT RACE

Research indicates that when racial minority youth have personally explored the meaning of their racial membership for themselves, have a positive view of their race, and a secure identification as a member of that race, they have higher self-esteem and more positive mental health outcomes than youth who are not able to these steps (Seaton, Scottham, & Sellars, 2006).

Transracial adoptive parents that are seen in treatment likely will fall somewhere on a continuum with respect to their understanding that "race matters," and that in addition to all of their other parenting tasks and responsibilities, they have unique responsibilities to this important fact. Some families will deny that race is important ("I am colorblind" or "love is enough"); others may sense that race is important, but they may not quite know how or what they should be doing. On the other hand, some transracial adoptive families may place greater emphasis on race than their child is comfortable with.

Therapists must help parents understand the importance of helping their children with "racial socialization," which is critical to fostering children's positive racial identity. Parents may be unaware of the unintended ways they may compromise their efforts to instill in children the values of their race. Racial socialization includes helping parents learn how to help their children cope with racism. This can be a daunting task because white parents frequently do not have the life experiences that equip them to prepare their children for racism.

Karen, adoptive mother of 16-year-old Kyra adopted from Ethiopia at age 6 years, was uncomfortable when Kyra started spending time at her friend Emily's house. Emily is African American, with two older teen brothers. Karen wondered whether there was proper supervision. Upon exploration in therapy, it became clear that Karen had not really considered that her daughter might "date" a black man. She also admitted that she would not have questioned her daughter's judgment or safety if Emily's family was Caucasian.

Seventeen-year-old Mark, adopted as an infant from Korea, was traveling with his Caucasian adoptive family in North Dakota one summer. Stopping at a restaurant, it seemed to Mark that it was taking an awfully long time for his family to be seated. He began to notice other "parties" being seated ahead of his family who had entered the restaurant after his family. Mark commented to his mother that he thought maybe something racist was happening. His mother dismissed his concerns and told him that he was being ridiculous and paranoid. As more time passed, Mark's father inquired about the wait and was told their table would be ready soon. It was not. Rather than confront the situation, Mark's family left and found another place to eat. No word was spoken about this incident until Mark brought it up in therapy. Mark's parents were helped to acknowledge that Mark's perception was accurate. His mother cried as she said she just felt so helpless about how to handle what had happened or even to talk about it, not wanting to either believe it or hurt Mark. Therapy helped Mark's parents open up the dialogue and plan for how they would work together to deal with any future racist incidents.

Therapists can support transracial adoptive parents in talking with their children about racial issues, even if their child does not bring up the subject. Parents can use natural opportunities, such as a television programs or newspaper articles that talk about race in some way. Therapists can help parents develop ways to let their child know that they feel comfortable discussing race, including the positive aspects as well as the difficult topics.

If their child is a victim of a racial incident or as problems in the community because of the unkind actions of others, therapists can teach parents ways in which to support their children. The therapist can help parents develop tools that they can give their children to deal with these situations. Above all, the therapist can help parents respond to their child's hurt feelings by allowing the child to talk about the experience with the parent and acknowledging that the parent understands (Leslee et al., 2009, TAC Module 12).

A therapist can support transracially adoptive parents in connecting their child to people who reflect the child's racial and ethnic heritage. Therapists can encourage families to participate in adoptive family support group events that often provide places where children will meet and interact with other children and adults of their own racial and ethnic heritage.

### EFFECTIVE THERAPEUTIC APPROACHES, TOOLS, AND STRATEGIES: TRANSRACIAL AND INTERCOUNTRY ADOPTIONS

The following, although not exhaustive, are treatment approaches, models, and interventions that have proven to be effective in treating intercountry and transracial families. Many of these tools can be incorporated easily into the therapist's previous clinical training and clinical constructs in which they practice.

### Psychoeducation for Parents

Much of the work with parents is helping them understand what is behind the troubling, distressing symptoms, and behaviors of their children are demonstrating. For adoptive parents, trying to understand a child's history can be heartbreaking. Psychoeducation for parents is provided in therapy around key aspects of the adoption experience for children and adolescence, including the following:

- How to understand the ways children and teens process adoption from a developmental perspective.
- How to talk with children and teens about adoption (telling the adoption story) from a developmental perspective.
- How to understand the implications of trauma experiences or histories on brain development and behavior, as well as the impact of institutionalization.
- How to understand the impact of prenatal drug and alcohol exposure.
- How to help children and teens process loss and grief.
- How to employ effective parenting strategies, including appropriate discipline with traumatized children.
- How to promote attachment with their children.
- How to promote self-esteem and positive racial identity through racial socialization.
- How to become a multiracial family, including how to incorporate their child's ethnic, cultural, and racial heritage into the family experience.
- How to help children cope with racism.

### Theoretical Basis for Dialectical Behavior Therapy

The focus of dialectical behavior therapy (DBT) is on helping the client learn and apply skills that will decrease emotion dysregulation and unhealthful attempts to cope with strong emotions, difficulties that many internationally adopted children and adolescents experience as a result of their traumatic beginnings. Usually, DBT includes a combination of group skills training, individual psychotherapy, and phone coaching, although there are exceptions. Parents involved in DBT are asked to monitor their child's symptoms and use of learned skills daily, and their progress is tracked throughout therapy. Four main types of skills are covered in DBT skills training: mindfulness, distress tolerance, emotion regulation, and interpersonal effectiveness (Dimeff & Linehan, 2001).

### Trauma-Informed Treatments

#### TRAUMA-FOCUSED COGNITIVE BEHAVIORAL THERAPY

Trauma-focused cognitive behavioral therapy (TF-CBT) is an evidence-based treatment approach shown to help children, adolescents, and their caregivers overcome trauma-related difficulties. It is designed to reduce negative emotional and behavioral responses following child sexual abuse, domestic violence, traumatic loss, and other traumatic events often experienced by internationally adopted children.

The neurosequential model of therapeutics (NMT) developed by Dr. Bruce Perry and Christine Dobson at the Child Trauma Academy in Houston, Texas, is most widely used treatment with traumatized and maltreated children. For more information about this approach to assessment and clinical intervention, see chapter 5, "A Neurodevelopmental Perspective and Clinical Challenges."

#### W.I.S.E. UP!<sup>SM</sup>

During the middle childhood years, adoptees encounter questions and comments from peers about adoption. In addition to feeling uncomfortable and upset, these questions may trigger additional feelings of loss and grief. These questions from the "outside" may trigger questions that children have "inside" that they may not be developmentally ready to think or talk about. For children in intercountry and transracial adoptions, they can be especially troubling when they refer to those aspects of the child's adoption story, or reflect racist attitudes and bias. Some of the questions and comments that children may hear are as follows:

> "Who/where is your real mother? How come she didn't keep you?"
> "I hear you were left in an orphanage. What was wrong with you?"
> "How can that be your mother? Her skin isn't dark like yours."
> "How much did your parents pay for you?"

"Why are your eyes so weird/strange?"
"Do you speak Korean?"
"I think Asian girls are really sexy."

C.A.S.E developed an empowerment tool that can be used to prepare children for adoption-related questions and comments. W.I.S.E. UP! can effectively assist children and teens manage these intrusive, insensitive, extremely hurtful situations. Children learn that they can choose how to respond with four options: "W," walk away or ignore what is being said; "I," it's private and I don't have to answer; "S," share something about their adoption story; or "E," educate others about adoption in general without sharing personal information. Children and teens explore their feelings about these questions and in which circumstances they are likely to choose one option over another or any combination of these four options.

The W.I.S.E. UP! Powerbook may be used as a clinical tool with families and children to help them prepare to effectively manage the challenge of unwanted questions or comments. Each book includes an insert with guidelines for clinicians for using the W.I.S.E. UP! program with children in therapy. Instructions for parents' use with children are included as well.

### GROUP THERAPY

Group therapy has a distinct advantage for adopted children and teens: It provides a social milieu for growth and emotional healing; it provides opportunities to identify with other kids and normalize experiences. "I'm not alone!" helps children and teens release stigma and shame, and it validates the universality of their issues. Groups may offer the opportunity to meet other transracially or internationally adopted children and see how they are part of a "larger adoption community." C.A.S.E. uses a scripted group schedule for its group therapy. For more information, see *Beneath the Mask: Understanding Adopted Teens* (Riley & Meeks, 2006).

*Beneath the Mask* was written for both parents and clinicians. It provides an in-depth understanding of the developmental challenges and psychological issues that adopted adolescents and their families experience. Clinicians will find a step-by-step approach to conduct an adoption-competent clinical assessment, effective clinical strategies, treatment resources and therapy tools. Numerous case examples are provided that illustrate the complex dynamics and common themes presented in clinical work with intercountry and transracial adoptive teens and their families.

## CASE ILLUSTRATION: TOO MANY LOSSES TOO SOON

### History

Lida is a 16-year-old girl who was adopted from Russia at the age of 7. Her parents had a birth son Adam who was 3 years older than Lida. Lida lived with her birthparents for the first 4 years of her life, was removed due to neglect, and placed in an orphanage for 3 years. Lida's birth parents were both alcoholic. Lida's adoptive parents described the conditions of the orphanage as "horrific."

Shortly after having her children removed, Lida's birthmother died from alcoholism. Lida's birthfather was still alive at the time of her adoption. Lida's adoptive parents were told by the orphanage staff that Lida and her older brother Alex, who was living in the same orphanage "were not close." They later learned from Lida that this was not true—that she and her brother were very close, and that it was extremely traumatic to have been separated from him. Lida told her parents that Alex had instructed Lida not to talk to them when they came to adopt her in the hope that they would not take her away.

### Presenting Problem

Lida entered therapy when she was 13.5 years old. Her parents were concerned that her early life experiences were causing the behaviors affecting their daughter but could not obtain validation from other professionals they had seen. The presenting issues were lying, stealing, defiance, poor boundaries, attention-seeking behavior, and difficulty with social relationships. Lida's parents had sought therapy in the past for their daughter and described it as being nonproductive with little change in presenting issues. Parents were recommended to employ "tough love" strategies to "gain control as parents" and "show their daughter that they were in charge."

When asked her view of what was happening, Lida shared, "I have anger issues and I lie sometimes." She identified sibling conflicts and the desire to get along better with her brother, that she loved him despite his hurtful comments to her (i.e., "I wish you were never born"), which she said, "force me to get revenge!" Lida admitted to being very worried that this difficult relationship was all her fault. She recalled that the first thing she did when she came from Russia was hit her brother, and she felt guilty and confused by her actions.

During elementary school, Lida was falling behind academically. Following an assessment conducted through her school when she was in the third grade, she was diagnosed with learning disabilities that affected her reading comprehension and fluency. She receives special educational supports to support her learning issues.

Treatment with this family included referral for a neuropsychological evaluation to further assess the impact of postinstitutionalization and in utero alcohol exposure, as well as individual therapy with Lida, and family therapy with and without Lida present.

The evaluation reflected the implications of the 3 years that Lida lived in an orphanage, revealing deficits in executive functioning, and in language development—all of which were contributing to her poor academic performance. Furthermore, having expertise in working with postinstitutionalized children, the evaluator also shared her concerns regarding the attrition of Lida's Russian language before English language had developed. This often presents a significant educational challenge for school-age internationally adopted children as they have to learn a new language concurrently with new academic content. This understanding provided much needed clarity to Lida's parents who desperately wanted to help Lida succeed academically but had been told by other professionals that Lida was just lazy.

**Individual Treatment Tools and Strategies**

A few weeks after starting therapy, Lida blurted out that she wanted to kill herself in math class after becoming frustrated while taking a quiz. She was seen immediately by her therapist to assess risk of self-harm. Lida revealed that she was feeling sad because, a few months before starting therapy, her friend's mother died and she had attended the funeral. The funeral triggered thoughts about her birthmother and the fact that she had not been able to attend her funeral. Lida never had the chance to say goodbye. Tears rolled down her face as she allowed herself to talk about her profound loss and express her conflicted feelings surrounding her "abandonment" and disloyalty. Lida had never shared these feelings with anyone.

Therapy supported the acknowledgment and processing of her grief. With regard to disloyalty, Lida feared sharing her grief with her parents as she worried that they would feel she was not grateful about being adopted and that she loved

### CASE ILLUSTRATION: TOO MANY LOSSES TOO SOON (CONTINUED)

her birth family more than them. Lida described crying herself to sleep at night as she tried desperately to remember what her birthmother and brother looked like. It was impressive to learn that Lida had been keeping a secret journal that helped her to soothe herself and process her difficult and bewildering history. Her writings revealed her significant trauma and intense feelings of loss and grief. She wrote about terrifying incidents involving her birth parents' drinking, which included memories of physical and verbal aggression as well as a fire that accidentally was set by her mother.

One of the clinical tools that have been extremely helpful when unresolved loss is present is the creation of a Loss Box. Although this tool has been used in other treatment modalities, we have found it to be useful in guiding children and teens through the psychological task of grief work.

Lida was open to this process and focused her attention on identifying the loss of her birth family—a powerful memory for internationally placed children whose early years were spent with their birthparents. Unfortunately, as with many children adopted internationally, Lida did not have any pictures of them. With the help of the therapist, Lydia was able to "recreate" from memory and use collaging as a tool to make a "snapshot" of what she remembered her birth parents looked like, and she placed those pictures in the box. Lida filled the box with pictures of the town she was raised in as well as the orphanage, which she found on the Internet. She also used clay to create symbols that represented her memories as a child in Russia.

In therapy, Lida was also provided with the opportunity to explore the use of rituals as a way to memorialize her birthmother. She chose to tie a message to a to a helium balloon to be released every year on the anniversary of her mother's death.

### Family Treatment

The focus of the work with Lida's parents had several goals: (1) to help them understand the underpinnings of their daughter's grief and how grief can be behaviorally manifested in children; (2) to equip the parents with knowledge around parenting a child with a trauma history to enable them respond to Lida's challenging behaviors in appropriate, effective, and healing ways; and (3) to help Lida share her feelings with her parents.

In individual treatment, Lida was able to unpack the sadness she felt that was underlying her behavioral difficulties. In sessions with her parents, she was able to share her feeling of loss and grief, her need to remember and acknowledge her birth family, and her fears around getting close to others. Lida and her parents explored her unconscious fear of getting close to them and of losing them as she did her birth family. Her defiance and acting out behaviors served the purpose of pushing them away, which also reaffirmed her sense of inadequacy and her belief that she was "unworthy."

In embracing Lida's grief, Lida's parents were able to explore with her the possibility of searching for her birth brother in Russia. Although her mother was supportive, Lida's father needed support to resolve his fear that such an undertaking might overwhelm Lida and exacerbate both her behavior and the secure attachment she was continuing to build with her parents.

Individual and family therapy also addressed the impact of prenatal exposure to alcohol. Lida was never formally diagnosed with fetal alcohol spectrum disorder, but it is likely that this exposure contributed to her learning and executive function challenges, including impulse control and judgment. (http://www.cdc.gov/ncbddd/fasd/facts.html)

## CASE ILLUSTRATION: CONNECTIONS

### History

Michael, age 10, was born in Ethiopia and adopted at the age of 7 years old by his parents who have a 14-year-old daughter by birth. His adoptive parents are both Caucasian. Michael was raised by his birth mother until the age of 4 years old when she died of AIDS. Michael witnessed his birth mother's decline in health and was with her in the hospital when she died. Before being placed in an orphanage, he lived for a year at this military field hospital where he was sexually abused and witnessed blood, death, and dismemberment on a daily basis.

### Presenting Problem

Michael was referred at age 9 years old, following two inpatient hospitalizations for violence against his peers, homicidal comments, suicidal thoughts, and

**CASE ILLUSTRATION: CONNECTIONS** (CONTINUED)

running away. Michael's parents came to therapy feeling hopeless and stating that they were thinking about dissolving their adoption. Parents shared that hospital staff were recommending residential treatment and inferred that he likely could not attach because of the extent of his early trauma.

### Treatment Tools and Strategies

While helping adoptive parents explore their thoughts of relinquishment is important, it is equally important to give them hope that through the process of treatment, a child can be helped to turn around and learn to trust and bond with them. Too often, parents who adopt children internationally who present as Michael did lack the knowledge they need to be effective as parents. Their ability to understand and feel hope can help them meet the challenges. Parenting a child with a history of traumatic experiences requires a skill set that is not intuitive. The therapist shared with Michael's parents that their responses to Michael need to be counterintuitive. When someone comes at us with anger, hostility, or aggression, our knee-jerk response is to fight or fly, which is exactly what traumatized kids are doing all the time. The therapist serves as a teacher for the parents providing them with psychoeducation about complex trauma and posttraumatic stress disorder (PTSD).

The treatment plan for Michael and his family focused on using the TF-CBT to address the issues of complex trauma and PTSD. A significant part of TF-CBT is psychoeducation, teaching the parents as well as the child about the facts of expected behavior, such as the ones they were witnessing. The parents learned that the impact of trauma on Michael's brain development resulted in the fact that his chronological age was different than his true emotional age—which was closer to 4 years old. His parents became more hopeful about Michael's ability to heal as their understanding increased around his unusual and destructive behavior. Play therapy was utilized during TF-CBT sessions to enhance the trauma-focused goals.

Therapist met with the parents for a month before working with Michael. Daily, he would threaten to kill them, sometimes when they were trying to get closer to him emotionally, but especially when they were having disagreements. He seemed to constantly miscue threats in his social life. It did not matter if people were trying to be friendly or if they were simply indifferent toward him.

He would read their facial expressions, body language, and speech as hostile. He automatically would go into the normal "fight, flight, or freeze" mode that all people exhibit when a perceived threat is at hand. Through the use of role-plays, therapists discussed ways in which the parents could work on their emotional regulation in response to his behaviors.

When Michael began coming to sessions with his parents, the therapy continued to focus on building a secure attachment through play-based interaction. Michael loved to spin in circles and swing for hours, often isolated himself from other children, and would engage in what looked like obsessive, repetitive play. Prior assessments concluded a diagnosis of autism.

It was quite clear that Michael was not autistic but that his body and brain were craving repetitive and consistent sensory stimuli. Consistency and repetitive actions can assist with rewiring the brain when children have experienced neglect and trauma. When it became clear that Michael was experiencing sensory integration issues as well, a referral was made to an occupational therapist. The therapist encouraged the parents to spin with him and to join in his play to engage him before trying to direct him toward playing or doing something that they wanted him to do. Michael's parents began understanding that his play calmed his sensory system. It was important that the parents understood and joined with him in this type of play as a way to work toward establishing a more secure attachment. As play therapy continued to enhance child and parent interaction, filial therapy, Theraplay®, DIR®/Floortime, and parent–child interaction therapy techniques all were utilized. Sand tray therapy was also used with Michael (see figure 10.1). Many children are unable to vocalize their emotional state as a result of trauma involving extreme neglect or abuse. Incorporating the element of a familiar medium, the sand, allows a child to instantly achieve a sense of comfort and security. With little instruction from the therapist, the child is free to play and develop his or her own expression of situations. Often, the children will experience a sense of independent play and will begin making assumptions and behavior changes without cues from the therapist. This method of therapy serves as a valuable and powerful outlet for children and an incredibly insightful method of gaining access to their traumatic experiences.

As the parents' level of anxiety decreased, so, too, did their son's. Michael seemed increasingly settled each time they came for sessions. His parents were noticing that his aggressive behaviors were decreasing and they began to see a

**CASE ILLUSTRATION: CONNECTIONS** (CONTINUED)

FIGURE 10.1 **Sand-tray therapy with Michael.**

different behavior in him, including smiles and occasionally laughter. The parents said for the first time since they had adopted him 2 years ago, he suddenly was appearing to be more relaxed and started looking at them more and sustaining eye contact. He was more engaged and became more creative in his play with his parents and peers. He was allowing family members to physically close to him; he permitted hugging, rubbing his back and shoulders, holding hands, and kissing on the cheek. The connections had begun.

**CASE ILLUSTRATION: HEALING THE HURT**

History

Julia is an active and engaging 8-year-old girl who was adopted from Guatemala at 23 months. She was born with a cleft palate and has had several corrective surgeries since coming home. Nothing is known about the circumstances surrounding Julia's relinquishment. Julia was placed in an orphanage as a newborn, and then had three foster home placements before returning to the orphanage before her adoption.

## Presenting Problem

Julia's adoptive parents sought services from C.A.S.E. when Julia was 6 years old because of excessive tantruming during which Julia could become physically aggressive, often hitting, kicking, and biting her mother. In addition, Julia's parents were concerned about poor sleep habits, saying Julia continued to wake every 2 to 3 hours at night. At the time treatment began, Julia was receiving preschool-based speech therapy services to address a diagnosed expressive language delay.

## Treatment Tools and Strategies

The focus of treatment has been on supporting Julia's parents to address challenging home behaviors, to help Julia better regulate her affect and behaviors while learning to utilize age-appropriate strategies for managing feelings of anger and frustration, and to support Julia in beginning to explore her adoption story. Julia's parents have both been engaged in treatment. Initially, however, her mother was much more open to psychoeducational interventions focused on increasing the parents' understanding of the developmental trauma and its impact on current behavior and socioemotional development as well as how early losses, deprivation, and inconsistent or unpredictable care may influence one's ability to regulate affect and tolerate frustration. Although Julia's father loved his daughter, it was difficult for him not to view much of her misbehavior through the lens of his own childhood: "manipulative, willful, disrespectful behavior received strict and firm punishment." He saw his wife as being too soft. Treatment helped him adjust his understanding embracing a more "positive parenting style," which is linked to positive adjustment in internationally adoptive families when their children have histories of maltreatment.

Julia's parents have worked hard to set age-appropriate (socioemotional age, not chronological) expectations for their daughter and have become skilled at understanding Julia's negative behaviors as a way of expressing strong and often-overwhelming feelings and fears that she has not been able to articulate more directly. Dad was able to respond with more warmth and positive discipline responses and received ongoing support in treatment to recognize his own triggers.

## CASE ILLUSTRATION: HEALING THE HURT (CONTINUED)

When Julia entered kindergarten, several months after beginning treatment, the school expressed concern about Julia's academic performance and reported that she struggled with transitions, had difficulty during unstructured class time, and could be impulsive and aggressive with her peers. Both the school and pediatrician felt that Julia met the criteria for attention deficit hyperactivity disorder (ADHD). As a result, and because of some continued challenges at home, a comprehensive neuropsychological evaluation was recommended to help paint a more complete picture of Julia's academic and emotional strengths and challenges.

The evaluation revealed significant speech and language delays and indicated that Julia also showed delayed development in early reading, writing, and math skills. Although challenges were noted in Julia's overall executive functioning, the criteria for ADHD were not met. The psychologist who conducted the testing believes that much of the impulsivity and poor problem solving is the result of social immaturity and a "primed stress response" system that better fits the diagnostic criteria for PTSD and children who were adopted internationally with histories such as Julia. As a result of the evaluation, Julia's parents decided to move Julia to a smaller, private school where she repeated her kindergarten year and received more intensive, targeted speech and language services with a private practitioner. Julia began thriving in school as her increasing social emotional maturity and blossoming language skills allowed her to better manage the social and academic demands of school.

Much of the individual therapy work with Julia, given her age, has been through play. Several consistent themes emerged in her play throughout treatment, focusing mostly on safety and protection, as well as sickness and healing. Julia has engaged in play with the "bad guys" since beginning treatment, and this play has evolved tremendously as Julia has begun to integrate her adoption story and early life experiences. A baby always has been at the center of her play, and notably, Julia chose a baby of color reflecting her racial connection as a transracial adoptee. (Children as early as 2 and 3 years of age begin to notice differences among people. They have learned to classify, and they tend to sort based on color and size. What we know is that young children cannot decipher multiple racial classifications and can get confused about the names of racial groups and the actual color of their skin. The therapist acknowledged how the baby's skin color was the same as Julia, and future work will help Julia understand how people with different skin tones can be part of the same family.) During play, there were always "bad guys" who would try to hurt the baby. At first, the baby did not have a protector, and Julia's play was disorganized and chaotic. Over time, Julia used animal figurines to help keep the baby safe, not allowing the "bad guys" to hurt or take the baby. More recently, Julia has become the "protector," ensuring that no harm comes to the baby during play.

Medical play has been the second area that has been seen consistently in treatment. Julia always takes on the role of the doctor, performing many of the same surgeries that she herself has had to endure. She is meticulous in her role, often engaging the therapist and her parents as nurses and other doctors to help with the procedures. Julia increasingly engaged in this type of play following a surgery she underwent during her time in therapy.

Play has been incredibly healing for Julia, as she has been able to take on the role of "protector" and "healer." She has been able to assume roles that represent "power" and "control," and in doing so, she has begun to work through some of the feelings of helplessness, which were associated with her life in Guatemala. Julia is thriving socially and academically in school. Her parents have seen great improvement in her ability to tolerate and manage frustration and report increased emotional maturity in many areas. Treatment continues to work on helping Julia's parents address challenging home behaviors and allows Julia the opportunity to continue to integrate and process her story.

CASE ILLUSTRATION: SEARCH FOR SELF

### History

Lui Li was adopted at age 16 months from an orphanage in China following three other "living situations." Little information regarding early history was available other than that Lui Li had been in an orphanage after being abandoned. At the time of placement, Lui Li was malnourished and had a history of scabies that resulted in constant scratching that continued beyond the treatment of scabies.

**CASE ILLUSTRATION: SEARCH FOR SELF** (CONTINUED)

In 2006, Lui Li began pulling her hair compulsively, which resulted in significant hair loss.

A psychological evaluation was conducted in 2001, which reported that Lui Li is a "complex child with many resources and strengths but also with special vulnerabilities and 'failures' in adaptation. Her adjustment falls within the neurotic realm, but is complicated by her tendency to somatization and perhaps budding characterological issues. She is a quite sensitive, imaginative child whose current cognitive functioning does not reflect her optimal level of performance . . . she shows limited ability to regulate affect which increases her predisposing to anxiety and depression." Nowhere in this evaluation is adoption ever mentioned or the implications of early deprivation and trauma on neurodevelopment. The recommendation was for "intensive individual intervention." Lui Li's mother reported that following this report, her daughter was involved in "traditional therapy" for more than 3 years with minimal progress.

Early developmental milestones for Lui Li are hard to identify because of placement age. This lack of information can pose challenges for professionals working with internationally placed children, often having to formulate a diagnosis and treatment plan without historical information. Her parents reported that she was not speaking Chinese at placement and seemed to understand English fairly easily. Her first intelligible statement was "do it myself."

Lui Li walked at 16 months, and it was not clear whether she had walked independently before adoption, but parents noted that she was well-coordinated and had strong fine motor skills. Lui Li was reported to be a healthy eater but had a history of hoarding food.

**Presenting Problems**

Lui Li was referred for therapy at 12 years of age as her parents were concerned about her not being as "close" to her mother as she would like her to be.

Lui Li presented with chronic anger outbursts, distractibility, oppositional defiant behaviors, depression, anxiety, and self-injurious behaviors. She clawed her skin with fingernails on extremities and stomach, used razors for cutting, and pulled large clumps of hair out of head. Hair pulling began in spring 2006. In 2006, Lui Li was diagnosed by the collaborating psychiatrist who confirmed the diagnosis of trichotillomania and anxiety disorder, and prescribed Lexapro to treat anxiety.

Lui Li was described as exhibiting anger for no clear reason, being controlling and manipulative, having a poor understanding of social cues, lacking empathy for others, and being socially abrasive, all resulting in her having a hard time making and keeping friends. She also would lie with no remorse. Teachers described her social interactions as ranging from bullying to being overly or inappropriately silly. In the classroom, she had trouble managing her behaviors.

Lui Li's parents were concerned that she was not able to demonstrate a variety of coping skills other than anger or "checking out." Lui Li reportedly cried daily and was unable to describe her feelings following these "crying storms." Sometimes she was seen as being "unresponsive" with no change in consciousness or mental status. She was hypervigilant regarding safety and extremely cautious in new situations.

At the time of intake, Lui Li presented as a young girl who was overly intense, had low levels of adaptability, lacked trust in others, and could not tolerate seeking comfort from anyone. She had a hard time bouncing back when distressed with high emotional reactivity. She had a negative view of herself and took her pain out on others and herself.

**Treatment Tools and Strategies**

Lui Li was seen in therapy from 2006 to 2011, at which time she was in the 11th grade. It is critical to understand Lui Li's behaviors in context of the contributing factors: early familial losses, environmental instability, and suspected abuse. All of these factors can significantly disrupt developing stages of cognitive and psychosocial development, including the development of attachment to parental figures, positive self-image, and trust in others. Lui Li's history and responses suggest an attachment disorder that was affecting family and peer relations. It was also necessary to view her behaviors through a neurodevelopmental lens, regarding her stress response. As she inaccurately perceived "threats," her fight or flight response was easily activated, and she was slow to soothe herself, expending a level of energy that resulted in emotional depletion. Lui Li would talk about how tired she was and how hard she worked at school to try to focus on her work. Given the complex clinical presentation, early treatment protocols consisted of DBT to treat the self-injurious behaviors as well as a behavioral treatment approach for the treatment of trichotillomania.

## CASE ILLUSTRATION: SEARCH FOR SELF (CONTINUED)

Lui Li's hair pulling resulted in significant hair loss, which added to her social isolation and feelings of difference. "I started to pull when I was 11 years old. In time, I had several bald spots, which I could no longer hide. All the hair form my crown was gone and my mom started to worry. She told me that I was going to see a therapist and I started to yell and said, 'NO, I DON'T WANT TO GO TO ANOTHER STUPID THERAPIST.' A few days later, we arrived at C.A.S.E. and my therapist helped me with my hair pulling and other issues like adoption. I learned so many things about 'trich' and strategies to manage it. I learned that it was not my fault, and I should not be ashamed. I was not the only person in the world who had it. Remember it's not your fault."

As issues of attachment, trauma, and trichotillomania (TTM) were effectively addressed, Lui Li was able to unearth and acknowledge her feelings of betrayal towards her birthmother. "She left me to figure life out on my own." "She abandoned me, left me in the middle of a field, what kind of person would do that?" "There must have been a child that was better than me." "You throw away garbage not a baby." "Most of the time I feel worthless, sad and unwanted." Lui Li felt conflicted and guilty for not feeling "grateful" that she was adopted, that she had been "saved." "My cutting helps me to put my pain into something physical." Given a safe place to hold these powerful emotions, Lui Li went on to reveal her feelings of difference as she was only one of four Asian kids in her grade. "I feel so different. I don't look like my parents, they don't look like me. Kids stare at me, they call me names. I'm not sure where I fit in.

One day Lui Li brought the lyrics of a song, "Reflections," by Christina Aguilera.

Look at me
You may think you see
who I really am
But
you'll never know me
Every day, is as if I play
apart
Now I see
If I wear a mask
I can fool the

world
But I cannot fool
my heart
Who is that
Girl I see
Staring straight back at me?
When will my Reflection show
Who I am inside?
I am now In a World
where I have to Hide my heart
And what I believe In
But somehow I will show the world
What's Inside my heart
And be loved for who I am

The line "Who is that girl I see, staring straight back at me" was the foundation for the mask work. Lui Li deeply pondered how she possibly could figure out who she was when she had no idea who brought her into the world, what they were like, or how she was like or different from them. This overwhelming vastness of unanswered questions shadows the critical developmental milestone of identity formation. Further complicating her quest for identity was the role being transracially adopted played: "What does it really mean that I am Asian?" Lui Li was able to honestly tell her parents about the extreme racism and bullying that she was experiencing, and the assumptions people made about her because of the color of her skin. In therapy Lui Li shared her mask with her parents, which revealed the pain she endured as reflected in the color black, but also her slow acceptance of which she was using pink and glitter to represent aspects of herself that she was slowly embracing through her therapy.

Lui Li terminated therapy in 11th grade, feeling that she had grown in so many ways: "I don't see myself as a kid that no one wanted, I have a family." She is currently in her second year of college, doing extremely well. She continues some hair pulling but as she says, "I have learned to manage my trich and continue to use the problem solving skills I learned, especially around dealing with my feelings in a different way."

## CONCLUSION: FINDING AN ADOPTION-COMPETENT THERAPIST

Intercountry and transracial adoptive families need and deserve access to professionals equipped to address their unique needs. Advocacy for congressional funding for adoption-competent postadoption training and support services is a priority for C.A.S.E. and our partner organizations.

Every day C.A.S.E. gets calls from desperate parents around the country searching for a therapist who understands adoption. We hear stories of time wasted with mental health professionals who often not only were not helpful but also exacerbated a family's distress. We feel for these families' frustration and offer several ideas to help locate an appropriate therapist. In addition to the following resources that may help identify appropriate resources, parents can learn the questions to ask to determine whether a therapist is adoption competent and specifically has the knowledge, training, and skill to effectively treat intercountry and transracial adoptive families.

Parents can consult the following resources for therapist recommendations:

- Agency social workers involved in the child's adoption
- State or local mental health associations
- Public and private adoption agencies
- Local adoptive parent support groups, including ones from your child's country of origin or for transracial adoptive families (www.pact.org)
- Specialized postadoption service agencies
- State adoption offices
- National and state professional organizations
- Family preservation services for adoptive families resource lists (https://www.childwelfare.gov/pubs/f_therapist.pdf)

This chapter affirms that we are making strides by acknowledging "adoption competency" as a valued body of knowledge that is essential when treating those whose lives have been touched by adoption. During a recent training, an adoptive mother began to talk about her teenage daughter who was struggling. This mother shared that they had seen many therapists and that her daughter was experiencing bullying at school related to racism and adoption. She wanted advice as to how to find a therapist that was adoption competent. The mother said that her daughter had written the following poem, and she obtained her daughter's permission to share it. Hopefully, this chapter will have encouraged more practitioners to see the value in seeking adoption-competent training to address the complexity adoption presents with young people like Maya who have so much to say if we will listen.

WHERE I'M FROM

Maya, age 12

I am from the town of Animal Lovers and gardeners
From Forever 21 and H&M
I am from the town full of flowers
beautiful, colorful
smelling like sweet pollen
I am from the basil
the tomatoes
red and shiny
I am from compliments and kindness
from "you should treat others how you want to be treated"
to the "you should treat everybody equally"
I am from the Shabbat blessings on Fridays
I am from Huizhou, China
from rice and noodles
from the mixed cultures and traditions
from the family members that bring the traditions to life
I am from a home of different cultures and unique family.

**DISCUSSION QUESTIONS**

1. What are the mental health challenges presented by transracial and intercountry adoptees?
2. What is the relationship between the adoptee's preadoption history and experiences and their mental health challenges?
3. What questions can you integrate into your assessment process that would enhance the adoption competency of your work with adopted children, youth, and their families?
4. Why is it imperative that parents be involved in treatment? What evidence-based and evidence-informed treatments are effective with this population?

5. How are racial, ethnic, and cultural differences between the adoptee and family best addressed in treatment to result in positive outcomes around identity formation and racial socialization?

**REFERENCES**

Arneaud, S., Hayes, K., Hoekstra, R., Jackson, R., Kerr, B., Lakin, D., and Wasserman, K. (1996). *Adoption support and preservation services*. Southfield, MI: Spaulding for Children.

Atkinson, A., & Gonet, P. (2007). Strengthening adoption practice, listening to adoptive families. *Child Welfare, 86*(2), 87–104.

Atkinson, A. J., Gonet, P. A., Freundlich, M., & Riley, D. B. (2013). Adoption competent clinical practice: Defining its meaning and development. *Adoption Quarterly, 16,* 156–174.

Barth, R. P. & Brooks, D. 2000. Outcomes for drug-exposed children eight years post-adoption. In R. P. Barth, D. Brodzinsky, and M. Freundlich (Eds.), Adoption and prenatal drug exposure: The research, policy and practice challenges, (pp. 23–58). Washington, DC: CWLA and Donaldson Adoption Institute.

Boss, P. (2000). *Ambiguous loss: Learning to live with unresolved grief*. Cambridge, MA: Harvard University Press.

Bowlby, J. (1969). *Attachment and loss: Attachment*. New York: Basic Books.

Bowlby, J. (1973). *Attachment and loss: Separation, anxiety and anger*. New York: Basic Books.

Bowlby, J. (1988). *A secure base: Clinical applications of attachment theory*. London: Routledge.

Briere, J., Kaltman, S., & Green, B. L. (2008). Accumulated childhood trauma and symptom complexity. *Journal of Traumatic Stress, 21*(2), 223–226.

Brodzinksy, D. M. (2013). *A need to know: Enhancing adoption competence among mental health professionals*. New York: Donaldson Adoption Institute.

Brodzinsky, D. M., Schechter, M. D., & Henig, R. M. (1992). *Being adopted: The lifelong search for self*. New York: Doubleday.

Brodzinsky, D. M., Smith, D. W., & Brodzinsky, A. B. (1998). *Children's adjustment to adoption: developmental and clinical issues*. Thousand Oaks, CA: Sage.

Carlson, V., Cicchetti, D., Barnett, D., & Braunwald, K. (1989). Disorganized/disoriented attachment relationships in maltreated infants. *Developmental Psychology, 25*(4), 525–531.

The Casey Center for Effective Child Welfare Practice. (2003). Strengthening families & communities: *Promising practices in adoption competent mental health services: A white paper.* Retrieved from http://www.aecf.org http://www.aecf.org/resources/promising-practices-in-adoption-competent-mental-health-services/

CBS/Associated Press. (2012). *Mom who sent adoptive child back to Russia ordered to pay child support.* Retrieved from http://www.cbsnews.com/news/mom-who-sent-adoptive-child-back-to-russia-ordered-to-pay-child-support

Center for Adoption Support and Education (C.A.S.E.). (2007). *Training for adoption competency.* Burtonsville, MD.

Courtois, C. A., & Ford, J. D. (2009). *Treating complex traumatic stress disorders: An evidence-based guide.* New York: Guilford Press

Dimeff, L., & Linehan, M. (2001). *Dialectical behavior therapy in a nutshell.* Retrieved from http://www.dbtselfhelp.com/DBTinaNutshell.pdf

Evan B. Donaldson Adoption Institute. (2010). *Keeping the promise: The case for adoption support and preservation.*

Fahlberg, V. (1979). *Helping children when they must move.* Detroit, MI: Department of Social Services.

Falicov, C. J. (1998). Family sociology and family therapy contributions to the family development framework: A comparative analysis and thoughts on future trends. In C. J. Falicov (Ed.), *Family transitions: Continuity and change over the life cycle* (pp. 3–54). New York: Guilford Press.

Feigelman, W. (2000). Adjustments of transracially and inracially adopted young adults. *Child and Adolescent Social Work Journal, 17,* 165–183.

Freundlich, M. (2006). Research on post adoption services: Implications for practice, program development, and policy. In M. M. Dore (Ed.), *The post adoption experience. Adoptive families' service needs and service outcomes* (pp. 283–301). Washington, DC: Child Welfare League of America and Casey Family Services.

Freundlich, M. (2009). *TAC curriculum, Module 9.* Center for Adoption Support and Education.

Freundlich, M., & Lieberthal, J. K. (2000, October 16). *The gathering of the first generation of adult Korean adoptees: Adoptees' perceptions of international adoption.* Retrieved from http://adoptioninstitute.org/publications/the-gathering-of-the-first-generation-of-adult-korean-adoptees-adoptees-perceptions-of-international-adoption/

Grotevant, H., & Brodzinsky, D. (2009). *TAC curriculum, Module 4.* Center for Adoption Support and Education.

Hajal, F., & Rosenberg, E. B. (1991). The family life cycle in adoptive families. *American Journal of Orthopsychiatry, 61,* 78–85.

Hirschi, T. (1969). *Causes of delinquency.* Berkeley: University of California Press.

Howard, J. A., & Smith, S. L. (2003). *After adoption: The needs of adopted youth.* Washington, DC: Child Welfare League of America.

Howard, J. A., Smith, S. L., & Ryan, S. D. (2004). A comparative study of child welfare adoptions with other types of adopted children and birth children. *Adoption Quarterly, 7*(3), 1–30.

Hughes, D. (2009). Attachment-focused treatment for children. *Clinical pearls of wisdom* (pp. 169–181). New York: Norton.

Jennings, A. (2004). *Models for Developing Trauma-Behavioral Health Systems and Trauma-Specific Services,* National Technical Assistance Center for State Mental Health Planning, National Association of State Mental Health Program Directors, Alexandria, VA.

John, J. (2005). *Black baby white hands: A view from the crib* (2nd ed.). Silver Spring, MD: Soul Water Rising.

Kubler-Ross, E. (2014). *On death and dying: What the dying have to teach doctors, nurses, clergy, and their families.* New York: Simon & Schuster/Touchstone Book.

Kubler-Ross, E., & Kessler, D. (2014). *On grief and grieving: Finding the meaning of grief through the five stages of loss.* New York: Scribner.

Landers, S., Forsythe, L., & Nickman, S. (1996). *Massachusetts Department of Mental Health training and adoptive family stabilization project final report.* Boston: Massachusetts Department of Mental Health.

Lenerz, K., Gibbs, D., & Barth, R. P. (2006). Postadoption services: A study of program participants, services, and outcomes. In M. Dore (Ed.). *The postadoption experience: Adoptive families service needs and service outcomes* (pp. 95–110). Washington, DC: Child Welfare League of America.

Leslee, L., O'Connor, R., McRoy, R., Brooks, D. & Baden, A. (2009). *TAC curriculum, Module 12.* Center for Adoption Support and Education.

Malchiodi, C. A., & Crenshaw, D. A. (2014). *Creative arts and play therapy for attachment problems.* New York: Guilford Press.

McDaniel, K., & Jennings, G. (1997). Therapists' choice of treatment for adoptive families. *Journal of Family Psychotherapy, 8*(4), 47–68.

McRoy, R. G., Grotevant, H., & Zurcher, S. (1988). *Emotional disturbance in adopted adolescents.* New York: Praeger.

Meese, R. L. (2005). A few new children: Post-institutionalized children of intercountry adoption. *Journal of Special Education, 39*, 157–167.

Pavao, J. M. (1992). Normative crisis in the development of the adoptive family. *Adoption Therapist 3*(2), 1–4.

Price, D. A., & Coen, A. S. (2012). *Colorado residential child care facilities outcome measures study.* Retrieved from http://www.childabuse.org/document.doc?id=138

Reitz, M., & Watson, K. W. (1992). *Adoption and the family system.* New York: Guilford Press.

Riley, D., & Meeks, J. (2006). *Beneath the mask: Understanding adopted teens.* Burtonsville, MD: C.A.S.E. Publications.

Rosenthal, J. A., & Groze, V. K. (1992). *Special needs adoptions: A study of intact families.* Westport, CT: Praeger.

Rosenthal, J. A., & Groze, V. K. (1994). A longitudinal study of special-needs adoptive families. *Child Welfare, 73*(6), 689–706.

Sass, D. A., & Henderson, D. B. (2000). Adoption issues: Preparation of psychologist and evaluation of the need for continuing education. *Journal of Social Distress and the Homeless, 9*(4), 349–359.

Sass, D. A., & Henderson, D. B. (2002). Adoptees' and birth parents' therapeutic experiences related to adoption. *Adoption Quarterly, 6,* 25–32.

Schooler, J. E., & Norris, B. L. (2002). Secrecy in adoption and the high cost it required. In J. E. Schooler & B. L. Norris (Eds.), *Journeys after adoption: Understanding lifelong issues* (pp. 3–15). Westport, CT: Bergin & Harvey.

Seaton, E. K., Scottham, K. M., & Sellers, R. M. (2006). The status model of ethnic identity development in African American adolescents: Evidence of structure, trajectories and well-being. *Child Development, 77*, 1416–1426.

Simmel, C. (2007). Risk and protective factors contributing to the longitudinal psychosocial well-being of adopted foster children. *Journal of Emotional and Behavioral Disorders, 15*(4), 237–249.

Simon, R. J., & Alstein, H. (2002). *Adoption, race, and identity: From infancy to adulthood.* New Brunswick, NJ: Transaction.

Smith, S. L. (2014). *Keeping the promise: The case for adoption support and preservation.* Retrieved from http://adoptioninstitute.org/wordpress/wp-content/uploads/2014/05/Keeping-the-Promise-Case-for-ASAP1.pdf

Smith, S. L., McRoy, R., Freundlich, M., & Kroll, J. (2008). *Finding families for African American children: The role of race and law in adoption from foster care.* New York: Donaldson Adoption Institute.

Trenka, J. J., Oparah, J. C., & Shin, S. Y. (2006). *Outsiders within: Writing on transracial adoption.* Cambridge, MA: South End Press.

Twohey, M. (2013). *The child exchange: Inside America's underground market for adopted children.* Americans use the Internet to abandon children adopted from overseas. Reuters Investigates.

United States. Department of Health and Human Services. Substance abuse and Mental Health Administration. Center for Mental Health Services. (2004). *Models for developing trauma-informed behavioral health systems and trauma specific services.* Alexandria, VA: National Association of State Mental Health Program Directors, National Technical Assistance Center for State Mental Health Planning.

Vandivere, S., Malm, K., & Radel, L. (2009). *Adoption USA: A chartbook based on the 2007 National Survey of Adoptive Parents.* Retrieved from http://aspe.hhs.gov/hsp/09/NSAP/chartbook/index.pdf

Wilson, J. Q., & Hernstein, R. J. (1985). *Crime and human nature.* New York: Simon & Schuster.

# Transracial and Intercountry Adoptions

*CONCLUSIONS*

▸ ROWENA FONG AND RUTH G. McROY

MORE THAN 30 YEARS AGO, Deborah Silverstein and Sharon Roszia (1982) explained the lifelong impact of adoption as follows:

> Adoption is a lifelong, intergenerational process which unifies the triad of birth families, adoptees and adoptive families forever ... all triad members, regardless of the circumstances of the adoption or the characteristics of the participants. (Silverstein & Kaplan, 1982)

Lifelong processes accompany the adoption journeys for adopted persons, adoptive parents and families, and birth parents involved in transracial and intercountry adoptions. Silverstein and Roszia (1982) identified the core issues for adopted persons, birth parents, and adopted parents as follows: loss, rejection, guilt and shame, grief, identity, intimacy and relationships, and control and gain (see the table). Throughout the years, the existence of intense and unresolved emotions surrounding grief, loss, guilt, shame, rejection, control and gain, and intimacy and relationships most likely continue to exist. The circumstances causing these emotions and the manifestation of these emotions, however, may have changed in the past three decades. For example, in countries such as China, the cultural values of shame and "loss of face" (Fong & Wang, 2000) would have been a major deterrent disallowing a Chinese couple to leave a child in an orphanage, hospital, or police station because children are so highly valued because of the expectation that children care for their elders. But since 1979, the single-child policy of China has forced couples to rethink the valuing of a

Seven Core Issues of Adoption

| | ADOPTEE | BIRTH PARENT | ADOPTIVE PARENT |
|---|---|---|---|
| 1. Loss | • Fears ultimate abandonment<br>• Loss of biological, genetic, and cultural history<br>• Issues of holding on and letting go | • Ruminates about lost child<br>• Initial loss merges with other life events<br>• Leads to social isolation<br>• Changes in body self-image<br>• Relationships losses | • Infertility equates to loss of self and immortality<br>• Issues of entitlement lead to fear of loss of child and overprotection |
| 2. Rejection | • Placement for adoption as a personal rejection<br>• Can only be "chosen" if first rejected<br>• Issues of self-esteem<br>• Anticipates rejection<br>• Misperceives situations | • Rejects self as irresponsible and unworthy because she permitted the adoption<br>• Turns these feelings against self as deserving of rejection<br>• Comes to expect and cause rejection | • Feeling of being ostracized because of procreation difficulties<br>• May make partner the scapegoat<br>• May expel adopted child to avoid anticipated rejection |
| 3. Guilt and Shame | • Feels deserving of misfortune<br>• Ashamed of being different<br>• May take defensive stance<br>• Anger | • Party to guilty secret<br>• Shame and guilt for placing child<br>• Feeling of being judged by others<br>• Double bind: Not okay to keep child—not okay to place him | • Ashamed of infertility<br>• May believe childlessness is a curse or punishment<br>• Religious crisis |
| 4. Grief | • Grief overlooked in childhood or blocked by adult leading to depression and acting out<br>• May grieve lack of "fit" in adoptive family | • Grief acceptable for only a short period<br>• Grief may be delayed 10 or 15 years<br>• Lacks rituals for mourning<br>• Sense of shame blocks grief work | • Must grieve loss of "fantasy" child<br>• Unresolved grief may block attachment to adopted child<br>• May experience adopted child's grief as rejection |

| | | |
|---|---|---|
| 5. Identity | • Deficits in information about birth parents, birthplace, and so on may impede integration of identity<br>• May seek identity in early pregnancies or extreme behaviors to create a sense of belonging | • Child as part of identity goes on without knowledge of self and self-worth<br>• May interfere with future parental desires | • Experiences a diminished sense of continuity of self<br>• "Role handicap"—I am a parent/I am not a parent |
| 6. Intimacy and Relationships | • Fears getting close and risking reenactment of earlier losses<br>• Concerns over possible incest (e.g., with an unrecognized sibling)<br>• Bonding issues may lower capacity for intimacy | • Difficulty resolving issues with other birth parent may interfere with future relationships<br>• Intimacy may equate to loss | • Unresolved grief over losses may lead to intimacy and marital problems<br>• May avoid closeness with adopted child to avoid loss |
| 7. Control and Gains | • Adoption alters life course<br>• Aware of not being a party to initial adoption decisions, in which adults made life-altering choices<br>• Haphazard nature of adoption removes cause-and-effect continuum | • Relinquishment seen as an out-of-control, disjunctive event<br>• Interrupts drive for self-actualization | • Adoption experiences lead to "learned helplessness," in which sense of mastery is linked to procreation<br>• Lack of initiative |

*Source:* Silverstein and Roszia (1982), http://www.adoptionsupport.org/res/7core.php.

child, especially if he or she has a disability (Johnson, 2012). This population limitation policy has resulted in males—who traditionally are more highly valued than females in Chinese culture—also to be abandoned. Thus, Chinese birth parents have not been able to be openly unified with their biological child and have suffered shame and loss of face for abandoning highly valued sons. Birth parents, adopted children, and adoptive parents all continue to face challenges of loss and shame, as well as other core issues related to intercountry and transracial adoptions. Problems with rehoming, the private practice of adoptive parents to place their adopted child via Internet and social media outlets into a new adoptive home without legal assessment or oversight, may be reflective of the current challenges faced by adoptive parents and children that would encompass many, if not all, of the core issues of adoption (see table).

In reexamining these seven core issues, some of the challenges may remain the same, but some of these challenges now may be different for triad members in inracial, transracial, and intercountry adoptions.

1. Loss Issues: All triad members suffer losses. But in cases in which adoptions are closed and do not promote or allow openness in contact or communication among triad members, ambiguous loss can become an even greater issue for triad members. According to author Pauline Boss (2000), when there is no verification of death, ambiguous loss freezes the grief process and prevents closure. Boss offers six guidelines for resiliency in a cyclical model: (a) finding meaning, (b) tempering mastery, (c) reconstructing identity, (d) normalizing ambivalence, (e) revising attachment, and (f) discovering hope (see chapters 9 and 10).
2. Rejection Issues: Disruptions and dissolutions in transracial and intercountry adoptions tend to heighten the rejection issues for all triad members. But in the issue of rehoming, in which illegal activities occur while placing a child in another adoptive home, rejection reoccurs without supports for resolution (see chapter 2).
3. Guilt and Shame Issues: Guilt is the feeling of responsibility with remorse about an offense committed, whether real or imagined whereas shame is the feeling of an improper act done by oneself or another. Cultural values associated with shame to self and family complicates the healing for triad members affiliated with those ethnic cultures (see chapter 7).

4. Grief Issues: Grief is associated with the healing of loss, but resolution toward grief issues are complicated in cases of rehoming, child abduction, and child laundering. (see chapter 2).
5. Identity Issues: Identity is the fact of being who one is. Historically, identity issues referred to concerns about the lack of knowledge about oneself (e.g., medical history). Currently, however, identity seems to be focused more on how to put together the multiple entities on knowing who one is, as an individual adopted person, and for the adoptive family to know how to be and function as a transracial family (see the introduction and chapters 4, 6, 7, 8, and 9).
6. Intimacy and Relationship Issues: Historically, these issues focused primarily on the relationship, or lack thereof, with the birth parents (see chapters 1, 3, and 5). Currently, intimacy and relationships focus on maintaining the connectedness to family via kinship care and sibling placements. Either through formal or informal kinship adoption, the goal is to keep the adopted person connected to the birth family for the sake of identity and relationships to birth relatives (see the introduction).
7. Controls and Gains Issues: Historically, these issues were related to the concern about lack of awareness or information or participation in knowledge and decision making, Currently, the control and gains issues are more seriously affected by fraud and coercive practices related to abduction and child sales (see chapter 2).

These seven categories of core issues might remain the same in transracial and intercountry adoptions but present more complexities and challenges for parents and professionals.

The approaches, guided by theoretical frameworks, need to be reevaluated to handle the complex and multiple traumas triad members often face. Historically, attachment theory was the primary theory associated with adoptions. But intersectionality is another appropriate and useful theory that is developed from feminist theory and involves the process of integrating multiple identities. In several chapters, the authors mentioned the need for the intersectional lens (chapter 4) with gay, lesbian, bisexual, and transgendered families; intersecting identities in ethnic identity formation chapter 6), intersectionality in school settings where multiple identities are interconnected (chapter 9). In addition, other theories, discussed in chapter 6, which are useful for understanding identity, include the bicultural identity integration model related to ethnic identity formation and the need to scaffold the child's identity. These concepts, the intersectionality of identity and the scaffolding identity, also seem applicable not just to the adopted person but also to the adoptive family and all of its family members. Becoming a transracial family with all family members fully agreeing and understanding its implications in adopted person connected to the "culturally competent person but also to the adoptive family and all of its family members. Becoming a transracial family

More research is needed to continue to expand our knowledge and understanding of transracial and intercountry adoptions and to develop innovative and evidence-based practices, policies, and resources (Schwartz et al., 2014). We acknowledge, support, and respect families who make the choice to adopt children who may have been abandoned, abused, or traumatized through institutional care or multiple moves in foster care and who also come from a different cultural or racial background than the parents (Hanna, Tokaski, Madera, & Fong, 2011). It is essential that supports are in place to increase parenting success and to make a commitment to these families to facilitate and strengthen the family unit through the availability of culturally and adoption-competent clinicians, educators, and others who can promote positive outcomes for these parents and children (McGlone, Santos, Kazama, Fong, & Mueller, 2002). Future suggested directions and recommendations include the following:

Intercountry Adoptions

1. Enforce Hague Intercountry Adoption Act (HCIA) policies despite country of origin, limited resources, and child protection capacity to foster a solid partnership and practices to promote ethical intercountry adoptions.
2. Develop both ethical and efficient systems in addressing the problem of the slowdown of the adoption process while children are languishing in institutional care or encountering other difficult circumstances as they wait for an adoptive placement.

Transracial Adoptions

1. Recruit a diverse pool of potential foster and adoptive parents who can meet the needs of these children, given the overrepresentation of African

American children in the child welfare system and in keeping with one of the provisions in the Multiethnic Placement Act (MEPA).
2. Provide training for adoption staff to be not only knowledgeable but also both adoption and culturally competent in keeping within the MEPA's requirements.
3. Develop strategies for agencies to adequately prepare transracial adoptive families and provide adoption-specific supports to help families address the significance of racial and cultural identity for their adopted children and to find ways to help them feel more connected to their heritage and identity (Vonk & Angaran, 2003).

## Gay and Lesbian Adoptions

1. Use culturally responsive approaches to working with lesbian and gay families, often referred to as "gay-affirmative" or "lesbian- and gay-affirmative" practice models as recommended, such as the Expanded Family Life Cycle model developed by McGoldrick, Carter, and Garcia-Preto (2010).
2. Work with lesbian and gay populations and acquire an understanding of both the "normative" developmental and life-cycle issues that individuals, couples, and families face as well as the unique issues experienced by those with diverse orientations, identities, and expressions.

## Neurodevelopmental Perspectives and Trauma

1. Provide attention, enrichment, nurturing and developmentally informed early intervention services to help the vast majority of institutionalized children to make significant developmental progress.
2. Use special education services as they remain needed as indicated for previously institutionalized children many years post-adoption, despite post-adoption gains in cognitive functioning.
3. Help children learn about their country and culture of origin because it is important, as is allowing and encouraging peer and mentor relationships with other children who share similar racial, cultural, or ethnic backgrounds as the adopted child (Ortega & Faller, 2011).
4. Decrease stress on the entire family system by family members becoming equally interested in learning about; respecting; and, in some cases, adopting their child's cultural norms and traditions, even if the child is still learning those norms and traditions.

## Ethnic Identity Formation

1. Seek opportunities for ongoing self-reflection, which should be viewed as a critical foundational task and process in which adults (parents and professionals) engage, and examine attitudes and beliefs about cultural and racial differences.
2. Communicate about adoption, in keeping with the child's developmental stage.
3. Balance multiple identities, while considering the importance of balancing family identity with supporting the development of children's multiple identities.
4. Emphasize preplacement and postplacement training or group-based supports or professional consultation for families.

## Medical

1. Offer preadoption counseling and advice, which are key to addressing challenges that should be anticipated, so families are prepared to meet a child's likely needs.
2. Assess comprehensively a child's status after arrival. This involves attention not only to medical issues but also to the psychological processes involved in incorporating a child successfully into the family.
3. Inform parents of the necessity to enculturate and racialize their children.
4. Remain vigilant to help identify problems that may appear at key developmental horizons or advancing age.

## School

1. Create environments inclusive of many kinds of families, including multiracial and nontraditionally formed families.
2. Strive for equity for all students, particularly with students with differing needs and experiences.
3. Pay attention to attrition rates for students of color or special education needs.
4. Have faculty and administrations be open to hearing from experts within the adoption community about the sensitivities of adopted children and

their needs, creating adoption-sensitive educators who incorporate adoption content and resources into the curriculum.
5. Ensure that school environments with students with different capacities and challenges are valued equally.
6. Prioritize research on transracial and international adoption and the impact on school settings; in particular, focus on research that promotes evidence-based teaching strategies and interventions that inform and lead to adoption-competent practices in the school.

## Adoption-Competent Mental Health Professionals

1. Help families locate an appropriate culturally competent therapist who has the knowledge, training, and skills to effectively treat international and transracial adoptive families.
2. Prepare and support transracial and intercountry adoptive families to deal with problems related to loss and grief, attachment, and trauma history as well as parenting a child of a different race.
3. Promote awareness for families and clinicians to know about effective therapeutic approaches, such as psycho-education for parents, trauma-informed treatments (such as trauma-focused cognitive behavioral therapy), group therapy, or the W.I.S.E. UP Powerbook, a clinical tool to help families prepare their children for managing the challenge of adoption-related questions and comments.

## Mental Health

1. Develop clinical applications based on theory that are specifically designed to effectively treat adoption-related mental health issues for all adoption stakeholders, including those affected by transracial or international adoption.
2. Conduct rigorous research to develop evidence-based best practices in the treatment of mental health issues that have been developed and specifically validated with transracial and international adoptees, birth parents, and adoptive families.
3. Develop and implement comprehensive adoption-competency training programs for clinical practitioners-in-training and all clinical practitioners, including education and awareness training regarding attitudes and

judgments about adoption that contribute to the stigma that accompanies adoption.
4. Design and implement empirical research that more effectively and fully accounts for and identifies the racial, cultural, and other disparities that are hallmarks of transracial and international adoption.
5. Conduct research with birth families of color and international birth families whose children were adopted transracially or internationally to best understand the mental health issues that affect these families.

## CONCLUSION

This book on transracial and intercountry adoptions calls for the development of and implementation of more research, training, evidence-based practices, and policies related to transracial and intercountry adoptions. Evidence shows that the seven core issues of adoption persist in these types of adoption, but expanded culturally competent practices are needed because of the complex issues involved in the intersections of ethnicity and race, sexual orientation, religion, physical abilities, and country of origin, which affect all triad members and their families. Training for adoption-competent professionals is necessary for all workers in child welfare, school, medical, mental health, and legal settings servicing individuals and families in transracial and intercountry adoptions. A multisystems approach is necessary to connect all helping professionals to understand common concerns, hopefully share information, and understand the necessity for cultural competent practice and cultural humility in servicing children and families experiencing transracial and intercountry adoptions. Additional research is still needed about the following: issues affecting birth family relationships or lack of relations with adopted persons; ethnic identity formation and the impact that the adoptive family and sibling relationships have on identity development; and the impact of the HCIA, MEPA–Interethnic Adoption Provisions, and Indian Child Welfare Act legislative policies. The complex needs of transracial and intercountry triad members are great, but multiple efforts and strides toward improvement are occurring, as evidenced in this book.

## DISCUSSION QUESTIONS

1. What kinds of theoretical frameworks are associated in working with children, youth, and families in transracial and intercountry adoptions?
2. What recommendations are there for professionals who work in schools, medical, and mental health facilities when they service children and youth who have been adopted through transracial and intercountry adoptions?
3. Give examples of using a multisystems approach in working with children, youth, and families experiencing transracial and intercountry adoptions.

## REFERENCES

Boss, P. (2000). *Ambiguous loss: Learning to live with unresolved grief.* Cambridge, MA: Harvard University Press.

Fong, R., & Wang, A. (2000). Adoptive parents and identity development for Chinese children. *Journal of Human Behavior in the Social Environment, 3,* 19–33.

Hanna, M., Tokaski, K., Madera, D., & Fong, R. (2011). Happily ever after? The transition from foster care to adoption. *Adoption Quarterly, 14*(2), 107–131.

Johnson, K. (2012). Challenging the discourse of intercountry adoption: Perspectives from rural China. In J. L. Gibbons & K. S. Rotabi (Eds.), *Intercountry adoption: Policies, practices, and outcomes* (pp. 103–118). London, England: Ashgate Press.

McGlone, K., Santos, L., Kazama, L., Fong, R., & Mueller, C. (2002). Parental stress with adoptive parents. *Child Welfare, 81*(2), 151–172.

McGoldrick, M., Carter, B., & Garcia-Preto, N. (2010). *The expanded family life cycle: Individual, family, and social perspectives* (4th ed.). Boston: Allyn and Bacon.

Ortega, R. M., & Faller, K.C. (2011). Training child welfare workers from an intersectional cultural humility perspective: A paradigm shift. *Child Welfare, 9,* 27–49.

Schwartz, A., Cody, T., Ayers-Lopez, S., McRoy, R., & Fong, R. (2014). Post adoption support group: Strategies for addressing marital issues. *Adoption Quarterly, 17*(2), 85–11.

Silverstein, D., & Kaplan, S. (1982). *Life Long issues in adoption.* Child WelfareInformation Gateway. Retrieved: http://www.fairfamilies.org/2012/1999/99LIfelongIssues.htm.

Vonk, M. E., & Angaran, R. (2003). Training for transracial adoptive parents by public and private adoption agencies. *Adoption Quarterly, 6*(3), 53–62.

## CONTRIBUTORS

ROWENA FONG, ED.D., MSW, is the Ruby Lee Piester Centennial Professor in Services to Children and Families at the University of Texas at Austin, School of Social Work. She received her B.A. from Wellesley College, MSW from the University of California at Berkeley, and Ed.D. from Harvard University. Dr. Fong has served as educator, center director for Asian American studies, researcher, school social worker, residential treatment caseworker, preschool teacher, and administrator. Since 2010, she and Becky Harding, past President of Families of Children (FCC) from China, Austin chapter, have codirected the FCC/UT Chinese Culture Camp for children and siblings adopted from China in Austin, Texas. Dr. Fong's primary areas of research and scholarship have been in child welfare, specifically transracial and intercountry adoptions, racial disproportionality and disparities, domestic and international victims of human trafficking, and culturally competent practice. She has published nine books and numerous articles in these areas and on other subjects related to Asian American children and families, primarily Chinese American children and families, and about immigrants and refugees.

RUTH G. MCROY, PH.D., MSW, is the first holder of the Donahue and DiFelice Endowed Professorship at Boston College Graduate School of Social Work. Before joining the Boston College faculty in 2009, McRoy was a member of the University of Texas at Austin School of Social Work faculty for 25 years and held the Ruby Lee Piester Centennial Professorship. She received her B.A. and MSW degrees from the University of Kansas and her Ph.D. from the University of Texas at Austin. Over the years, she has served as a professor, research center administrator, clinical practitioner, researcher, consultant, and child welfare trainer. Her primary research and practice interests include adoption and foster care, racial and ethnic diversity, transracial adoptions, kinship care, family preservation, adoptive family dynamics, sibling placement issues, open adoptions, respite care, and other forms of postadoption services. McRoy has published numerous articles and ten books on such topics as transracial adoptions, special needs adoptions, openness in adoption, and many others.

ANN E. SCHWARTZ, PH.D., received a B.A. in sociology from Trinity University in San Antonio, Texas, and an M.A. in sociology from the University of Arizona in Tucson, Arizona. She completed a Ph.D. in social work at the University of Texas at Austin and was awarded a dissertation grant from the Fahs-Beck Foundation for Research and Experimentation. She is a professor of sociology at Concordia University Texas in Austin, Texas. Her professional fields of interest include child welfare policy, kinship care, foster care, ethnic identity, and adoption. She has published and presented on issues related to the impact of kinship and nonkinship foster care on the personal and ethnic identity development of African American adolescents. Currently, she is working with the Texas-Minnesota Adoption Research Project, focusing on the longitudinal experiences of birthmothers. In addition to teaching and research, Dr. Schwartz also coordinates the Service-Learning Program at Concordia, Texas. Previously, she administered a grant-funded initiative aimed at preparing students for service in the child welfare system through a partnership with Lutheran Social Services of the South. She has also served as assistant to the vice president of academic services at Concordia.

HOLLEE MCGINNIS, MSW, is a doctoral candidate in social work at Washington University in St. Louis. Her dissertation, funded by the Korea Foundation and U.S. Fulbright, focused on the mental health and academic outcomes of adolescents in orphanages in South Korea. Before returning to school she was the policy director at the Donaldson Adoption Institute. She received her B.A. from Mount Holyoke College and her MSW degree from Columbia University, and completed a postmaster's clinical social work fellowship at the Yale University Child Study Center. She has been active in the field of international and transracial adoption as a community organizer, policy analyst, and researcher. Her work has focused on racial or ethnic and adoptive identity among transracial adoptees, adoptive parenting issues, adoption policy, birth search and reunion, global child welfare, and substitute care for orphans. She has published numerous essays in anthologies, books, media, and peer-reviewed journals.

KAREN SMITH ROTABI, PH.D., MSW, MPH, has worked in child welfare in a number of countries that include the United States, the United Kingdom, Belize, and Guatemala. She focuses on child protection responses and family support, emphasizing prevention and social policy. Along with Judith Gibbons, Rotabi edited *Intercountry Adoption: Policies, Practices, and Outcomes* (Ashgate Press,

2012). Rotabi is an associate professor of social work at the United Arab Emirates University. Her publications can be found at https://unc.academia.edu/KarenSmithRotabi.

CARMEN MÓNICO, PH.D., MSW, MS, is assistant professor at Elon University's Human Service Studies. Her dissertation research inquired experiences of Guatemalan women whose children were abducted and trafficked for intercountry adoption. Together with Karen Rotabi, she analyzed practices of search and family reunion of "disappeared" children during El Salvador civil war. Her full biography is available online at http://www.elon.edu/directories/profile/?user=cmonico.

AMY GRIFFIN, PH.D., MSW, is a currently a Society for Research in Child Development (SRCD) and American Association for the Advancement of Science (AAAS) Congressional Fellow in the office of U.S. Senator Al Franken. She completed her doctorate in social work at Boston College. Dr. Griffin's research focuses on dually involved youth, a population of youth who are involved in both the juvenile justice and child welfare systems. Additional research projects and articles have included transracial adoptions, home evaluations for prospective adopters, and multimethods research. Dr. Griffin graduated with a B.A. in psychology from Boston College and then received her MSW from the School of Social Policy and Practice at the University of Pennsylvania.

DEVON BROOKS, PH.D., MSW, is an associate professor in the School of Social Work at the University of Southern California. He served previously as associate dean for faculty affairs and as chair of the faculty. He earned his Ph.D. and MSW from the School of Social Welfare at the University of California, Berkeley, and his B.A. in psychology from George Mason University. Dr. Brooks's research interests revolve around foster care and adoption, child maltreatment, and public child welfare organizations. Particular areas of research interest include transracial adoption, lesbian and gay adoption, engagement, and child welfare organizational capacity and professional development. Other areas of interest and scholarship pertain to diversity, intersectionality, and intercultural competence and to distance education and training. Dr. Brooks teaches MSW and doctoral courses both in the classroom and virtually. He typically teaches courses on research, human behavior, diversity, and sexual orientation. He codeveloped and coteaches a global immersion course on social innovation, engagement, and impact and has provided group-based field instruction. Additionally, Dr. Brooks is heavily involved in curriculum development, implementation and evaluation, and in reaffirmation and reaccreditation. Other teaching and curricular areas of interests revolve around program, course, and syllabus development; student professional competencies and learning outcomes; distance education and continuing professional development; faculty mentoring; and academic integrity. Dr. Brooks has served on numerous committees at the University of Southern California and within the School of Social Work, as well as on professional organizations, including the Council on Social Work Education, the Society for Social Work Research, the National Association of Social Workers, and the National Association of Black Social Workers. He consults, presents, and publishes widely. Currently, Dr. Brooks is working on two books—one on intercultural social work practice, education, and research and the other on social work assessment, evaluation, and research.

DONI WHITSETT, PH.D., LCSW is a clinical professor and the associate director of faculty development at the University of Southern California (USC) School of Social Work. She earned her doctoral degree in social work from USC and her MSW from Case Western Reserve University. Treating individuals, couples, and families, her clinical practice experience spans more than four decades. Dr. Whitsett's teaching, research, and practice interests include trauma, human sexuality, and cult-related issues. Over her 20 years at the USC School of Social Work, Dr. Whitsett has taught both foundation and advanced courses in practice, behavior, and mental health both in the classroom and virtually. She taught the human sexuality course required for licensure for mental health practitioners in California for more than 15 years and currently teaches an elective on human sexuality at the School of Social Work. She regularly provides leadership in the courses she teaches and to the numerous curriculum committees on which she serves. Dr. Whitsett is a coinvestigator on a grant titled Sexual Functioning in the Military. Dr. Whitsett has published in professional journals and has been an invited speaker and presented nationally and internationally on trauma, cult-related topics, and online education. She helped to organize two conferences in Australia and has taught mental health courses in China.

JEREMY T. GOLDBACH, PH.D., joined the University of Southern California (USC) School of Social Work in 2012 after completing both his M.A. and Ph.D. in social work at the University of Texas at Austin (UT-Austin). His dissertation, "Toward the Prevention of High Risk Behavior in Sexual Minority Adolescents," explored the relationship between minority stress and marijuana use by lesbian, gay, and bisexual adolescents. His work at UT-Austin was funded through the Substance Abuse and Mental Health Services Administration Center for Substance Abuse Prevention, specializing in prevention science.

He currently holds funding through the National Institute of Child Health and Human Development for psychometric instrument development (2014–2016) and through the Trevor Project, to explore suicidality among LGBTQ adolescents (2015–2016). Dr. Goldbach has been funded by the National Institutes of Health Clinical and Translational Science Institute to pilot an intervention for Latino youth and families, and through the Zumberge Small Grant program to explore stress and behavioral health outcomes in racially and ethnically diverse lesbian, gay, and bisexual adolescents. Dr. Goldbach currently serves as project evaluator with the National Association of Social Workers HIV/AIDS Spectrum: Mental Health Training and Education of Social Workers Project. His practice background includes both clinical and community organizing. Before returning for his doctoral education, Goldbach oversaw a large community-organizing project in Texas that funded thirty-two community coalitions to reduce substance use concerns through environmental, policy-based strategy. His teaching interests include direct social work practice, human behavior, and research with vulnerable populations.

BRUCE D. PERRY, M.D., PH.D., is the senior fellow of the ChildTrauma Academy, a nonprofit organization based in Houston, Texas, and adjunct professor in the Department of Psychiatry and Behavioral Sciences at the Feinberg School of Medicine at Northwestern University in Chicago. He serves as the inaugural senior fellow of the Berry Street Childhood Institute, an Australian-based center of excellence focusing on the translation of theory into practice to improve the lives of children. Dr. Perry is the author, with Maia Szalavitz, of *The Boy Who Was Raised as a Dog*, a bestselling book based on his work with maltreated children and *Born for Love: Why Empathy Is Essential and Endangered*. His most recent multimedia book, *BRIEF: Reflections on Childhood, Trauma and Society* was released in 2013. Over the past 30 years, Dr. Perry has been an active teacher, clinician, and researcher in children's mental health and the neurosciences holding a variety of academic positions. Dr. Perry has conducted both basic neuroscience and clinical research. His neuroscience research has examined the effects of prenatal drug exposure on brain development, the neurobiology of human neuropsychiatric disorders, the neurophysiology of traumatic life events, and basic mechanisms related to the development of neurotransmitter receptors in the brain. This work has examined the cognitive, behavioral, emotional, social, and physiological effects of neglect and trauma in children, adolescents, and adults. This work has been instrumental in describing how childhood experiences, including neglect and traumatic stress, change the biology of the brain—and, thereby, the health of the child. His clinical research over the past 10 years has been focused on integrating emerging principles of developmental neuroscience into clinical practice. This work has resulted in the development of innovative clinical practices and programs working with maltreated and traumatized children, most prominently the Neurosequential Model©, a developmentally sensitive, neurobiology-informed approach to clinical work (NMT), education (NME), and caregiving (NMC). Dr. Perry is the author of more than 500 journal articles, book chapters, and scientific proceedings and is the recipient of numerous professional awards and honors, including the T. Berry Brazelton Infant Mental Health Advocacy Award, the Award for Leadership in Public Child Welfare, the Alberta Centennial Medal, and the 2014 Kohl Education Prize. Dr. Perry was an undergraduate at Stanford University and Amherst College. He attended medical and graduate school at Northwestern University, receiving both M.D. and Ph.D. degrees. Dr. Perry completed a residency in general psychiatry at Yale University School of Medicine and a fellowship in Child and Adolescent Psychiatry at the University of Chicago.

ERIN HAMBRICK, PH.D., is the Child Trauma Academy's Inaugural Robin Fancourt Research Fellow. She was awarded her Ph.D. in Clinical Child Psychology from the University of Kansas in August 2014, following a predoctoral internship in pediatric health psychology at Children's Hospital, Colorado. Currently, she is a National Institute of Mental Health T32 Research Fellow through the University of Colorado School of Medicine, Department of Psychiatry. As part of this 2-year research fellowship, she is conducting research with the Kempe Center for the Prevention and Treatment of Child Abuse and Neglect and the University of Denver Graduate School of Social Work. During this fellowship she is coleading skills groups for Fostering Healthy Futures, an intervention being implemented at Aurora Community Mental Health Center. Dr. Hambrick's clinical interests include working with youth exposed to maltreatment or other forms of trauma (e.g., disaster, traumatic grief, medical trauma). She is particularly interested in the role of relational and strengths-based interventions, including mentoring interventions, for maltreated youth. She is trained in several evidence-based and evidence-informed interventions, such as Parent-Child Interaction Therapy, Psychological First Aid, and Fostering Healthy Futures. Dr. Hambrick's research interests include implementation of evidence-based treatments for maltreated youth and for youth affected by disaster. She currently studies the developmental impact of chronic maltreatment and trauma.

She has published several research articles on risk and resilience in children following adversity, and on implementation of evidence-based interventions.

ROBERT PERRY, B.S., is serving as the Robin Fancourt Fellow of the ChildTrauma Academy, a nonprofit organization in Houston, Texas. In this capacity, he conducts both clinical and preclinical neuroscience research. His most recent project is a comparison of neuroimaging (SPECT) with the heuristic functional brain maps created using the web-based neurosequential model of therapeutics (NMT) assessment process. Additional projects include the development of analysis algorithms for the ChildTrauma Academy's core clinical data set that will allow more in-depth examination of the impact of developmental adversity on a range of brain-mediated functions, and examination of the inter-rater reliability and fidelity of the NMT metrics across multiple clinical sites. Mr. Perry is a graduate of the University of North Carolina-Chapel Hill where he earned a B.S. in biology and psychology. He previously has worked as a clinical intern at the psychiatric residential treatment facility of the Alexander Youth Network in Charlotte, North Carolina, and as a research assistant for the ChildTrauma Academy. His research interests include the epigenetics of adversity, molecular mechanisms involved in various aspects of the stress response, neuroplasticity, and developmental neurobiology.

ELLEN E. PINDERHUGHES, PH.D., is associate professor in the Eliot-Pearson Department of Child Study and Human Development, Tufts University. Her research focuses on contextual and cultural influences on family socialization processes among culturally diverse families, particularly those raising children at risk for problems in development. She coedited (with H. N. Le) a special issue of *Applied Developmental Science* focused on culture, context, and parenting processes. She is one of several principal investigators of Fast Track, one of the National Institute of Mental Health's largest longitudinal prevention trials, which has been following more than 1,100 youth living in high-risk communities for more than 20 years. As an adoption researcher, she has published on readjustment processes among families adopting children from foster care as well as on transracial international adoptive families and their navigation of cultural and racial differences, in particular, ethnic–racial socialization and ethnic identity. As a senior research associate with the Adoption Institute, she coauthored a study of practices of adoption professionals and experiences of adoptive parents concerning international adoption and the impact of the Hague Adoption Convention on the Protection of Children and Co-operation in Respect of Intercountry Adoption. She served on the Institute of Medicine

Committee on Child Maltreatment and is on the editorial board of *Adoption Quarterly*.

JESSICA A. K. MATTHEWS, B.A., is currently a doctoral student in the Eliot-Pearson Department of Child Study and Human Development working with Professor Ellen Pinderhughes. While attending the University of California, Berkeley, Matthews majored in psychology and political science where she became interested in adoption. Matthews has been studying adoption, international adoption in particular, for the past 10 years. Now at Tufts University, she is pursuing her Ph.D. in applied child development focusing on early emotion regulation, identity formation, and the ethnic-racial socialization of international adoptees. Additional research interests include the complexities of transracial adoption, special needs adoption, and the development of children who do not regularly experience parental care worldwide.

XIAN ZHANG, M.S., is a doctoral student in Eliot Pearson Department of Child Study and Human Development at Tufts University. She obtained her B.S. in psychology and M.S. in psychoanalytic developmental psychology from University College London, England. She currently works with Dr. Ellen Pinderhughes in the Adoption and Development Project as a lab leader. Her research interests include cultural socialization and identity development in children from transracial adoptive families and immigrant families.

AMANDA L. BADEN, PH.D., is an associate professor in the Department of Counseling and Educational Leadership at Montclair State University in New Jersey. She was the recipient of the John D. Black Award in 2014 from the American Psychological Association and Division 17 (Counseling Psychology) for the Outstanding Practice of Counseling Psychology. She is a senior research fellow of the Evan B. Donaldson Adoption Institute, a member of the State Board of Psychology for New York State, on the editorial board for *Adoption Quarterly* and the *Journal of Social Distress and the Homeless*, and cochair of Biennial Adoption Initiative Conferences in New York City held at St. John's University. She is an adult adoptee from Hong Kong and her experiences both personally and professionally have lead her to focus her research and clinical practice on adoption triad members, transracial and international adoption issues, racial and cultural identity, and multicultural counseling competence. She has a clinical practice in Manhattan.

JONATHAN R. MAZZA, M.A., currently works as a crisis clinician in the emergency department at Morristown Medical Center in New Jersey. Jonathan received his M.A. in community counseling and has diverse clinical experience in the follow areas: psychiatric inpatient, crisis intervention services, homeless and at-risk youth agency, intensive outpatient, and medical psychiatric liaison. Mazza has presented on adoption research at numerous national and regional conferences, was a committee member for the Adoption Initiative organization, and helped coordinate two inspiring adoption conferences in New York City. Jonathan also was an editorial assistant for the *Journal of Counselor Preparation and Supervision* and was a graduate assistant at Montclair State University working under Dr. Amanda Baden and Dr. Edina Renfro-Michel.

ANDREW KITCHEN, M.A., is currently a psychiatric clinical screener at Trinitas Regional Medical Center in Elizabeth, New Jersey. Andrew received his B.A. in psychology and M.A. in community counseling at Montclair State University. He is currently a licensed associate counselor in the State of New Jersey. Andrew is an international adult adoptee, who was adopted from South Korea at the age of 6 months. He continues to work with a team of research assistants lead by his former professor, Dr. Amanda Baden, to continue to advocate for and improve the clinical treatment of adoptees within the mental health community. Kitchen has presented on adoption research at St. John's University, Rutgers University, and the 2014 American Psychological Association Conference in Washington, DC.

ELLIOTTE HARRINGTON, M.A., is currently a doctoral student studying counselor education at Montclair State University in Montclair, New Jersey. She holds an M.A. in community counseling also from Montclair State University. Harrington's areas of interest include pedagogy, family studies, and adoption, particularly the experiences of birth parents. She is a member of an adoption research team lead by Dr. Amanda Baden at Montclair State University. Harrington has been a speaker and presenter on the topic of adoption at various local, state, and national conferences. She is an adoptive mother through a domestic, open adoption.

EBONY WHITE, M.A., is a licensed professional counselor in the state of New Jersey as well as a national certified counselor. She currently works as a program director for a community mental health outpatient clinic in East Orange, New Jersey. Her area of interests is advocacy and social justice within the African American community, specifically related to fostering positive outcomes in children raised by female head of households in low-income communities. She is a doctoral fellow in the Counselor Education program at Montclair State University, where she works on a research team focused on multicultural issues in adoption, led by Dr. Amanda Baden. Her research has been presented at the

2014 NJCA Conference, Montclair State University Research Symposium, and recently the Diversity Challenge at Boston College.

DANA E. JOHNSON, M.D., is a professor of pediatrics and member of the Divisions of Neonatology and Global Pediatrics at the University of Minnesota where Dr. Johnson cofounded the International Adoption Program in 1986. His research interests include the effects of early institutionalization on growth and development and the outcomes of internationally adopted children. Dr. Johnson serves on the editorial boards of *Adoption Quarterly* and *Adoptive Families* magazine and has authored numerous scholarly works. He received the Distinguished Service Award and the Lifetime Achievement Award from Joint Council for International Children's Services, the Friend of Children Award from NACAC, and the Harry Holt Award from Holt International. Dr. Johnson has two birth daughters and an adopted son from India.

JUDITH K. ECKERLE, M.D., is an assistant professor in the Division of Global Pediatrics at the University of Minnesota. Dr. Eckerle is the director of the Adoption Medicine Program and sees clinic patients from foster care, domestically and internationally adopted children for medical assessments, and children for fetal alcohol spectrum disorder evaluations. Dr. Eckerle's research interests include investigating markers in children with early adversity that may be predictive of future cognitive outcomes. She teaches and mentors students and residents in the Adoption Clinic elective. She was adopted from Seoul, South Korea.

JAERAN KIM, PHD, LISW, is assistant professor of social work at University of Washington, Tacoma. Kim has worked with children, youth, and families in both private and public adoption. Kim's research foci include adoption stability, transracial and intercountry adoption, and adopted children with disabilities.

BETH HALL, B.A., is the director of Pact, An Adoption Alliance. She cofounded Pact in 1991 to combat the discrimination she witnessed against adopted children of color and their birth families. Pact is a nonprofit organization whose mission is to serve adopted children of color. She is the coauthor, with Gail Steinberg, of the book *Inside Transracial Adoption* (Jessica Knightly Publishing, 2013). She is the white adoptive mother of a Latina daughter and an African American son (both now young adults) and grew up with an adopted sister.

DEBBIE B. RILEY LCMFT, is the chief executive officer of the Center for Adoption Support and Education, Inc. (C.A.S.E.), an independent, nonprofit adoptive family support center in the Baltimore–Washington area. A nationally recognized adoption expert and dynamic public speaker, Riley has 35 years of professional experience, including extensive health care management and administrative expertise, designing and developing nationally acclaimed adoption-competency programs, direct delivery of specialized counseling services that affords her the broad knowledge and expertise needed to promote mental health training, child advocacy, and public policy development. Riley created a continuum of innovative, culturally responsive evidenced-informed programs to improve the behavioral outcomes of foster and adopted youth and their families, which has become a nationally recognized model. Riley consults with national child welfare agencies on complex child welfare issues and systems of care enhancement. For more than a decade she has built and implemented a framework for training an adoption-competent mental health workforce nationally. She is the founder of the Training for Adoption Competency (TAC) curriculum, which currently is taught in thirteen states. Through a recent federal 5-year grant awarded to C.A.S.E from the U.S. Department of Health and Human Services, Administration for Children and Families, Riley serves as the principal investigator to establish a National Adoption Competency Mental Health Training Initiative (NTI). The initiative will build the adoption-competency capacity of child welfare professionals and mental health practitioners that serve youth moving toward permanency as well as youth living in permanent adoptive or guardianship homes. The NTI will develop state-of-the-art evidence-informed adoption competency web-based curricula for each group with quality improvement components for use on a national basis. She is coauthor of the book, *Beneath the Mask: Understanding Adopted Teens.*

ELLEN SINGER, MSW, LCSW-C, is a senior adoption-competent therapist and educator for the Center for Adoption Support and Education (C.A.S.E.) in the Washington metropolitan area. She obtained her MSW from the University of Illinois/Jane Addams College of Social Work in Chicago, Illinois. Before joining C.A.S.E. in 1998, Singer worked for several adoption placement agencies and family service and mental health centers. She provides clinical services for prospective parents considering adoption or third-party reproduction, foster and adoptive parents, adult adopted people and their families, and expectant and birth parents and their families. She facilitates adoptive parent support groups and provides training to parents, community groups, educators, child welfare, and mental health professionals. Singer is the editor of C.A.S.E.'s monthly e-newsletter and is the author or coauthor of numerous articles for parent and professional newsletters and magazines, including *Adoptive Families, Fostering Families, Adoption Today, Family Therapy* (publication of the

American Association for Marriage and Family Therapy), *Pediatric Nursing*, and *North American Council on Adoptable Children*. She has contributions in *Adoption Parenting: Creating a Toolbox, Building Connections*, edited by Jean Macleod and Sheena Macrae (EMK Press, 2006) and in *The Foster Parenting Toolbox: A Practical, Hands-On Approach to Parenting Children in Foster Care*, edited by Kim Phagan-Hansel (EMK Press, 2012). Singer is an adoptive mother.

# INDEX

AAP. *See* American Academy of Pediatrics
AAP Council on Foster Care, Adoption, and Kinship Care (COFCAKC), 242
abandonment, 48, 56, 202; China's notability for child, 219; relinquishment and child, 219–20
abductions, legal assistance for child, 43–44
abilities, of TRAs/ICAs, 295–96
Aboriginal and Torres Strait Islander Child Placement Principle, 6
abusive care, 126–49
acceptance, 303–4
accreditation, 26–28, 30; of adoption agencies, 52; medical information disclosures and, 31–33; social information disclosures and, 31–33, 46; TRA training standards and, 32
ACE. *See* Adverse Childhood Experiences
"activity dependence," 129
"Acuerdo," 25–26
ADHD. *See* attention deficit hyperactivity disorder
Adichie, Chimamanda, 158
adolescence, 317
adopted teens, 337; identity development crisis of, 291; mental health services used by, 291–92
adoptees, 10–11; accuracy of medical and social information of, 244; ADHD and, 197; adult adjustment of female, 204; adult adjustment of male, 204; adult adjustment of nonadoptees and, 203–4; age and mental health of, 195, 197, 200–202, 204; assessing cultures of, 251–52; attachment difficulties of nonadoptees and, 199–202; behavioral problems in normal ranges, 328; case study and India's, 202; Caucasians as, 202; Chinese, 200; Colombian, 215–16; communication changes with growth of, 178; communication with listening and warmth for, 161; CS and African American, 170, 172; CS and Korean, 172; CS and special needs', 171, 248; cultural support needs of, 34, 51–52, 56–57, 148, 165–66; depression of nonadoptees and, 198; developmental tasks of, 286; diverse community challenges of, 293; eating and sleeping issues of, 288–89; education in medical issues of, 243; educators limited understanding about, 281–82; emotional obstacles facing, 293; Ethiopian, 333; ethnic identity and Korean, 168–71; family comparisons of adoptees and non-, 160; ICAs and health of, 251–52; identity development of immigrant, 169–70; identity formation of nonadoptees and, 204–6; Koreans as, 71, 97, 168–69, 251, 333–34; language development of, 289; LGA, TRA and experience of, 111–14; medical assessments, after arrival of, 252–54; mental health and comparing nonadoptees with, 196–207; mental health issues and Dutch, 198; mental health issues and Swedish, 196, 198, 200; mental health issues of, 196–207; mental health research of nonadoptees

adoptees (*continued*)
and, 206; mental health services and, 195–207; neurodevelopmental perspectives of, 365; ongoing medical assessments of, 254–56; parental support for birth family interest of, 178; parent's visible differences with, 280–81; PfB and perceptions of, 173–74; preadoptive history of, 195–96; PTSD, self-esteem, and trauma of nonadoptees and, 199; Romanian, 199, 212; school behavioral problems of, 286; school experiences of, 278; siblings and, 302–3; substance abuse of nonadoptees and, 198–99; suicide of nonadoptees and, 199–200; teachers' sensitivity to needs beneficial for, 180. *See also* transracial adoptees; transracially and internationally adopted children

adoption, 161–62, 178, 220–23, 264, 307; African American demographics for, 76–77; blacks in foster care and, 71, 76–80, 238–39; bullying related to racism and, 352–53; Canadian moratorium on, 49; children's varied experiences of, 287–88; competent mental health professionals and, 315–53; core capabilities of relational neurobiology and, 138–39; core issues of, *360–61*, 362–63; as cultural experience in U.S., 237; culturally competent practices in, 368; data compiled for report on, 96, 238–41, 249; definition of inracial, 96; delays in, 33; developmental milestones in, 290; development disruptions and, 287; Ethiopia's corruption in, 49; fall of Communism in Eastern Europe and, 240; focus of research on, 194; foster care and black children, 71, 76–80, 238–39; gay couple's experience of, 110–14; gays, lesbians and, 70, 365; global level, 249; Guatemala's unethical and illicit, 42–43; Haiti and fraud in, 41–42, 60; humanitarian disasters and, 248; ICAs, TRAs and triad themes in, 224–25; illicit and unethical, 38, 40–44; incompetent mental health services and failed, 317; independent, 30; interdependent, 29; intersectional lens of, 95–96; liberalization of Chinese policy for, 240; lifelong impact of, 359–60; as manifestation of love and empathy, 126; medical issues in, 241–43; medical professionals' role in, 243–45; mental health professionals and, 367; MEPA and, 76–78; neurodevelopmental perspective policy in, 146; open, 220–23; pediatrics' support and, 241; personal experiences and, 278–79; preference of younger aged children for, 48, 56, 77, 83; protection by policy and implementing measures, 39, 59–60; Russian Federal Law No. 167-FZ banning same-sex couple, 24; single parent, 81, 99, 101; by singles, 202; understanding, 2; United Kingdom's moratorium on, 49; U.S. accounted for half of total, 96; U.S. citizenship and, 256; whites and foster care, 70–71, 219, 238–39; whites' preferences for, 101–2. *See also* domestic adoptions; Hague Convention for Intercountry Adoption; intercountry adoptions; international adoptions; kinship care; lesbian and gay adoptions; post adoptions; transracial adoption; transracially and internationally adopted children

adoption agencies, 277; accreditation of, 52; financial resource management for, 52; financial transparency of, 51; HCIA impact on professionals and, 51–53; unrealistic demands placed on, 84

Adoption and Safe Families Act, 1

adoption competency: adoptive families' need of, 318–19; assessment process and, 327; clinical toolkit for, 328; defining, 320–22; finding mental health professionals with, 352–53; practice integration into, 325–28; TAC and, 109, 324–25; temperament of the family

INDEX                                                                385

system and, 319, 327–28; therapeutic
  approaches, themes and examples of,
  330–34; training importance for, 353
adoption fraud: in Cambodia, 40–41; case
  examples of, 40–43; in Haiti and Chad,
  41–42, 60
adoption kinship network: components of,
  193–94; mental health services survey,
  322–23; professionals and, 224
*Adoption Medicine: Caring for Children
  and Families* (Mason, Johnson, &
  Prock), 242
adoption service providers, 319; diligent
  recruitment and, 30; evaluations on,
  27–28; medical professionals and
  orientation of, 264; prosecutions
  allowed for, 52–53
adoption visibility: exosystem in, 162–63;
  macrosystem in, 163–64; mesosystem
  in, 162–63; TRA families and
  importance of, 162–64
adoptism, 11–13, 282
adoptive families: adoptees's developmental
  tasks and, 286; adoption competency
  needed by, 318–19; affirmative approach
  for, 109; child developmental problem
  risks and, 105–6; comparisons of nonadoptive and, 160; contextual approach
  for, 109; continuum of care and, 328–
  29; demographics and outcomes of, 107;
  ecological context changes within TRA',
  159–64; educators having partners of,
  295; elements of communication critical
  for, 161–62; family life cycle and, 108–9;
  identity development and integration
  of birth and, 165, 169; identity
  development within transracial, 167–
  69; issues related to racial differences
  in, 316; PfB complications for TRA,
  174–75; prerequisite home studies of,
  54–55; school's inclusive environments
  benefiting, 304–5; training of, 54
adoptive identity, 165–66
adoptive parenthood: case study of,
  215–16; risk factors contributing to
  stress of, 212–13; stress assessments

of, 212; transitioning into, 210–11;
  understanding sources of stress in,
  212–13
adoptive parents, 295; African Americans
  and colorblindness of, 258–60; anxiety
  assessments of, 214; assessing depression
  in, 213–14; coping with racial bias,
  211–12; feelings during transitioning of,
  211; HCIA, IAA and, 31–32; intimate
  relationship satisfaction of, 214–16;
  issues and interests impacting, 31–32;
  mental health issues of, 208–16;
  national survey, 1, 69, 76, 238, 240–41;
  postadoption mental health concerns
  of, 211–12; preadoption contact with,
  243–45; preadoption mental health
  concerns of, 208; as predominantly
  white, 167–68; religious beliefs
  motivating and, 249–50; resolving
  infertility issues of, 209–10; transition
  to parenthood, 210–11; unrealistic
  demands placed on, 84
adulthood: adoptee and nonadoptee
  adjustment in, 203–4; case study of
  adoptee in, 207; deportation of adoptee
  in, 164; identity development study in,
  10–11; transition into, 263
Adverse Childhood Experiences (ACE),
  263
advocates, 306–7
Africa, 197, 220; CS and adoptees of, 172;
  non-signing of HCIA in, 49
African Americans, 3, 136–38, 238–39, 333;
  adoption demographics for, 76–77;
  adoptive parents' colorblindness and,
  258–60; bias between whites and, 157;
  birth families, 29, 31; child suspensions
  of, 284; civil rights movement and
  attention to, 72; CS and adoptee,
  170, 172; disproportionality in
  representation, 4, 72, 78–80, 238; foster
  care and, 75, 238–39; kinship care and,
  7–8; MEPA's impact on adoptions
  of, 76–78; problems of child welfare
  services and, 72; racial integration and
  attention to, 72. *See also* blacks

age, at adoption, 195, 197, 200–202, 204
aggression, 133
Aguilera, Christina, 350–51
Alaska Native Americans, 79
Alford, K., 9
ambiguous loss, 290, 320
American Academy of Pediatrics (AAP), 241–42, 250–51
American College of Obstetrics and Gynecology, 245
American College of Pediatricians, 250–51
anxiety disorder, 214, 348
arousal response, stress-response system, 131–33
Asia, 200
Asian Americans, 3, 155, 166
Asians, 70, 101, 168–69
assessments: adoption competency process and, 327; adoptive mother anxiety, 214; adoptive parenthood stress, 212; adoptive parents' depression, 213–14; decisions and, 307–9. *See also* medical assessments
Association for Women's Rights in Development (AWID), 94
attachment disorders, 128, 171, 196, 207, 286, 329, 349; of adoptees and nonadoptees, 199–202; child attachment and, 56
attachment theory, 319–20, 363–64
attention deficit hyperactivity disorder (ADHD), 137, 197, 202, 295, 346
autism, 129, 343
AWID. *See* Association for Women's Rights in Development

Baden, A. L., 58–59, 167–68, 283
Bailey, J. D., 53, 56
Banaji, M. R., 158–59
Bastard Nation, 262
behavioral problems, 144–46; adoptees in normal range of, 328; case studies involving therapy for, 338–51; cognitive challenges interrelated with, 128–29; educators and, 288; in schools, 286; sensitized stress-response system and, 134, *135*, 136, 142–43; top ten reasons for seeking help for, 329–30
belonging, sense of, 136–38, 140, 142–43, 205–6
*Beneath the Mask: Understanding Adopted Teens* (Riley & Meeks), 337
*Beyond Culture Camp: Promoting Health Identity Formation in Adoption* study, 10
BIA. *See* Bureau of Indian Affairs
bias: adoptism and, 282; adoptive parents coping with racial, 211–12; children with disabilities and, 294; of classmates, 282–83; health care professionals and, 250–51; on identity aspects, 93–94; intent and impact aspects of, 284; microaggressions from, 283–84; against TRA/ICA children, 279–80; tribalism related to, 149; whites and African American, 157. *See also* preparation for bias
biological child, 305
bipolar disorders, 198
biracial, 207
birth culture, 201–2, 204–6, 207, 212
birthdays, 298–99
birth documents, 256, 261
birth families: African American, 29, 31; falsehood of child's future return to mother in, 219; HCIA, IAA and, 28–31; HCIA's impact on, 53–54; issues and interests impacting, 28–31; parents' support for adoptees interest in, 178
birth parents, 287, 291; foster care and parents of color as, 219–20, 238–39; mental health issues and, 216–23; promise of financial security to, 219
blacks, 70–71, 76–80, 101, 238–39
body mass index (BMI), 22
Boss, P., 290
Boss, Pauline, 320
boundaries, human, 140–42
Brabender, V. M., 212
Brodzinsky, D. M., 161–62, 323
Bronfenbrenner, U., 159
Bucceri, J. M., 156–57

INDEX

Bucharest Early Intervention Project, 263
bullying, 202, 352–53
Bureau of Consular Affairs, 20–21
Bureau of Indian Affairs (BIA), 72, 74
Butler-Sweet, C., 206
Byers, L. G., 7

Cambodia, 40–41, 60–61, 99
Canada, 29, 49
Capodilupo, C. M., 156–57
Carl, Helen, 249
Carter, B., 108
C.A.S.E. *See* Center for Adoption Support and Education
C.A.S.E. model: attachment theory in, 319–20; family systems theory in, 319, 327–28; grieving process in, 320; Trauma-informed treatment in, 320
case planning, 51
case study: of adoptive parenthood, 215–16; of adult adoptee, 207; behavior problem therapy in, 338–51; on connections, 341–44; gay couple adoption experience, 110–14; healing from hurt, 344–47; of Indian adoptees, 202; infertility of adoptive parents, 209–10; on LGA and TRA family, 110–14; losses, multiple and frequent, 338–41; mental health issues, 202–3; open adoption and relinquishment, 220–22; relational sensitization, 144–46; searching for self, 347–51; sense of belonging in relationships, 136–38
Caucasians, 9, 69, 136–38, 202, 238–39, 333. *See also* whites
CDHS. *See* Colorado Department of Human Services
Center for Adoption Support and Education (C.A.S.E.), 318–21, 337, 345, 352
Central American Orphanages, 127
central authority, HCIA, 21
Chad, 41–42
Chapin, Dwight, 241
Child Citizenship Act, 164, 256

child development, 105–6; HCIA, IAA and, 28–33; HCIA's impact on, 55–58; issues and interests impacting, 33
child laundering, 3; in Cambodia, 40–41; Guatemala and, 42–43
children, 39; abandonment of, 48, 56; acceptance experienced by, 303–4; adoption experiences varied of, 287–88; adoption preference for younger aged, 48, 56, 77, 83; advocates for, 306–7; African American suspensions of, 284; bias and disabled, 294; biological, 305; birth mothers and falsehoods of returning, 219; buying of, 55; as cultural beings by healthy sense of self, 157–58; disabilities and discrimination against, 294; educational outcomes of, 274–75; educators and trajectories of, 309–10; in foster care and adoption of blacks, 71, 76–80, 238–39; human rights defenders protecting, 43–44; ICA in China and special needs, 48; identity struggles of bicultural, 143; LGA and teasing of, 94; LGAs and positive outcomes of, 103–5; medical issues of postinstitutionalized, 242, 252; racial differences of, 285; risk factors of postinstitutionalized, 242, 252; school's assessment decisions of, 307–9; special education for institutionalized, 147–48; teasing of LGA, 104–5; trauma before placement of, 106. *See also* transracially and internationally adopted children
Children's Bureau, 258
Children's Home Society, 246
child rights: ICA and pre-adoption, 39; international private law and, 38–40
child trafficking, 2–3; IAA allowing prosecutions for, 52–53; New Life Children's Refuge in Haiti, 41–42
Child Trauma Academy, 137, 145, 336
Child Welfare League of America (CWLA), 71–73, 246
child welfare systems: disproportionate representations in, 79–80; problems of African Americans and, 72

China, 20, 167, 199–200, 359–60, 362; adoption policy liberalization of, 240; child abandonment notable in, 219; FCC and, 277; ICA requirements of, 21–22; LGAs and two-tiered system of, 100–101; medical systems in, 244; one-child policy and, 48, 56; post war orphans from, 97; problems and length of institutional time in, 317; special needs children and ICA in, 48; TRA and, 98–99, 240
Chinese, 172
Christian Alliance for Orphans, 250
Cicchini, M., 218
CICIG. *See Comision Internacional contra la Impunidad*
citizenship: ITRAs and, 163–64; U.S. adoption and, 256; USCIS and, 25, 28–29; visas and forms for, 164
"civilized oppression," 82
Civil Rights Act, Title VI violation of, 80
civil rights movement, 72, 74
classmates, 282–83
classroom assignments, 297–98, 301
cleft palate, 344
Clifton, J., 218
"clinical toolkit," 328
clinicians, 92–94
closed adoption, 220–23
CNA. *See* National Adoption Council of Guatemala
COA. *See* Council on Accreditation
coercive practices, 2–3, 41–42. *See also* adoption fraud; force, fraud, and coercion pattern
COFCAKC. *See* AAP Council on Foster Care, Adoption, and Kinship Care
cognitive challenges, 128–29, 147–48
Cohen, J. S., 206
colic, 213
Colombia, 215–16
Colorado Department of Human Services (CDHS), 26
colorblindness, 258–60
*Comision Internacional contra la Impunidad* (International Commission Against Impunity in Guatemala) (CICIG), 42–43
Commission on Civil Rights, U.S., 77
communication, 304–5; adoptees adjusting by listening and warmth in, 161; adoptees' growth and changes in, 178; adoptive families' critical elements of, 161–62; developmental considerations in, 161–62; developmental stages for, 161–62; language barrier method and, 246–47; medical professionals' awareness for optimal, 249; methods for cultural sensitivity and, 245–47; parents and adoption, 178; PfB parental support and, 173–76
complaints, submittal of, 31
"complex trauma," 332
connections, case study, 341–44
consent. *See* informed consent
contextual concepts, 109, 126–30; ecological, 159–64; microsystem as first level in, 159–60; of relinquishment, 218–19
control issues, 363
Council on Accreditation (COA), 26–28, 30
counseling, 30
Courtois, C. A., 332
Crenshaw, Kimberlee, 276
Cross, S. L., 7
Crumbley, J., 285
CS. *See* cultural socialization
cultural beings: children's healthy sense of self as, 157–58; lessons learned in adjusting as, 156–58; resources for growth as, 158–59
cultural competence, 13–14, 194; models for ICA practices in, 58–59; in social work, 58–59
cultural humility, 194, 202, 210, 217, 219; culturally competent practice and, 13–14; social workers' knowledge and, 84
culturally competent practice, 368; cultural humility and, 13–14; theoretical framework of, 13–14
cultural sensitivity: checklist for awareness and, 245–46; communication methods

and, 245–47; preadoption counseling and checklist for, 245–46
cultural socialization (CS), 168; African American adoptees and, 170, 172; African Americans' adjustment and, 170; Chinese and, 172; considerations for, 179; Korean adoptees and, 172; for LGAs responsive to, 108–10; as outcome of kinship care, 6–7; parents' racial and cultural attitudes important to, 171–72; special needs' adoptees and, 171, 248; TRAs, E-RS, and, 170–73
cultural support, 34, 51–52, 56–57, 148, 165–66
"cultural tourism," 172
culture, 93, 172; assessing adoptees', 251–52; birth, 201–2, 204–7, 212; competent practices of, 368; definition of, 245; holidays and, 300; ICWA and, 6, 12; identification, 247–49; India's, 171; intrauterine environment and establishing, 251; LGAs diversity and, 101–2; values of, 359–60, 362; white, 166
"culture keeping," 172
curriculum, diverse, 296–97, 306
Curtis, C. M., 82
Curtis, R., 205
custody, Internet, 317–18
CWLA. *See* Child Welfare League of America

"Danger of a Single Story, The," 158
data: global adoption reports and, 96, 238–41, 249; multiple sources for research, 90. *See also* demographics; research
Day, A. G., 7
DBT. *See* dialectical behavior therapy
De Bellis, M., 130
delays, adoption, 33
demographics: adoptive families' outcomes and, 107; African American adoption, 76–77; gays in adoption, 70; ICAs, 19–21, 97–98; of international adoptions, 97–98; for LGAs, 90–91; LGAs originating factors and, 99–100; MEPA passage and TRA, 69–70;

pediatric professionals and racial, 258; transracial domestic adoption history and, 238–41
Denby, R., 9, 82
Denmark, 255
Department of Health and Human Services, U.S. (DHHS), 70–71, 74
Department of Homeland Security, U.S., 25
Department of State, U.S. (DOS), 19, 25
deportation, 164
deportation, of adult adoptees, 164
depression, 207, 221–22; of adoptees and nonadoptees, 198; adoptive parent assessments for, 213–14; postpartum, 213–14
deprivation, early, 263
developmental adversity, 136; clinical challenge of, 130–31; functional consequences of, 128–29; neurodevelopmental consequences of, 129–30
developmental stages: adoption communication, 161–62; child's risk for problems in, 105–6; salience of sexual orientation and, 104–5
development disruptions, 287
DHHS. *See* Department of Health and Human Services, U.S.
dialectical behavior therapy (DBT), 335–36
differences, racial, 280–81, 285, 292, 316
DIR®/Floortime, 343
disabilities, 294
disasters, humanitarian, 248
discrimination: children with disabilities and, 294; of classmates, 282–83; microaggressions from, 283–84; against TRA/ICA children, 279–80
disease, infectious, 253–54
disengagement, 279
disproportionality: of African American representation, 4, 72, 78–80, 238; child welfare systems representing, 79–80; definition of, 4; of Native American representation, 75, 79–80; poverty and placement, 79–80
dissociation, stress-response system, 131–33

District of Columbia, 100
diversity, 292–93, 306; LGAs and cultural, 101–2; TRA, LGA and international, 101–2
divorce, 113–14, 201, 207
DNA analysis, 262–63
DNA fraud, 43–44
Dobson, Christine, 336
Docan-Morgan, S., 174, 279
domestic adoptions: definition for, 95; history and demographics of transracial, 238–41; increase in, 1, 96–97; reasons for choosing ICAs instead of, 247–48
dominant society, 274
Donaldson Adoption Institute, 279
DOS. *See* Department of State, U.S.
Doss, Helen, 249
dyslexia, 296

early deprivation, 263
Eastern Europe, 19, 197, 212, 276, 294; adoptions and fall of Communism in, 240; case study of adoptee from, 144–46; medical systems in, 244
ecological context, 159–64
economy, 8
Edinburgh Postnatal Depression Scale (EPDS), 213
Edison, Thomas, 296
education, 243; C.A.S.E. and, 318–21, 337, 345, 352; children's outcomes of, 274–75; IDEA and, 294; IEP, 276; multicultural, 305; psycho-, 335; services for special, 147–48; TRA/ICA children outcomes of, 276; TRA/ICA children's setting for, 284–85
educators, 281–82, 286, 288; adoptive parents as partners for, 295; children's trajectories and, 309–10
"elephant in the room," 57
"Embracing Otherness, Embracing Myself," 158
emotional distress, 210
emotional obstacles, 293
empathy, 126
environments, inclusive, 304–6

EPDS. *See* Edinburgh Postnatal Depression Scale
equity, 305–6
Erikson, Erik, 204
E-RS. *See* ethnic-racial socialization
Escobar, Ana, 43–44
Ethiopia, 20, 167, 301; adoptee from, 333; adoption corruption in, 49; ICA requirements of, 22–23
ethnic identity: formation, 366; foster children and, 7; ICAs and formation of, 10–11; identity development of racial and, 166–69; kinship care and, 7–9; Korean adoptees and, 168–71; manifestations of, 166–67; parental advocacy for developing, 180; parents' self-reflection and, 177; recommendations for promoting TRAs', 176–77; self-reflection for promoting, 176–77; suggestions for professionals developing, 181–83; TRA and formation of, 10–11; TRAs and ICAs and development of, 154–84
ethnic–racial socialization (E-RS), 170–73
Europe, 29
evaluations, 27–28
Evan B. Donaldson Adoption Institute, 10, 30–31, 81, 219, 318, 323
exosystem, 162–63
Expanded Family Life Cycle, 108–9

Fallon, A. E., 212
*Families Are Different*, 302
Families with Children from China (FCC), 277
family, 1, 92; divorce and gay couple's, 113–14; identity challenges of LGA and TRA, 115; LGA, 103–7; LGAs and TRAs case study on, 110–14; life cycle, 108–9; multicultural, 33; non-adoptee and adoptee comparisons of, 160; outcomes of LGA, 114–15; therapy, 114; TRA and, 84, 110–15; TRAs and context changes within, 159–64; trees, 297
family systems theory, 319, 327–28
*Far from the Tree* (Solomon), 256–57

Farr, R., 70
FASD. *See* fetal alcohol spectrum disorder
Father's Day, 299
FCC. *See* Families with Children from China
Feagin, J. R., 285
Feast, J., 218
Feigelman, W., 203–4, 317
females, adult adjustment of, 204
fetal alcohol spectrum disorder (FASD), 255
Field, J., 221
Final Rules, 26
finances: resource management of, 52; security of, 219; stress and, 208; transparency of adoption agencies', 51
first parents. *See* birth parents
Fish, L., 127
Fisher, Florence, 261
Foli, K. J., 214
food insecurity, 288–89
force, fraud, and coercion pattern, 2–3, 39–44, 53, 60
Ford, J. D., 332
Foreign-Born Adoption Clinic, 246
foster care, 1, 3, 237; African Americans and, 75, 238–39; birth parents of color and, 219–20, 238–39; blacks and adoptions within, 71, 76–80, 238–39; COFCAKC and, 242; ethnic identity and children in, 7; kinship care and, 5; parental rights termination and, 220–23; whites and, 219–20, 238–39; whites and adoptions within, 70–71, 219–20, 238–39
*Fostering Health: Healthcare for Children and Adolescence in Foster Care*, 242
fraud, 2–3; DNA, 43–44; Haiti's adoption, 41–42, 60. *See also* adoption fraud; force, fraud, and coercion pattern
Froberg, D., 214
*From Home to Homeland* (Jacobs, Ponte, & Wang), 173

Gair, S., 213
GAO. *See* Government Accountability Office, U.S.

Garcia-Preto, N., 108
Gates, G. J., 90–91
gay adoptions, 70, 365
gays, 365; in adoption demographics, 70; case study, 110–14; as parents, 105–7
gender, 93
general health, 253–54. *See also* mental health
Gibbons, J. L., 27–28
Gjerdingen, D. K., 214
global adoption: data compiled for reports of, 96, 238–41, 249; surrogacy and, 2
Glover, Danny, 296
"Goldilocks" effect, 134
Goodman, E., 199–200
Government Accountability Office, U.S. (GAO), 76–77, 83
grandmothers, 7
Greenwald, A. G., 158–59
grief: grieving process in C.A.S.E. model, 320; issues, 330–31, 338–41, 363
Groark, C. J., 127
group therapy, 337–52
Groza, V., 29
Guatemala, 20, 167; child laundering and, 42–43; CNA of, 25–26; HCIA implementation in, 44–46, 60; ICA requirements of, 25–26; subsidiarity principle as law focus of, 45–46; unethical and illicit adoptions in, 42–43
*Guide to Good Practice*, 29, 54

Hague Adoption Convention, preamble, 33
Hague Complaint Registry (HCR), 31
Hague Conference on Private Intercountry Law, 29
Hague Convention for Intercountry Adoption (HCIA), 3, 12, 164; adoption agencies and impact of, 51–53; Africa's non-signing of, 49; birth families and, 28–31; birth families and impact of, 53–54; central authority oversight requirements by, 21; child development and impact of, 55–58; development and purpose of, 39; enforcement of

Hague Convention (*continued*)
justice lacking in, 60; Guatemala's implementation of, 44–46, 60; IAA and, 28–33; ICA and implementation consequences of, 53; ICA practice in U.S. changed by, 19; ICA requirements and, 21–26; misconceptions of, 46–50; practical application and impact of, 50–55; for prevention of abduction and sales in ICA, 39; professionals and impact of, 51–53; reduction of international adoption and, 98–99, 240; subsidiarity principle for continuum of care by, 39; TRAs and ratification of, 169; U.S. agencies and professionals impacted by, 26–28; U.S. implementation of, 44–45
Hague Convention on Rights of Child and Multi-Ethnic Placement Act, 193
Hague Intercountry Adoption Act (HCIA), 364
Hague Permanent Bureau, 50, 54
Haiti, 41–42, 60
Hall, Beth, 11, 277, 306
Hambrick, Erin, 12
Hansen, M. E., 76
HCIA. *See* Hague Convention for Intercountry Adoption; Hague Intercountry Adoption Act
HCR. *See* Hague Complaint Registry
healing from hurt, case study, 344–47
health care professionals, 250–51
healthy developmental experiences, 133–38
healthy human functioning, 139–40
heritage trips, 172–73
heterogeneous stress responses, 134
Hispanics, 7, 70, 101
Hoebel, A., 251
Holder, A. M., 156–57
holidays, 300
Holland, 198
Hollingsworth, L. D., 56
Holt, Bertha, 249
Holt, Harry, 249
homeland tours, 277
home studies, 54–55
homosexual orientation, 103–5
"honeymoon period," 253
horizontal identity, 256–58
Howard, J. A., 211–12
Howe, D., 56
Huang, B., 199–200
Hubinette, T., 57–58
humanitarian disasters, 248
human rights defenders, 43–44
humans: boundaries of, 140–42; survival and needing other, 138–39
hysterosalpingography, 209

IAA. *See* Intercountry Adoption Act
IAT. *See* Implicit Association Test
ICAs. *See* intercountry adoptions
ICWA. *See* Indian Child Welfare Act
IDEA. *See* Individuals with Disabilities Education Act
identity, 115, 281; adoptive, 165–66; balancing of multiple, 179; bias on aspects of, 93–94; bicultural children's struggles with, 143; competent clinicians needed for matrix of, 92–94; concerns for loss of personal, 262; culture, 247–49; formation, 2, 12, 204–6; horizontal and vertical, 256–63; intersecting, 155; intersectionality for vulnerability of complex, 93–94; racial, 166–69; scaffolding of, 12, 364. *See also* ethnic identity
identity development, 292, 363; adult adoptees and study for, 10–11; crisis in, 291; definition for, 165; exploring issues in, 301–2; of immigrant adoptees, 169–70; importance of self-reflection and TRA, 183; integration of birth and adoptive families in, 165, 169; ITRAs' cultural and adoptive, 165–66; racial and ethnic identities and, 166–69; scaffolding emerging sense of self in, 160; suggestions for professionals on ethnic, 181–83; within TRA families, 167–69; of TRA/ICA children, 275; TRAs and complications of, 164–69

INDEX 393

IEP. *See* Individualized Education Plan; Interethnic Adoption Provisions
Illegal Immigration Reform and Immigrant Responsibility Act, 164
illegal practices, 2
immigrants, 169–70
impact, in bias, 284
Implicit Association Test (IAT), 158–59
inclusive environments, 304–6
independent adoptions, 30
India, 20, 171; case study on adoptee from, 202; ICA requirements of, 25
Indian Adoption Project, 6
Indian Child Welfare Act (ICWA), 3, 6, 11–14, 74; choices allowed for child placement by, 75–76
Indian culture, ICWA and, 6, 12
Individualized Education Plan (IEP), 276
Individuals with Disabilities Education Act (IDEA), 294
infectious disease, 253–54
infertility, 208; case study of adoptive parents', 209–10; postadoption depression and, 213
informed consent, 30–31
inracial adoptions: CWLA and placement preferences for, 73; definition of, 96
"institutional autism," 129
institutional care, 195–96
institutionalized children, 242; adverse prenatal exposures of, 127, 252; special education services indicated for, 147–48
institutions: destructive practices of, 127–28, 252; racism and, 284; sentiments of society's, 11
integration, racial, 72
intent, in bias, 284
Intercountry Adoption Act (IAA), 26; adoptive parents and, 31–32; birth families and, 28–31; child development and, 33; HCIA and, 28–33; prosecutions for child trafficking allowed by, 52–53; reduction of international adoption and, 98–99, 240
intercountry adoptions (ICAs), 1–4, 364; Bureau of Consular Affairs' demographics for, 20–21; China's requirements for, 21–22; cultural competence models for practices of, 58–59; decrease in, 2, 19, 240; defining inclusions for, 14; definition of, 95; demographics for, 19–21; development of ethnic identity for, 154–84; domestic adoptions and reasons for, 247–48; Ethiopia's requirements for, 22–23; evolution of transracial domestic and, 238; formation of ethnic identity and, 10–11; Guatemala's requirements for, 25–26; HCIA and requirements of, 21–26; HCIA for prevention of abduction and sales in, 39; HCIA implementation consequences and, 53; health of adoptees in, 251–52; history and changes of TRAs and, 193; increases in, 240; India's requirements for, 25; instead of domestic adoptions, reasons for, 247–48; intersectionality concept for TRA and, 92–94; intervention services and progress of, 147–48; literature themes of adoption triad and, 224–25; loss and grief issues in TRAs', 330–31, 338–41, 363; medical service issues for TRAs and, 237–64; mental health services challenging TRAs and, 193–226; neurobiological development and adverse experiences of, 126–49; post World War II, 38, 238–39; preadoption adversity and, 127–28; pre-adoption children's rights and, 39; Republic of Korea's requirements for, 24; risk due to crisis in mental health and, 316–17; Russian moratorium on, 47–48; Russia's requirements for, 23–24, 240; scope and context of, 126–30; social attention of, 57; South Korea and downturns of, 50; special needs children in China and, 48; therapeutic approaches for TRAs and, 330–51; transcultural dimension of, 56–58; transracial dimension of, 56–58; trauma issues in TRAs', 332; UAA and, 26–27; U.S. downturn of, 46–47, *47*

Intercountry Adoption Universal
  Accreditation Act (UAA), 26–27, 31
interdependent adoptions, 29
Interethnic Adoption Provisions (IEP),
  73–75, 239
International Adoption Clinic, 247
international adoptions, 238–39; countries
  banning, 99; decline of, 97–98, 240;
  demographics of, 97–98; HCIA and
  reduction of, 98–99, 240; IAA and
  reduction of, 98–99, 240; TRA, LGA
  and diversity within, 101–2. *See also*
  intercountry adoptions
International Commission Against
  Impunity in Guatemala. *See Comision
  Internacional contra la Impunidad*
International Law Permanent Bureau, 50
international laws, 12
international private law, 38–40
international transracial adoptees (ITRAs),
  168; citizenship and, 163–64; cultural
  and adoptive identity development of,
  165–66
Internet, 317–18
intersecting identities, 12, 155
intersectionality, 276, 363–64; adoption
  through, 95–96; approaches and
  perspective of, 92–94; complex identity
  vulnerability recognized by, 93–94;
  highlights of, 93; importance of multiple
  factors recognized by, 93; TRA, ICAs
  and concept of, 92–94
intervention services, 136–37, 147–48
intimacy barrier, 138–39, *141*; human
  boundaries and, 140–42; personal space
  violations and, 142
intimacy issues, 363
intimate partners, 214–16
intrauterine environment, 251
Italy, 170
ITRAs. *See* international transracial
  adoptees

Jacobs, D., 173
Japan, 97
*John Doe v. Hamilton County Department
  of Human Services*, 78

Johnson, D. E., 242
Johnson, K., 219
Judge, S., 212
justice, 60

KAAN. *See* Korean Adoptee and Adoptive
  Parent Network
Kaiser Permanente Health Maintenance
  Organization, 263
Kao, G., 276
Katch, Jane, 289
*Keeping the Promise: The Case for Adoption
  Support and Preservation*, 318, 323
kidnapping, 42
Kim, JaeRan, 11, 276–77
kinship care, 71; African Americans and,
  7–8; cultural socialization as outcome
  of, 6–7; defining practices and statistics
  of, 6; ethnic identity and, 7–9; foster
  care and, 5; grandmothers as majority
  in, 7; Hispanics and, 7; low-income
  economy and, 8; Native Americans and,
  5–6; responsibility associated with, 9
Klatzkin, Amy, 303
knowledge: mental health issues and
  professionals', 223–25; social workers'
  cultural humility and, 84
Kopera-Frye, K., 7
Korea, 99; adoptees from, 71, 97, 168–69,
  251, 333–34; CS and adoptees of, 172;
  medical systems in, 244; post war
  orphans of, 97; Republic of, 20, 24;
  South, 50, 276–77, 285
Korean Adoptee and Adoptive Parent
  Network (KAAN), 277
Koreans, 71, 97, 168–71, 251, 333–34
Korean War, 71
Kubler-Ross, Elisabeth, 320
Kyle, F., 218

laboratory screenings, 253–54
language, 305; barrier, 246–47;
  development, 289; issues, 345; medical
  assessments for issues, 255, *255*;
  outcomes, 252
Latin America, 197, 200
Latinos, 3

lawlessness, low-resource countries and, 60–61
Lee, R. M., 162, 168
legal assistance, for child abductions, 43–44
lesbian, gay, bisexual, transgender (LGBT), 90, 108, 113–14
lesbian and gay adoptions (LGAs), 365; acceptance and growth of, 91–92; adoptee's experience in TRA and, 111–14; approach and implications for professionals in TRA and, 108–10; case study on family of TRA and, 110–14; children's positive outcomes of, 103–5; children subject to teasing of, 104–5; China's two-tiered system and, 100–101; CS responsive approaches for, 108–10; cultural diversity within, 101–2; demographics and originating factors of, 99–100; demographics for, 90–91; families of, 103–7; family outcomes of, 114–15; identity challenges and families of TRA and, 115; implications for professionals in TRA and, 108–10; international and TRA diversity within, 101–2; issues associated with, 90–115; placement barriers for, 100–101; professionals working with families of, 92; research findings for, 102–3; teasing of children in, 94
lesbian couples, 70
lessons learned, as cultural beings, 156–58
Lev, A. I., 92–93
Levy-Shiff, R., 204, 211
LGAs. *See* lesbian and gay adoptions
LGBT. *See* lesbian, gay, bisexual, transgender
Lifelong Families Model, 109
Lim, E., 214
Logan, J., 218
loss, 2; ambiguous, 290; box therapy tool, 340; case study of multiple and frequent, 338–41; TRAs', ICAs' grief issues and, 330–31, 338–41, 363
Loss Box, therapy tool, 340
love, 126

low-resource countries, 60–61
loyalty, 292

macrosystem, adoption visibility, 163–64
males, adult adjustment of, 204
Malott, K., 70
marital problems, 210, 213
Marshall Islands, 218
Mason, P. W., 242
master's level social workers (MSWs), 52
Matsumura, S., 218–19
Matthews, Jessica A. K., 12
McCall, R. B., 127
McCreery Bunkers, K., 29
McGinnis, H., 168, 211–12
McGoldrick, M., 108
McRoy, R. G., 8
medical assessments: adoptees' after arrival, 252–54; adoptees' ongoing, 254–56; for speech and language issues, 255, *255*
medical information: accreditation standards for disclosures of, 31–33; accuracy of adoptees' social and, 244
medical issues, 366; in adoption, 241–43; education for adoptees', 243; of postinstitutionalized children, 242, 252
medical professionals: adoption practice and orientation of, 264; cultural identification and, 247–49; ICAs' and TRAs' service issues with, 237–64; optimal communication awareness for, 249; role in adoption of, 243–45
medical systems: in China, 244; in Eastern Europe, 244; in Korea, 244
Meeks, J., 291–92, 337
mental health, 106, 367–68
Mental Health Inventory (MHI), 214
mental health issues: of adoptees, 196–207; adoptees' age and variables predicting, 195, 197, 200–202, 204; adoptees compared with nonadoptees for, 196–207; of adoptive parents, 208–16; birth parents and, 216–23; case study, 202–3; Dutch adoptees and, 198; ICAs and risk due to crisis of, 316–17; practice and policy for, 223; professionals' knowledge and, 223–25;

mental health issues (*continued*)
  recommendations for professionals of, 224–25; relinquishment and birth parents', 217–18; Swedish adoptees and, 196, 198, 200
mental health professionals, 367; adoption competency integration into practice of, 325–28; finding adoption competent, 352–53; need for adoption-competent, 315–53; neurodevelopmental perspective and, 147–48; resource recommendations for finding, 352; TAC and evaluation highlights for, 324–25
mental health services, 291–92; adoptee and nonadoptee research, 206; adoptees and, 195–207; adoption kinship network survey, 322–23; failed adoptions and incompetent, 317; ICAs and TRAs challenges with, 193–226
MEPA. *See* Multiethnic Placement Act
MEPA-IEP. *See* Multiethnic Placement Act and Interethnic Adoption Provisions
mesosystem, in adoption visibility, 162–63
Mexican Americans, 3, 221–22
MHI. *See* Mental Health Inventory
microaggressions, 283–84
microsystem, 159–60
Middle East, 197
"miracle question," 114
Mistry, J., 170
mood disorders, 198
moratorium: Canadian adoption, 49; ICAs and Russian, 47–48; United Kingdom's adoption, 49
Mother's Day, 299
Mott, S. L., 214
MSWs. *See* master's level social workers
multicultural education, 305
multicultural family, 33
"multiculturalization," 58
Multiethnic Placement Act (MEPA), 3, 12, 239, 365; African American adoptions and impact of, 76–78; failure of adoption barrier removal by, 77; IEP amendment of, 73–75; passage of, 74–75; TRA demographics post passage of, 69–70
Multiethnic Placement Act and Interethnic Adoption Provisions (MEPA-IEP), 74–75; problem of implementing, 83; research on, 83; violations of, 77–78, 80, 84
multiple identities, 179
Murphy, Y., 94

NAACP. *See* National Association for the Advancement of Colored People
NABSW. *See* National Association of Black Social Workers
NACAC. *See* North American Council on Adoptable Children
names, 299–300
"narrative burden," 278–79
NASW. *See* National Association of Social Workers
NASW Standards for Cultural Competence, 13–14
National Adoption Attitudes Survey, 248
National Adoption Competency Mental Health Training Initiative, 109
National Adoption Council (CNA) of Guatemala, 25–26
National Adoption Information Clearinghouse, 70
National Association for the Advancement of Colored People (NAACP), 73
National Association of Black Social Workers (NABSW), 73, 206, 238, 257, 258, 260
National Association of Social Workers (NASW), 13
National Consortium for Post Legal Adoption Services: Adoption Support and Education, 319
National Foster Care Adoption Attitudes Survey, U.S., 237
national laws, 12
National Longitudinal Survey of Adolescent Health, 199
National Survey of Adoptive Parents, 1, 69, 76, 238, 240–41

National Survey of Child and Adolescent Well-Being (NSCAW), 7
National Urban League, 73
Native Americans, 3, 136–38; Alaska, 79; disproportionality in representation of, 75, 79–80; kinship care and, 5–6
*Need to Know: Enhancing Adoption Competence Among Mental Health Professionals, A* (Brodzinsky), 323
Neil, E., 218
Nelson, C. A., 130
Netherlands, 29
neural networks: healthy human functioning associations and, 139–40; heterogeneous stress responses and, 134
neurobiological development: abusive care and, 126–49; adverse experiences' impact on ICAs and TRAs, 126–49; traumatic experiences and mechanisms influencing, 129–30
neurodevelopment: activity dependence as fundamental in, 129; adoption policy and program implications from, 146; caregivers and professionals understanding, 147–48; consequences of, 129–30; perspectives in, 365; trauma on, 348; viewing through lens of, 349
Neuropsychological testing, 254–55
Neurosequential Model of Therapeutics Metrics (NMT), 136–37, 336
New Life Children's Refuge, 41–42
Newton, Thandie, 158
Ng, N., 298
NMT. *See* neurosequential model of therapeutics; Neurosequential Model of Therapeutics Metrics
non-adoptees: adoptee mental health comparisons with, 196–207; family comparisons of adoptees and, 160
normative crisis, 287
North American Council on Adoptable Children (NACAC), 73
Norway, 276
Nosek, B. A., 158–59
NSCAW. *See* National Survey of Child and Adolescent Well-Being

OCR. *See* Office of Civil Rights
Office of Children's Issues, 26
Office of Civil Rights (OCR), 74, 77–78
one-child policy, China's, 48, 56
"One-Family United Nations," 249
open adoption: case study of relinquishment and, 221–22; *vs.* closed adoption, 220–23; reunion and positive effects of, 221; stress decreased in, 220–21
Open Door Society, 238
Oppositional Defiant Disorder, 137
orphanages. *See* institutions
orphanages, mortality and morbidity in, 241, 317. *See also* institutions
orphans: Chinese post war, 97; Japanese post war, 97; Korean War, 71; post war Korean, 97; US Visa issuance to, 49–50

Pact Family Camp, 277, 283
Padilla, A. M., 169
PAIR. *See* Pre-Adoption Immigration Review
Palacios, J., 159–60, 163
panic attacks, 221–22
parenthood: adoptive parents' transition to, 210–11; different race, 333–34; TRAs and impact of, 189
Parenting Stress Index (PSI), 212
parents: adoptee's interest in birth family and, 178; adoptee's visible differences with, 280–81; communication about adoption and, 178; ethnic identity and self-reflection for, 177; gay and straight, 105–7; homosexuality, 103–5; PfB support and communication of, 173–76; psychoeducation for, 335; racial and cultural attitudes important to CS, 171–72; recruitment, 80–81; rights of, 220–23; single, 81, 99, 101, 207. *See also* adoptive parents; birth parents
Parents to Adopt Minority Youngsters, 238
Paton, Jean, 261
Patterson, C., 70
Pearson, F., 205

pediatrics: adoption support in, 241; professionals' racial demographics in, 258
permanence, 292
Permanency and Adoption Competency Certificate, 109
Perry, Bruce, 12, 336
Perry, Robert, 12
personal experiences, 278–79
personal identity, 281
personal space violations, 142
personal timelines, 298–99
PfB. *See* preparation for bias
Phinney, J. S., 166
physical characteristics, 285–86
Pierce, Chester, 283
Pinderhughes, Ellen E., 12
Pinderhughes, E. P., 283
placement, 97; children and trauma before, 106; ICWA as allowing choices for, 75–76; LGAs and barriers for, 100–101; poverty and disproportionate, 79–80; professionals' training for TRA, 181–82; racial background, 73; standards for case planning in, 51. *See also* Multiethnic Placement Act; Multiethnic Placement Act and Interethnic Adoption Provisions
play therapy, 342–44, 346–47
policy, 240; adoption and neurodevelopmental perspective, 146; China and one-child, 48, 56; implementation of protective measures, 39, 59–60; implications for practice and, 82; mental health issues practice and, 223; one-child, 359–60; organizations for sealed record, 261–62; TRA regulating, 73–74
Pollack, D., 76
Ponte, I. C., 173
Position Statement Against Transracial Adoption, 257
Positive Adoption Language, 246–47
postadoptions, 213, 323–25; mental health concerns in, 211–12; professional support for, 316; services for, 11, 241

postpartum depression (PPD), 213–14, 222
posttraumatic stress disorder (PTSD), 199, 342, 346
poverty, 79–80, 219
PPD. *See* postpartum depression
Pre-Adoption Immigration Review (PAIR), 22–23
pre-adoption status, 39; adoptive parents and contact while in, 243–45; checklist for counseling while in, 245–46; ICAs adversity and, 127–28; institutions' destructiveness and adversity in, 127–28, 252; medical review while in, 243–45; mental health and, 208; multicultural family training while in, 33
preamble, Hague Adoption Convention, 33
prenatal exposures: institutionalized children's adverse, 127, 252; to substances, 128, 196
preparation for bias (PfB), 170; critical for TRAs and racism, 175–76; discussions regarding, 179–80; parental communication and support for, 173–76; perceptions of adoptees and, 173–74; self-esteem and stress levels relating to, 175; TRA adoptive families' complications for, 174–75; TRAs and, 173–76
prerelinquishment maltreatment, 195–96
problems, developmental, 105–6
Prock, L. Albers, 242
procreation, 138
Procuraduría General de la Nación, 25–26
professionals, 258; adoption kinship network and, 224; adoption medicine and role of, 243–45; consultations with TRA, 182–83; ethnic identity development suggestions for, 181–83; HCIA and, 26–28, 51–53; LGA and TRA implications for, 108–10; LGA family working with, 92; mental health issues and knowledge of, 223–25; neurodevelopmental perspective and, 147–48; placement training for TRA, 181–82; post adoption support for mental health by, 316; prosecutions allowed for, 52–53
prosecutions, 52–53

protection: policy and implementing measures for adoption, 39, 59–60; of vulnerable beings, 138–39
PSI. *See* Parenting Stress Index
psychoeducation, 335
"psychosocial dwarfism," 130–31
PTSD. *See* posttraumatic stress disorder
puberty, 255

Quiroz, P. A., 171, 172

race, 93, 171–72; adoptive families and issues related to, 316; children and differences of, 285; inracial placements and, 73; integration, 72; matters, 307; parenting of different, 333–34; placements of different, 73; TRA and distribution variances of, 70; TRA/ICA children and history about, 300–302
Race Forward, 306
racial achievement gap, 306
racial characteristics, 285–86
racial disparities, 284, 305
racial identity, 166–69
"racial socialization," 333
racial society, 257–58
racism, 208, 220, 283; bullying related to adoption and, 352–53; incidents, 333–34; institutional, 284; PfB as critical for TRAs and, 175–76
Raleigh, E., 276
rape, 199
real-life experiences, 276–77
recruitment: diligent, 30; parental, 80–81
"reculturation," 172
"Reflections," 350–51
regression, stress-response system, 133
rehoming, 2, 3, 317–18
Reitz, M., 319
relational neurobiology: adoption and core essential capabilities of, 138–39; species survival and, 138
relational sensitization, 144–46
relationships: issues of, 363; satisfaction of intimate partner, 214–16; sense of belonging case study for, 136–38

religious beliefs, 249–50
relinquishment, 342; case study of open adoption and, 221–22; child abandonment and, 219–20; context of, 218–19; forced, 317–18; mental health issues of birth parents and, 217–18
Removal of Barriers, 73–75
Republic of Korea, 20, 24
research, 225; data from multiple source, 90; focus of adoption-related, 194; LGA, 102–3; mental health of adoptees and nonadoptees, 206; on MEPA-IEP, 83; TRA outcome requests for, 82
resource gap, 306
resources, 52, 60–61; for finding mental health professionals, 352; for growth as cultural beings, 158–59
Respectful Adoption Language, 246
responsibility, kinship care, 9
responsive system of care, 318–19
reunions, 221
Riley, D., 224, 291–92, 337
risk factors: adoptive parenthood and stress, 212–13; of postinstitutionalized children, 242, 252
Roby, J. L., 39–40, 218–19
Romania, 199; adoptees from, 212; problems and length of institutional time in, 317
Roszia, Sharon, 359
Rotabi, K. S., 27–28
Ruck, M. D., 283
Russia, 20; ICA moratorium of, 47–48; ICA requirements of, 23–24, 240; problems and length of institutional time in, 317; TRA and, 98, 240
Russian Federal Law No. 167-FZ, 24
Russian Federal law No. 727-FZ, 23–24
Ryan, S., 211–12

safety, sense of, 148
same-sex couples, 24
Samuels, G. M., 305
sand-tray, 343, *344*
Sargent, Porter, 29
scaffolding identity, 12, 364

Schmidt, C., 70
schools: adoptees and limited understanding of, 281–82; adoptees' behavioral problems in, 286; adoptees' experiences in, 278; child assessment decisions in, 307–9; children experiencing acceptance in, 303–4; classroom assignments in, 297–98; core issues for, 366–67; diverse curriculum for, 296–97; ecology and environment of, 302–7; equity and inclusion in, 305–6; inclusive environments in, 304–5; public, 282; racially charged history in, 300–302; TRA/ICA children and nondiverse, 292–93; zero tolerance policies of, 282
Schwartz, A., 7–8
sealed records, 261–62
Seattle Adoptions International, 40–41
self-esteem: of adoptees and nonadoptees, 199; case study of searching for, 347–51; PfB and, 175
self-reflection: ethnic identity and parents, 177; for promotion of ethnic identity, 176–77; TRA identity development's importance and, 183
Sennott, S. L., 92–93
sensitization: behavior problems and stress-response, 134, *135*, 136, 142–43; case study on relational, 144–46; stress and stress-response, 134, *135*, 136, 142–43
sexism, 220
sexual abuse, 106, 136, 200
sexual orientation, 93, 104–5
siblings, 302–3
Silverstein, Deborah, 359
single-child policy, 359–60
single parents, 81, 99, 101, 207
Slap, G., 199–200
sleep deprivation, 213
sleeping disorders, 288–89
Smit, E. M., 211
Smith, S. L., 211–12
Smolin, D. M., 41
social attention, 57

social information: accreditation standards for disclosures of, 31–33, 46; accuracy of adoptees' medical and, 244
social work, 58–59, 84
social workers, 82; cultural humility and knowledge critical for, 84; as lacking familiarity with TRA findings, 84; MSW and, 52; NABSW and, 73, 206, 238, 257–58, 260; NASW and, 13
Social Work Practice, 13–14
society, 11, 274
Solomon, Andrew, 256–57
Solomon, B., 303
South, S. C., 214
South Asia, 202
South Korea, 50, 276–77, 285
special education services, 147–48
species survival, neurobiology and, 138
Speech and Language Pathologist, *255*
speech issues, 255, *255*, 345
Spencer, Marietta, 246–47
State Dependence of Developmental Window, 134, *135*
state-dependency: disruption, 133–38; functioning under, 131, *132*
statistics. *See* demographics
status levels, 155
Steinberg, G., 306
stepchildren, 237
stereotypes, 166, 205
Steward, R. J., 58–59
straight parents, 105–7
stress, 148, 207; adoptive parenthood and understanding, 212–13; adoptive parenthood assessments for, 212; adoptive parenthood risk factors for, 212–13; financial, 208; hormones, 128; open adoption and decreased, 220–21; PfB and, 175; PSI and, 212; PTSD and, 199, 342, 346; sensitization response and, 134, *135*, 136, 142–43; toxic, 252
stress-response systems: altered, major and interactive, 131–33; arousal response and dissociation, 131–33; regression, 133; sensitization and, 134, *135*, 136, 142–43
stuck spots, 292

INDEX   401

subsidiarity principle: for continuum of care by HCIA, 39; Guatemalan law focus on, 45–46

substance abuse, 106, 202, 207, 220; of adoptees and nonadoptees, 198–99; prenatal exposure of, 128, 196; prenatal exposures to, 128, 196

successful development, sense of safety for, 148

Sue, D. W., 156–57

suicides: of adoptees and nonadoptees, 199–200; Sweden's intercountry adoptee, 57, 200

support groups, 113–14

surveys. *See specific surveys*

survival, 138–39

survival, human, 138–39

Survivors Foundation, 43–44

Sweden, 57, 168, 196, 198, 200

TAC. *See* Training in Adoption Competency

TAC evaluation highlights, 325, *326*

TAC model, postadoption training, 323–25

tantrums, severe, 171

Tatum, B. D., 285

teachers, 180, 307

teasing, 94

TED Talks, 158

"temperament of the family system," 319, 327–28

Tenebaum, H. R., 283

teratogens, 128

terminology, 275

"Terminology of Adoption, The," 246

TF-CBT. *See* trauma-focused cognitive behavioral therapy

theoretical framework: of adoptism, 11–13; of culturally competent practice, 13–14

therapists. *See* mental health professionals

Theraplay®, 343

therapy, 114, 207; adoption competency themes and, 330–34; case studies involving behavior problem, 338–51; DBT and, 335–36; group, 337–52; ICAs, TRAs and effective, 330–51; Loss Box tool, 340; neurodevelopmental lens in, 349; play, 342–44, 346–47; sand-tray, 343, *344*; TF-CBT, 336–37, 342; tools and strategies for, 339–47, 349–51; trauma-informed treatments in, 320, 336–37

Tieman, W., 196

Tirella, L. G., 276

Title VI, violation of Civil Rights Act, 80

tools, 328; Loss Box, 340; therapy strategies and clinical, 339–47, 349–51

top ten behaviors, 329–30

Torino, G. C., 156–57

"tough love," 338

"toxic stress," 252

TRA. *See* transracial adoption

TRA/ICA. *See* transracially and internationally adopted children

training, 33, 225, 353; of adoptive families, 54; TAC model and postadoption, 323–25; TRA and lack of mandatory, 32, 81–82, 181–82

Training and National Certification for Adoption Competent Mental Health Practitioners, 320–21

Training in Adoption Competency (TAC), 109, 324–25

transcultural dimension, 56–58

transnational adoptions. *See* intercountry adoptions

transracial adoptees (TRAs), 110–14; colorblindness and, 258–60; complex trauma issues in ICAs and, 332; context changes within families of, 159–64; development of ethnic identity for, 154–84; E-RS, CS and, 170–73; ethnic identity issues in development of, 154–84; ethnic identity recommendations for promoting, 176–77; experiences and complexities of, 154–56; HCIA ratification and, 169; heritage trip pros and cons of, 172–73; history and changes of ICAs and, 193; identifying as whites, 168; identity development complications of, 164–69; impact of parenting and, 189; importance of

transracial adoptees (TRAs) (*continued*)
adoption visibility in families of, 162–64; issues upon entering adolescence and, 317; literature themes of adoption triad and, 224–25; loss and grief issues in ICAs and, 330–31, 338–41, 363; lower racial/ethnic identities of, 168; medical service issues for ICAs and, 237–64; mental health services challenging ICAs and, 193–226; misread signals and cues of, 146; neurobiological development and adverse experiences of, 126–49; PfB and, 173–76; PfB as critical for racism and, 175–76; preparing for, 261; in racial society, 257–58; self-reflection and identity development's importance for, 183; therapeutic approaches for ICAs and, 330–51; vertical identity for, 258–63; white environments and, 202–3

transracial adoption (TRA), 1–4, 11–14, 29, 275, 280, 297, 364–65; accreditation standards for training in, 32; adoptee's experience in LGA and, 111–14; adoption visibility and, 162–64; case study on family of LGA and, 110–14; China and, 98–99, 240; conclusions and implications for, 83–84; consultations with professionals in, 182–83; defining inclusions for, 14; definition of, 69, 96; demographics post passage of MEPA, 69–70; families and, 84, 110–15, 159–64, 174–75; formation of ethnic identity and, 10–11; history of, 71–73, 96–97; ICAs and, 92–94; identity challenges and families of LGAs and, 115; identity development and, 167–69, 183; implications for professionals in LGA and, 108–10; international and LGA diversity within, 101–2; issues affecting, 78–79; lack of mandatory training for, 32, 81–82, 181–82; placement training for professionals in, 181–82; policies regulating, 73–74; racial distribution affected by, 70; research requests for outcomes of, 82; Russia and, 98, 240; of single whites, 101, 202–3; social workers as lacking familiarity with, 84; U.S. whites and placements of, 97. *See also* transracial domestic adoption

"transracial adoption paradox," 168
transracial dimension, 56–58
transracial domestic adoption: evolution of ICAs and, 238; history and demographics of, 238–41
transracially and internationally adopted (TRA/ICA) children: abilities of, 295–96; bias and discrimination of, 279–80; birthdays and timelines of, 298–99; classroom assignments for, 297–98; cultural holidays and, 300; disability assessment of, 294; diverse curriculum benefiting, 296–97; educational outcomes of, 276; educational setting of, 284–85; identity development of, 275; names and, 299–300; nondiverse school challenges of, 292–93; physical and racial characteristics of, 285–86; racially charged history and, 300–302; real-life experiences and, 276–77

TRAs. *See* transracial adoptees
trauma, 2, 128, 350, 365; of adoptees and nonadoptees, 199; children and pre-placement, 106; complex, 332; mechanisms and neurobiological development in, 129–30; on neurodevelopment, 348; preadoptive, 315; PTSD and, 199, 342, 346
trauma-focused cognitive behavioral therapy (TF-CBT), 336–37, 342
trauma-informed treatment: in C.A.S.E. model, 320; in therapeutic approaches, 336–37
tribalism, 149
trichotillomania (TTM), 348–51
triggering language, 305
trips, heritage, 172–73
Triseliotis, J., 218
TTM. *See* trichotillomania

UAA. *See* Intercountry Adoption Universal Accreditation Act
United Kingdom, adoption moratorium of, 49

United Nations, 96
United Soviet Socialist Republic, dissolution of, 240
United States (U.S.), 97; adoption and citizenship in, 256; adoption as cultural experience in, 237; downturn of ICAs to, 46–47, *47*; half of total adoptions accounted by, 96; HCIA changing ICA practice in, 19; HCIA implementation in, 44–45; U.S.-Russia Adoption Agreement and bans in, 23–24
U.S. agencies: Final Rules and, 26; Hague Convention impact on professionals and, 26–28
U.S. Citizenship and Immigration Services (USCIS), 25, 28–29
U.S. Intercountry Adoption Act, 44–45
U.S.- Russia Adoption Agreement, 23–24

validation, 290–91
Van Ausdale, D., 285
vertical identity, 256–63
visas, 49–50, 164
Vonk, M. E., 58–59
vulnerable beings, protection of, 138–39

Wang, L. K., 173
war orphans, 97

Watson, K. W., 319
Westhues, A., 206
"Where I'm From," 353
white environments, 202–3
whites, 69; adoption preferences of, 101–2; adoptive parents as predominantly, 167–68; bias between African Americans and, 157; culture of, 166; foster care and, 70–71, 219–20, 238–39; ITRAs identifying as, 168; stereotypes and, 166; TRA placement with U.S., 97; TRAs of single, 101, 202–3
Wiscott, R., 7
W.I.S.E. UP!, 336–37
W.I.S.E UP Powerbook, 367
women, human rights and, 43–44
Wood, L., 298
Woolston, Clare Herbert, 259
World War II, 261; ICA post, 38, 238–39; international adoptions' growth after, 98, 238–39
Wrobel, G. M., 161
Wu, J., 170

Young, M. I., 82

Zhang, Xian, 12
Zoé's Ark, 42
Zurcher, L. A., 8

GPSR Authorized Representative: Easy Access System Europe, Mustamäe tee
50, 10621 Tallinn, Estonia, gpsr.requests@easproject.com